ρ

# STRONG INSTITUTIONS IN WEAK POLITIES

# Studies on Contemporary China

The Contemporary China Institute at the School Oriental and African Studies (University of London) has, since its establishment in 1968, been an international centre for research and publications on twentieth-century China. *Studies on Contemporary China*, which is edited at the Institute, seeks to maintain and extend that tradition by making available the best work of scholars and China specialists throughout the world. It embraces a wide variety of subjects relating to Nationalist and Communist China, including social, political, and economic change, intellectual and cultural developments, foreign relations, and national security.

Editorial Advisory Board:

Volumes in the Series:

# Strong Institutions in Weak Polities

## STATE BUILDING IN REPUBLICAN CHINA, 1927–1940

JULIA C. STRAUSS

CLARENDON PRESS · OXFORD
1998

Oxford University Press, Great Clarendon Street, Oxford OX2 6DP

Oxford New York
Athens Auckland Bangkok Bogota Bombay
Buenos Aires Calcutta Cape Town Dar es Salaam
Delhi Florence Hong Kong Istanbul Karachi
Kuala Lumpur Madras Madrid Melbourne
Mexico City Nairobi Paris Singapore
Taipei Tokyo Toronto Warsaw
and associated companies in
Berlin Ibadan

Oxford is a trade mark of Oxford University Press

Published in the United States
by Oxford University Press Inc., New York

British Library Cataloguing in Publication Data
Data available

Library of Congress Cataloging in Publication Data
Strauss, Julia C.
Strong institutions in weak polities:
state building in Republican China, 1027 1010/ Julia C. Strauss.
p. cm. — (Studies on contemporary China)
Includes bibliographical references and index.
1. Bureaucracy—China. 2. China—Politics and
government—1928–1937. 3. China—Politics and
government—1937–1945. I. Title. II. Series: Studies on
contemporary China (Oxford, England).
JQ1510.S785 1998
320.951'09'04—dc21 97–46972 CIP

ISBN 0–19–823342–6

1 3 5 7 9 10 8 6 4 2

Typeset by Pure Tech India Ltd, Pondicherry
Printed in Great Britain
on acid-free paper by
Biddles Ltd, Guildford and King's Lynn

*Dedicated to the Memory of*
*Joseph and Rosalie Strauss*

# ACKNOWLEDGEMENTS

Any work clocking in at over ten years in the making receives a great deal of help along the way. I would like to thank those who provided the consistent support, encouragement, and criticism that kept this project on track throughout its many stages of evolution.

The first order of thanks goes to David Leonard and Frederic Wakeman, who sat on my Ph.D. committee at the University of California at Berkeley. David Leonard suggested the topic, kept an eye on both the detail and the wider conceptual framework of the dissertation, insisted that chapters be submitted in good time, and constituted a dissertation discussion group that went a long way in overcoming the isolation of the early stages of writing. Frederic Wakeman contributed his time, infectious enthusiasm, and a vast knowledge of the research, both published and unpublished, on republican and late imperial China.

The second order of thanks is due to William Kirby, who commented generously on the entire manuscript in two of its major post-dissertation incarnations, and offered especially helpful suggestions for the revision of the material on the Ministry of Foreign Affairs.

Tim Brook and R. Bin Wong usefully reviewed the whole work. Hong Yung Lee, Elizabeth Perry, Laurence Schneider, Charles Strauss, and Jeffrey Wasserstrom commented on particular drafts of chapters. Stevens Tucker contributed astute criticism throughout, and saved me hours of frustration in the computer room. John Dower and Cornell Fleischer provided perspective on the process of writing in general, and Sue Appleton Hughes's expert copyediting prevented an uncounted number of writing embarrassments.

A grant from the Committee for Scholarly Communication with the People's Republic of China supported my field research in Nanjing and other cities from August 1987 to through June 1989. Upon returning to Berkeley, the Department of Political Science provided teaching assistant-ships, and recommended for a Chancellor's Dissertation Fellowship, which kept me in rent and cat food for the months of writing up. The Depart-ments of History and East Asian Studies at Washington University in St Louis and the Department of Political Studies at the School of Oriental and African Studies in London provided congenial environments and support-ive colleagues for the multi-phased process of revision.

Many in China were extremely generous with their time, support, and advice. A special thanks must go to Professor Cai Shaoqing, my *daoshi*, of the History Department at Nanjing University, who spent numerous hours arranging my way through the bureaucracy. Professor Wu Yiye, also of

Nanjing University's history department, offered a very useful review of classical Chinese as well as a unique perspective of Chinese history. Zhu Jin, my 'research assistant' and friend, showed me the ins and outs of the local book stores and libraries, and was a delightful companion in research trips to Shanghai and Beijing to conduct interviews. The staff at the No. 2 Historical Archives in Nanjing, whom I saw every day and came to think of as family, were extremely patient as they continued to ferret out stacks and stacks of archives—even when they couldn't quite understand why I was straying so far from my original outline. In Taiwan, I benefited from the hospitality of the Institute of Modern History at the Academia Sinica, and the knowledge of staff at the Guoshiguan Archives. Mr Wang Hua-chung, of the Examination Yuan, took a particularly kind interest in my work, and directed me to many of his friends and acquaintences for interviews.

One of the most rewarding aspects of this research was interviewing retired bureaucrats who had worked for the National Government in the 1930s and 1940s. On both sides of the Taiwan Straits, I found these gentlemen to be unfailingly charming, forthcoming, and willing to contribute whatever they could. Their reminiscences gave a formerly rather abstract topic life and body, and greatly added to whatever feel and texture for organizational culture that is conveyed in these pages.

Finally, I would like to thank those nearest and dearest: Jeffery Kapellas, for his much-appreciated editing assistance and deep affection; the US and London sets of cats, for providing useful reminders of life away from the computer; and the executives at Columbia Records, whose reissue of Glenn Gould's marvelous renditions of Bach's keyboard works on CD has provided the perfect background music for writing text.

JCS

London
June 1997

# CONTENTS

# Introduction: Institution-Building and State Transformation in China

In the 450 years between the dawn of the Age of Exploration and the decolonization waves of the mid-twentieth century, the European state system developed, consolidated, and expanded to encompass the rest of the globe, with momentous consequences for the non-European world. Between the sixteenth and twentieth centuries, the surviving members of the European state system achieved something remarkable: the global transformation of the political and economic landscape through the indirect influence of trade, the threatened use of force, and outright conquest. By the late nineteenth century, the rest of the world had been drawn into an international system of states and an international economy, defined by Europeans and largely dominated by them as well. Through the extraordinary and destructive dynamism of a small group of states in north-west Europe, Western ideas of state sovereignty became dominant in the international system, areas not under the direct or indirect control of European and Europe-derived powers decreased, and places not subject to the opportunities and vagaries of the world market largely disappeared.

The impact of these revolutionary developments on the non-European world was overwhelming, and the age of European dominance irrevocably altered non-Western states and societies in myriad ways. Europeans created new states and new administrations everywhere they went. In the sparsely settled Americas, they exterminated or enslaved indigenous peoples, physically taking over and creating European-derived states. In the more populated parts of Africa and Asia, where such strategies were unfeasible, Europeans set up colonial administrations. Even in those areas that escaped formal colonial rule, such as Ottoman Turkey, Japan, and China, the impact of European expansion had a strong echo effect: indigenous elites and rulers saw their neighbours succumb to Western power, keenly felt the West's economic and military pressure, and struggled hard to maintain their independence, typically by playing one European power against the other while attempting to strengthen their local administrative capacities. By the turn of the twentieth century, the world was covered with states that were either originally European, imposed artificially by Europeans, or attempting to replicate the Europeans' success. In both absolute and comparative terms, state building and its supporting processes of institution building have had a lasting impact on the global political landscape.

The issues considered in this work are as longstanding as the processes of state building in the non-Western world, and are particularly relevant to those states with strong indigenous traditions of statecraft and rule that survived intact into the modern era: China, Japan, Ottoman Turkey, Iran, Ethiopia, and Thailand. In environments characterized by resource scarcity, small pools of potentially qualified personnel, and/or widespread external hostility to an increased central government presence, how can a state previously content with fairly minimalist goals of self-maintenance develop strong, proactive organizations capable of implementing new agendas of centralization and economic development? In societies in which the reach of the state is limited and intermittent while the claims of kith and kin are immediate and powerful, how can critical organizations inculcate their members with norms strong enough to transcend the individual's short-term interests and personal loyalties? In short, how can pre-existing administrative organizations be reconstituted and transformed to build a new type of state when institutional capacity is inherently fragmented, ambiguous, and weak?

## STATES, INSTITUTION BUILDING, AND CORE ACTIVITIES

In one form or another, states have existed since the beginning of recorded history; and while authors vary in their respective emphases, there is substantial agreement on the minimal attributes of states and 'stateness'. Most draw on Weber's definition of the state as a 'compulsory organization with a territorial basis' that possesses an 'administrative staff [that] successfully upholds the claim to the monopoly of the legitimate use of physical force in the enactment of its order' and 'regulates more generally the interrelations of the inhabitants of the territory'.[1] By definition, a state is a centralized entity. Within a given territory, its organizations are formally coordinated with each other, distinct from other organizations in society, and claim authority over other these other organizations through its monopolies on authoritative rule making and the use of legitimate force. In its dealings outside its own territory, the state also claims exclusive authority to represent its society internationally.[2]

From the time of the great nineteenth-century sociologists onward, it has been recognized that central administrative structures, along with military and judicial organizations, are among the state's most critical components of extraction, coercion, and coordination,[3] organizing and carrying out 'core activities' without which the state could not exist. Neither military, administrative, or judicial state structures are exactly coterminous with the state itself. Few would argue that the Inland Revenue is exactly the same thing as the United Kingdom: the former will never sign a peace treaty, develop a weapons system, or administer aid to families with dependent children. But all can agree that the Inland Revenue is a crucial supporting component of the larger state, without which continued functioning in these other arenas of activity would be next to impossible. Administrative organizations hold the state together, providing the backbone that makes centralization possible. They collect the taxes, administer the justice, and, since the late nineteenth-century, have taken on a wide variety of new responsibilities and tasks, from redistributing wealth, to promoting economic development, to regulating industries, to guaranteeing social insurance, to establishing national educational bodies, to promoting public health.[4]

The first imperative of all state-building activity is to exert control over a territory: without a relatively secure central base from which to operate, there can be no state, and without at least primitive military and administrative organizations, there can be no centralized control over an area. As military and administrative organizations are the agents through which the state externally differentiates itself from other groups in society, most early state-building action has revolved around 'organizing the means of coercion' within a given area, guarding against incursions from without, and securing the revenue to make internal coercion and external security possible.[5]

For states in highly competitive environments, the likelihood of survival declines appreciably if the state does not either inherit or create reasonably effective, well functioning supporting state organizations in these core activities of coercion, extraction, and administration; thus, aspiring state makers across the board tend to place exceptionally high premiums on the modernization of the military and the creation of effective mechanisms for tax raising. Like organizations in any place or time, the supporting bureaucracies of the state that make the tax collection, judicial administration, and provision of social services possible are dualistic, with both functional and affective components. As entities designed and created to achieve goals, they are purposefully oriented towards realizing certain ends, but as bounded realms of social interaction, they are subject to the vagaries of human behaviour.[6] For an organization to be successful over an extended period of time, it must become institutionalized on both affective and functional dimensions. Since highly coercive measures are unlikely to produce high performance over any sort of long run, the organization must first elicit the internal commitments of staff to its goals and projects by 'infusing [them] with value beyond the technical requirements of the task at hand'.[7]

Organizations become internally institutionalized and stable in so far as they socialize their members into administrative ideologies, reward those who believe in the organization's values, and effectively carry out the tasks deemed important, replicating those values for subsequent generations of employees within the organization. As instruments designed for purposive action, administrative organizations are also expected by those inside and outside the organization to make visible progress towards achieving its goals. But organizations do not exist in vacuums. They stake out particular 'domains' (or policy environments) regarding the actions they will pursue and the clientele they will serve, they possess technologies for promoting organizational goals, and they operate in specific 'task environments', which encompass 'everything in the external environment which are relevant or potentially relevant to goal setting and goal attainment'.[8]

An organization's domain, task environment, and technologies have a strong objective influence on the likelihood of goal achievement, which in turn affects internal infusion with value, institutionalization and organizational morale. A organization that aspires to become well institutionalized must launch a two-front attack, simultaneously building internal commitments and organizational culture while externally realizing enough of its goals to stay in operation. In environments in which the domains of state administrative organizations are shifting rapidly, where the technologies are uncertain and external task environments are hostile and unpredictable, internal institutionalization and stabilization is, by definition, exceptionally difficult. These, of course, are exactly the types of conditions typical to non-Western states attempting to transform their administrative organizations into proactive, effective institutions.

In reality, states have more often than not fallen short of achieving the basic attributes suggested by the Weberian definition of the term: centrality, a monopoly on the legitimate means of force and binding rule making, and even the exclusive right to speak for the sovereign state internationally have not come easily or automatically. The feudal state in medieval Europe had nothing that even approached a monopoly on the legitimate use of force; some state administrations are so thoroughly the creatures of a particular class or group in society that the whole idea of state autonomy is sometimes called into question.[9] Even the question of international representation may become blurred: in cases of civil war, a government claiming the sovereign right to manage its own affairs may not be accorded either *de jure* or *de facto* recognition by other states or external groups.

But even though states have varied tremendously in the degree to which they have exhibited the key Weberian properties of 'stateness', most states (or proto-states) have, when feasible, sought to become more 'state-like' by centralizing control over their territories, achieving a degree of autonomy from groups in society, becoming the internationally recognized legitimate authorities for the physical areas over which they claim jurisdiction, and in the twentieth century moving into domains of broad social regulation and social insurance.

Particularly before the nineteenth century, the historical record is full of examples that suggest the difficulties of successful state building. Under pre-modern conditions of production, transport, and resource extraction, states normally could realize only these more minimal attributes of 'stateness'. At best, they could muster enough of the military and administrative organization to maintain a veneer of centralized control over a territorial area. Lacking the projective capacity to send central agents down to the truly local levels, where the bulk of the population lived, they ruled in a *de facto* partnership with local elites and notables. Regardless of their formally despotic power, they could not hope to vigorously control and regulate the relations between groups in society. Outside the highly competitive system of European states that began to emerge in the early modern period, until fairly recently the vast majority of states have had to be content with a loose degree of control and self-maintenance even while they typically claimed to be the sole source of legitimate political power in the territories over which they exercised nominal absolute rule.[10]

For all pre-modern states, even the most long-lived and successful, simply maintaining a bare modicum of 'stateness' could be precarious. Since central administrative structures were limited in their extent and reach and extractive capacity was severely circumscribed, states devoted much of their effort to maintaining some sort of equilibrium between centralized authority and local realities. Withdrawal of support from local notables often fragmented the state from within, and the development of new military technology or the rise of predatory neighbours perenially threatened from without. Continued existence at a minimum depended on the state's capacity to successfully defend itself, with invasion and conquest constantly looming as threats. With the advent of new technologies, new forms of organization, and newly successful predators, pre-modern states large and small rose and fell, only intermitently exercising much of a direct presence at the local level. For all the splendour they may have accumulated at their cores and all the authority they commanded in the abstract, traditional states were, in comparison with their twentieth-century counterparts, fairly fragile.[11]

The particular social and geopolitical circumstances of early modern Europe produced a new sort of state, one that was constrained to generate efficient extractive administrations domestically to provide for external security. Anomalous factors such as the feudal legacy, slow accretion of power under a number of different kings, the continued existence of corporate rights and privileged groups, and a traditional (if often imperfect) separation between temporal and ecclesiastical power all contributed to the inability of any to establish a lasting hegemony over the continent. Charles Tilly suggests that, in Europe's late medieval environment of highly competitive proto-states, state building was largely a function of war making and a desperate struggle for survival. Between the fifteenth and twentieth centuries, the landscape became littered with examples of those states that ultimately failed and were absorbed by bigger, more powerful neighbours. With the exception of England (which had the luxury of being able to depend on its relatively cheap navy for war making), in the European context of highly competitive proto-states, success in war was in turn closely related to the state's ability to field effective administrative organizations able to extract the resources necessary to maintain increasingly expensive military technology (such as standing armies), and to pacify recalcitrant groups within its putative boundaries.[12] Although the process was not in full swing until the added boost of the Industrial Revolution, European states began concurrently to *implode* in internal generative capacity and *explode* in bursts of externally oriented activities such as exploration, commerce, and colonial ventures in the sixteenth and seventeenth centuries.[13]

When European states met non-Western states and societies, the usual result was the destruction of the latter and the establishment of some sort of colonial administration. But for those who, through some combination of luck, skill, scale, and geographical isolation, managed to avoid direct colonization, very serious questions of state building and institutional transformation arose. How could strong states capable of standing up to the West be built? How could traditionally limited state administrations be reconstituted to carry out new tasks while retaining their legitimacy? What values would ultimately be encoded in these new state organizations?

Although Turkey, Iran, Thailand, Ethiopia, Japan, and China are all equally good candidates for research into these questions of state and institution building, the scope of this study is confined to the institution-building efforts undertaken in China during the Republican period (1912–49), and focuses in particular on the years between 1927 and 1940, when the National Government under the Guomindang (Nationalist Party) made the greatest, although still incomplete, strides towards state reintegration and central state rebuilding of any Chinese government between the fall of the empire in 1912 and the establishment of the People's Republic of China in 1949. China was, in the early twentieth century, the longest-lived example of a non-Western culture, civilization, and organized political entity in the world, one whose imperial institutions had crumbled and whose political future was still uncharted.

Far from being an historical footnote of no consequence, the Republican period in general and the activities of Nationalist state and institution builders in particular are important for two reasons. Despite the Nationalists' eventual defeat in the civil war of the late 1940s, these were the years in which the institutional foundations for the subsequent evolution of the twentieth-century Chinese state were laid down. Further, the activities of the National Government offer an exceptionally well documented and accessible case study for comparative state and institution building, as Nationalist state and institution builders were dogged, perhaps to an extreme degree, by a set of dilemmas common to state and institution builders the world over.

After half a century of reform efforts within the framework of the Celestial Empire failed to produce a rejuvenated and centralized China, the imperial system finally collapsed in 1911–12, leaving in its wake a set of fragmented military, political, and social organizations, and a proliferation of unanswered questions as to how to put the polity back together on a sound, and recognizably 'modern', basis. Given the weak state of China's central administration, how could imperialist encroachment best be turned back? How would republicanism and revolution be defined and operationalized? What was the most effective means to national wealth and power? How could a strong state be built? For elites in early twentieth-century China, the solutions to these questions were not of mere academic interest: they were a matter of national identity and survival. National identity and survival, in turn, depended on rapidly developing state institutions capable of taking on new tasks, and drastically increasing efficiency, effectiveness, and projective capacity, when nearly everything in the immediate environment served to undermine central institution building.

Like prospective institution builders elsewhere, state-building elites in Republican China were accorded no *tabula rasa*. Even as they struggled against it, the legacy of the late imperial state and society continued to exhibit a powerful influence on its Republican era heirs: providing the raw materials with which to work, offering deeply held symbols of legitimation, and constraining choices.

## SUMMARY AND OUTLINE

Substantively, this work analyses patterns of attempted institution building in central state administration in Republican China (1912–49). It was during this period that the Chinese state disintegrated under the warlords (1916–27), was partially reintegrated by the Nationalists under Chiang Kai-shek (1927–37), largely disintegrated again under the impact of the Sino-Japanese War (1937–45), and underwent the trauma of full fledged civil war, which culminated in the triumph of the Communists and the flight of the Nationalists to the island of Taiwan (1945–9). While the political and administrative elites of the early Republic (1912–27) were no less concerned with state building and institution building than were the next generation of Nationalists and Communists, the regional militarism and political fragmentation of the warlord era in the 1910s and 1920s for the most part precluded effective central institution building. Since it was not until the Nationalists succeeded in establishing a proto-state in the lower Yangzi Valley in 1927–8 that sustained *central* government efforts in institution building were possible, the descriptive chapters deal primarily (although not exclusively) with the time frame between 1927 and 1940, as it was during these years that the Nationalists made their greatest, although still incomplete, progress towards their announced goals of state reintegration, institution building and national development.[14]

My findings indicate that, for states confronting objectively unfavourable conditions for institution building, such as was the case for Republican China, success in institution building is contingent and unusual, but by no means random. Nationalist China, as a weak state operating in hostile environment with external and internal sources of competitive pressure, concentrated the lion's share of its attention on exactly those 'core' activities associated with state building in early modern Europe: on building up an effective military, focusing on resource (particularly tax) extraction to finance the military, and developing foreign relations to try to bring about a less precarious international environment by establishing a credible international presence, negotiating with other states, and joining alliances.

What is often overlooked is the degree to which the Nationalists were surprisingly *successful* in carrying out these critically important components of the state building process during the 1930s. Most of the standard assessments of Republican China tend to be highly critical of the Nationalist regime, reading the government ineffectiveness, corruption, and military weakness that led to eventual defeat in the late 1940s back into the 1930s and early 1940s.[15] More sympathetic analyses of the Nationalist era have at best considered the Nationalist strategy of state building to have long-term promise until fatally undercut by the Japanese invasion of 1937.[16] But whether critical or sympathetic, all of these works are primarily interested in explaining the Nationalist defeat in 1949 rather than evaluating what the regime attempted, given the context and constraints of its own times, in order to overcome its very real weaknesses.

I suggest that over a medium term, between the late 1920s and roughly 1940, not only were supporting state organizations of the National Government as different from each other as the Ministry of Finance and the Ministry of Foreign Affairs successful, but their success hinged on two closely related variables: insulation of the organization from external pressures, and general perceptions of the organization as successful in meeting its goals. In a hostile external environment rent with patronage politics, success depended first on the degree to which the organization was able to insulate itself from the external environment while promoting the bureaucratization and professionalization of its personnel within. To maintain insulation against external pressures, the organization had to 'buy' its legitimacy through its effectiveness in carrying out services necessary to the survival of the state. High performance in goal implementation, in turn, was in part a reflection of organizational insulation and bureaucratization, but was also positively correlated with two other factors: the degree to which the organization's tasks were specific and divisible, and the degree to which the organization was able to establish domestic control over its policy domain. Once established, a well insulated organization could creatively recast pre-existing symbols of legitimacy and statecraft, further boosting internal morale and prestige without.

This work synthesizes a variety of archival, secondary and interview materials into four in-depth case studies of central administrative organizations in the Nationalist state: the Examination Yuan, the Sino-Foreign Salt Inspectorate, the Ministry of Finance, and the Ministry of Foreign Affairs.[17] Through the development of these case studies, the analysis focuses on two critical factors in institution-building success in hostile environments: the interaction between the incipient professionalization promoted by the organization's internal personnel policy, and its external results in goal implementation and achievement.

After reviewing the basic agenda of the late imperial Chinese state, the recasting of that agenda during the last years of the dynasty, and a description of the environment in which the Nationalists came to power in the late 1920s in Chapter 1, Chapter 2 focuses on the National Government's civil service personnel and examination systems as implemented by the Examination Yuan and the Ministry of Personnel. The goals of the Examination Yuan stood more as an ideal statement of intent for the design and operations of the National Government than it was a concrete guide to its workings, while the Examination Yuan's weaknesses and tactical retreats illustrated in microcosm the difficulties of the larger Nationalist strategy of co-option and inclusion in institution building. The Examination Yuan did regularly hold open civil service examinations in the 1930s and 1940s, but examinations never became what ideally they 'should' have been: the primary channel of recruitment into the civil service. This chapter also describes the limited gains made by the Examination Yuan and Ministry of Personnel as the units entrusted with implementing the state's ideals of technocracy, depoliticization, and quality control in the civil service at large. Since the Examination Yuan's *raison d'être* and organizational goals were in a domain over which it could not directly enforce compliance, it remained a weak organization, one that for the most part relied on moral suasion and normative appeals to institutionalize its values. In spite of their longstanding legitimacy in traditional Chinese culture and statecraft, open civil service examinations could not be effectively institutionalized without strong organizational boundaries, and ultimately depended on autonomous bureaucratic organizations outside the Examination Yuan to see that it was in their interests to accept new recruits qualified by the examination process. Substantive power and the capacity to build strong, professional institutions remained with the organizations themselves rather than in an external coordinating body like the Examination Yuan.

Chapters 3 and 4 describe the activities of one such body, the Sino-Foreign Salt Inspectorate. The Salt Inspectorate was a prefecturally organized tax collecting body whose effectiveness made it a veritable model of institution-building success. By self-consciously pursuing strategies of bureaucratization, rationalization, and professionalization, the Inspectorate systematically insulated itself from an environment it perceived to be hostile, unpredictable, and politicized. In focusing on a domain in which it could achieve visible and important results, it operated at such a high level of effectiveness that it remained one of the few organizations that retained a nationwide network during the anarchy of the warlord years (1916–27), and proved to be an indispensible source of revenue once it was taken over by the National Government during the Nanjing Decade. Because it was in part established by foreigners and retained a unique system of shared authority between Chinese and foreign tax inspectors, the Salt Inspectorate was an anomalous organization, whose particular structures were hardly likely to be replicated directly by a Chinese government that had come to power on the strength of its nationalism and anti-imperialist credentials.

Chapter 5, which considers all of the Ministry of Finance's tax collecting sub-organizations, provides a partial corrective to the anomalous example of the Salt Inspectorate. While the leadership of the Ministry of Finance borrowed heavily from contemporary Western ideals of centralization and efficiency, and explicitly set out to replicate Salt Inspectorate-style rationalization, bureaucratization, and effectiveness, there was no discernible foreign presence in the direct operations of the Ministry. Cobbled together from the remnants of pre-existing finance administrations, the Ministry of Finance began the Nanjing Decade more a *de facto* coalition of semi-autonomous sub-organizations than a smoothly operating, tightly centralized machine.

The activities of the Ministry of Finance illustrate two important trends in the institution-building processes of the 1930s. First, it attempted to mirror the types of state-building strategies being employed throughout the state at large: takeover of weak or illegitimate organizations, deployment into arenas weakly held by competing organizations, co-optation and gradual amalgamation of medium-strength bodies, and a declaration of monocratic authority while looking the other way for areas in which central power could not effectively reach. Second, the Ministry of Finance did contain one sub-organization, the Consolidated Tax Administration, which was without a heavy foreign advisor presence *and* gradually institutionalized and internally bureaucratized to produce impressive results by the mid-

1930s. The experience of the Ministry of Finance suggests that successful institution building need not depend directly on outside influence to instil and insulate core values, and may have more to do with organizational technology, manageability of domain, and the subsequent willingness of political leadership to refrain from micro-management.

Chapter 6 turns to the Ministry of Foreign Affairs, an elite, generalist organization whose patterns of institution building were in some ways quite different from those of the more technically oriented Salt Inspectorate and Ministry of Finance. Like the Salt Inspectorate, it maintained its organizational boundaries quite well, and achieved substantial results. But unlike the Salt Inspectorate and Finance, many of its activities were not particularly amenable to specific breakdown, and its control over domain was at best partial: political leaders frequently did intervene to recalibrate the general thrust of foreign policy throughout the Nationalist period. Furthermore, Foreign Affairs did not rigorously exclude anything that smacked of Party indoctrination, and instead opted to incorporate the norms of Party loyalty while still managing to maintain its high standards and recruit from the best and the brightest.

Chapter 7 concludes with an analysis of institution-building strategies in central state organizations in Nationalist China, and suggests future avenues for research. Institution-building strategies in Republican China, with all their failures and successes, have a significance that goes far beyond the particulars of the history of the state in Republican China. The types of problem faced by China during this period were far from unique, and it is entirely possible that the range of institution-building responses produced by China's central administrative elites has close analogues in other, similarly situated, non-Western states. However, principles that can be generalized to other contexts must first be well grounded in an understanding of the particulars from which they rise, and this work attempts to be equally faithful to both by developing its concepts in the context of specific administrative histories.

We will begin with an overview of the late imperial and early Republican legacy inherited by the Nationalist institution builders of the late 1920s and 1930s.

# 1

## From Presiding to Centralizing State: The Late Imperial Legacy and Institution-Building Dilemmas

### INTRODUCTION

Governance and statecraft in late imperial China was implemented within a political, institutional, and ideological context of extraordinary staying power. The key political features of the agrarian empire—an Emperor and ruling house, a bureaucracy staffed by a literati elite, and the socializing role of Confucian ethics—had, with modifications, survived such cataclysms as changes in dynasty, alien rule, and periods of political disintegration. These political and institutional arrangements were both long-lived and sufficient to meet the challenges posed by the immediate political environment, until the combination of internal social pressures and external imperialism of the mid-nineteenth century began to generate strains beyond its capacity to respond effectively. By any standard, China was an exceptionally successful non-Western state, with goals that, while significantly different from the goals of states in early modern Europe, remained remarkably consistent until the first years of the twentieth century.

In an extraordinarily long-lived marriage of Confucian ideological justification and tacit admission of the technical limitations of administering a vast agrarian empire, administration in the Celestial Empire was geared towards the maintenance of cosmic harmony and order from the mid-fourteenth to the end of the nineteenth century.[1] Although the late imperial Chinese state claimed exclusive political legitimacy and had no concept of 'legitimate' competing nodes of political authority, it was usually content to reign and loosely regulate rather than vigorously rule. For the most part, emperors and bureaucrats pursued activist intervention only when it was perceived that the natural, proper order of things was set to spiral out of equilibrium, with unchecked official corruption, famines or natural disasters, or banditry. Of course, circumstances that could be interpreted as destabilizing were often present, and under these conditions the late imperial state was capable of vigorous action, as it was in the eighteenth century with the establishment and maintenance of a complex system of state granaries.[2]

But even when actively intervening, the *raison d'être* of the late imperial Chinese state was to *yi an* (literally, to 'hand down tranquillity to posterity'). *Yi an*, in turn, connoted a stable state of affairs in which the elements of the hierarchically organized social order (scholar–gentlemen, peasants, artisans, and merchants) would coexist peacefully and go about their business properly, bringing about a state of balance that would be, in the ideal, unchanging. Thus, at the age of 9, the Kangxi Emperor (r. 1662–1722) wrote: 'I have no desires except that I wish the nation to enjoy peace and order, and the people to be content with their occupations, so that all will be able to live together in grand harmony.'[3]

Ideally, from emperor on down the hierarchy to the district magistrate, 'Grand Harmony' would be realized through the morally proper personal conduct of the 'gentleman' (*junzi*) who staffed the administrative system. His *modus vivendi* was to regulate, educate, and harmonize the relations between different groups and the state with as little direct government intervention as possible. A typical passage from a Ming tract on administration, still widely read until the end of the nineteenth century, read:

What is needed in administration at the present time is to keep troublesome business at a minimum, not add to it; to preserve the rules, not change them; to bring about tranquillity in all situations, not to stir them up; and to relax and simplify the control of the people, not to tighten and complicate it.[4]

For the late imperial Chinese state, benevolent government was minimal government: it kept taxes low, granted remissions, and provided grain relief to the common people in times of distress and famine; it legitimated quite extensive *de facto* deconcentration of power by tolerating the need to be responsive to the 'particular needs of the situation' on the part of the local magistrate; and it regulated social relations primarily by personal example, education, and moral suasion, resorting to coercion only when other means had failed.

Given China's physical size and internal diversity, even achieving relatively modest goals of system maintenance and harmonizing was no easy task. The centralized Confucian bureaucracy maintained the cohesiveness of the vast, heterogeneous empire by administering the realm, and serving as a bulwark of order, standardization, and universalism in a society in which virtually all social action was informed by particularist groups (e.g. family, lineage, old school ties, secret societies). With variable success, the universalistic orientation of the bureaucracy was reinforced in two ways: through the hierarchical structure of imperial bureaucracy itself, and by the intensive pre-entry socialization of its members.

Formal state structure in late imperial China was highly bureaucratic in Weberian terms: hierarchically organized, functionally differentiated at the central level, and given to statute making and use of precedent. Under the Emperor and his advisory policy-making bodies (the Grand Secretariat and, later in the Qing, the Grand Council) in the capital, the central Six Boards (of Civil Appointments, Revenue, Rites, War, Punishment, and

Works) engaged in rule making, issuing orders, and checking on the activities and compliance of the lower levels. At the bottom of the official hierarchy, prefects and district magistrates served as the embodiment of state authority in the far-flung counties of the Empire, and were immediately responsible to centrally appointed provincial governors and governors-general; while financial commissioners, judicial commissioners, and several circuit intendants all reported directly to the central government on provincial affairs.

At its centre, the imperial bureaucracy exhibited an exceptional degree of functional differentiation, with the central Six Boards organized into subdepartments entrusted with specific tasks.[5] But since system maintenance, rather than maximal efficiency, was the central administration's key goal, the central bureaucracy was also characterized by a good deal of shared authority, redundancy, and overlap. Functions were differentiated to process the large volume of documents coming in from the provinces, but responsibility was diffused rather than concentrated to provide the higher-ups with a number of independent sources of information and analysis.[6]

Since the metropolitan bureaucracy was designed to enforce uniformity and standardization, maintain control and responsiveness among the rank and file, and generally combat the natural centrifugal tendencies of an organization spread so thinly over such a vast area, the bulk of the central bureaucracy's activities were proscriptive rather than prescriptive or proactive. Initiation of programmes, works, and experiments was seen as something best left to the discretion of the officials in the provinces who were presumably familiar with local circumstances. Imperial central administration was occupied primarily with information gathering and control: receiving and writing reports, rule making, auditing, and meting out rewards and demerits.[7]

In addition to controlling its bureaucrats through direct rewards and punishments, the imperial Chinese state indirectly fostered identification with its preferred goals by holding open civil service examinations as the primary route of recruitment into the bureaucracy.[8] By testing ancient texts written in classical Chinese and skills such as poetry composition and calligraphy, the state was able to select generalist Confucian gentlemen well versed in a universalistic culture that stressed an idealized past, the proper ordering of things on the basis of virtue, self-cultivation in the present, and obedience to hierarchical authority. Through the open civil service examinations, the state was able to standardize the values and educational experiences of its prospective bureaucrats while institutionally gluing the upwardly mobile to the state itself as the guarantor of prestigious official careers.

The competitiveness of the examinations was nothing short of murderous, and the 'wastage' was enormous: in 1850, only 0.05 per cent of the eligible lowest degree holders passed the provincial level *juren* examinations that qualified (but did not automatically guarantee) one for a substantive post, and the chances of getting through all three sets of examinations to the palace examination were but 1 in 6,000 for those with the lowest *shengyuan* degree.[9] With such long odds to combat, families aspiring to retain or increase their status started their sons on the road to 'Examination Hell' early. Success on the examinations required rote memorization of the over 400,000 characters that constituted the *Four Books*, the *Five Classics* and assorted commentaries, requiring years of preparation.[10] Boys of the gentry began their classical education at around the age of 7, spending literally their whole lifetimes in pursuit of advanced degrees and eventual office-holding. Rarely was the lowest *shengyuan* degree attained before the age of 21, success on the difficult provincial *juren* examination, if forthcoming at all, occurred in the early thirties, and a *minimum* seven- to ten-year wait between provincial examination success and substantive appointment was not uncommon.[11]

Given the long years of training and waiting for such uncertain success, the examination system in practice heavily favoured the already well-off gentry, despite its formal openness to all. Typically, it would be only they who had the resources to invest in the necessary years of education for their sons. The peasant eking out a subsistence living would scarcely have the leisure to learn to read and write, much less afford the expense of tuition and the loss of the productive labour of his sons in the fields. The rare exceptions to the rule of gentry-dominated examination success served largely to perpetuate one of the most enduring myths of social mobility in imperial China: the career open to talent.[12]

For all its widely acknowledged shortcomings, the civil service examination system in imperial China served as the lynchpin of state and elite perpetuation. Through open civil service examinations, the state created a self-confident, literate cadre of bureaucrats with remarkably similar values and pre-service experiences. Despite differences in diet, local custom, and dialect, the classically trained literati throughout the Empire had far more in common with each other in terms of culture and values than they did with the masses of illiterate peasants and artisans of their own local areas.[13] By making performance on impersonally administered examinations the prerequisite to the only socially prestigious career, the late imperial state was able to in part pre-coopt large numbers of local elites whose commonality of interests with the state would otherwise have been much less. Even though the vast majority of prospective literati bureaucrats failed the examinations, every male with the ambition and family resources to do so devoted years to studying the same canonical texts, creating standards for elite values that went far beyond the minority who passed the examinations and achieved office. Direct central state penetration of local areas always remained problematic, but since the local district magistrate and the local gentry tended to hold the same literati culture in common, there was at least the possibility of reaching a *modus vivendi* between the local representative of the state and local elites.

The Confucian bureaucracy was an exceptionally long-lived and self-replicating institution. From the Song dynasty until 1905, its formal structures of hierarchy and control maintained a modicum of administrative unity and standardization, while its rigorous examination system created a cadre of influential individuals pre-socialized into Confucian literati values congenial to bureaucratic perpetuation. But even with these two means of fostering integration and universalism, the state remained 'pervasive but weak', by twentieth-century standards, particularly with respect to finance and local administration.[14]

It was in the districts that the official representatives of the imperial state had the closest contact with the common people, and it was here that the stresses and strains inherent in the state's relatively modest goals of balancing and harmonizing were most visible. The functional differentiation of the Metropolitan bureaucracy was not formally replicated in field administration, where the magistrate was the sole legitimate governmental authority in an area that could include up to several hundred thousand people. Although the long years of studying poetry and Confucian classics hardly prepared the aspiring magistrate to handle the specifics of fiscal, judiciary, or administrative problems, the district magistrate was expected to be a master of interpersonal relations. Folk characters such as the wise official Baogong served as positive models of exemplary magisterial behaviour,[15] able to 'see into the heart of the situation', arrive at proper judgements, serve as a 'father and mother official' to all those in the district, and carry out state dictates. In practice, this meant that all formal responsibility for resolving litigation, tax collection, local security, and assorted emergencies fell to one individual.[16]

Unless he succeeded in resolving all outstanding criminal cases and forwarding tax quotas in full to the provincial authorities each year, the magistrate was unlikely to receive a positive rating when the triennial *daji* evaluations were held, and the threat of impeachment for not conforming to regulations and orders hung over his head at all times. The organizational imperatives of the state bureaucracy made things even more difficult. The centralized reporting and control system tended to quell most risk-taking and initiative; the law of avoidance (which forbade any official to serve in his home province) practically ensured that the magistrate would be unable to communicate with the vast majority of the inhabitants of the area in which he was the sole figure of state authority; and the low level of remuneration left him with no alternative but to condone informal (and quite often uncontrolled) fee-taking to make up the difference.

Given these very real structural constraints, actual performance in local administration tended to depend on the magistrate's ability to coordinate and control the three unofficially recognized groups who processed the bulk of the paperwork and were the actual implementors of most administrative action: the *yamen* (magistrate's residence) clerks and runners, the magistrate's own private secretaries (*muyou*), and the local gentry elite. While the support of all three of these groups was necessary, only the private secretaries, who were personally hired by the magistrate, had a consistent incentive to work in the magistrate's interests. Both petty sub-officials (yamen clerks and runners) and the local gentry were at least as likely to obstruct the magistrate as they were to aid him.

Clerks, runners, and other petty officials comprised a semi-permanent, local administrative staff that provided the actual interface between the yamen and the rest of the district, filing documents, posting edicts, processing litigation, and collecting taxes. Sub-officials were indispensible to the magistrate, who depended on them for their knowledge of the local dialect and customs.[17] But the yamen staff's low social status and miniscule formal salaries led inevitably to informal fee-taking and corruption, while their virtual stranglehold over local information meant that effective supervision was at best sketchy and at worst impossible.

The position of the local gentry was more ambiguous. As local notables, the gentry had every incentive to evade taxation, keep their holdings off the tax rolls, settle local disputes in their own favour, and beg special favours at the yamen. But, as elites with classical education who aspired to the high status conferred by examination success and officeholding, they usually held at least some of the literati high culture in common with the magistrate, and often could be prevailed upon to direct their natural leadership in the community to ends in accordance with those of the state. In order to implement any substantial administrative project such as dike maintenance, relief grain distribution, or restoration of shrines, the district magistrate had to have some sort of viable working relationship with the local gentry. The district magistrate's resources—both human and financial—were limited: even when supplemented by his administrative staff of secretaries and clerks, he was an outsider whose reach did not extend very far beyond the yamen walls without the active collaboration of local elites. Despite the integrating factors of standardized Confucian education and a centralized network of bureaucratic control, the imperial state's projective capacity— particularly in its own countryside—was practically limited by a lack of resources, a weak financial base, ambiguous partners and subordinates, and the intensive particularism of the society over which it ruled.

Confucian literati officials were also caught in an irreconcilable tension between two different value systems: the norms of a universalistic bureaucracy, which demanded uniformity and impartiality, and the even more

pervasive norms of a society, in which loyalty and the fulfilment of obligations to strong personal networks of kin, friends and neighbours remained
the most important imperatives. Once a native son had achieved a position
of such high status, he would invariably be besieged by relatives, friends,
and neighbours to provide them with scarce resources—employment,
favours, and donations. It was a rare individual that could openly refuse
such requests: an official career was temporary, while family and local ties
lasted beyond one's lifetime.[18]

While Confucian state doctrine trumpeted the virtues of impartiality (*xu*)
and carefulness (*shen*), it also recognized the importance of filial piety (*xiao*)
and human feelings (*renqing*). Most officials could ill afford to alienate the
dense social networks from which they had come and to which they would
eventually return by appearing to be 'lacking in human feelings'. Nowhere
was the contradiction between these two different value systems more aptly
expressed than by Wang Huizi, a mid-Qing official who wrote the widely
disseminated *Xuezhi Yishuo* (Opinions on Apprenticeship in Government),
when he sighed, 'Follow the law and you will destroy personal affection;
follow personal affection and you will abuse the law.'[19] Often the pressures
on the individual bureaucrat did not present choices in terms of clear rights
and wrongs: rather, the bureaucrat had to balance between two, only partially reconcilable, types of 'right'. The rules and proscriptions of the bureaucratic state, the interests of the locality to which the bureaucrat was posted,
and the demands of kith and kin back home rarely neatly converged.

Social norms that reified status hierarchy and displayed 'sensitivity to
human feelings' were also replicated in the bureaucracy itself:[20] gift-giving,
courtesy calls, and elaborate greeting and sending off for superior officials
were omnipresent features of informal bureaucratic culture. Despite
repeated proscriptions against gift-giving, the central bureaucracy was
unable to stamp out practices so widely legitimated in society at large.
Given the wide-ranging formal responsibilities of officials and the structural
weaknesses that made carrying out the letter of those responsibilities so
difficult, promotions, demotions, and impeachments in the bureaucracy
were in all likelihood as much a reflection of how well the individual kept on
the good side of his superiors as they were indicators of objective administrative excellence.[21] While the imperial Chinese state selected its personnel
on the basis of the impersonal criteria of examination success and had an
exceptionally well elaborated and formal code of law and administrative
procedure, the informal culture of the Confucian bureaucracy was unable
to maintain exclusively universalist, impartial norms.

These, then, were the primary characteristics of the late imperial Chinese
state: committed to the stability, order and cosmic harmony of a vast,
heterogeneous empire, it was none the less systemically and normatively
constrained in fulfilling its goals. The contradictions between a universa-

listically oriented, cosmopolitan bureaucracy and the localized, diverse, highly particularistic society in which it operated were never completely resolved. In prosperous times of good harvests and vigorous emperors, as was the situation for most of the eighteenth century, a dynamic balance was established between the natural tensions existing between these dual-value systems. But stresses of any kind, such as increasing population, bad harvests, or decline at the centre, tended to magnify the structural weaknesses of the presiding state and tip the balance towards particularism.

## THE RANGE OF RESPONSE AND THE NINETEENTH-CENTURY CRISIS

The nineteenth century brought a series of additional crises to the late imperial state. Population pressure, the increase of real taxes on the peasantry (arising from the appreciation of silver *vis à vis* copper), and the humiliations and disruptions engendered by Western imperialism and economic penetration led to all the classic external manifestations of dynastic decline: increased banditry, corrupt and ineffective local administration, and the spread of uncontrolled heterodox sects. When central military units collapsed before the Taiping rebels in the early 1850s, the dynasty had no alternative but to allow loyal provincial officials hitherto undreamed-of discretion to form effective local armies to put down the rebellion, accelerating a process that would prove to be a long decline of central power.

The responses of the Qing government and its provincial viceroys to the twin threat of internal rebellion and external pressure resulted in the growth of a set of *ad hoc* organizational structures parallel to, but never completely integrated with, the formal Confucian bureaucracy in the second half of the nineteenth century. The interest in the creation of limited alternative organizations came first from reformist provincial viceroys, who advocated the establishment of a series of 'self-strengthening' enterprises such as arsenals, shipyards, and military schools to promote military modernization. But the achievements of the military enterprises and the new modern schools were mixed.[22] The Metropolitan bureaucracy and the Court never threw its full weight in support of the self-strengthening projects, whose implementation was piecemeal and uncoordinated, invariably depending on the uneven strength and sponsorship of provincial leaders. Careers in arsenals and shipyards lacked the prestige of established careers in the traditional civil service, continuously suffering from high turnover and lack of sustained leadership.[23]

Concurrent with this limited movement for military modernization from the top down, the second half of the nineteenth century witnessed a remarkable explosion of new types of administrative organization from the bottom up. The Taiping crisis greatly expanded the amount of official degrees available for purchase, and the growing numbers of individuals who bought degrees created a vast resevoir of 'expectant officials' (*houbu*).[24] These purchasers of degrees, along with individuals 'recommended' by high-ranking provincial officials, were often assigned to the growing number of local offices and projects that were springing up everywhere in the late nineteenth century—*lijin* bureaus to administer the new local taxes on the inland transport of goods, reconstruction bureaus, local gazeteer bureaus, and foreign affairs bureaus. The expectant officials were also prevalent in the local versions of 'foreign'-inspired (*yangwu*) offices—telegraph bureaus, steamship companies, and cotton mills.

Although *ad hoc* administrative organizations proliferated in the late nineteenth century, a position in the self-strengthening enterprises or local administrative bureaus never commanded the prestige of the 'regular' official career. The enterprises and local specialized bureaus were irregular organizations created (or allowed to develop) to meet specific needs that the formal bureaucracy was ill-equipped or unwilling to handle on its own. As marginal organizations whose norms were unproven and unincorporated into the regular bureaucracy, they were accorded neither adequate leadership nor central support, and remained poorly coordinated with each other and the central bureaucracy. Careers in these supporting and *ad hoc* organizations were seen to be a poor second best, and were frequently used by the ambitious as springboards into the regular official bureaucracy. Until the imperial civil service examinations were abolished in 1905, most individuals continued to memorize the classics and practise eight-legged essays in the hope of examination success and an eventual career in the regular bureaucracy. For the central state, too, the fundamental norms of balance and harmony endured until the end of the century, despite rapid social change, the proliferation of *ad hoc* bureaus in the provinces, and deepening military, political and administrative crisis.

### THE *XINZHENG* ERA: RECASTING AGENDAS IN THE CENTRAL STATE, 1902–1911

In the wake of renewed imperial encroachment, the defeat of the Boxer Uprising, and rising nationalist demands for national pride and power, in the early years of the twentieth-century Qing court abruptly shifted course and proceeded fundamentally to re-orient the agenda of the central state, adopting a series of far-reaching measures known as the *xinzheng* ('new government') reforms. The *xinzheng* reforms established a fundamentally different template for political organization, state agenda, and political evolution in China: it projected nothing less than the rapid transformation of an agrarian empire, committed to balancing and presiding, into a centralized, commercial, dynamic, and modern country. In the years between 1903 and 1908, the Confucian civil service examinations were abolished; the central government 'Six Boards' were reorganized into modern ministries; military, educational, and police reform was promoted; plans were drawn up to directly project central government power much further into the provinces than had ever before been the case; and commissions were appointed to draw up programmes for the phased implementation of constitutional reform.[25]

If the *xinzheng* programme represented a fundamental shift in central state goals and agenda, the objective circumstances for realizing those new goals were distinctly unfavourable. The raw materials that aspiring central-izers had to work with—weak central institutions, the perennial tension between universalism and particularism, substantial power concentrated in the hands of provincial viceroys, a weak fiscal base, and limited direct projective capacity—remained fundamentally unchanged. Furthermore, the *xinzheng* central reformers had to contend simultaneously with new, provincially based alternative visions for national development, and to some extent incorporated these visions into the larger *xinzheng* project. Local and provincial elites had filled the vacuum left by the waning of central state power after the Taiping Rebellion; these same elites grew increasingly activist, vocal, and involved in a wide range of new projects by the turn of the century, establishing modern schools, recovering railroad rights, and convening provincial assemblies.[26]

Not surprisingly, these groups had their own conceptions as to how China should pursue the creation of wealth and power. The *xinzheng* reform package was, in fact, exceptionally ambiguous on the issue of local and provincial self-government. Memorials flew thick and fast on the advisability of representative government throughout the *xinzheng* era, the Qing established a preparatory commission for constitutional government (Xianzheng Bianchaguan) in 1907, and drafted multiple plans for the gradual transformation of the imperial system into a constitutional mon-archy; but the role that provincial and local assemblies would play in the policy process was left unclear when the general thrust of the other parts of the *xinzheng* programme was to consolidate and project central power. Designed to transform China rapidly into a strong, modern country, the *xinzheng* centralizing reforms ironically provoked widespread resistance and alienation in the provinces, and eventually contributed to the provincial gentry's withdrawal of support during the 1911 Revolution.

Ultimately, the dynasty proved unable to cope with the simultaneous rise of regional power, growing nationalism among the provincial gentry, and increasing demands to render the country strong and powerful, and it fell in 1911–12 to an uneasy coalition of northern militarists and southern repub-licans, who proclaimed the establishment of the Republic of China. But, while the 1911 Revolution was able to topple the Qing dynasty and decisively end the system of imperial rule, it did not quickly create a convincing set of replacement political institutions, and still less did it usher in the anticipated goods of republicanism: modern representative democracy, national unity, and renewed vigour in combating China's international weakness and underdevelopment. The political elite split between northerners, military figures, and those who had been strongly identified with the former imperial government, who tended to favour vigorous recentralization, and southerners, returned students, and those active in the new provincial assemblies, who usually pressed for greater representation and federalism.[27] And, once Yuan Shikai failed in his bid to crush the southern republicans and establish strong central control in 1916, no remaining group was militarily, politically, or institutionally strong enough to impose its vision on the rest of the country, initiating a progressively descending spiral of militarism, political fragility, and internal disintegration.[28]

With the onset of warlordism, internal political fragmentation, and continued external pressure, the remainder of the Republican period did not lack for aspiring centralizers whose goals, orientation, and agenda directly descended from the *xinzheng* reforms so belatedly undertaken by the Qing in its last decade of rule: despite the political change from Empire to Republic, there was broad continuity of central state agenda from the late Qing through the Republican period. Like the last generation of imperial reformers, most political executives in the Republican period took a fairly statist approach to national integration in the quest to make China strong and powerful, stressing military modernization and educational reform, encouraging commerce, and strengthening central government bodies. In addition, the vast majority of the top political players in both the Beiyang (1916–27) and Nationalist (1927–49) eras were socially conservative military men who had a consistent collective distaste for all forms of political participation that they could not directly control.

Unfortunately for the post-1911 governments of Republican China, the last years of the Qing passed on to its successor regime a set of structural weaknesses every bit as consistent as the new *xinzheng* agenda of central state and institution building, with a gap between central state goals and implementing capacity that was, if anything, even larger in the early Republic than it had been in the twilight years of the Qing. The old problems of weak central administration, weak resource extractive capacity, a non-unified military, ambiguous loyalty of central government personnel, and increasingly localist provincial elites worsened, compounded by the political disintegration and regional militarism of the 1910s and 1920s. Under these circumstances, dramatically increasing the central state's institutional capacity remained problematic.

The bureaucratic elites of the Republic were as much influenced by the traditions and practices of the late imperial state as they were constrained by the political pressures of contemporary reality. Even the self-consciously revolutionary Nationalists, who came to power significantly after the 1911 Revolution, continued to be powerfully influenced by many of the ideals and the institutional heritage of the late imperial Chinese state. Long after the political disintegration of the empire, the sheer weight of thousands of years of Chinese statehood, tradition, and cultural pride continued to exhibit a strong influence on the mind-set and actions of twentieth-century bureaucratic elites even as they struggled to implement new ideas, new programmes, and new goals in building a modern state.

BACKGROUND TO THE ESTABLISHMENT OF THE NATIONAL GOVERNMENT

When it established the National Government (Guomin Zhengfu) as the central government of China in April 1927, the Guomindang (Nationalist Party) was a weak, fractured entity still struggling with unresolved questions regarding its own identity. As a revolutionary party reorganized along Leninist lines by Soviet advisors in 1923–4, the Guomindang was unequivocally committed to national reunification, anti-imperialism, national dignity and salvation, and economic development. In practice, the Guomindang was a bewildering collection of groups and factions upon which a thin veneer of Leninist discipline had been lain. The best methods for achieving the laudable goals on which all could agree proved to be insurmountably far-ranging, with the Communists on the far left (who had been ordered by Moscow to cooperate with the Guomindang and accept Guomindang membership) advocating class struggle and radical social transformation, the 'left' Guomindang gravitating towards mass movements and social transformation but stopping short of endorsing class struggle, the revolutionary military elite (trained at the newly established Whampoa Military Academy) favouring chain-of-command discipline and focusing on securing military stability, and groups on the far right inherently distrusting the mass mobilization methods of the Communists and the 'left' Guomindang. Not only did these groups all promote different strategies for the achievement of national dignity and power, they were themselves shot through with personality-based networks of kinship, friendship, sworn brotherhoods, and old school ties. Thus, the history of the Northern Expedition to unify the country (launched by the Guomindang's National Revolutionary Army from its base in Guangzhou in July, 1926 and officially completed with the occupation of Beijing in June, 1928) and the concurrent formal establishment of the National Government in Nanjing in April of 1927 were crucial to the subsequent patterns of attempted institutionalization during the 1930s.

At what ought to have been the moment of its greatest success, as the National Revolutionary Army reached the big cities along the Yangzi River, the precariously maintained coalition openly broke apart. While the 'left' Guomindang established a provisional government in Wuhan, Chiang Kai-shek headed east to exploit the vast resources of Shanghai, the commercial heart of China. In so doing, Chiang tilted definitively towards the right. He entered into an alliance with the Shanghai capitalists and underworld, condoned the massacre of thousands of Communists in the city, established his own government in Nanjing, and set about extirpating Communist and leftist influence within the Guomindang and in the areas that it militarily controlled.[29]

In retrospect, it seems surprising that the Nanjing government survived at all; in mid-1927 it was faced with enemies on all sides and dissension within its own ranks. The issues with which it initially had to deal included the existence of (1) a rival government set up by an equally credible wing of the Guomindang in Wuhan, (2) a group of ultra-conservatives in the Guomindang who claimed sole legitimate authority, and (3) a forbidding number of powerful independent militarists in the north who stood between Nanjing and the overriding goal of national reunification under its aegis. The Wuhan government crumbled from lack of incoming funds, the new centre–right coalition under the leadership of Chiang Kai-shek reprimanded and re-included the hardline conservatives, and it then opted for a policy of cooptation and accommodation with the northern warlords. In exchange for the militarists' formal acceptance of the flag of the new National Government, they were brought into the government, given high positions, and, in the many instances in which the new government was unable to make good its claims to sovereignty in the provinces, were allowed *de facto* continued control over regional taxes and administration.

The process by which the National Government was tentatively established in 1927–8 had a resounding impact on the future direction of the regime. With the purge of the Communists and the Left, and the inclusion of warlords, industrialists, and various local elites whose commitment to any sort of revolutionary principles was highly questionable, the National Government under a Guomindang dominated by Chiang Kai-shek turned definitively away from bottom-up organization and social mobilization and opted instead for a top-down, elitist approach of simultaneous centralization and cooptation as the prevailing strategy to lead China from weakness, fragmentation, and humiliation to the national goals of unity, wealth, and power.

The circumstances for so doing in the late 1920s were hardly conducive to success. The struggle for unity had exposed irremediable divisions within the revolutionary movement; the upper echelons of the National Government and the Nationalist Party were still riven with cross-cutting factional cleavages and personality clashes; the territory to which the new government pretended included only two and a half provinces under the direct control of the National Government; and the combination of continued threats from within and an extraordinarily hostile international environment meant that the regime could not relax its already substantially heavy military slant. Military and fiscal weakness, in combination with the political elite's real belief in the organic unity of the Chinese people, and an increasing fear of open divisions and 'chaos' (*luan*) led the regime to include virtually all those who did not openly oppose the new government beneath a thin veneer of formal authority.

In addition, many of the basic operations of the newly established National Government exhibited a curiously schizophrenic character. Once the Guomindang had narrowed the definition of 'revolution' to mean a statist 'revolution from above', the vast majority of the actions and policies of the government continued the top-down, centralizing, state-building imperative that had first emerged with the *xinzheng* reforms in the last years of the dynasty, pursued by Yuan Shikai during the early Republic, and pretended to by a host of Beiyang governments in the years since 1916. The legitimating ideology of Sun Yat-sen could not be completely jettisoned by the Nationalist Party he created and reorganized, however. Even as it sought to re-centralize military and administrative control, the Nanjing regime promoted a cult of Sun's thought as the moral and ideological underpinning of its own rule.

The ideas underlying these two quite different visions of state reconstitution were only uneasily reconcilable. Sun's thought, such as it could be compressed into a legitimating canon for an increasingly militarily dominated and socially conservative regime, were far from consistent and therefore were exceptionally open to a fair amount of redefining and reinterpretation after he passed from the scene. But in the *Fundamentals of National Reconstruction* and *The Three Principles of the People*, which were the major documents repeatedly used to ground and legitimate Guomindang domination of state and society, Sun stressed the idea that local self-government ought to be implemented after a period of time in which the people were properly trained by the revolutionary party in the arts of self-government. There is no question that he envisioned a new government with powers that were divided both in the central government itself and between the central and regional governments.[30] On the other hand, the centralizing imperative characteristic of the state-building efforts that were begun in the very late Qing and early Republic stressed a strong executive that reduced all other elements in the political system to an advisory and handmaiden status in the interests of standardization, integration, and the creation of a strong central state.

Sun's ideas about 'Five Power Government' drew heavily from American political concepts about the desirability of divided power, and stipulated the eventual organization of the central government with five separate but equal supreme government bodies, which would comprise the Executive, Legislative, Judicial, Examination, and Censorial Yuan. Equally, despite the due establishment of these five organizations as the basis of the National Government in the late 1920s, the bulk of central government action in the Nationalist years was, as it had been for the earlier Beiyang, Yuan Shikai, and *xinzheng* central governments, heavily slanted towards statism, central control, and central institution building, with the bulk of real power vested in *ad hoc* military commissions with no formal constitutional status, and in the Executive Yuan.

The institutional ambiguities of the Nationalist era were not confined to the relative distribution of power between centre and regions: they were inherent to the makeup of the regime itself. Despite the formal separation of the Guomindang (Nationalist Party) and the Guomin Zhengfu (National Government) that was established in 1927, the relations between the two organizations were similarly characterized by redundancy and confusion, particularly at the top, as typically the leading figures in the government were also leading figures in the Guomindang Central Executive Committee and/or in important military organizations. With such overlap in two hierarchically organized bodies, the question of whether government policy was determined on the basis of decisions made in the upper echelons of the Guomindang, the National Government, or simply on the basis of informal arrangements between the key elite that shared positions in both underscored the lack of institutionalization from above.

Certainly at the apex of the political system, party, state, and personalities all merged to produce policy orientations for state organizations to carry out. But, in contrast to the Chinese Communist Party in the People's Republic some twenty years later, the Guomindang, however much it may have wished to do so, was never able to act as a shadow government with Party committees that emasculated state organizations from within. Guomindang influence in the National Government's state organizations was indirect, implemented by virtue of responsibility to either the Executive Yuan or to a minister who took his cues from decisions reached by the Guomindang Central Executive Committee. Except at the very top, the Guomindang and the National Government remained separate and readily distinguishable entities throughout the Nanjing Decade. However, the overlap between the personalities and informal groups with dual membership in both the Nationalist Party and the National Government both generated confusion over authority and prevented institutionalization at top decision-making levels, as those in the key elite often held multiple positions in party, government and military organizations.

In few policy areas of the fledgling government were the government's goals, the stresses and strains of its inherited institutional weaknesses, and the difficulties posed by its inclusive and co-optive strategy of state reintegration more visible and more problematic than in the design and execution of the national personnel system, and it is to this topic that we now turn.

# 2

# The Civil Service and State Building: The Examination Yuan in the 1930s[1]

INTRODUCTION

This chapter analyses the establishment of the National Government's formal civil service system in the 1930s as a symbol and reflection of a much wider process of attempted state building and institutionalization. After nearly twenty years of state disintegration and warlordism, it was during the late 1920s and 1930s that the Guomindang under Chiang Kai-shek entered its most vigorous period of national integration, consolidation, and state building. Although nearly uninterrupted threats to the state from within and without (recalcitrant warlords, Communist revolutionaries, and Japanese aggressors) enabled the military to justify a continued preponderance in governmental affairs,[2] the establishment of an effective central state administration was seen to be an equally crucial component of the regime's medium to long-term viability. Once the military situation stabilized, it was the central government civil servants who were often entrusted with much of the real implementation of policy. In areas as diverse as tax collection, flood control, household registration, land surveying, and education, it was incumbent on the newly constituted government to foster a cadre of these agents of the state that was both effective in policy implementation and highly responsive to the central executive.

While the formal civil service system of the new National Government was geared to the practical necessities of securing an effective and loyal bureaucracy, it also reflected a series of legitimating ideals. In a culture with a long tradition of bureaucratic rule and disdain for the military, the formal civil service system established in the Nanjing Decade reflected the regime's key values of standardization, rationality, and orderly control—values that were conceptualized as providing both desirable linkages with a proud past and the means to lead China into a glorious and modern future. The reality of the National Government's civil bureaucracy often fell far short of the ideals and principles reflected in the drafts of rules, regulations and laws it so regularly churned out, and the constant shortfalls in implementing the centralizing ideals of national civil service policy illustrated in microcosm the problems inherent to the Guomindang's co-optive approach to state building.

Even though reality proved disappointing, the aspirations embodied in those rules and regulations remained important as the standards against which reality was measured, towards which reformers continued to strive, and around which much discourse regarding the nature of the modernizing state coalesced. As a statement of *intention* as to the nature and composition of a newly reconstituting state, personnel policy in the National Government displayed both striking continuities and sharp breaks with the past. Like socially conservative governments the world over, the Nanjing regime did not hesitate to enlist the aid of the past in promoting its version of the future.

### THE EXAMINATION YUAN AND ITS ANTECEDENTS

As the central government organization entrusted with standardizing the national personnel classifications and holding civil service exams, the Examination Yuan owed its existence to Sun Yat-sen's conception of 'Five Power Government' as outlined in his April 1924 speech, 'The Fundamentals of National Reconstruction'. This speech in turn served as the legitimating basis of the Organic Law of the Republic of China, first promulgated by the Guomindang in October 1928. Thus, several years before the National Government was established in Nanjing, the establishment of a national civil service recruited on the basis of objective examinations was an established part of Guomindang ideology.

The Nanjing Government formalized its commitment to this goal in Article 37 of the Organic Law of 1928, which stated that the Examination Yuan was to be established as the 'highest examination organ of the national government [that] shall take charge of examinations and determine the qualifications of public service'. In addition, 'all public functionaries [should] be appointed only after having, according to law, passed an examination and their qualifications for public service having been determined by the Examination Yuan'.[3] After key preparatory laws and regulations were drafted in the late 1920s, the Examination Yuan was formally inaugurated on 1 January 1930, thereby joining the other four yuan of the National Government.

Sunist ideals about 'Five Power Government' and structural division of power to the contrary, the Examination Yuan was in other respects directly descended from the Yuan Shikai and Beiyang governments in Beijing of the early Republic. During the immediate post-imperial period, central government policy towards its own civil service contained two key planks: increasing standardization and efficiency under strong executive control, and open civil service examinations as a means by which to attract 'men of talent'. Continuing in the trajectory established by the late imperial *xinzheng* reformers who promoted the integration of the curriculum of the 'new schools' (of law, administration, and engineering) with a completely revised system of national civil service exams,[4] Yuan Shikai and the later Beiyang governments that adopted his central government personnel system virtually *in toto* attempted to build a strong central civil service highly responsive to the executive and recruited on the objective basis of experience and examination success. The interlocking imperatives of strong executive control over the prospective agents of the state, attracting 'men of talent' to central government service, and the desire to determine qualifications of excellence on the basic of objective criteria (preferably examinations as the 'Regular Path') were identifiably part of post-imperial central government policy in China as early as 1913–14.

Only eight months after the Emperor's abdication, Yuan Shikai issued a law that outlined the new rank classifications for the civilian bureaucracy under the Republic, and in 1914 he issued a Presidential Order detailing the qualifications and salary scales for particular ranks that remained largely unchanged until establishment of the Nanjing Government in 1927–8. By 1915 he had outlined a new set of regulations for the administration of civil service examinations at both the central and provincial levels.[5] This system of rank and grading classification was the first step in the central government's attempts to build a standardized, integrated bureaucracy under firm executive control.

In terms of rank classification, the civil service under Yuan Shikai was divided into those with status grades (analogous to a system of commissioned officers) and an equally large group of secretaries, copyists, and office workers without formal career status. From highest to lowest, the former were subdivided into the three general grades of 'selected' (*jianren*), 'recommended' (*jianren*), and 'delegated' (*weiren*) appointments: within each of these grades there were a number of different ranks or 'steps' that determined one's specific level and salary. While a small number of 'special' (*teren*) appointments for very high positions (such as the heads of ministries) were exempt from meeting the qualifications established for the other career positions, the backbone of the central government ministries was, at least in theory, covered by civil service qualification requirements. Between them, the appointees to the selected, recommended, and delegated grades included everyone from the division chiefs, councillors, and executive secretaries (who served the Minister directly) to the section chiefs and everyday section members who handled the bulk of the ministry's work. According to the personnel regulations, holding more than one appointment and serving in one's native area were both forbidden. Furthermore, except for the 'special appointment' political officials, bureaucrats were to be protected from arbitrary dismissal, regular promotions on the basis of competence and performance were to be established, and malfeasance in office was to be promptly punished by a special committee for the discipline of public officials. Through these regulations, the central government attempted to build a standardized system of rank classifications in which it could effectively manipulate incentives and sanctions to gain the responsiveness and increased performance of its civil bureaucracy.

Attempts to identify and recruit 'men of talent' willing to work for the central government in the early Republic under Yuan Shikai were hampered by two interrelated factors. The new 'standards of excellence' were far from clear, and in the 1910s there was still a relative scarcity of individuals appropriately trained abroad or in the new schools. Even on paper, the qualifications for the appointment of civil officials were exceptionally inclusive. The route to the highest 'selected' grade could be either through currently holding a position in a 'selected' or 'recommended' grade, or passing an examination with the 'selected' designation. Qualifications for the 'recommended' appointment were even looser—passing the civil service exam, holding a current 'recommended' position, having held an equivalent rank under the Qing, holding a university degree in law, economics, or politics, or having had five years of administrative experience all sufficed.[6]

Whether the personnel regulations under Yuan Shikai and the successor Beiyang governments did in fact serve as a screening device or were merely an *ex post facto* rationalization for bestowing official titles and status on those already in office is a question that awaits further research.[7] The regulations do clearly illustrate that in the absence of an effectively functioning civil service examination system, the central governments in the early Republic felt compelled to turn to two different pools of potential administrative talent: bureaucrats with previous experience, and graduates of modern schools both in China and returning from abroad. Although the constellation of influential groups in government circles changed considerably with the ascendance of the Guomindang in 1927–8, similarly returned students and men of practical administrative experience continued to be important recruiting grounds for appointees to the middle and upper reaches of the civil bureaucracy for the remainder of the Republican period.

After having served as one of the late Qing officials most involved in the attempted reform and eventual abolition of the late imperial civil service exams,[8] Yuan Shikai laid out a plan for a revived version of an examination and training system for both the central bureaucracy and local administration as soon as he could after taking over the presidency of the Republic. In 1915 he issued regulations for the eventual administering of a *gaokao* (upper civil service examination for appointment to the central government bureaucracy) and *pukao* (general civil service exam for appointment to provincial and local positions). Even though Yuan was forced from power and died in disgrace as the arch-villain of the modern period[9] before his programme for national examinations could be implemented, when the first *gaokao* under the Republic was held in June 1916, it bore a remarkable likeness to the Yuan Shikai plan of the year before.

The *gaokao* combined with a two-year on-the-job apprenticeship was designed to be a system that blended rigorous pre-entry selection with a healthy dose of practical training. A specially constituted examination committee (*dianshi weiyuanhui*) of academics and relevant specialists drew up examination questions for each area speciality, and then served as graders for the written examination papers. The examinations themselves were meant to be thorough. A preliminary exam tested general history, composition, and document handling: second and third sittings covered a wide variety of special topics such as law, government, shipbuilding and agronomy. Success on these three written exams and a final oral exam led to provisional assignment to a ministry for a two-year training period and an eventual appointment with a 'recommended' grade.[10]

Yuan Shikai's personnel system remained on the books essentially unchanged until the Nanjing government took power in 1927, even though the years between 1916 and 1927 were politically unstable in the extreme, with the country collapsing in endless wars waged by provincial militarists, and new governments being formed seasonally in Beijing. Yet in the midst of this systemic breakdown, the central bureaucracies of the Beiyang governments continued minimally to function: mail was delivered, schools continued to grant degrees, foreign loans were concluded, ambassadors were exchanged, and occasionally even national civil service exams were held according to the pattern that had been first laid out during the Yuan Shikai years.

When the Nanjing government had established a serious national military presence and was casting about to reconstitute the central state apparatus, it invented neither personnel classifications nor the basic structure of its civil service system from thin air; it drew heavily from the immediately preceding Beiyang and Yuan Shikai governments. If Sun's 'Fundamentals of National Reconstruction' offered the broad vision behind the creation of the Examination Yuan as the organization in the 'Five Power Government' system to be entrusted with examining and regulating the civil service, the particulars of an already quite elaborate system of personnel classification and civil service examinations developed by the previous generation of late Qing and early Republican centralizing reformers provided the basis upon which concrete measures and laws for a national personnel policy were further developed by the Nanjing government.

## THE EXAMINATION YUAN IN THE 1930s: INSTITUTIONAL CLAIMS, TACTICAL RETREATS, AND INCREMENTAL GAINS

In theory, the Examination Yuan that came into formal existence on 1 January 1930 ought to have played the dominant role in all aspects of the

National Government's civil service. It was by law the highest examining organization in a republic in which all civil servants were to be formally appointed only after having passed an examination. It also had the authority to determine the qualifications for each of the civil service classifications and formally to register the official appointments.[11] If it had truly functioned as its regulations stipulated, the Examination Yuan would have exerted a strong influence in the national government as a strong supporting arm of the central executive. But in reality, the Examination Yuan was a weak organization, with neither its own independent base of power nor the consistent backing of other entities in the government, and its decidedly mixed performance mirrored the weaknesses of the National Government and the drawbacks inherent to its strategy of co-optation.

While the Examination Yuan had the authority to issue laws and regulations on national personnel policy, it lacked the backup of effective rewards and sanctions through which it could encourage (and, if necessary, enforce) compliance. On the date of its formal inauguration, it had no influence to speak of in the rest of the National Government's civil administration, whose various ministries and commissions jealously guarded their autonomy with respect to their own staff. It was only over a period of years that the Examination Yuan could, by moving very slowly and carefully, make good *any* of its claims to formal and legal authority over the national civil service.

Despite its unevenness in goal implementation, the Examination Yuan remains a fascinating topic of inquiry. As this organization developed during the years between 1930 and 1940, it exhibited in microcosm the attempted implementation of the National Government's top-down strategy of state reconstruction, the tactical retreats mandated by its inclusiveness, its partial successes, its crucial cultural and symbolic linkages to past and future, and a final shift in orientation towards partification and militarization that would prove ineffective in stopping demoralization and decline during the Sino-Japanese War.

The Examination Yuan was a relatively small organization with perhaps only 200 full-time career employees and an equal amount of support staff during the 1930s.[12] Its formal organization reflected two quite different spheres of activity. Under the Examination Yuan's highest administrative level of President, Secretariat, and Board of Councillors were two subordinate organizations. A very small, permanent Commission on Examinations (Dianshi Weiyuanhui) handled general administrative affairs and created *ad hoc* subordinate committees, Xiangshi Weiyuanhui, to deal with the particulars of administering any given exam; a much larger, permanent, Ministry of Personnel (Quanxu Bu) handled matters for the civil service as a whole—promulgating the *Law on Civil Service Appointments* of 1933, evaluating the credentials of individual appointees, and establishing uniform pay scales and retirement benefits.

These two sub-organizations of the Examination Yuan addressed two quite different aspects of the National Government's personnel policy, aspects that were linked only tenuously. Through the subjects that it tested for, the examination system, as overseen by the Commission on Examinations, served as a symbolic wish list as to how the state conceived of itself via its national civil service. The Ministry of Personnel, on the other hand, was geared towards practical implementation of the state's standardization and centralization of control over its various parts. Of these two activities and separate organizations within the Examination Yuan, the examining function was invariably accorded higher symbolic status.[13] Since the positions on the Commission were so few, occupying one of them seems to have been a matter of some honour. In contrast, the Ministry of Personnel had a much lower profile, dealing with a huge volume of routine tasks such as checking of credentials and registration of civil servants. However, because the Ministry of Personnel's successes and weaknesses so closely mirrored those of the National Government as a whole, the following analysis reverses the traditional order of presentation.

The Ministry of Personnel was, by the standards of organizations in the National Government, exceptionally weak. To it fell the relatively thankless task of attempting to standardize, codify, and check on the qualifications of the thousands of career officials distributed throughout the various other government yuan and ministries that made up the National Government. The Ministry of Personnel's mission was to act in the general interest of the National Government, transcend the parochial interests of specific ministries, and enforce a minimum of across-the-board quality control with respect to appointments and promotions. The Ministry of Personnel rank-ordered its tasks and goals to include: (1) standardization of ranks and salaries; (2) review of public servants already in office; (3) review of new appointments; (4) registration of public servants and those who passed the examinations; (5) allocation of those who passed the examinations; (6) welfare work among public servants; and (7) training of public servants and the matter of rewards and penalties.[14] Within this ambitious set of objectives, even the completion of just the first and second tasks by such a small organization was an enormous administrative undertaking.

By the time it finally succeeded in getting its version of the *Law on Civil Service Appointments* approved by the Legislative Yuan in 1933, the Ministry of Personnel was completely occupied with a huge backlog of simple routine work: reviewing the qualifications of all those currently in office. By 1928–9, all the assorted central government yuan, ministries, and commissions were fairly bursting with personnel of highly divergent backgrounds, and the situation in the provinces was considerably more 'irregular'. Although the talents of individual administrators ranged from the highly trained to the functionally incompetent, virtually all bureaucrats with acting appointments in the late 1920s and early 1930s had come by their positions in the same way: through personal networks and private recommendation. The criteria for involvement in different networks varied enormously: individuals came by their positions on the basis of military service or loyalty to the Guomindang, through associations with former militarists or other elites now part of the central government, on the basis of previous central government service during the Beiyang period, and even on the strength of their professional and technical capabilities. Both the highly qualified and the completely unqualified were ultimately dependent on the same factor: the ability to tap into the networks of those with the power to allocate positions.

Since the National Government had deliberately adopted a policy of inclusion and co-optation, the rigorous enforcement of impersonal methods of civil service recruitment was among the many luxuries that it could not afford. Except for the very highest appointments, recruitment in the late 1920s and early 1930s operated on the principle of sub-infeudation. Individuals, informal groups, and factions would be brought into the government and rewarded with high positions in ministries (or divisions of ministries) over which they exercised the functional right of appointment. The types of individuals recruited at the upper–middle and middle reaches of the civil bureaucracy varied a great deal from ministry to ministry, from department to department, and even from time period to time period as the bosses at the top, with their differing emphases and orientations, changed.[15]

Even given the political necessities of the day, the National Government appears to have been exceptionally wide-ranging in its initial hiring of personnel, even going so far as to adopt a deliberately inclusive attitude towards a group to which it was in no way politically obligated—the former Beiyang government bureaucrats. Not only did the National Government central ministries accept large numbers of former Beiyang bureaucrats,[16] but some of the draft regulations being circulated throughout the Executive Yuan ministries in 1929 suggested that the qualifications of those who had passed the examinations under the Beiyang governments ought to be honoured for entry into the National Government. It was even felt in some quarters that those who had come up through the previous system in general should have precedence in hiring over mere college graduates who were without real experience.[17]

Government service in the 1930s was a high-status occupation with correspondingly generous salaries and benefits, and it was an occupation to which many aspired, as until the early 1940s prices remained relatively stable. Renumeration for even low-level section members was sufficient to support a family, and those with 'recommended' appointments could typically maintain large households with servants (see Tables 2.1 and 2.2).[18]

**TABLE 2.1.** National Government Civil Service Classifications

| Grade | Rank | Monthly salary (yuan) |
|---|---|---|
| *teren* ('special' appointment) | | 800 |
| *jianren* | 1 | 680 |
| ('selected' appointment) | 2 | 640 |
| | 3 | 600 |
| | 4 | 560 |
| | 5 | 520 |
| | 6 | 490 |
| | 7 | 460 |
| | 8 | 430 |
| *jianren* | 1 | 400 |
| ('recommended' appointment) | 2 | 380 |
| | 3 | 360 |
| | 4 | 340 |
| | 5 | 320 |
| | 6 | 300 |
| | 7 | 280 |
| | 8 | 260 |
| | 9 | 240 |
| | 10 | 220 |
| | 11 | 200 |
| | 12 | 180 |
| *weiren* | 1 | 200 |
| ('delegated' appointment) | 2 | 180 |
| | 3 | 160 |
| | 4 | 140 |
| | 5 | 130 |
| | 6 | 120 |
| | 7 | 110 |
| | 8 | 100 |
| | 9 | 90 |
| | 10 | 85 |
| | 11 | 80 |
| | 12 | 75 |
| | 13 | 70 |
| | 14 | 65 |
| | 15 | 60 |
| | 16 | 55 |

*Source*: Chen Tai-chi, 'Examination Yuan', in *The Chinese Yearbook 1935–36*, ed. Kwei Chungshu (Shanghai: Commercial Press).

TABLE 2.2.   Price Indices for Prewar Shanghai, 1930–1937

| | Price index |
|------|-------|
| 1930 | 100.0 |
| 1931 | 110.3 |
| 1932 | 98.0 |
| 1933 | 90.5 |
| 1934 | 84.7 |
| 1935 | 84.0 |
| 1936 | 94.6 |
| 1937 | 112.7 |

*Source*: Chang Kia-ngau, *The Inflationary Spiral* (New York and London: MIT Press and John Wiley), 371, table A-1 (based on data compiled by the National Tariff Commission).

Although degrees of professional competence and factionalism varied greatly from ministry to ministry, the numbers of individuals attracted to the state bureaucracy far outnumbered available positions, and the political imperative to bring as many powerful groups as possible into the government meant that many technically qualified individuals never got government posts, while many other functional incompetents were awarded sinecures. The inclusiveness of the National Government in this start-up period in the late 1920s significantly diluted its fervour and effectiveness at the outset, and continued to cast long shadows well into the 1930s.

In attempting to set minimal standards for official government classification, the Ministry of Personnel exhibited the same weaknesses that prompted the National Government to allow such a diverse lot on to its payroll on the basis of ascriptive qualifications in the first place. While the government's real power was still weak in the late 1920s and early 1930s, it preferred a strategy of top-down co-optation and informal coalition building under a façade of formal hegemony to a strategy of consolidation within a much narrower range of attempted control. The Ministry of Personnel pretended to the goals of standardization and centralization (with ritual obeisances to the need to 'attract talent' to government service), but the specifics of the Law on Civil Service Appointments betrayed the inherent weaknesses of the regime in its continued inclusion of those whose support it felt it could not do without.

The law was in many ways strikingly reminiscent of similar laws promulgated by Yuan Shikai in 1912–14. The classification scheme and salary scales were similar, and the broad categories of civil servants as either selected, recommended, or delegated were identical. The later addition of a larger number of steps or ranks ( *ji* ) within each grade ( *deng* ) did not much change the general levels of prestige and remuneration for each. If anything, the formal civil service qualifications for the National Government in the early 1930s were even more inclusive than had been those of the Yuan Shikai and Beiyang governments in the 1910s and 1920s. Those eligible for a 'selected' appointment included those currently holding a position with such a designation, those having acted as state officials for a year or more, those having 'rendered meritorious service to the Revolution for ten or more years', and those who had written well-known literary works or made inventions of recognized eminence. Qualifications for 'recommended' appointments were fulfilled by those passing the upper civil service examinations, those currently holding such a position, those having held a delegated appointment for three or more years, those having served the Republic for seven or more years, and graduates of universities and colleges in China or abroad. For the lowest commissioned grade of 'delegated' appointments, one could qualify by passing the lower-level, ordinary Examination Yuan exam, by currently holding a delegated position, by having served the revolution for five or more years, or by being a graduate of an upper-level special school.[19]

While Article 10 of the Law on Personnel stipulated a preference for appointees who had passed the official examinations, this provision was not backed up by other regulations or controls. Overall, the criteria for the qualifications for different grades were broad enough to grant official status to the vast majority of those already in office—irrespective of how they originally came by their posts. Technical competence and experience were certainly among the qualities valued and selected for. But even on paper, objective, technical, and educational qualifications were not given exclusive precedence for appointment: service to the revolution and an applicant's currently held position constituted equally valid claims.

The enormous number of drafts of the Law on Civil Service Appointments that were circulated and discussed between 1928 and 1933 suggest that the final product was the result of a long process of bargaining and progressive widening of qualifications. In this process, the powerful Executive Yuan (under which the vast majority of the functional ministries and civil servants were to be found) seems to have played a dominant role. Even before the Examination Yuan and Ministry of Personnel were formally established, drafts of regulations on the appointment of personnel quite similar to the later law were circulated to the ministries by the Executive Yuan. In November 1930, less than a year after the Examination Yuan was formally established, the Executive Yuan ordered its subordinate ministries and commissions to either retain or demote their personnel in accordance with these guidelines.[20] In this way, the right of actual checking and verifying qualifications was done by the ministries, who would then send their final reports on to the Registration Department of the Ministry of Personnel. Presumably, the Ministry of Personnel took exception to this further truncation of its already modest powers. Although the provisions for the qualifications for rank were substantially the same in the drafts and in the final law, the issue of who had the final power of review and determining classification remained unresolved until early 1933, when the law was passed in favour of the Ministry of Personnel.

Even so, the ministries under the Executive Yuan were extremely slow to submit the credentials of their personnel. In mid-1933, the Ministry of Personnel complained of foot-dragging and repeatedly issued extensions and exhortations to the ministries to turn in their supporting documentation forthwith.[21] After roughly a year and a half, the Ministry of Personnel succeeded in reviewing nearly 4,000 new appointments, a mere 361 of which were rejected as not being up to standard.[22] It appears that the Ministry of Personnel did manage gradually to extend its influence with respect to this basic review of personnel qualifications throughout the 1930s. By 1936 virtually all the organizations under the Executive Yuan had submitted their personnel documents for review, and by the early 1940s even those Party organizations involved in government operations had been sufficiently pressured to forward the qualifications of their employees.[23]

Throughout this period, even while its influence grew incrementally, the Ministry of Personnel had no direct means by which it could force a dismissal or a demotion in the Executive Yuan ministries. In the words of one former Ministry of Finance bureaucrat, 'If the Minister wanted to make a certain appointment, there wasn't a thing the Ministry of Personnel could to prevent it!'[24] Since temporary 'acting' (*daili*) appointments were not subject to the regular Ministry of Personnel review process, an individual whom a ministry particularly wanted to retain could be given a series of active 'temporary' posts, thus avoiding the scrutiny of the Ministry of Personnel.

As it exhorted the ministries to comply with its review, the Ministry of Personnel had but one, rather backhanded, actual sanction by which it could encourage compliance. It could (and sometimes did) withhold approval of the formal appointment of an individual it deemed not up to standard. Without the proper documentation from the ministries, it could threaten to not officially register anyone at all. The indirect evidence suggests that, over the course of the 1930s, the Ministry of Personnel was at least partially successful in establishing a new norm of formally conferred official 'standards' in the civil service bureaucracy. Individuals *did* hanker after the prestige of an official appointment: not coming up to 'regular' Ministry of Personnel standards (loose and inclusive as they were) was felt to be a great loss of face. The few who failed the Ministry of Personnel's review were supposed to resign, and in fact, these individuals tended to be slowly phased out by their work units after not receiving their official certificates of appointment.[25]

Although the Ministry of Personnel did achieve a measure of limited success in making its power of review and registration of civil servants more than an automatically forthcoming rubber stamp, review and registration was but one of the ways in which the Ministry attempted to foster standardization and control of the civil bureaucracy. Ultimately far more ambitious were its plans to establish an impersonal system of annual evaluations (*kaoji*) upon which pay raises and promotions would be based for the entire civil bureaucracy. In 1934 regulations on annual evaluations were issued to the ministries, at the end of 1935 the first Ministry of Personnel sponsored evaluations were held, and by early 1936 the system was codified into formal law.

In this annual review of personnel performance, the actual evaluation and filling in of forms was devolved to the lowest possible level. The Ministry of Personnel did little more than design the forms and send them along to the relevant personnel office in the individual ministries. This office would in turn pass the forms along to the supervisors of the departments and sections to be filled out, would hold a meeting to discuss the results, and would then present these to the Minister for his seal before returning its decisions to the Ministry of Personnel. This *kaoji* system delegated virtually all the discretionary power of evaluation to the immediate supervisors of those being evaluated in the ministries; by the time the results got back to the Ministry of Personnel, the latter had little more to do than register the decisions made elsewhere.[26]

Nevertheless, there were two ways in which the institution of an annual evaluation system in the ministries lent itself an ongoing process of standardization, rationalization, and central control. Since the Ministry of Personnel's forms were geared to grade overall performance, the categories to be evaluated included work effectiveness (50 per cent), knowledge (25 per cent), and deportment (25 per cent). These broad categories were further subdivided into specifics such as 'drafting documents', 'managing subordinates', 'willingness to accept responsibility', and 'handles work properly' (for work effectiveness); 'special achievements' and 'experience' (for knowledge); and 'carefulness', 'fairness', and 'dependability' (for deportment). Each sub-category was assigned a maximum number of points that could be earned. The overall score was to be linked directly to rewards (raises and promotions) and penalties (reprimands, demotions, and in extreme cases, dismissal).[27]

The reduction of overall performance to numbers and categories was a clear attempt to depersonalize an administration noted for its high level of personal networks. The numbers and categories on evaluation forms had the additional advantage of appearing to be 'scientific' and 'objective'. Although it is by no means certain that the annual evaluations served to de-personalize organizational life to the extent that its promoters had hoped, the system did work fairly well as a means of control in the mid-to late 1930s; the annual evaluations were coupled with strict quotas on the percentages of promotions permitted from 'designated' (*weiren*) to 'recommended' (*jianren*), and from 'recommended' to 'selected' (*jianren*) appointments.[28] Barring cases of extreme incompetence, most civil servants in the National Government were expected to advance grades within ranks fairly regularly under normal circumstances, although the big jumps in status from a 'delegated' to a 'recommended' appointment (or from a 'recommended' appointment to a 'selected' appointment) were very difficult to come by: enforced quotas allowed only 5 per cent of the delegated appointees to be promoted to the grade of 'recommended', and a maximum of 10 per cent of the 'recommended' grade bureaucrats to be promoted to a 'selected' appointment.[29]

By keeping the percentages of real promotions low and establishing a system in which justification for a promotion was, if not objective, then at least committed to paper on the basis of numerical evaluations, the Ministry of Personnel managed to foster some structural control and partially to impose plans for standardization and scientific management over the civil service at large. Furthermore, in keeping the numbers of recommended and selected appointments down, the Ministry of Personnel helped to maintain the continued prestige and high status of the upper civil service in the mid-to late 1930s.

Although the main agenda of the Ministry of Personnel—standardization and control of the National Government civil service—made incremental gains during the 1930s, the results it achieved never came close to realizing the goals to which it aspired. As a weak organization with a limited set of sanctions at its disposal, it was all the Ministry of Personnel could do to enforce a set of vastly watered-down standards that permitted the inclusion of warlords, party faithful, and in many cases all sorts of relatives and hangers-on. The examination system inaugurated with the first higher civil service exam of 1931 never provided more than a small fraction of the recruits into the civil service, because the Ministry of Personnel had no power of assignment: it could only *recommend* examinees to the ministries for positions.[30] Within the ministries, even the many who possessed professional qualifications or had relevant experience typically got their jobs through personal connections—the recommendations of friends and relatives.

The vast disjuncture between the Examination Yuan's powers of examination and its power of assignment to positions, combined with an inclusive set of criteria that validated the vast majority of individuals who had found their way into the National Government during the late 1920s, made for a national personnel system that was reactive and minimalist rather than proactive and maximalist. The Ministry of Personnel took some tentative first steps, with some modest success, in promoting new norms of objectivity and impersonal competence through the annual evaluations for civil service personnel; it also managed to establish a new set of norms in favour of quality control and minimal standards. But it did not serve as a proactive system of recruitment itself. A truly well functioning civil service examination system that made performance on impartially administered exams a prerequisite for official appointment could have played this sort of proactive role. But in the 1934 revision of the Organic Law, even the polite fiction that 'all civil servants shall be appointed only after having passed an examination' was quietly dropped in the recognition of the state's weak institutional capacity to enforce such a provision across the board. As a result, standards, levels of commitment, and degrees of factionalism varied dramatically from ministry to ministry—with consequential unevenness in the performance of the National Government central bureaucracy as a whole.

## THE 'ADMINISTRATIVE EFFICIENCY' SCHOOL

These interrelated problems were recognized and extensively discussed by a loose coalition of contemporary academics, journalists and government officials whose assorted writings and analysis could be called the 'Administrative Efficiency' school.[31] Led by a former member of the 'left' Guomindang, Gan Naiguang, and supported by reformist government officials concentrated in the Ministry of the Interior, the 'Administrative Efficiency' reformers pushed for the establishment of a central Committee on Administrative Efficiency as an advisory body to the Executive Yuan in mid-1934. Between 1934 and 1936, the committee published periodicals in Chinese and English pertaining to administrative efficiency and reform, hosted conferences, and drew up multitudinous plans for reform—in the central archives, for the provincial governments, for local tax administration, and for the integration of 'Bandit Suppression Areas'.

The writings of the 'Administrative Efficiency' group were highly practically oriented; their recommendations for realizing administrative efficiency reflected both a tremendous admiration for the civil services in the West and an overpowering desire to centralize administrative authority and standardize operations in a China that was still institutionally weak, fragmented, and anything but centralized and standardized. Typical articles dealt with plans for the reform and standardization of documents and forms, reform and implementation of an examination system, the desirability of supplementary education for government officials, and the possibilities of imitating certain types of Western institutions such as the US Civil Service Commission.[32] The Administrative Efficiency school equated the 'scientificization' (*kexuehua*) of administration with centralization on the basis of objective, impersonal criteria. They also explicitly appealed to the principles of (Western) scientific management: the goal of reform was to simplify and unify procedures in order to use less resources and time in accomplishing more production and results.[33]

With their desire to raise administrative efficiency by scientific management methods, the Administrative Efficiency reformers singled out the prevalence of ascription in government offices (such as position based on private or party connections) for particular opprobrium. In virtually every article, they bitterly criticized the continued existence of personalistic ties in the bureaucracy, warned against its pernicious effects, and offered practical recommendations as to how to circumvent it. One author waxed particularly sarcastic in his characterization of the normal recruiting process as practised in the ministries:

Normally, employers only ask after one's connections, not after one's skills. Their calculation for hiring is as follows: (relatives + old friends + acquaintances) + (position distribution + individual background) = the sum total [of this appointment system].[34]

The reformers urged the rooting out of personalism; breaking the power of informal groups by giving unannounced competence tests to those already with positions to identify those bureaucrats 'of inferior quality seeking safety in numbers by hiding amongst the group'; recruiting solely on the basis of a working civil service examination system; instituting a strong system of yearly *kaoji* evaluations; and guaranteeing tenure to regular officials to 'encourage the spirit of public service'.[35]

Although many of the Administrative Efficiency reformers were themselves members of the Guomindang, they were ambivalent about the way in which the Guomindang had the potential to exercise power through the government bureaucracy and networks of patronage. With their stress on scientific management, impersonal, Weberian bureaucracy, objective technical competence, legal proceduralism, and the institution of a strict division between political leaders and technical administrators, the Administrative Efficiency group stood in implicit opposition to Guomindang partification of the civil bureaucracy, and occasionally would go so far as to say so directly. In the words of Gan Naiguang, in his introductory article to *The Chinese Administrator*, 'appointments of Civil Servants—through whatever method they may come about—should be governed by objective standards. Considerations of personal relationship or party affiliations *must be thrown overboard*' (emphasis added).[36]

On the other hand, the views of the Administrative Efficiency school were sympathetic to the increased centralization of administrative and executive power in general, and to the strengthening of examination personnel systems in particular, thus finding a natural constituency in the Examination Yuan and, to a lesser extent, in the Executive Yuan. The revival of an effective civil service examination with strong links to the higher education system, the guaranteed employment of those who passed the examinations, and the institution of rigorous evaluation and review in the government bureaucracy were central to the Administrative Efficiency reform package and could logically be expected to be implemented through the Examination Yuan. The goals of the Examination Yuan, the Ministry of Personnel, and the Administrative Efficiency school dovetailed around the ideals of central control, standardization, and objectively determined individual qualifications in the name of science, efficiency, and the speedy national reconstruction of China.

Existing in an environment of weak institutions, where lip service was paid to the ideals of unity and objectivity but most real influence was still tied up with factions and groups that had gained strongholds in the ministries, this modestly centralizing/reformist coalition did manage to achieve some tactical victories (such as the promulgation of the Law on Personnel Appointment) during the mid-1930s. A new norm of annual evaluation on the basis of objective competence was inaugurated, and in at least some organizations technical competence and excellence in work performance became increasingly important criteria for recruitment and promotion. Moreover, the number of civil service examinees in the ministries slowly climbed as examinations were held more regularly. But even while these reformist trends made slow headway, the underlying system remained largely unchanged.

When the war with Japan broke out in 1937, the Examination Yuan and the Ministry of Personnel were significantly stronger than they had been in 1931. But even so, the vast majority of civil servants had obtained and still went about obtaining their positions on the basis of whom they knew rather than through an open exam. Most units could boast of only one or two individuals who had passed the exams, and many had none at all.[37] An evaluation system had been set up, but the significant promotions tended to be made quite apart from the formal evaluations.[38] More examinations were held and placement became less of a problem, but the Examination Yuan was still powerless to directly assign successful examinees to substantive posts.

In short, even at the end of the 1930s, personalistic ties in recruitment (and, to a lesser extent, in promotion) were still of primary importance in the civil service of China. Government administration was far from the scientific discipline that the Administrative Efficiency school had hoped to see realized. Reality still fell far short of hopes and ideals. Although all could agree in theory on the necessity of attracting talent and promoting on the basis of objective considerations, in practice very few were willing to upset their own networks of personal ties for the sake of a less immediate, more abstract principle. Even while the standards for new appointees and promotions did, on the whole, rise during the 1930s, the vested interests of many in the central government worked against the strict institutionalization of an effective examination system.

## EXAMINATIONS AS SYMBOLIC IDEAL

Whatever the shortcomings of the National Government's actual record on depersonalizing its own central government civil service, the ideal of a national civil service based on open examinations as the 'regular path' (*zhengtu*) remained extraordinarily powerful throughout the 1930s (and indeed, for the remainder of the Republican period). Like the national personnel system, the examination system did slowly begin to institutionalize during the 1930s. As the decade wore on, more examinations were held and the absolute numbers of those in the ministries with examination credentials increased. However, since the examinations never contributed more than a fraction of the total number of civil servants,[39] it was chiefly as an ideal and a symbol that the examinations were so important.

The institution of civil service examinations was one of the few means available that could bridge the gap between China's proud past and her uncertain steps into a 'modern' future. The association of civil service examinations with the late imperial Chinese state had been very strong for centuries. In one form or another, examinations had been a primary source of recruitment into the civil service of the Chinese state since at least the Tang Dynasty (618–907), and laudatory treatments of the subject by Chinese authors typically tried to push the pedigree of civil service examinations back even farther to the Han Dynasty.[40] At the same time, civil service examinations were a prominent feature in the government systems of the advanced, wealthy, and modern West. The civil service examination was that rarest of cultural institutions; it was sufficiently malleable to look simultaneously backward to a proud past *and* forward to a progressive future. As such, civil service examinations were such a symbol of great positive valence that they could attract a substantial cross-section of the political and administrative elites in Republican China.[41]

In the immediate post-imperial period, politicians who were mortal enemies (such as Yuan Shikai and Sun Yat-sen) both envisioned a reconstituted Chinese state in which civil service examinations figured prominently. In the succeeding generation of the 1930s and 1940s, the National Government's very inclusiveness accommodated a range of sub-groups ranging from the 'left' Guomindang (Gan Naiguang) to other more narrow technocrats who contributed to the Administrative Efficiency writings or worked in the Examination Yuan and Ministry of Personnel, to individuals on the far right like Dai Jitao, who was the head of the Examination

Yuan—all of whom, at the very least, paid lip service to the ideal of civil service examinations.[42]

Civil service exams could be positively validated both with the traditionalist vocabulary of providing a 'regular path' by which a 'career was open to talent'[43] and through the progressive criteria of efficiency and expertise. Through the institution of open civil service examinations, even an arch-progressive Administrative Efficiency proponent could write (one suspects with some relief) about at least *one* topic in which something indigenous to China was borrowed by the currently 'advanced' West, and transformed into an entity both recognizably efficient and modern. Wrote Shen Jianshi, 'The abuses of the [previous examination system] were not with the principle of the examinations themselves. *Previous times* had exhibited a *good system* in which examination was the regular path to appointment'[44] (emphasis added). Further, like the Confucian bureaucrats who had not spent the long years of studying in vain, those who came in via the examination route were commonly awarded 'regular' status.[45] With such a variety of legitimating bases, civil service examinations (and the upper civil service exam in particular) provided a potential unifying symbol around which many different groups clustered to work through their various visions about the direction of the post-imperial, post-warlord Chinese state.

The examination system introduced by the National Government in the early 1930s reflected a hodgepodge of ideals as to the optimal constitution of a national civil service. From the outset, three very different sets of exams were planned: an upper civil service exam (*gaokao*) for entry into the central government upper civil service with a recommended appointment (*jianren*); a special set of exams requested on an occasion-by-occasion basis to fill immediate needs (*tekao*), also for recommended appointments; and an 'ordinary' exam (*pukao*) for entry into the central or provincial bureaucracy with a delegated appointment, (*weiren*).

Beginning with the first upper civil service exam of 1931, the Examination Yuan planned to hold upper civil service and ordinary civil service exams in alternating years, to be supplemented with special exams as requested by the relevant ministries when the need arose. The Examination Commission decided when examinations would be held and constituted an *ad hoc* Supreme Examination Committee (Dianshi Weiyuanhui) usually composed of government officials, which in turn created another *ad hoc* Assistant Examination Committee (Xiangshi Weiyuanhui). This committee, whose members were usually university professors and middle-to-upper-level bureaucrats, dealt with the bulk of the preparatory work and the initial grading of the exams, while the Supreme Examination Committee used the final red ink to assess the examinations.[46] While the Examination Yuan held the formal authority, initiated the examination cycle, and validated the results, the real administration of the national civil service exams was delegated to *ad hoc* committees of experts constituted specifically for the purpose of holding that particular exam.

Through their composition of their questions, the procedures by which they were administered, and the mythology that surrounded them, the upper civil service examinations held during the 1930s reflected the both the basic agenda and methods of implementation for the reconstituting state. Although the categories of examination questions sometimes shifted in proportional importance, the types of knowledge selected for inclusion in the examinations remained unchanged throughout the 1930s and into the 1940s. From the very first examination cycle of 1931 until the end of the Republican period, the civil service examinations held by the Examination Yuan paired cultural conservatism with two much newer types of qualification: loyalty to the Party–State, and objective technical competence.

The exams were divided into three. A written first exam tested general knowledge, Chinese language, clarity of thought, and Party principles. A second exam tested for objective knowledge and critical analytical ability in specialized areas (such as general administration, education, finance, or foreign affairs). There was a final oral exam. With the exception of the newly added section on Party principles, the rough composition of these civil service exams was similar to that originally outlined by Yuan Shikai in the mid-1910s. In both schemes, a large general knowledge/Chinese language section ensured that the upper civil service was literate and cultured, while the questions on specific subject areas provided for the selection of individuals with high degrees of professional, 'modern' training and experience.[47]

All applicants, including those who were conspicuous 'examination successes' with the highest scores of their year, agreed that these exams were very difficult.[48] For any given upper civil service exam cycle, only roughly 100 of several thousand would pass all three parts. The overall pass rate of the upper civil service examination between 1931 and 1940 was a mere 8.61 per cent, and the vast majority of those who did pass barely did so, with scores in the 60–70 per cent range.[49] To have even a chance to pass, the examinee had to demonstrate knowledge of the legitimating doctrines and inner workings of the National Government and the Guomindang, be well grounded in the elite classical culture, *and* have an extensive academic mastery of a specialized area.

The general knowledge items were the first tested and were designed to be particularly difficult. Most questions leaned towards the historical and the archaic, and required active use of classical Chinese. Questions such as '"Virtue obtains position, ability directs office and salary secures achievement." Discuss, using classical Chinese' were typical. Other questions commonly asked for essays on Mencius' views of statecraft, Confucius' 'Four Teachings', or discussions of traditional aphorisms such as 'Men of learning should manage the affairs of All Under Heaven' (attributed to the founding Ming Emperor in the mid-fourteenth century).

'General knowledge', as constructed on the upper civil service examinations, presumed the ability to link knowledge of the past with contemporary circumstances. One particularly interesting question on the *gaokao* of 1931 asked the examinee to 'Discuss the following: (1) How the Executive Yuan enforces its orders to the provinces and instructs its subordinate organizations. (2) The Executive Yuan's historical and cultural antecedents. Be sure not only to discuss damage [done by previous administrative systems to the country] but also to concentrate on how [previous executive systems] safe-guarded culture and the purity of the country.'[50] Evidently, the heavy use of classical Chinese and archaic subjects weeded out a fair percentage of candidates at the very beginning. Even as late as the 1936 exam, significant numbers of people took one look at the examination questions, got up, and left the room in despair.[51]

'General knowledge' also always included a sub-section on 'Party Principles' (*dangyi*), which in the late 1940s and 1950s would become 'The Three Principles of the People' (*sanmin zhuyi*). Almost all of these questions required a fairly thorough knowledge of Sun Yat-sen's more important speeches and documents, and occasionally questions on the content of recent Party Congresses or proclamations were asked as well. Even in these cases, the examinee was expected to refer back to the ultimate canon of Sun Yat-sen whenever possible. The answers assumed by questions such as 'How ought one to go about re-establishing the position of the Chinese people?' (1931 exam) thus linked a general goal to which all were committed (restoring the power and pride of the Chinese people) with Sun Yat-sen's unchallengeable principles and, by extension, with the National Government and the Guomindang's current programmes for realizing them.[52] To answer virtually any of the questions on Party principles, the candidate was to write an essay extolling the current agenda of the State through the vehicle of Sun's thought. The way in which the themes of modernization, economic construction, order, and anti-communism were expected to be discussed strongly implied loyalty both to the Party and to the State's agenda and methods.

For those who successfully completed the rigorous first day of examinations, the second day offered equally challenging questions in a variety of sub-fields. This part of the examination tested factual knowledge of given subject areas, and was also felt to be quite difficult by those who took it. One examinee who later went on to a very high position in the Ministry of Personnel remarked of the education sub-field on the 1933 exam: 'The examinations were *very* thorough—even a Ph.D. in education would have had a hard time answering everything!'[53] Questions were, in fact, quite comprehensive. The education speciality required the individual to prepare for the sub-fields of educational theory, educational history, educational administration and administration, education statistics, normal, technical, social, and village education, educational psychology, investigation into educational problems, and the construction of course curricula. On this particular exam, the education sub-field asked for an essay involving a detailed comparison of educational systems in the USA, Europe, and China both before and after the First World War.[54]

Between the general knowledge, the Party principles and the special subject sections, the examination questions were designed to reward the relatively few who, like the institution of the examinations itself, had the equipment and flexibility to look backward to a solid grounding in history and culture, to function in the present by submitting to the ideals and authority of Party and State, and to contribute their technical abilities and knowledge in leading China into the future.

The procedures and ceremonies surrounding the administration of the exams were even more revealing in their symbolic linkages to the past. The way in which the examinations were graded exhibited a longstanding fear of bias on the part of the evaluators. The questions were graded blind, and, like those in charge of the imperial examinations, the graders on the Assistant Examination Committee were literally locked up in the Examination Yuan and not allowed any contact with the outside world for days, until the results were fully tallied and cross-checked. In a formal procession reminiscent of that following the imperial examinations, the results of the exam were announced when the Head of the Examination Yuan, Dai Jitao, formally unlocked the grading cells of the members of the Examination Committee and Assistant Examination Committee. All then marched out the Examination Yuan gate and posted a 'Golden Roll' of the names of the successful examination candidates in rank order on a red banner upon which Dai had written the characters 'For the sake of the country, seek the able and virtuous.' After Dai bowed, firecrackers were set off and the crowd surged forward to find out who had placed where on the list. The next day there were further formal ceremonies, first at the Sun Yat-sen mausoleum, and then within the gates of the Examination Yuan itself. During the latter ceremony, the first, second, and third highest scorers on the exams were presented with special commemorative gifts and calligraphy paraphernalia.[55]

In general tenor and specific ceremonial, the procedures surrounding the announcement of the successful examinees attempted to recreate the spirit that animated the final phase of the late imperial examination cycle. In both periods, the successes were relatively few in number and had come through a gruelling set of examinations everyone knew to be extraordinarily competitive. The ceremonial publicized and reified those successes as members of a status group apart, re-emphasized the group's close links to the state, and underscored the longstanding legitimacy of the whole process. Dai Jitao himself acknowledged these post-exam festivities as a 'showcase for showing off talent'.[56]

Even the architecture of the buildings in the Examination Yuan complex revealed a similarly syncretic amalgamation of culturalist looking backward and marching forward into the brave new world of modern statehood. The complex itself was modelled after a traditional Chinese palace with several separate buildings, courtyards, and gardens. To re-emphasize the traditional primacy of civilian over military, Dai Jitao (who was himself much influenced by the pacifist strains of Buddhism) refused to allow outside police or military guards anywhere near the gate of the Examination Yuan. Instead, he had his own corps dress in the style of traditional military guards. Archaeological and cultural objects were scattered throughout the grounds; the Yuan's atmosphere had the ambiance of a modern government office and the coloured detail of an old-time yamen.[57]

The couplets and aphorisms inscribed on the stone pillars and across the transverse beams of the Examination Yuan's buildings betrayed a similar conflation of traditional values and new state goals. The signs in front of the main gate and main office read in a fairly traditional vein: 'He who enters this gate, let him not be out for winning promotion and getting rich: he who exits this gate, let him have the leisure to cultivate himself and succor the people' (main gate), and 'Intelligence and humaneness are formulated only in the midst of adversity: one should be pure, cautious and diligent in one's actions' (main office). Others were much more syncretic in their application of traditional vocabulary to new ends. The sign in the Hall of Ceremonies read: 'Only by *restoring fundamental morality* and intellectual capability can we save China, create true equality and freedom, and *quickly catch up to world cosmopolitan culture*' (emphasis added).[58]

The ideal of an examination system provided a highly positively charged symbol around which otherwise quite diverse groups of Chinese elites could cluster. Objective, state-run examinations as an integral part of a 'regular path' and a 'career open to talent' were ideals long in existence in China and doubly legitimated by the contemporary example of the Western civil service systems. Since open civil service examinations provided a positively charged symbolic arena into which many were drawn, it was possible for the examination system to begin to take hold in the mid-1930s through a process of gradual inclusion. The steady expansion of the upper civil service exams into new administrative areas, the increasing frequency of special examinations, and a partial shift in the profile of the typical successful examination candidate all attest to the partial, albeit incomplete, institutionalization of the examination system during the 1930s.

In 1931, the year in which the first *gaokao* was held, the examination system contained very little beyond intent, symbolism, and ceremonial.

The Ministry of Personnel did not as yet formally exist, and the Examination Yuan, itself only recently created, had no influence to speak of in the ministries. Some successful examinees were never assigned appointments at all, and the evidence suggests that many were accepted only very grudgingly. The ministries were already staffed with individuals of varying qualifications, virtually all of whom had attained their positions through recommendations and personal connections. Those who took the examinations in the early 1930s tended to be the leftovers—those without the influence and 'pull' to obtain an appointment in the usual way.[59]

Although the examination successes of 1931 and 1933 were not particularly well connected, as a group, they were very bright young men in their mid-to late twenties who had attended the better public and private universities in China.[60] After having come through such a set of difficult examinations and participated in the same legitimating ceremonies, they were quick to develop a sense of quasi-corporate solidarity. In early 1932 there were still some of their number who had not been assigned a position, a number of others who had already been arbitrarily dismissed from their jobs, and many who had not been yet been accorded the recommended appointment status that was their due. Those who had passed with the highest grades for each of the sub-fields on the first upper civil service exam, along with some of the other less distinguished successes, wrote a joint letter of protest to the Examination Yuan in which they outlined their grievances and requested job security and immediate conferral of recommended appointment status. In June 1935 very much the same group wrote yet another letter to the Examination Yuan. On this occasion they cited the prevalence of non-examinee appointments in the ministries, and urged the Yuan to implement its own regulations by ensuring that those who passed the exams were appointed before anybody else.[61]

Although the examinees of 1931 and 1933 were less than satisfied with their treatment in the ministries in the early 1930s and were not particularly happy about the state of personnel appointments even in 1935, other evidence indicates that the examination system was, in fact, beginning to stabilize in the mid-1930s. At this time the number of special subjects offered as part of the *gaokao* steadily expanded. In 1931 one could choose from one of five areas: general administration, education, finance, police administration, or foreign affairs. On the 1933 exam police administration was dropped,[62] but three new areas—auditing/accounting, statistics, and judicial administration—were added. By the 1935 exam, inclusion of public health, (economic) construction, and upper-level postal administration brought the number of specialized topics on the civil service exam to ten. With the specially administered 1936 exam in honour of Chiang Kai-shek's fiftieth birthday, the number of sub-fields dropped back down to a hard core of six: general administration, education, finance, auditing/accounting, statistics, and judicial administration. However, this exam was a specially offered sitting and an exception to the otherwise quite general trend towards the widening scope of the upper civil service exam; after 1936, the trend of including larger numbers of special subjects was reasserted.[63] The *modus operandi* of the Examination Commission seems to have been that, when it was in doubt, it ought to add another subject to the *gaokao*.

Furthermore, by the mid-1930s some of the functional ministries began to avail themselves of the Examination Yuan's services. In 1934 several ministries requested that the Examination Yuan hold special examinations (*tekao*) to fill their needs for technically trained personnel in such areas as accounting and judicial administration. By the 1936 special sitting of the upper civil service exam, allocation of successful examinees was no longer a serious problem. At least in some cases, the Examination Yuan and the relevant ministry were by this time sufficiently coordinated that there was no practical distinction between a *tekao* (formally requested of the Examination Yuan by the ministry to fill specific shortages of personnel) and the regular sub-fields of the *gaokao*. Those who chose finance as a sub-field on the 1936 upper civil service examination thought of themselves as taking a *tekao*; they tested exclusively for entry into a new department that was in the process of being created at that time.[64]

By the mid-1930s the civil service examination system, like the national personnel system of which it was an ostensible component, was gradually becoming regularized. The Examination Yuan and at least some ministries had begun to arrive at a state of mutually beneficial coordination and cooperation; as the Examination Yuan increasingly offered examinations to qualify the personnel for which there was a demand in the ministries, the ministries correspondingly proved more willing to hire those who had passed the examinations. As this trend towards stabilization and co-ordination proceeded in tandem with the extension of the personnel system, the profile of those who attempted the exams shifted. In contrast to the early 1930s, when the typical examination candidate was a bright young man without the private connections to obtain a post, by the late 1930s between a third and a half of the examination successes had already been in substantive positions in government organizations for some years.

Success on the *gaokao* carried with it a big leap in upward mobility for the vast majority of everyday section members who were blocked by the strict quotas on promotions to 'recommended' status. Since passing the upper civil service examinations conferred *jianren* ('recommended') appointment status after a relatively short probationary period, those already with positions in the civil service used the examination system as a means of breaking through the promotion bottleneck between the vast mass of *weiren* ('delegated') appointments and the much higher in status *jianren* ('recommended') appointments.[65]

## REFORM, EXPANSION, AND COMPETING PRIORITIES, 1937 AND AFTER

The incremental development of an inclusive and largely technocratic examination and civil service system ended abruptly in 1937, when the Japanese invaded central China and precipitated the retreat of the National Government to Chongqing, in the far interior. Directly and indirectly, the war created the conditions under which the Nationalist Party would attempt to reinvigorate and dramatically expand the central state bureaucracy. Unfortunately for all concerned, efforts at bureaucratic reinvigoration faltered with exponential growth. Immobilism, inflation, and military defeat combined with rapid expansion of government organizations to produce a decline in the prestige and ineffectiveness of the civil service for the remainder of the 1940s.

Party leaders who doubled as government political executives began openly to question the loyalty, commitments, and implementing capacity of their own upper civil service as early as 1938–9. From the time the dust began to settle in Chongqing in late 1938, the regime was keenly aware of its military and administrative weaknesses: it had lost its best trained military core in the autumn of 1937, had lost its economic base in the Jiangnan, and had removed itself to a region of the interior in which its roots were shallow to non-existent. A temporary accommodation with the Communists to the north had been reached, but the agreement was expedient and was felt to be damaging to the regime's grounding on the principle of anti-communism.

In this atmosphere of deeply felt institutional weakness, the Guomindang launched a broadly based programme of inculcation into martial values and Party norms 'from above' via a strategy of highly controlled, one-month 'training courses' (xunlianban) to bring at least the middle to upper reaches of the government bureaucracy into line. A whole range of xunlian courses, some run by the Central Training Institute (Zhongyang Xunliantuan), some completely managed by the ministries themselves, and some run as joint ventures between the Central Political University (Zhongyang Zhengzhi Daxue) and sub-units of particular ministries, aimed to bring the three pronged goal of militarization, partification, and increased technical capacity to the remainder of those who could in any way be in a position entailing discretionary decision-making in the government.[66] One interviewee remembered xunlian as consisting largely of military drill during the morning, and afternoon sessions of 'political study' (zhengzhi xuexi)— Sun Yat-Sen's more important works, current Guomindang policy directives, the all-important distinction between Sun's 'Principle of People's Livelihood' and communism, and the wartime collaboration with the Communists as a purely tactical necessity.[67]

Even before the civil service began to grow exponentially in the early 1940s, the Party leadership had turned decisively away from the largely Weberian and technocratic approach to the state administration that was characteristic of the early to mid-1930s, with a number of measures designed to partify (*danghua*) and militarize (*junshihua*) government administrators. One of the first things to be altered was the process of the civil service examinations, which were now reoriented towards ensuring the political responsiveness and Party loyalty of the new cadre of successful examinees. Although the *gaokao* had always required an essay on Guomindang ideology for the general knowledge segment of the exam, during the 1930s the questions on party principles (*dangyi*) comprised just one two-hour sub-section during a whole day of testing on general knowledge, and was weighted as being significantly less important than the aggregate of the other general knowledge questions or the full day of testing on specific technical sub-fields.[68]

Even if in practice there were many different routes into the government bureaucracy, before the onset of the Sino-Japanese War the examination system assumed implicitly that in principle examination success was a sufficient qualification by *itself* for a government position at a relatively high entry level. For those who got through the first two days of written exams, the final oral exam was very much a formality: very few individuals were eliminated at this late stage.[69] If examination success did not guarantee a position in the bureaucracy in the 1930s, this was widely felt to be a regrettable departure from principle, and almost no one seems to have openly questioned the appropriateness of a system of proven examination success to be followed by a short probation and official appointment, until the war years.

These previous working assumptions were substantially modified with the first major post-retreat upper civil service examination of November 1938. For the duration of the Sino-Japanese War, examination success was a desirable but by itself insufficient qualification for a medium to upper-ranking government appointment in the National Government of China. Guomindang Party authority, exercised through the Central Executive Committee (Zhongyang Zhixing Weiyuanhui) and the Supreme National Defence Committee (Guofang Zuigao Weiyuanhui), decided in favour of a new procedure known as the 'preliminary examination/re-examination' (*chushi-zaishi*) system. In this scheme, those who qualified for the upper civil service examination, upper-level special civil service examinations, or judicial administration examination for an appointment at the *jianren* level took a first set of examinations (with questions and sections similar to those of the exams in the earlier part of the decade) and were then obliged to attend the Guomindang Central Political School (Zhongyang Zhengzhi Xuexiao), soon to become a full fledged Central Political University

(Zhongyang Zhengzhi Daxue) for a three-to nine-month course of 'training' (xunlian). After completing the training course, the examinee then took a 're-examination' (zaishi) which, if passed, provided the formal qualification for a jianren civil service appointment.[70]

The Central Political School (later Central Political University) was, in turn, 'established by the [Guomindang] Party... for the purpose of revolution and national construction... and training committed cadres [zhengzhi xuexiao shi dang li de xuexiao, fu you geming jianguo... peiyang jingmingde ganbu]'.[71] Although in practice the training courses run at the Central Political University varied substantially in relative mixes of 'functional' (yewu), 'political' (jingshen), and 'military' (junshi) training, as did the length of the training courses, this supplementary 'training' (xunlian) period was designed primarily to ensure political loyalty to the Guomindang and its wartime policies. Individuals were sent to the Central Political University as part of functionally specific groups based on the examination just taken, with special training 'groups' (zu) in finance, in accounting and statistics, in legal administration, in general administration, and so forth. This gave technically inclined ministries some scope for interjecting supplementary functional training for their prospective new recruits. Large parts of each day were devoted to a standardized programme of military drill and political indoctrination in which Sun Yat-sen's thought, contemporary government directives and objectives, and small group discussions predominated.[72]

Using this sort of controlled indoctrination to increase the loyalty and responsiveness of the bureaucracy was an early Guomindang forerunner of a set of institution-building strategies that would become more common, more stringent, and, at least in the short term, significantly more effective under the Chinese Communist Party in the 1950s.[73] But for the Guomindang, the drive to partify, indoctrinate, and standardize the thoughts and values of those in the civil service proved ineffective, for it coincided with a tremendous expansion in the size of the bureaucracy, which doubly and triply aggravated the wartime conditions of institutional weakness that led the Party leadership to turn to a programme of indoctrination to mobilize commitment in the first place. Uncertain communications and large de facto degrees of deconcentrated authority made the never easy task of rapidly assimilating, training, and socializing such a large influx of new personnel that much more difficult.

During the early 1940s, the National Government's respective sub-organizations grew at a pace that would have been unimaginable only a few years before, when the catchwords for administrative reform were 'streamlining', 'amalgamating', and 'reorganizing' in an effort to 'increase administrative efficiency'. In order to staff the many new regional and local centres in hitherto poorly controlled areas of the interior, the government stepped up both formal and informal methods of recruitment into the bureaucracy.

The numbers of individuals qualified by the civil service examination had been purposely kept low throughout the 1930s. The upper civil service exam, for example, had been offered only once every other year during the 1930s (with the exception of the 1936 special exam), and had passed somewhere between 100 and 150 individuals for each sitting. In contrast, the upper civil service exam was offered at least once, and sometimes twice, a year between 1939 and 1945, and passed an average of between 300 and 400 candidates in any given year. The list of special topics offered on the examinations continued to expand, ultimately including the fields of economic administration, national construction, land administration, and cooperative administration. The pace of the special examinations was augmented during the war years as well; in every year between 1939 and 1945, at least one special examination was held for either finance or judicial administration, and in a number of years special examinations were held for both.[74]

Although less easy to quantify, the war years also saw an increase in informal recruitment. Particularly in the technical or semi-technical fields such as economics and accounting, skilled people were in short supply. During the early 1940s government offices that had turned away qualified individuals in droves during the 1930s found themselves in the unaccustomed position of recruiting directly from the universities and technical schools that had relocated inland, and even were willing to overlook the leftist credentials of experts whom they felt they needed.[75] Irregular appointments, acting temporary appointments, and widespread lateral entry further increased the difficulties of organizational socialization and institutionalization.[76]

Expansion and attempted politicization were the two trends that characterized the National Government civil bureaucracy during the 1940s. While the civil service examinations qualified ever larger numbers of individuals, the formal examination system counted for increasingly less in practice. Although originally designed to uphold quality control while cementing the status bond between the successful examinee and the state he served, ever larger numbers of examination-qualified individuals could not stop the larger-trend wholescale de-institutionalization in a system now characterized by chaotic expansion, uncertain and irregular promotion and control, and largely ineffective top-down attempts at indoctrination. In addition, the continued military stalemate and the stubbornly rising inflation of the early to mid-1940s contributed to an overall organizational paralysis and decay that irremediably sapped government morale and effectiveness, with effects that lasted well past 1945.

CONCLUSION

Although the examination system roughly paralleled the state administration it serviced, with a process of slow consolidation in the 1930s and sharp acceleration during the Sino-Japanese War, examinations never at any time served as the primary channel of recruitment into the National Government in Republican China. To a greater or lesser extent, personal ties and old boys' networks of various sorts continued to be the primary points of entry into the system. The examination system did incrementally acquire some amount of prestige in the 1930s, but it didn't become what it 'should' have been—the process by which nearly all incoming civil servants acquired their positions—until the mid-1960s, in Taiwan. However, as a symbolic ideal, the examination system remained important to a wide variety of elites as a means by which some degree of traditional culturalism could be legitimately linked with forward-looking progressivism.

In a much reduced, weakened form, the Examination Yuan also recreated some of the dynamics of the traditional Chinese civil service examination system. It fostered a small, highly prestigious group of examination successes whose status was closely linked to validation by the state. In the late 1980s, very elderly gentlemen on *both* sides of the Taiwan Straits could still recite in detail the questions they wrote on, name the names of all those still living who took the examination along with them, and muster clear recollections of who passed and in what order on a given examination over half a century earlier.[77]

The operations of both the examination system and the Ministry of Personnel had much more to do with the intent, ideals, and systemic weaknesses of the National Government than with the realities of organizational life in the various ministries and commissions where the majority of civil servants were to be found. Although the National Government civil service system made some significant advances during the 1930s, the government's earlier and wider strategy of co-optation precluded the early institutionalization of a centrally effective civil service personnel policy, and this was reflected in the Ministry of Personnel's tactical retreat from stipulating the examination qualification as a prerequisite for government position in the mid-1930s. At best, the Ministry of Personnel possessed a series of linked ideals and plans for centralizing, regularizing, and rendering state organizations efficient as it alternated its own orientation between a proud past and an uncertain but modern future. The substantive power over appointment and promotion remained in the ministries, where the realities of recruitment, socialization, and institutionalization were played out in specific policy environments, against the backdrop of particular organizational cultures and goals. And these cultures and goals, varied as they were, are the subjects of subsequent chapters.

# 3

## Overcoming Institution-Building Dilemmas: The Sino-Foreign Salt Inspectorate

### INTRODUCTION

The first part of this work explored the central problem of the post-imperial Chinese state: institution building. Faced with a wide variety of new demands and tasks, including the establishment of new educational systems, military reorganization, the response to Western imperialism, and economic development, state-building elites in Republican China were confronted with a dilemma that has plagued developing countries the world over: how to create strong, proactive central organizations in environments in which institutional capacity is weak and fragmented.

This institution-building dilemma was an omnipresent feature of early twentieth-century China. The Republic of China had inherited from its imperial predecessor a system in which a weak fiscal base had seriously impeded the *de facto* reach of the central state. Because the state lacked the resources to adequately salary its regular officials and fund a vast working sub-bureaucracy and multitudinous *ad hoc* supporting organizations, it tolerated nearly universal, albeit informal, fee-taking to make up the shortfall. Although the actual financial burden of informal fees exceeded that of official, regular taxes,[1] fee-taking was not officially recognized by the central government. Since it remained unchecked and unregulated, the informal taxation system filled the legitimate fiscal requirements of local bureaucratic administration, while easily shading into what was popularly perceived as corruption, 'pocket lining', and abuse of office. By the turn of the twentieth century, proliferating local bureaucratic organizations at the level of the ward led to the local imposition of *tankuan*, or 'irregular levies'. As the name suggests, the *tankuan* were assessed on an *ad hoc* basis, frequently without oversight or authority from higher levels of state organizations.[2] Whether informal or ad hoc, the funds generated in this manner remained unavailable to the central government.

At the same time, the individual state administrator was caught between the conflicting cultural ideals of state service, impartiality, and universalism on the one hand, and filial piety, human feelings, and the need to provide for one's own on the other. Without mechanisms and incentives to reinforce the former and dampen the latter tendencies, state organizations had much difficulty inculcating their members with organizational norms strong enough to transcend immediate, short-term interest and personal loyalties.

At both the central and provincial level, political and administrative elites in early twentieth-century China continually, and at times desperately, searched to overcome the familialism and clan orientation of Chinese society in an effort to weld together 'a loose sheet of sand' into a proud, dynamic nation, experimenting with a wide variety of approaches to resolve this central dilemma of institution building.[3] As suggested in the Introduction, the Guomindang under Chiang Kai-shek variously attempted to utilize revolution, Leninist organization, military dictatorship, foreign-expert-inspired reform, mass campaigns, and fascism as conscious strategies of institution and state building. Each of these strategies attracted believers and adherents, but for the most part these different experimental strategies had only limited success.

Throughout the 1930s, the Guomindang put social revolution on indefinite hold; their Leninist party organization weakened as it was invaded by cliques and informal personalistic networks, their mass campaigns (such as the New Life Movement) met with popular apathy or derision, their fascist Blue Shirt movement alienated professionals and intellectuals, and the more sweeping of the Western-adviser-based reform programmes that they invited (such as the Kemmerer Commission's recommendations for overhauling the financial and banking system) proved difficult to implement. Despite the clear orientation of the Nationalists towards centralization of power, control, and standardization and some real gains made in achieving these goals, the existing norms of the society in which the regime was embedded in the short term sanctioned familialism, cliquism, and the conflation of public interest with private gain.

Despite this wider social nexus so profoundly unfavourable to the processes of institution building, several administrative organizations in the Republican period managed to overcome this longstanding institution-building dilemma on a country-wide basis. Three such organizations, all of which were notable for their hybrid foreign and Chinese staffing, their relative autonomy from the rest of the 'regular' Chinese government, and their close associations with foreign imperialism and pressure on China, stand out: the Inspectorate General of Maritime Customs, established in the mid-nineteenth century before being amalgamated with domestic customs offices to form the Customs Administration; the Postal Administration, begun as a subsidiary operation of Maritime Customs before being reorganized with French assistance at the beginning of the twentieth century, and finally the Sino-Foreign Salt Inspectorate, a tax collecting agency which was created in 1913.

Of these three organizations, the Salt Inspectorate is notable for several reasons. It was the last established of the joint Sino-foreign civil service organizations in an era of rising nationalist sentiment and corresponding European decline. Unlike the Customs Administration, it operated largely in remote inland locations with a broad range of pre-existing arrangements for salt production and taxation. Lastly, its history, with various name changes and reorganizations, covered virtually the duration of the Republican period, from 1913 until 1949.[4]

Against all expectations, the Salt Inspectorate very quickly became a veritable model of a successful, well-institutionalized, high-prestige organization that elicited the loyalty and commitment of its Chinese and foreign staff even as it operated in an extremely turbulent, often hostile, environment. In a period in which much of the rest of China collapsed into warlordism, the Salt Inspectorate remained one of only two tax-collecting organizations (the other being the Customs Administration) that continued consistently to operate on a national level. Throughout the Republican era, it provided all of the central regimes, from the Yuan Shikai and Beiyang to the Chiang Kai-shek central governments, with their second most important source of tax funds. Furthermore, even when virtually independent of the Chinese central government in the 1910s and 1920s, it made substantial headway in continuing to pursue in broad outline the central government's post-*xinzheng* state-building goals of centralization, efficiency, rationalization, and penetration. In so doing, the Salt Inspectorate provided a working example for other, similarly situated, state organizations to emulate. In so far as the key factors behind the Salt Inspectorate's successful institution-building efforts were generalizable strategies of bureaucratization, organizational insulation, and objective goal implementation, the Salt Inspectorate 'model' was of potentially even greater relevance than its many admirers suspected.

## BACKGROUND TO SALT TAX ADMINISTRATION

Historically, the salt gabelle had been the major source of non-land-based tax for the Chinese empire. Even during the latter half of the nineteenth century, when revenues from the salt tax declined relative to those from the rapidly expanding maritime and inland customs administrations, salt remained an important and stable source of tax funds. But precisely because the salt tax monopoly was a longstanding institution, which had evolved slowly in conjunction with the imperial Chinese state over a period of centuries, it reflected the features of late imperial finance that centralizing rationalizers found so problematic by the early twentieth century. Like the late imperial state of which it was a part, the salt gabelle possessed formal and exclusive authority over all aspects of the salt tax, but only an uneven ability to enforce those claims. Officially, the salt tax mirrored the cornerstone of imperial benevolence through the principle of low taxation to the people. In actual practice, the state tended to concentrate its attention on those least capable of resisting: highly visible rich salt merchants to whom the state had 'entrusted' the salt monopoly at the top of the tax pyramid, and the poor peasants subject to the abuses of informal surcharges and tax-farming at the bottom.[5]

Administratively, the salt gabelle was, of necessity, highly decentralized. The different salt-producing areas of the empire were physically widely dispersed, and highly heterogeneous in terms of production techniques, marketing, and customary arrangements made with local salt merchants. Since the state lacked the ability to institute a uniform tax rate or set of procedures, it based its salt tax policies on what it *could* easily control: appointment of high-ranking salt commissioners to the salt districts, and the so called *yin'an* system whereby salt merchants were guaranteed rights to procure salt and paid the tax on the transport of salt along easily monitored rivers and waterways.[6] Although specific arrangements varied from district to district, each official salt-producing district was assigned a monopoly 'circuit' in which only its salt could legally be sold. Typically, specially privileged salt merchants bought vouchers from the salt office which legally enabled them to transport specific quantities of salt upriver to designated salt receiving areas. The real degree of central government involvement in the salt tax varied from place to place. In a few unusual districts, the official salt offices controlled all aspects of the salt trade from production to retailing, while in others, salt merchants were so entrenched that the imperial state's local salt office could barely enforce the tax payments that were its due. In most areas, the official government 'monopoly' masked a substantial degree of sub-contracting to merchants.

Since the tax was determined on a district-by-district basis and was levied on the transport rather than the production of salt, the *yin'an* system was characterized by great local flexibility and highly inegalitarian levels of taxation. Duties varied, as did the number of tax assessments per shipment of salt. Those closest to the salt works paid relatively little in tax, while those in the remote, often much poorer, areas of the interior far from the salt works paid much more.

Salt that could evade official control—either through private production, smuggling along the waterways, or use of overland routes—escaped taxation altogether. The prevalence of riverine smuggling, or 'owling' (*xiao*), prompted the *ad hoc* creation of paramilitary units ('salt police') in many areas. Like most of the late imperial sub-bureaucracy, the salt police lacked adequate fiscal support; in many cases the payoffs they received from the 'owls' to turn a blind eye constituted their only regular source of funds.

At all levels, the revenues collected were prone to leakage. High ranking but inadequately salaried salt officials were able to make fortunes during their tenures, thus exacerbating a chain reaction of corruption at lower levels. Tax leakage was as much a result of decentralized imperial administration as it was of systemic corruption. Much of the salt revenue surplus in a given area was retained locally or provincially. Districts and provinces levied *ad hoc* surtaxes on the main salt tax to provide appropriations for locally determined projects—from modernized 'new armies' to local temples and foundling hospitals. Even in relatively good years for salt production and distribution, the central government received only a fraction of the revenues actually collected. By the late nineteenth and early twentieth centuries, as the dynamic balance between the centre and the regions shifted decisively towards the provinces, the percentage of the collected tax that was ultimately remitted to the central government diminished: in 1900, gross reported salt tax collections stood at around 24 million taels, with 9 million taels remitted to the central government; ten years later, in 1911, the year the dynasty fell, gross reported collection was up to 40 million taels, with remittance to the central government standing at the unchanged 1900 quota of 9 million taels.[7]

With steadily increasing expenses for new schools, modern armies, railroads, and the like, both central and provincial leaders began to turn to the salt tax as a potential source of extra funds. The last years of the dynasty saw a number of steps aimed at increasing the efficiency of the far-flung, notoriously inefficient salt administration through processes of standardization and control. Proposals were floated to replace the cumbersome system of multiple local taxes and permits with one consolidated tax at the site of production (*jiuchang zhengshui*). Provincial officials pushed for increased state involvement in all aspects of the salt monopoly, and the central government even succeeded in establishing a new, national bureau known as the Yanwu Shu (the Salt Office), with the authority to handle all salt affairs.[8]

Although these reforms were part of what might be called a discourse of rationalization and centralization for salt administration in the first decade of the twentieth century, in practice they were systematically undercut by entrenched interests which gained from customary arrangements at every level of the system. Salt merchants were opposed to increased government involvement in any aspect of the salt administration; provincial leaders cast a jaundiced eye on relinquishing their quite substantial discretion over the salt tax to a new, central organization; and the assorted sub-bureaucracies attached to different sectors of the salt gabelle had every reason to resist any sort of rationalizing and intrusion from above. By the time the dynasty collapsed in 1911, the proposed reforms had not been implemented to any considerable degree: the Yanwu Shu remained a weak organization and the *jiuchang zhengshui* method of tax assessment a distant ideal.

In spite of central growing awareness of the need to systematically extract more revenue in order to recentralize and rebuild the country in the last years of the Qing, the salt gabelle in the early twentieth century was still a dispersed, decentralized patchwork of *ad hoc*, customary practices which defied neat categorization. The projective capacity of the state was at this time still extremely limited; much as it might have desired to increase its revenues, the central state had neither the physical resources nor the will to field a staff that could directly administer the salt tax. Hundreds of years of *de facto* power-sharing with local elites further legitimated minimal central involvement, as did the arcaneness, variability, and quirkiness of the arrangements in each particular sub-administration, which drove waves of would-be central standardizers nearly to distraction. Even well into the 1930s, when central authorities went to investigate the Zhejiang salt administration, they found that sub-districts were sharply divided between areas with very high and very low tax rates. When they asked local people why this was the case, those asked simply responded that 'the custom has always been like this'.[9]

Aside from the establishment of a national salt administration organization (the Yanwu Shu) that had neither the opportunity nor the means for effective action, none of the ideas for centralizing and systematizing the salt tax had found much practical expression by the time of the dynasty's fall. The continued efforts of the early Republican government to recentralize and prevent local appropriations of salt revenue did not meet with any greater success.[10] Institutional capacity remained weak in a policy environment that was diverse, heterogeneous, and cross-cut with networks of local and regional privilege.

## THE ESTABLISHMENT OF THE SINO-FOREIGN SALT INSPECTORATE, 1913

The Sino-Foreign Salt Inspectorate, the organization that would become one of the main pillars of national finance for the Republican Chinese state, was established in 1913 as a totally unforeseen byproduct of the collision between the two worlds of international finance and Chinese domestic politics in the aftermath of the dynastic collapse of 1911–12. The early Republican government was in immediate danger of defaulting on a number of large loans contracted by the late dynasty to finance railroad construction. In addition, the dominant military and political figure in north China, Yuan Shikai, was attempting to consolidate his power and bring a secessionist revolutionary movement in the south to heel. The interests of the conservative strongman and the international banking consortium coincided. Yuan Shikai wanted immediate resources to establish his control over the rest of the country, and the international banks had an interest in protecting past investments by supporting a stable Chinese government favourable to Western business interests.[11]

The result of protracted negotiations was a package deal known as the Reorganization Loan. Under its terms, the outstanding loans left over from the Qing were refinanced, the Yuan Shikai government was given the then substantial sum of £25 million in ready cash, and provision was made for the reorganization of the salt gabelle under joint Sino-foreign administration to provide the extra revenue to guarantee and service the new debt. As part of the Reorganization Loan agreement, Yuan Shikai agreed to the establishment of a joint Sino-Foreign Salt Inspectorate (Yanwu Jihe Zongsuo), to be staffed by parallel levels of Chinese and foreign administrators.[12]

From a late twentieth-century perspective, this sort of arrangement, in which a nominally sovereign government under external pressure accepted a hybrid foreign–Chinese run administration with a large measure of *de facto* autonomy, seems bizarre, smacking of imperialism and worse; by the standards of the late nineteenth and early twentieth century, it was an unusual but by no means unheard-of organizational response to a particular complex of administrative problems common in non-Western countries. Although India was fully colonized by the British, the Indian civil service had long been organized along similar lines. Late imperial states that were like China in not being colonized outright but saddled with heavy external debts and weak internal fiscal capacities, such as the Ottoman and Persian empires, also featured jointly run, civil-service-based tax collectorates that were in place until sufficiently strong nationalist leaders arose to abolish them.[13] In China itself, both the Customs Administration and the Postal Service provided examples of hybrid bureaucratic organizations that had been instituted in the nineteenth century and by all measures were still running strong in the early twentieth.

Originally, the Salt Inspectorate was authorized to have a fairly limited scope: it was entrusted solely with the actual collection and deposit of the salt tax into a central account to service the Reorganization Loan debt. The separate, central government Yanwu Shu (Salt Office) retained authority over all other 'administrative' aspects of the salt gabelle, including salt production, transport, and sale. Formally, the Salt Inspectorate was to remain subordinate to the Yanwu Shu.

Given that previous attempts to reform the salt administration had been conspicuous in their failure to get off the ground, few in 1913 expected that the fledgling Salt Inspectorate would be able to do more than meet its minimal obligations to service the Reorganization Loan debt. However, to general surprise, the Salt Inspectorate was able to forward salt tax receipts both to the group bank account for the Reorganization Loan and to the Chinese central government within a year of its establishment. Net salt

**Table 3.1.**  Salt Tax Collections by the Inspectorate, 1913–1927

|       | Gross revenue (standard silver dollars) | Net revenue (standard silver dollars) |
|-------|-----------------------------------------|---------------------------------------|
| 1913  | 19,044,200  | 11,471,000 |
| 1914  | 68,485,300  | 60,410,000 |
| 1915  | 80,503,400  | 69,278,000 |
| 1916  | 81,064,800  | 72,441,000 |
| 1917  | 82,245,800  | 70,627,000 |
| 1918  | 88,393,700  | 80,607,000 |
| 1919  | 87,822,500  | 80,607,000 |
| 1920  | 90,052,400  | 79,064,000 |
| 1921  | 94,883,100  | 77,988,000 |
| 1922  | 98,106,700  | 85,789,000 |
| 1923  | 91,706,700  | 79,545,000 |
| 1924  | 87,908,600  | 70,544,000 |
| 1925  | 91,931,600  | 73,634,000 |
| 1926  | 86,317,200  | 64,287,000 |
| 1927  | 59,753,300  | 57,905,000 |

*Source*: P. T. Chen, 'Public Finance', in *The Chinese Yearbook 1935–36* ed. Kwei Chungshu (Shanghai: Commercial Press), 1298.

revenue jumped from 11,471,000Y in 1913 to 60,410,000Y in 1914 (the first full year of the Salt Inspectorate's operation), and gradually increased to a pre-National Government high of 85,789,000Y in 1922, before the disruptions of the warlord period began to have a seriously dampening effect (see Table 3.1).[14]

Although no one had anticipated it, the Salt Inspectorate was, practically from the outset, efficient enough in its tax collection to have a healthy surplus even after the annual debt obligations had been met. Within a very short time, Inspectorate offices had branched into activities as diverse as the construction of salt depots (to make control easier and smuggling more difficult), road improvements (for ease of transport), the development of new salt evaporation techniques (to raise quality in production), and occasionally even the administration of rudimentary examinations for divisions of salt police.[15]

The Salt Inspectorate then went on to become one of the most successful national-level organizations in Republican China. It provided subsequent central governments in the Republican period with a steady flow of tax receipts, steered through the years of internal anarchy and warlordism in the 1920s, survived its abolishment and reconstitution under the Guomindang in 1927–8, managed to absorb other salt organizations under the Nationalist Ministry of Finance during the 1930s, and only began a long decline during the years of the Sino-Japanese War in 1937–45.

This initially high degree of effectiveness and quick extension of organizational action directly resulted from the values, principles, and practically oriented administrative strategies of the Salt Inspectorate's first Foreign Chief Inspector, Sir Richard Dane. In 1913, just before his appointment with the newly forming Salt Inspectorate, Dane had retired from a long career in the Indian civil service, where he had last served as inspector-general of excise and salt. As such, his ideas about finance and organizational effectiveness were set squarely in the traditions of British liberal capitalism and a generalist colonial civil service. Dane was a firm believer in the pursuit of administrative efficiency for its own sake, in a politically neutral, centralized civil service as the only way to achieve this efficiency, and in free trade as the appropriate mechanism to create additional resources for the administrative machine to tap.

In the early Republican period, Chinese centralizing reformers could easily concur with all but the last sentiment, but they had failed in their efforts to establish a strong, non-corrupt, centrally administered salt gabelle. Ironically, it was Dane, the outsider with the backing of the quasi-imperialist group banks, who succeeded in institutionalizing an effective tax agency which long outlasted the period of his stewardship and became the second most important source of funds for the centralizing Republican state.

Dane was able to do this by applying the principles of rational bureaucratization to both the *internal* dynamics of the Salt Inspectorate as it struggled to establish itself as a separate entity, and the *external* acts of the organization as it sought to operationalize its goals. Bureaucratically determined 'strategies of insulation' were geared towards establishing and protecting the internal organizational integrity of the Inspectorate, while goal implementation focused on the specific ways in which organizational ideology was concretized and evaluated. These two methods were tightly linked. In early twentieth-century China, only a well insulated organization with a keen sense of its own mission could carry out efficient, centralized tax collection, and the organization's success in operationalizing that goal tended further to boost its internal morale and its capacity for insulation.

### BUREAUCRATIC STRATEGIES OF INSULATION

Knowing no Chinese, but a good deal about colonial finance and administration from his previous career as the Inspector-General of Excise and Salt for the Indian civil service, Sir Richard Dane arrived in China in 1913 with the express purpose of reorganizing the traditional salt gabelle. Like the Chinese late imperial reformers before him, he quickly diagnosed the problems of the salt administration: decentralized tax collection, lack of standardized tax rates, local leakage, and the existence of too much non-taxed salt. Unlike the imperial reformers, however, Dane was able to wrest for himself a fair amount of discretionary authority as Chief Foreign Inspector. He widened the early Inspectorate's range of legitimate action by portraying himself as neutral in mediating disputes between the Chinese government and the group banks.

Within months of Dane's arrival, the Inspectorate central organization had gained the power to collect the salt tax, authorize the transfer of revenue to the group banks, forward the surplus to the Chinese government, and audit the district offices. In so doing, the Inspectorate promulgated a new series of regulations that amounted to a new programme for the entire salt administration.[16] Once accorded actual authority over tax collection and the release of salt revenue to the group banks and the Chinese government, Dane had the financial means to insulate the Inspectorate from an otherwise inhospitable, hostile environment, and to lay the foundation for a successful, reformist administration.[17]

When Dane and the first set of district inspectors went out to the field in 1913–14, they found a tax collection system riddled with corruption, nepotism, and inefficiency:

The principle function of the checking offices was apparently to provide employment for the needy relatives of higher officials. The Station's sole source of income was the commission the employees could collect from the merchants for passing excessive quantities of salt, since the funds allotted for expenses and wages were customarily retained by patrons higher up... [while] ... the Salt Police [whose ostensible duty was to prevent salt smuggling] depended on the sale of salt to supplement their wages.[18]

The Inspectorate's first task was to replace this pyramid of corruption and immobility with an organization that took as its core values the bureaucratically inspired norms of efficiency, objective impersonality, and performance achievement in a geographically dispersed, prefectural administration. Concretely, this meant that the Inspectorate under Dane (and subsequent foreign and Chinese chief inspectors) had to hold all substantive control over the recruitment and promotion of personnel, thus establishing a stable system of incentives to encourage socialization into organizational norms and goals.

Once the Salt Inspectorate had claimed for itself a legitimate sphere of action and authority, it was faced with the classic problem of all deconcentrated prefectural administrations: how to attract and retain a cadre of field officers committed to vigorously promoting centrally determined organizational goals in a wide variety of situations all far from the central office. Like the United States Foreign Service, the British Colonial Office, and the prefects of Louis XIV, the Inspectorate had to prevent its staff from 'going native' and being drawn into local networks of privilege and favouritism while simultaneously promoting positive identification with the goals of the central organization. The Inspectorate accomplished this through bureaucratic methods of organizational insulation: in 1913–14, Dane directly transposed a strict British civil service system to the Salt Inspectorate, where it remained the cornerstone of organizational integrity and esprit until well into the 1940s.

In the hostile and politicized environment of early twentieth-century China, the most important practical feature of the Inspectorate strategies of insulation was the organization's ability to maintain near complete autonomy from the rest of the Chinese government. To reinforce insulation, the Inspectorate independently recruited both foreign and Chinese staff, and adamantly resisted politically inspired appointments in the central office and the districts. The appointment of the Chinese Chief Inspector was in theory the prerogative of the Chinese government, but in practice, the Inspectorate pressed for the appointment of an official expert in salt affairs, preferably from its own ranks. In this regard, the Inspectorate was successful until 1928, the year the National Government took over the Inspectorate and placed it under the formal authority of the Ministry of Finance.

Since the Inspectorate had independent access to the funds it collected before it authorized releases to either the group banks or the Chinese central government, it could, quite literally, 'afford' to maintain a completely separate system of rank classifications, with considerably higher salary scales for lower and middle-level officials than for those used in the regular Chinese government offices.[19] The mere existence of such a distinctive system of personnel classification with rankings that were inherently non-convertible into the regular Chinese government bureaucracy further reinforced the organization's sense of separateness. (see Table 3.2). The Inspectorate also offered its personnel steady, if slow, advancement through its elaborate system of grades, an extraordinary degree of job security, and a series of personnel benefits that would be considered enlightened even by the standards of late twentieth-century Western business management.

In pursuing bureaucratic, rule-oriented strategies of insulation, the Salt Inspectorate, either by luck or design, very adroitly tapped into longstanding symbols of great legitimacy for Chinese bureaucratic elites. It utilized the traditional ideals of open civil service examinations and the *zhengtu* (regular path of advancement), reinforced the deeply held sense of the civil service bureaucrat as a high-status position with special responsibilities, and turned these sentiments to new organizational goals of efficiency and centralization of power. By rigorously adopting impersonal standards of entry

**Table 3.2.** Personnel Classification and Monthly Salary Scales

| Nationalist Government | | | Salt Inspectorate | | |
|---|---|---|---|---|---|
| Grade | Rank | Salary (yuan) | Grade | Rank | Salary (yuan) |
| teren ('special' appointment) | | 800 | A | a | 800 |
| | | | | b | 750 |
| | | | | c | 700 |
| jianren ('selected' appointment) | 1 | 680 | | d | 650 |
| | 2 | 640 | | e | 600 |
| | 3 | 600 | B | a | 550 |
| | 4 | 560 | | b | 500 |
| | 5 | 520 | | c | 450 |
| | 6 | 490 | | d | 400 |
| | 7 | 460 | C | a | 350 |
| | 8 | 430 | | b | 300 |
| jianren ('recommended' appointment) | 1 | 400 | | c | 250 |
| | 2 | 380 | D | a | 220 |
| | | | | b | 200 |
| | 3 | 360 | | b | 200 |
| | 4 | 340 | | c | 175 |
| | 5 | 320 | | | |
| | 6 | 300 | E | a | 160 |
| | 7 | 280 | | b | 140 |
| | 8 | 260 | | c | 120 |
| | 9 | 240 | F | a | 100 |
| | 10 | 220 | | b | 85 |
| | 11 | 200 | | c | 70 |
| | 12 | 180 | | d | 60 |
| weiren ('delegated' appointment) | 1 | 200 | | e | 50 |
| | 2 | 180 | | f | 40 |
| | 3 | 160 | | | |
| | 4 | 140 | | | |
| | 5 | 130 | | | |
| | 6 | 120 | | | |
| | 7 | 110 | | | |
| | 8 | 100 | | | |
| | 9 | 90 | | | |
| | 10 | 85 | | | |
| | 11 | 80 | | | |
| | 12 | 75 | | | |
| | 13 | 70 | | | |
| | 14 | 65 | | | |
| | 15 | 60 | | | |
| | 16 | 50 | | | |

*Source*: adapted from *The Chinese Yearbook, 1935–36*, ed. Kwei Chungshu (Shanghai and Chungking: Commercial Press), and *Yanwu Renshi Guize* (Regulations on Salt Administration Personnel), unpublished booklet (Caizheng Bu, date unknown, *c*.1950).

and promotion, the Inspectorate was able to structurally reinforce the parts of the traditional civil service ideal that stressed universalism and impartiality while managing to exclude the particularistic norms of providing for one's own that led to nepotism and corruption. Regularly held examinations provided one with the 'proper' means of entry into the organization; security of tenure and relatively high salaries led to 'regular' careers of quite high status; and strongly enforced bureaucratic regulations afforded the individual in the service a plausible excuse to turn down the particularistic claims of family and friends.

The Inspectorate's entire personnel system reified an ethos of objectivity, concrete measurability, and stability. It spent much of its energy translating these basic principles into practice through myriad rules and regulations. In contrast to the vast majority of state organizations in Republican China, which were noteworthy for the enormous gaps that existed between the intentions and regulations they committed to paper and actual practice, the Salt Inspectorate did *not* exhibit a very large differences between enunciated principle and real action. For example, as the regulations stipulated, once the Inspectorate was established, its Chinese staff, with very few exceptions, was recruited solely on the basis of an open general examination, and could begin a career only towards the bottom of the system of ranked classifications. This initial entry exam required a college, technical school, or normal school degree, but it was otherwise generalist in nature: it tested English, Chinese, mathematics, and the overall ability to write and process documents. For those who passed the initial exam, the Inspectorate ran a three-month training course in which it inculcated the fundamental principles and specifically required techniques and methods of salt administration. After the training period, another examination was given prior to actual appointment, and, depending on the results, successful applicants were accorded one of the lowest three ranks within the lowest grade and were assigned to a particular field office to fill a specific post.[20]

Lateral entry was not unheard of, but it was extremely rare, as it ran counter to the Inspectorate's strong preference for organizational stability through in-house socialization. Although the forty-odd foreigners employed by the Inspectorate took up their appointments at fairly high levels and regulations allowed initial appointments roughly one third of the way up the scale (at the E/a grade), the bulk of the Inspectorate staff began their careers in the Inspectorate towards the bottom of the organization by passing the entry exam, and were expected to work their way slowly but surely up through the system.

Although this near-exclusive reliance on recruitment through examination at the entry level began to fray slightly in the mid-1930s and came under serious pressure during the Sino-Japanese War in the 1940s, for the first twenty-four years of the Inspectorate's existence the organization did in fact adhere to its principles of entry at the bottom and promotion on the basis of seniority and experience. In a sample of some 104 bureaucrats who began their careers with the Inspectorate prior to 1927, only 6 began their careers with higher than the E/a classification permitted by the personnel regulations, and of these only 3 came into the organization after its initial start-up period in 1913–14. Of the 104, the vast majority (83) started off in the lowest three ranks, with a further 10 individuals who began their tenure in the Inspectorate higher up on the scale coming in to the organization in its first year of operation, when the need for staff at a variety of levels was obviously acute.[21]

Promotions and big increases in responsibility were not accorded to everyone, and were restricted by vacancies in positions with commensurate status. In both theory and in practice, those rewarded with promotions could *not* skip over the ranked steps in each grade: the deserving had to wait until a position at an appropriate level became available. The Inspectorate's personnel system thus institutionalized bias towards seniority and stability once minimum standards of objective competence had been met. Strict quotas limited the percentages of staff permitted to advance to the next rank,[22] dampening expectations of quick promotions and perhaps frustrating the most ambitious. This was indeed later recognized by the Salt Administration as one of its chief drawbacks: it 'lacked a forward looking spirit' (*quefa qiantu jingshen*) and 'constrained the development of talent' (*xianzhi caiju fazhan*).[23]

But if promotions were rare and the most ambitious were perhaps tempted to look elsewhere, the vast majority of those who worked in the Inspectorate could look forward to pay raises for as long as they remained with the organization and fulfilled its minimum performance requirements, and to guaranteed tenure except in cases of gross malfeasance. There were enough ranks (*ji*) within each broad grade (*deng*) to allow for fairly regular merit increases. Yearly evaluations to determine merit increases were drafted by each office's personnel review group, which then passed its recommendations on to the boss for approval.[24] Promotions were granted in two ways. In the bottom three ranks, an organization-wide written promotion exam (*shengdeng kaoshi*) was held annually, and if an applicant passed, he advanced to the next rank automatically. For the upper four levels in the organization, where quota restrictions made promotions much harder to come by, promotions were granted on the basis of an individual's ability, length of service, and willingness to be posted wherever he was needed. In this informal equation, seniority was the most important factor: those who had already demonstrated their consistency and loyalty to the organization tended to be those who were rewarded.[25]

The institutional preference for seniority and stability was reinforced in other ways as well. For those who stayed with the Inspectorate for longer than seven continuous years, there was the option of 'long leave'—a sabbatical year at close to full pay. Those remaining with the organization over the long term were also rewarded with increasingly generous terms for sick and personal leave, supplementary bonuses, and attractive pensions.[26]

To foster continued identification with the values and goals of the central organization and systematically to forestall incipient tendencies towards 'capture' by local elites, the Inspectorate frequently rotated its middle- to upper-level officials from district to district. Depending on the particular skills of the individual, tours of duty lasting between two and five years in any one location were interspersed with at least one very short-term posting of six to twelve months in a completely different location. Of some 27 high-level Inspectorate administrators who joined the organization before 1927,[27] 21 had at least one posting that lasted between three and five years, and 23 were sent on short-term assignments of one year or less. More surprisingly, the Inspectorate was even able to move its support staff to an unusual degree: of the 42 individuals who entered the Inspectorate before 1927 and never advanced beyond the lowest three grades, only 3 remained in one location for the length of their tenures. Nearly half of the lower-level personnel had at least worked in different branch offices within the same district, and only slightly less than half were rotated out of their home district at least once.[28] With its capacity to rotate and transfer even its clerical and support personnel, the Inspectorate managed to dampen the structural features that provided such a hospitable environment for much of the local bureaucratic corruption and collusion with local elites that characterized the late imperial and early Republican period.[29]

In addition to its many positive inducements (such as higher salaries and security of tenure) and neutral techniques (such as frequent rotation) of buffering the organization's staff from the particularistic demands of those outside the organization, the Inspectorate did not hesitate to institutionalize quick and unremitting sanctions against those who either failed in their duties or, worse, succumbed to the temptation to use their position for private gain. Unlike most Republican era state organizations, the Inspectorate's bureaucratized core values of civil service neutrality and performance achievement did not make exceptions for the social niceties of 'saving face'. The surviving forms from the Inspectorate make it quite clear that those individuals who acted in the belief that the regulations regarding the private use of public office did not apply to them were unceremoniously censured and, depending on the severity of the offense, dismissed without regard to their position or length of service.

In the sample of 185 who worked for the Inspectorate between the 1910s and the mid-1930s, there were 14 cases of dismissal. Of these 14 instances, 9 involved low-ranked staff involved in 'weighment and collecting', the stage at which the bags of salt were weighed and the salt tax collected.

The surviving records suggest that the Inspectorate appears to have been exceptionally rigorous in its censure of those caught in any type of activity it deemed corrupt or irregular, and did not grant exceptions to those who had either acquired high positions or had lengthy tenure in service. Of the 14 dismissed, 5 had been with the organization for ten or more years, 1 had reached the very high position of assistant district commissioner, and 1 had garnered a previous commendation for distinguished service.[30]

Had the Inspectorate been less vigorous in prosecuting and expelling those who were insufficiently socialized into the organizational norms of bureaucratic objectivity, all of the Inspectorate's other carefully constructed strategies of insulation would have been wasted: eternal vigilance was the price paid for impartiality. Because bureaucratic, rule-oriented impersonalism so demarcated the Inspectorate and set it off from the particularistic outside environment, Inspectorate administrators felt very strongly that their 'civil service traditions' were the heart and soul of the organization's distinctiveness and success. They defended these 'civil service traditions' with a tenacity bordering on the ferocious, as they genuinely believed that once these civil service traditions were compromised, organizational collapse would be imminent.[31] Therefore, an extraordinary amount of attention was devoted to maintaining the organization's core values of bureaucratic evenhandedness and objectivity.

For the most part, the Inspectorate's bureaucratic strategies of insulation around the central norms of impartiality and performance achievement were successful, in spite of widespread hostility in the surrounding society to the institutionalization of those values. Paradoxically, the decentralized, prefectural nature of the salt administration may have contributed to the organization's success. Since those concerned with their careers had to move (and move frequently) to locations that ranked among the least desirable in all of China, the insufficiently committed tended to select themselves out. In one report on the conditions of service in the Inspectorate even into the mid-1930s, one commentator wrote:

Salt production is not generally associated with concentrations of population, or congenial topographic or agricultural settings: rather the reverse. For instance, Panpin, the head office of the Lianghuai District [the most important salt producing area in China] . . . is situated about 30 miles away from the coast in the alluvial plain of the Yellow River, in country that is impassable in any form of wheeled conveyance in rainy weather . . . and which, on account of the poverty of the local population, has been notorious for generations as one of the worst bandit-infested areas of China.[32]

Other areas had even poorer inhabitants, more rampant banditry, worse communications, more intransigent local elites, and even lower standards of living. Because of its policies of insulation, the Salt Inspectorate managed to turn the very difficulty of the job and the undesirability of most of the locations involved to positive advantage. Buffered by relatively high salary levels, positively motivated by the likelihood of eventual rewards for increased performance, and frequently rotated to prevent local connections from ever growing too strong, Inspectorate officials did commit their careers and loyalties to the organization as a whole—even when it involved being sent to the true hardship posts such as Moheijing in rural Yunnan, where both local militarization and malaria were endemic.[33]

Both direct and indirect evidence points to the early establishment and continued operation of a highly motivated staff that internalized the Inspectorate's norms of bureaucratically determined neutrality, fairness, and technical competence. Given the extreme volatility of the political situation and the instability of most administrative organizations throughout the Republican period, people stayed with the Inspectorate for extraordinarily long periods of time. By the mid-1930s, the 'typical' high-level Inspectorate official had begun his career well before the Nationalist takeover in 1927, and had already been with the Inspectorate for an average of seventeen years.[34] This remarkable longevity was partially attributable to the Inspectorate's policies of slow advancement and promotion, but people were also obviously reluctant to leave what was considered to be a well paying, stable job with an unusually impartial and fair-minded organization.[35]

The Inspectorate's bureaucratic strategies of insulation, with their collective stress on seniority, impersonal fairness, and objective performance, attracted individuals who valued stability over rapid advancement. In exchange for the security and protection that the organization could provide, Inspectorate officials were happy to do good, careful work, and otherwise not attract too much attention to themselves or take great risks.[36] Somewhat surprisingly, for those who stayed with the organization, this bureaucratic conservatism and rule orientation did not to lead to either alienation or ennui, but instead fostered a certain pride and the satisfaction of belonging to an organization that provided for its members *and* made good its formal claims of efficiency and objectivity. Several retirees commented to the effect that 'The Inspectorate was really a wonderful place to work...we were just like one big family! But one drawback was that we seldom got the chance to know non-Inspectorate people.'[37]

Reports written by the foreign Inspectorate officials or external evaluators were equally laudatory. In contrast to the 'average' Chinese official, who either was on the take or fled at the first sign of trouble, Inspectorate officials were time and again singled out for praise for their dedication, steadfastness, and unwillingness to buckle to the pressures of local notables, marauding warlords, or the claims of family and friends.

To cite two examples, in late 1932 the American Vice-Consul in Yunnanfu (Kunming) reported admiringly that the local Chinese District Inspector, Guo Shaozong, had refused to turn over the Salt Inspectorate funds to the demands of Long Yun, provincial leader in Yunnan—'despite being threatened with imprisonment and persecution'.[38] In December 1937, as the Japanese army was advancing and the staff for the Lianghuai district office preparing to evacuate, the Chinese and Foreign District Inspectors wrote a joint memo in which they described a situation in which there was no money, no banking facilities, no military protection, little in the way of communication with the outside, and frequent bombing raids that necessitated working by candlelight. They concluded: 'we would like to take this opportunity to commend members of the Lianghuai staff, especially those retained for duty under the most trying circumstances, who generally have behaved throughout in a highly satisfactory manner.'[39]

By all accounts, Dane's initial actions to establish an autonomous, well-insulated organization provided the foundation for the Salt Inspectorate's startling success and longevity. But the bureaucratic, depersonalized strategies of insulation that were the core of the organization's integrity were further bolstered by the mixture of bureaucratic and professional ways in which organizational ideals were translated into strategies for goal achievement. Without objective results, the Salt Inspectorate could not have justified its continued existence to either its own members or its numerous external critics. Ultimately, the *manner* in which organizational goals were pursued protected the Inspectorate by allowing it to claim lack of political interest and neutral competence even as the external political environment became increasingly hazardous.

## BUREAUCRATIC AND PROFESSIONAL STRATEGIES OF GOAL IMPLEMENTATION

In terms of organizational ideology, the Salt Inspectorate adhered to an unchanging, consistent set of goals that had the advantage of being inherently amenable to bureaucratic rationalization and professional experimentation. In 1913 Dane drew up a list of what came to be known as the 'Fourteen Principles', in which he outlined the problems and appropriate remedies for salt administration. In addition to reiterating the necessity for 'strong civil service traditions' (which were, in essence, the bureaucratic strategies of insulation described above), Dane offered a quite detailed list on what *ought* to be done to reorganize the salt tax, and in some cases, even suggested how such reorganization should be pursued.

At a very early date in the organization's history, the major technical problems of the salt administration were reduced to two. First, the lack of effective, centralized administration allowed revenue to be locally siphoned off, surtaxes indiscriminately to be added, and wildly varying tax rates to continue to exist. Second, monopoly privileges to specifically designated salt merchants further contributed to market distortion and inefficiency. The prescribed solutions to these problems encompassed the establishment of central control over the salt works and tax collection, standardization and ultimate reduction of the salt tax rates, simplification of the salt tax through consolidation of the numerous levies on salt transport into just one tax assessed at the site of production (*jiuchang zhengshui*), and raising efficiency through the abolition of both public and private monopolies.[40] Although the Inspectorate had only varying degrees of success in realizing all of these goals (the imposition of free trade would prove to be particularly problematic), it did have, from the very outset, a clear programme of action that served as the standard against which all subsequent actions were measured. This 'programme' remained remarkably consistent, regardless of changes in leadership of the organization, until the outbreak of the Sino-Japanese War.

None of these medium-term organizational goals was particularly easy to implement. Even into the 1930s, the different salt producing regions were still characterized by variable rates for the basic salt tax and surtaxes: different regions also had wildly divergent local arrangements for the distribution of salt. However, as an organizational programme for institution building, these objectives were exceptionally amenable to professionalization at the top of the organization and bureaucratization for the rank and file. Dane's original list of organizational goals clearly laid out overarching principles, related means to ends, and was straightforward to operationalize. The nature of organizational goals and technology lent themselves to high degrees of 'specificity': 'the degree to which it is possible to specify the objectives of a particular activity, the methods for achieving them, and the ways of controlling achievement'.[41] Centralized receipt of salt funds, reduction and unification of tariff rates, and abolition of monopolies were fairly specific activities that were both definable and measurable in terms of their intentions and effects.

Once the organization's goals were established (and after Dane they became such an established part of the Inspectorate's ideological bedrock that no one ever seems to have questioned them), it was relatively straightforward to devise methods for achieving them, measuring the results, and advancing or tactically retreating as circumstances warranted.[42] Bags of salt, amounts of revenue collected, and percentages of revenue spent on administrative costs could be (and were) duly counted and reported every year, district by district and station by station, thus leading to fairly efficient bureaucratization of most Inspectorate operations. In any given year, the performance of the Salt Inspectorate could be readily correlated with external, universally accepted indicators of success or failure: the bottom line of this year's revenue receipts versus last year's revenue receipts.

In circumstances of variability—when the organization was unable to completely 'control achievement' and fully bureaucratize by formulating an impersonal rule, or when it saw the opportunity to expand its influence—the Salt Inspectorate allowed its senior staff a good deal of discretion and flexibility in implementing organizational goals: upper-level staff were presumed to be reliable professionals who could be trusted to make appropriate on-the-spot decisions.[43]

Because the Inspectorate's goals and technologies lent themselves to neutral criteria for evaluation, it was possible for the organization to take advantage of its decentralized operations and experiment with new methods of salt administration. Successful pilot projects could be quickly validated and, circumstances permitting, extended to other districts. For example, in the notoriously monopoly-controlled, smuggler-infested Huaibei region, one particularly vigorous Chinese district inspector, Miao Qiujie, who would some five years later become head of the Salt Administration, invested heavily in depot construction, roads, telephones, and other infrastructure to store the salt and easily monitor its transport, thereby bringing about a drastic reduction in 'banditry' and nearly doubling the releases of legal salt in a single year.[44] The Huaibei experiments were then extended to salt-producing districts in Hubei, Hunan, and Anhui. Once an innovation appeared to be successful in one district, it entered the canon of approved methods, was described in working reports and training manuals, and was attempted in other locations deemed suitable.[45]

On the other hand, the high specificity of most Inspectorate operations made it relatively easy to retreat temporarily from those goals or programme that could not be immediately realized. As long as minimal criteria were met (i.e. the continued collection of enough revenue to service the Reorganization Loan debt), progress towards other goals such as unification of tax rates, extension of the tax net, and abolishment of merchant monopolies could be realized in a piecemeal, two-steps-forward-one-step-back fashion. A rapacious warlord in one district or an annoyingly strong cartel of salt merchants in another could be temporarily accommodated. Tactical measures, such as having to buy off a warlord or continue partial reliance on salt merchants for distribution and marketing in one district at a given time, did not necessarily fatally compromise the integrity of the organization as a whole. Successful experiments in a given district could be extended to other districts, while the reverses of one district tended to be confined to that particular area. Even if the Inspectorate was put in a position of having to retreat on one front (such as turning over a substantial amount of its funds at gunpoint to a warlord), it could continue to pursue its other goals, such as raising the amount of revenue collected, suppressing smuggling, or increasing the efficiency of staff operations.

Outward-oriented bureaucratic strategies of goal implementation aided organizational stability and institutionalization in the way it shaped the range of action for both the organization's top leadership and its rank and file. Dane's original programme of organizational goals was not immediately realizable *in toto*, but it did lend itself to breakdown into sub-goals. As long as the district-level leadership maintained its professional and bureaucratic orientation, the exceptionally well defined organizational goals and methods for achievement made charismatic, visionary leadership at the top of the organization unnecessary and, in some ways, unwelcome. Dane was an administrator of exceptional vision and vigour, but his genius was to build the Inspectorate on a set of depersonalized, bureaucratic, and professional norms that could long outlast the tenure of any particular leader, including himself. After a mere four years, Dane left the Inspectorate, and was followed by a succession of colourless, faceless foreign chief inspectors whose assorted health problems, lack of 'vision', and tendencies to focus narrowly on regulations, figures, and details none the less seem not to have had a strongly negative effect on the organization as a whole.[46]

The measurable and divisible specificity of Inspectorate goals gave an additional boost to the organization's bureaucratic strategies of insulation. Because goals were so straightforward, specific, and directly measurable, it was easy to assess staff performance along objective, bureaucratically determined lines. Peculation and poor performance, as well as conscientiousness and vigour, were easily spotted by superiors and appropriately punished or rewarded. The unambiguousness of organizational goals and their straightforward reduction to specific tasks made it that much easier for the Inspectorate to inculcate ideals of objective performance in its staff. Because the Inspectorate could neutrally determine the criteria for performance and rewards, organizational authority itself became increasingly depersonalized.

For the Salt Inspectorate, bureaucratic strategies of insulation and a combination of bureaucratic and professional methods of goal implementation were mutually reinforcing. From the perspective of the organization's reformist leadership, these strategies made possible 'the emergence of a new type of Chinese official accustomed to facing facts and giving practical application to defined principles', whereas before 1913 'even the lowest of official employees [was] unwilling to take an active part in weighing salt, since this might be classed as manual labor derogatory to their dignity'.[47] Without a well insulated staff socialized into the norms of civil service and objective competence, the Inspectorate probably could not have cut through the tangle of local, vested interests and corruption to produce a tax surplus; but without a set of goals that lent themselves to objective evaluation and specific breakdown, the Inspectorate might not have been able to generate enough internal cohesiveness to maintain its autonomy and insulation.

The Inspectorate's main achievement was its ability appropriately to focus strategies of bureaucratization both inwardly and outwardly, transforming depersonalized, bureaucratic rules of principle into the organization's *modus vivendi*. In the words of one former salt official, 'It *seemed* like a very rigid system, but in fact the stress on rules and seniority got rid of much in-house competition. *Things were done according to regulations—the longer you were in the service, the more you knew*.'[48] The individuals who worked for the Salt Inspectorate committed themselves to the organization because its rigid bureaucratic procedures and strategies made still strongly held bureaucratic elite ideals of fairness, stability, and universalism a reality in an environment in which such ideals could seldom find any concrete expression.

## CONCLUSION

The Sino-Foreign Salt Inspectorate managed to accomplish a feat that few other organizations in early twentieth-century China could replicate. It possessed both the will and the means to insulate itself consistently from a highly particularistic environment as it coalesced around its core values of depersonalization and objective performance. Because organizational goals were agreed upon, divisible, and specific, the Salt Inspectorate's mission and internal culture were amenable to the organization's promotion of bureaucratization and professionalism as it sought to secure its survival. Very explicit programmes of bureaucratization and rule orientation were instituted to foster insulation and socialization into an ethic of performance achievement for the Inspectorate staff; a mixture of bureaucratic rule orientation and professional discretion gave the top echelon of the district administration the flexibility to improvise, balance differing commitments, and respond to contingencies in the environment. The close connection between internally oriented bureaucratic insulation and externally oriented bureaucratic and professional goal implementation enabled the Inspectorate consistently to perform at high levels, expand in scope, and withstand repeated shocks that a less insulated, less efficient, less effective organization could not have survived. How the Inspectorate was able to do so in an increasingly problematic, politicized external environment is the subject of the next chapter.

# 4

## The Salt Inspectorate in the Nationalist State: Tensions between Politics and Administration

### INTRODUCTION

The Salt Inspectorate overcame institution-building dilemmas by self-consciously adopting a two-front strategy of bureaucratization. The existence of an in-house civil service system fostered performance achievement and depersonalization of authority, which were critical components in the organization's attempts to insulate and buffer itself from a hostile external environment. Externally oriented, measurable, task-specific goal achievement enabled the Inspectorate to utilize its objective 'results' (i.e. the taxes it collected) to further insulate itself and turn back external attacks. Through insulation and bureaucratization, the Inspectorate sought to institutionalize itself in what was, in the early twentieth century, widely considered to be the only appropriate manner: as an administrative 'machine' that was as far removed from politics and personalism as possible.[1] In laudatory reviews of the Salt Inspectorate's institution-building accomplishments, the imagery was typically heavily mechanistic:

In fact, the whole machinery of the administration was put into simple and efficient working order so that all could see how the administration worked, the part that each cog was expected to play, and the regulations under which each was expected to play his part.[2]

For the Inspectorate, 'politics' was capricious, divisive, personality-based, unscientific, and unpredictable, while 'administration' was productive, objective, scientific, and, with a modicum of good luck, predictable.

In contrast to the Inspectorate, which had a very clear vision of its role as a limited, exclusive, administrative organization, the Guomindang conceived of itself and its role as extensive, inclusive, political, and, through the structures of the National Government, administrative as well. Whatever its internal factional differences may have been, the Guomindang saw the establishment of its political and administrative control over state structures, political discourse, and society at large as the first step in its developmental strategy of reintegrating the state. This attempt at rigorous reassertion of monocratic control drew much from the imperial past even as it attempted to implement modern, revolutionary national reconstruction and development.

Beyond a near obsession with unity and control, the Nationalist regime was mired in ambivalence regarding what constituted appropriate medium-term goals and methods of implementation. In practice, the regime was so inclusive that it simultaneously favoured elite-managed technocracy and popular mobilization; objective competence and Party indoctrination; and the principle of merit even as it acted out the reality of a developed spoils system. The reasons for this far-reaching inclusion went beyond even the Nationalist military and institutional weakness, which pushed the regime to attempt to co-opt other powerful groups. Since Sun Yat-sen, the Nationalist anti-imperialist 'revolution' had been predicated on the assumption that the interests and desires of the Chinese people were inherently unifying and constructive rather than selfish and destructive to the causes of nation building, and a set of bloody purges had been carried out against the Communists in 1927 because the conservative wing of the Guomindang ultimately could not stomach the 'divisiveness' of class struggle.[3]

For those who survived the purges and remained in the Guomindang and National Government after 1927, the inclusion of all those who did not openly oppose the principles of unity and construction was not merely craven tactical accommodation: it was a logical extension of deeply held norms. But inclusion and incorporation of very different groups into a centralizing state apparatus could not deny the existence of politics and parochial interests: it merely transferred the locus of politics from between the Party/Government and society to the inner reaches of the Party and Government, thus conflating politics, administration, and the pursuit of private interest. Since the scope of its action was so wide and the groups it incorporated so diverse, the Nationalists were extraordinarily eclectic, ambivalent, and sometimes self-contradictory in their medium-range strategies for institution building and development.

The Sino-Foreign Salt Inspectorate—limited, technically oriented, depoliticized, and *exclusive*—and the Nationalist Party—extensive, factionalized, and *inclusive*—were opposing images of each other. When the latter came to power and officially subsumed the former in 1927–8, it raised a question that was to plague both the Inspectorate and other technocratically inclined groups within the National Government throughout the 1930s and into the 1940s: would the politics of the Party invade and discredit 'scientific' and 'objectively oriented' technocratic administration, or would the example of 'objective' administration provide a salutory model to be emulated elsewhere in the Party and Government, ultimately shifting the basis of politics and regularizing the nexus between 'politics' and 'administration'?

## DRESS REHEARSAL: INSPECTORATE AND WARLORDS, 1917–1926

First as the Salt Inspectorate and then as the Directorate-General of Salt, the Salt Administration spanned the duration of the entire Republican period, and managed to continue operating even under the extraordinarily volatile political and military conditions of the warlord years (c.1916–27). During this era, the Beiyang government centred in Beijing was unable to extend its authority much beyond the immediate environs of the capital. Meanwhile, outside of Beijing regional militarists attempted to build power bases, entered alliances with each other, and fought increasingly larger, more serious, more expensive wars in order to aggrandize their own power, contain the influence of the others, and (for the largest regional players) aim to take control of the capital and therefore the central government themselves.[4]

The warlords were a highly heterogeneous lot, ranging from the outright rapacious, who were given free rein because of the anarchic and increasingly militarized times, to quasi-state builders like Yan Xishan in Shanxi and the Guangxi triumvirate, who attempted to develop the areas in which they had their power bases. However, even for the well-meaning, the anarchic structure of the political environment and the rules of the game pushed the regional militarist towards irregular levies (tankuan) and outright plunder. Since the individual warlord had to maintain a level of military preparedness and technology at least as advanced as that of his potentially aggressive neighbour, he was driven by the interests of immediate self-preservation to be enormously extractive in the areas under his immediate control. Resource extraction involved everything from outright looting to the taxation of opium, brothels, and scissors. Without money, personal armies could not be paid; without fairly regular pay, personal armies would weaken; and with a dissatisfied and weakened personal army, the individual leader could not expect to survive for long. As the warlord period wore on, regional battles tended to get larger, require more men and materiel, involve more ideological pretensions, and become more decisive for winners and losers. As a result, the search for stable resource bases accordingly intensified.

During this turbulent period, the Salt Inspectorate's district offices were among the few local organizations of resource extraction still effectively tied to a nationwide administration: their control over local tax funds and their undeniable efficiency led them to be particularly inviting targets for warlord depredations, particularly when warlord engagements grew larger and more destructive in the mid-1920s. The warlords were, by definition, not averse to using the means of violence to impose their will: in many salt-producing areas, including Jiangsu, Sichuan, and Yunnan, they invaded the local district offices, physically threatened the staff, and demanded payoffs. Until the Northern Expedition in 1926, Inspectorate offices so pressured typically opted to 'make the best of a bad situation' by negotiating a one-off deal with the currently threatening military figure.[5]

Although the Inspectorate viewed such arrangements with distaste, the terms reached could usually satisfy the minimal requirements of both parties. In return for allowing the Inspectorate to continue its work without interference, the warlord, who invariably had a pressing need for funds, received a substantial windfall. The Inspectorate office usually retained enough revenue to cover its own immediate administrative expenses and its share of the Reorganization Loan debt. The portion of the funds that went to the warlord encompassed the revenue normally earmarked for the 'central government', and, although each case was negotiated on an *ad hoc* basis, typically the warlord got half while the Salt Inspectorate office retained half of the funds that were available.[6] Such arrangements could be worked out because warlord operations were not known for their efficiency or stability in fiscal administration: the salt tax provided a potentially lucrative source of funds, and the Salt Inspectorate offices had already proven themselves to be much more efficient than anyone else in collecting this particular tax. In this way, local strongmen avoided the trouble of having to institute, even provisionally, a tax administration in an area about which they knew little and were ill equipped to be effective.

For its part, the Inspectorate adhered quite rigidly—even at gunpoint—to the bureaucratic strategies of insulation and goal implementation that were at the core of its efficiency and success. As long as bureaucratic insulation, autonomy, and some flow of resources to the central organization could be maintained, the attacks of the warlords were felt to be serious, but not in principle fatal, disruptions to the organization as a whole, particularly if they were confined to individual areas.

The figures on revenue releases to the central and local governments confirm a pattern of increasingly serious instability, politicization, and attacks on the Inspectorate throughout the 1920s. In 1922, the year of the Inspectorate's highest pre-Nationalist period collection, of 85,789,000Y net, somewhat more than half, or 47,193,23Y, was forwarded to the central government by the Inspectorate, with about one quarter, or 20,125,720Y, 'retained locally' without 'consent'. Only four years later, in 1926, Inspectorate net totals had declined by a third to 64,287,000Y, from which less than 9,000,000Y went to the central government, while local governments and warlords retained well over half, at 37,388,616Y.[7] By 1926 the Inspectorate was under sufficient stress from widening civil wars that some of its offices were beginning to close, and the Guomindang National Revolutionary Army forcibly shut down all the district offices in its path as manifestations of imperialism that needed to be swept away.

By mid-1927 to early 1928, the months in which it faced formal abolishment and reconstitution, the Salt Inspectorate had already had some ten years of direct experience in dealing with extreme conditions of political and military uncertainty, albeit on a localized and case-by-case basis. Over the unstable warlord era, it had developed an set of survival tactics, formally submitting and paying off those militarily or politically stronger, while appealing to its proven record of efficiency and effectiveness to otherwise be left alone to continue to do the job. In short, even *in extremis*, the Salt Inspectorate opted to buffer itself and contain the worst of the external turbulence as much as it could in order to maintain its organizational core of effective autonomy, technocracy, and depoliticization. With this repertoire already well established by the time of the Northern Expedition, the Inspectorate had a basic set of strategies ready for its incorporation into the Nationalist government.

ABOLITION AND INCORPORATION, 1927–1928

As a revolutionary, nationalist organization, the Guomindang was very much concerned with anything that smacked of imperialism or slights to China's national dignity, and was initially extremely hostile to the Inspectorate. In the view of many in the revolutionary movement, the Inspectorate was an imperialist organization that existed solely to exploit China and insult her sovereignty for the benefit of the international banks. Therefore, as the National Revolutionary Army marched north to the Yangzi River valley in 1926–7, it forcibly closed down district offices along the way, and in June 1927 Gu Yingfen, then briefly holding the Ministry of Finance portfolio, formally abolished the Salt Inspectorate just as the National Government under Chiang Kai-shek was being established in Nanjing.

But no sooner had the Inspectorate been officially closed than key figures in the Guomindang coalition began to lobby for the organization's re-establishment. By the autumn of 1927, Sun Ke (who briefly served as Minister of Finance), Zheng Hongnian (Vice Minister of Finance), and Wu Chaoqu (C. C. Wu, Minister of Foreign Affairs) were requesting talks with the Salt Inspectorate. These individuals may well have had slightly different agendas for wishing to consider restoration of the Inspectorate: Wu Chaoqu, for example, was almost certainly concerned about the diplomatic costs of appearing to repudiate the Reorganization Loan agreement, and Sun Ke clearly intimated that he wished to use the Inspectorate as a vehicle to appoint some seventy of his followers. But by late December, Sun Ke was out of the Ministry of Finance and Song Ziwen (T. V. Soong) was preparing to assume office. Even before receiving the Ministry of Finance portfolio, Song indicated his preference for honouring the Reorganization Loan agreement and using a reconstituted, non-patronage-based Salt Inspectorate as the organization to generate the necessary revenue.[8] Shortly thereafter, Song secured the Guomindang Central Executive Committee's approval for the restoration of the Inspectorate: by the winter of 1927–8 many of the Inspectorate district offices were being reopened, and roughly a year later, in late 1928, the Party's decision was formally promulgated by the government Legislative Yuan, by which point most of the district offices were up and running again.[9]

For the Salt Inspectorate, the arrangement concluded with the National Government Ministry of Finance must have seemed the logical extension of strategies already practised during the volatile 1920s. In exchange for being formally reconstituted, the Salt Inspectorate bowed to the superior political and military strength of the Nationalist regime. Having little choice in the matter, as neither the British nor the other foreign powers would or could do more than officially register concern that the Reorganization Loan repayment schedule continue to be met, the Inspectorate was incorporated into the National Government under the aegis of the Ministry of Finance.[10] Guomindang political control was exercised through the appointment of a new Chinese chief inspector, Zhu Tingqi, an individual with no prior experience in salt or tax administration.

Despite howls of protest from the Western banking and business interests, Frederick Hussey-Freke, the Foreign Chief Inspector, agreed to transfer responsibility for the loan repayments to the Ministry of Finance as the best that could be arranged under the circumstances. In return, the Inspectorate was, like the Customs Administration which was similarly incorporated at the same time, accorded the status of a *shu*—a semi-autonomous entity within the larger Ministry of Finance. In principle, the Inspectorate was allowed to retain its foreign personnel, was granted continued control and substantial autonomy over day-to-day operations and, apart from the appointment of Zhu Tingqi at the very top, its independent civil service system remained intact.

For the Guomindang, the immediate incentives for the re-establishment of the Salt Inspectorate were strikingly similar to those of individual warlords in allowing the Inspectorate to stay in business. In an environment characterized by continuing high levels of militarization, the Guomindang was bedevilled by weak supporting administrative structures in combination with a pressing need to raise ever larger amounts of revenue to finance a voracious military machine. Between the Northern Expedition, recalcitrant independent warlords, local rebellions, 'Bandit Encirclement' campaigns against the Communists, and laying the groundwork for an eventual showdown with Japan, the regime was engaged nearly continuously in some sort of military action or military preparation during the whole of the Nanjing Decade. The percentages of the national budget officially devoted to military expenditures were extraordinarily high—ranging from a high of over 50 per cent in 1928–9 to a low of 21.6 per cent in 1935–6 (see Table 4.1).[11] Particularly during the regime's early years, the Guomindang political leadership came to the same conclusion as had many of the local warlords: overriding its distaste for a foreigner-influenced tax collection

**Table 4.1.** National Government Official Military Expenditures

| Fiscal year[a] | Expenditures (in yuan) | % of total government expenditure |
| --- | --- | --- |
| 1928 | 210 | 50.8 |
| 1929 | 245 | 45.5 |
| 1930 | 312 | 43.6 |
| 1931 | 304 | 44.5 |
| 1932 | 321 | 49.7 |
| 1933 | 373 | 48.5 |
| 1934 | 368 | 34.4 |
| 1935 | 220 | 21.6 |
| 1936 | 322 | 32.5 |

[a] Fiscal year = 1 July–30 June.
*Source*: Hung-mao Tien, *Government and Politics in Kuomintang China, 1927–37*, 83.

agency was its need for the reliable income from the salt gabelle that only the Inspectorate could provide.

In spite of a range of institutional weaknesses that were analogous to those characterizing earlier warlord regimes, the National Government possessed a range of aspirations and intentions that went far beyond these. Although implementation was problematic and uneven, the Guomindang had a national programme for state building and reconstruction, a slowly developing capacity to reintegrate and enforce minimal standardization over larger and larger areas of the country, and a number of institution-building approaches that were considerably more politicized than anything ever attempted by most regional militarists. If the Inspectorate's strategies for handling its incorporation into the National Government remained fundamentally the same as they had been in previous dealings with warlord regimes, the political and institutional context was substantially altered by the events of 1927. Although the political and military situation in the late 1920s rendered continued immediate tax extraction a goal that could not be ignored, the Guomindang was not content with mere subsidies and buy-offs: it sought integration, unity, strength, and national pride. But because the methods and strategies for implementing these goals were far from consistent or uniform within the government, the Salt Inspectorate was afforded opportunities as well as constraints once it was incorporated in the evolving Nationalist state.

### INFORMAL POWER SHARING, 1928–1937

During the nine years between 1928 and 1937, relations between the Nationalists and the Salt Inspectorate were, for the most part, characterized by informal power sharing, with different groups in the Party and Government vacillating between the desire to suppress and the desire to emulate the Salt Inspectorate. Formally, the Nationalists held all the cards. The Inspectorate had ceased to exist as an independent entity and was now a 'subordinate and advisory body' to the Ministry of Finance; the Ministry of Finance had taken over the receipt of the salt funds and now managed the foreign debt itself; and the new Chinese Chief Inspector, Zhu Tingqi, was a Guomindang appointee whom the Salt Inspectorate regulars, at least initially, neither liked nor approved of.[12] However, the formal organization charts and the reams of regulations put out by the Ministry of Finance obscured a fundamental reality: all appearances to the contrary, the Inspectorate maintained a substantial degree of autonomy under the National Government.

Because the Salt Inspectorate had for so long been grounded in an ideal of depersonalized administrative competence divorced from politics, it could accept the existence of new political masters fairly easily, as long as the political leaders in question were content to give orders from outside the organization and not interfere with its administrative procedures or attempt to micro-manage implementation within. While accepting the formal authority of the new political masters, the Inspectorate quietly and continuously devoted a good deal of its energies to persuading Guomindang political masters to allow it its 'proper' sphere of influence in administration. Concretely, this translated into the Inspectorate's continued *de facto* autonomy over personnel and basic operations until the late 1930s.

The Inspectorate was able to do so for two related reasons. First, like individual warlords, the Nationalist regime really could not afford to 'kill the goose that laid the golden egg' by tampering with the Inspectorate too much. Second, while the strategies of the Salt Inspectorate in dealings with the Guomindang were defensive, consistent, and reflective of the organization's carefully constructed solidarity and unity of purpose, those of the Party and Government towards the Inspectorate were variable, inconsistent, and reflective of a number of fundamental ambivalences within the ruling elite. The longstanding obsession with unity dictated a broad policy of inclusion and power sharing with all those not in open revolt who could not be immediately replaced or bypassed. This resulted in the somewhat anomalous coexistence of mutually antagonistic groups within the Ministry of Finance: both the 'rationalizing' Salt Inspectorate and the Yanwu Shu.

Guomindang political elites were also frequently caught between mutually exclusive imperatives. Their desire to establish uniformity and control often collided with the immediate necessity of delegating authority to an organization capable of garnering the revenue to secure the state's survival. Less obvious, but no less real, was the perennial conflict between the search for efficiency and the effective emulation of successful Western (or Western-inspired) institutions on the one hand and the nationalistic impulse to negate the last vestiges of imperialism and national humiliation through top-down control and bottom-up mobilization on the other. These ambivalences were well summed up by one commentator:

[The Inspectorate's] existence as a collecting agency of foreign creditors was derogatory of China's sovereign right and particularly repugnant to Chinese nationalism...On the other hand, recognition must be given to the efficiency of the Inspectorate service, as testified to by the rapid increase of the salt revenue since its institution in 1913.[13]

For reasons of principle, different groups in the regime did have undeniable, legitimate differences of opinion with respect to anomalous organizations like the Inspectorate, and for individual reasons, those with any stake at all in the system had every immediate incentive to foster continued networks of patronage.

In the years between 1928 and 1936, the informal power sharing tacitly worked out between the Guomindang and the Salt Inspectorate enabled the latter to deflect most, although not absolutely all, pressures from other quarters to politicize the Inspectorate and render it a site for patronage. The Inspectorate was able to re-insulate itself by pleading its case to those in the government who were known to be sympathetic to its core values of depersonalization, efficiency, and effectiveness. It got the ear of Song Ziwen, the most powerful figure in Nationalist financial circles, by appealing to its previous 'ten years of good results', which were a function of its 'strong civil service traditions and experiences in salt administration', and it is clear that as a result of his admiration for the Inspectorate's success and efficiency, Song adopted a relatively hands-off policy towards internal Inspectorate operations.[14]

Since the core of the Salt Inspectorate's organizational integrity and external efficiency was widely recognized to be its depersonalized, autonomous civil service, it was in this particular area that the informal power sharing between government and organization was arranged. The Guomindang appointed a Chinese chief inspector who was unpopular with the Inspectorate staff, who immediately upon his appointment broke with 'tradition' and brought in an old teacher of his at a very high rank, and who did little to prevent the erosion of the authority and prestige of the foreign district inspectors;[15] but the Salt Inspectorate was allowed to maintain its separate recruitment and personnel system.[16] The Ministry of Finance had taken over direct receipt of the salt revenues and responsibility for handling the debt, technically leaving the Salt Inspectorate without independent funds. But the Ministry of Finance also very quietly set up a special internal fund from which the higher Salt Inspectorate salaries were paid.[17]

For the most part, the key components of the Inspectorate's success— bureaucratic recruitment by examination, frequent transfer, a slow rate of promotion, higher salaries, and evaluation on the basis of objective performance—remained unchanged until several years into the Sino-Japanese War.[18] With the resource base of its organizational insulation at least provisionally secure, the Inspectorate turned its energies back to the things it did best: efficiently collecting taxes, rationalizing procedures, amalgamating quirky districts, and implementing standardization where-ever possible.

Once incorporated into the National Government, the Salt Inspectorate behaved as one would expect of a self-styled efficient, non-political admin-istrative arm of the centralizing state. Most of the statistical evidence suggests that, in addition to pursuing its longstanding methods of salt administration, the Salt Inspectorate secured its survival through impress-ive responsiveness to its political masters. Some of the foreigners in the Inspectorate lamented the organization's loss of independent initiative during the Nanjing Decade:

The Inspectorate may be seen rather laboriously following whither it was being led by Minister Soong, without once attempting to outstrip its leader or even to keep pace with him and vigorously support and consolidate every step he took, or to urge his attention toward the abolition of the many objectionable monopolies which its experience had shown were harmful... [With the accession of Kong Xiangxi as Minister of Finance in 1933]...the Inspectorate has been somewhat blindly wielded as a weapon for producing increased revenues without sufficient knowledge or insistent advice as to how the weapon may best be used... [This]...has resulted in attention being concentrated almost entirely on the money aspects of the admin-istration...in general an apparent tendency to sacrifice past experience to the needs of the moment.[19]

There is little doubt that, throughout the 1930s, the Salt Administration was squeezed hard from above and usually produced what was demanded, and that, despite the complaints of those who longed for the good old days when the Inspectorate was not accountable to anything other than itself and the Group Banks, its submission to the will of its new political masters made excellent political and administrative sense. The central state needed more efficiency, more revenue, and less operating expenses. The district inspectors gritted their teeth, cut administrative costs, and, even though it went against the organizational norm of consolidating and reducing taxes, raised duty rates in many districts as much as seven times over the course of the 1930s.[20]

By virtually any set of criteria, the Inspectorate continued to be both impressively effective (bringing in more in absolute revenue) and more efficient (producing more revenue relative to administrative cost and relat-ive to the amount of salt produced) during the Nanjing Decade. At the end of 1929, only one year after its formal reconstitution, Inspectorate offices had been re-established in those areas under Nationalist control, and were producing enough revenue to nearly secure the annual debt. During the early to mid-1930s, the amounts of collected revenue climbed steadily: annual totals in the early 1930s were roughly 50 per cent higher than they had been in the early 1920s.[21] At the demand of the Ministry of Finance, a general retrenchment fostered increased 'administrative efficiency': between 1929 and 1933, the percentage of gross collected revenue spent on administrative expenses declined by a respectable 5.79 per cent in the districts where the central government and Inspectorate had good control.[22] The relative contribution of efficiency (reduction of administrative costs) and simple organizational effectiveness (pushing through and collecting) in securing increased taxes is difficult to determine, but Table 4.2 illustrates conclusively that throughout the Nanjing Decade the Salt Inspectorate remitted more to the central government Treasury on proportionally less produced salt, demonstrating both efficiency and effectiveness. Total revenue produced by the Inspectorate increased by over 50 per cent, while the amount of salt being taxed simultaneously declined by roughly 15 per cent.

Although informal power sharing between the Salt Inspectorate and the Nationalists was not without its internal tensions, the arrangements reached benefited both. With the exception of the foreign staff in the Inspectorate, who were the clear 'losers' over the long run in the Nationalist takeover of the Inspectorate, both the Inspectorate and the National Government expanded, consolidated, and grew in influence over the course of the 1930s. The Salt Inspectorate was, of course, on a much tighter leash than it had been before 1927–8. It no longer had the same range of discretion, and it was put into the service of the state in a much more systematic manner than it had been even under the very worst of the warlords (who tended to move on after a one-time extraction). But

Table 4.2.  National Government Salt Collections, 1928–1937

|      | Piculs collected ('000) | Tax collected ('000 yuan) |
|------|-------------------------|---------------------------|
| 1928 | 53,484 | 137,045 |
| 1929 | 60,898 | 143,366 |
| 1930 | 42,109 | 147,207 |
| 1931 | 43,994 | 154,145 |
| 1932 | 47,630 | 157,752 |
| 1933 | 47,062 | 160,693 |
| 1934 | 45,041 | 177,461 |
| 1935 | 52,674 | 185,416 |
| 1936 | 48,672 | 217,817 |
| 1937 | 42,663 | 217,905 |

Source: Ding Changqing et al., Minguo yanwu shigao, (Beijing: Renmin Chubanshe, 1990), 218–19.

by rising to the challenge and demonstrating its responsiveness and efficiency, the Salt Inspectorate was able to secure official approval to do within the National Government what it had informally attempted for years outside the Chinese government: to bring the other salt organizations operating in China under its authority.

The division between the 'collecting' (Inspectorate) and 'administrative' (Yanwu Shu) salt units had by the early 1930s long since ceased to have much meaning as the Inspectorate and the Yanwu Shu (Salt Office) had for years overlapped with respect to salt production, anti-smuggling measures, and transport activities. The Yanwu Shu had never mustered either the insulation or the effectiveness of the Salt Inspectorate, and was widely considered to be a disorganized, corrupt set of local organizations incapable of doing very much.[23] In persuading the Ministry of Finance to support it against the Yanwu Shu and the Salt Police, the Inspectorate combined appeals to its long standing track record of effectiveness with the Ministry's predisposition to raise general efficiency through amalgamation, standardization, and the elimination of organizational replication and overlap. By the early 1930s, the Inspectorate was able to convince the efficiency minded in the Ministry of Finance that the interests of the centralizing state would best be served by allowing the Inspectorate to absorb the other salt organizations, and to dominate the salt administration policy area in the name of the state. In 1931, Song Ziwen ordered the takeover of the Yanwu Shu by the Inspectorate, and in 1932–3 he approved the same fate for the salt police units.

The Inspectorate's absorption of the Yanwu Shu took place without much incident. The Salt Police, on the other hand, had been building their organizational capacity along similar lines of centralization and rationalization, and were considerably more problematic for the Inspectorate to digest. As early as 1930, the Inspectorate began to fund the salaries of the Salt Police, and in 1931 the Inspectorate established a special administrative office to handle the Salt Police's requisitions for uniforms, ammunition, and salaries. But even after their official incorporation into the Salt Inspectorate in 1932–3, as a group with a distinctly military orientation and training in the midst of a highly civilian, technically oriented organization, the Salt Police continued to control most of their own appointments and deployment through a new 'Preventative Office', which was officially part of the Inspectorate.[24]

During the 1930s, the Salt Inspectorate's staff vigorously objected to the intrusion of external political and personal appointments into their still relatively well-insulated and certainly highly distinctive system. In 1936 a clutch of Legislative Yuan delegates singled out the Salt Inspectorate's high salary scales and independent personnel system for attack, prompting the normally publicity-shy organization to '[be] willing to go public to answer the specific charges levelled'. More or less simultaneously, J.C. Croome ranted about the 'appointment of unqualified individuals to posts created especially for them... substituting patronage for justice'.[25]

Such fears notwithstanding, political and personally inspired appointments still seem to have been quite exceptional in the 1930s. Most of the differences in recruitment and appointment patterns between the pre- and post-1927 period stemmed from the Inspectorate's incorporation of the 'preventative function' (i.e. the Salt Police) rather than from any systemic intrusion of personalism and politics. During the 1930s, the policy against no lateral transfers weakened slightly; of the fourteen 'high' and 'near-high fliers' recruited after 1927, all started their appointments with the Inspectorate at considerably higher salaries than the regulation 160Y per month; but, with the exception of the four individuals with military backgrounds who worked exclusively in the new Salt Police divisions, the backgrounds of these 'high fliers' were not significantly different from those rare individuals in the pre-1927 period who had started with similarly high positions. Eight had received advanced degrees abroad, three were high-level transfers from the Ministry of Communications, and two were experienced accountants.[26] With the exception of those in the newly incorporated Salt Police sub-administration, the vast majority of the post-1927 recruits came into the organization in exactly the same manner as had those in the pre-1927 organization—through open examination, at the bottom.

The other features of the Salt Inspectorate's bureaucratic strategies of insulation and goal implementation did not change substantially from the pre-1927 period. Individuals' career patterns remained the same, transfers and promotions occurred with about the same regularity. The addition of a number of individuals entering at higher-than-normal levels probably lessened the organization's rigid insistence on seniority and longevity as the primary basis for rewards, but the incentives encouraging stability and seniority (such as the sabbatical and supplementary bonuses) remained in effect.[27] The Salt Inspectorate not only survived its abolishment and reconstitution; it did so with its personnel, organizational culture, and mechanisms for socializing subsequent generations largely intact. Since the Salt Police already had their own militarily oriented organizational culture and career patterns, the incorporation of the Salt Police probably put a greater internal strain on the organization than did any external, overt politicization, and the Inspectorate dealt with this potential problem by confining the Salt Police to remaining a recognizably distinct sub-group within the larger organization.

Although abolishment and incorporation by the Guomindang had been a serious shock to the Salt Inspectorate, the organization paradoxically survived by conservatively adhering to its core values of neutrality, efficiency, and effectiveness. In the substantially changed post-1927 political order, the Inspectorate continued to represent itself as a depoliticized administrative machine capable of performing important services to the state. An organization unable to accommodate new political leaders would not have been tolerated by the control- and unity-minded Guomindang, much less have been allowed to expand in influence and responsibility. While the Salt Inspectorate was allowed quietly to retain a good deal of its internal autonomy, and to continue to pursue a number of the goals to which it had always aspired (such as increasing its control over salt works, and raising efficiency and effectiveness), responsiveness to new political masters dictated that it pursue certain goals (increasing control, and raising the absolute and relative amounts of tax revenue) to the partial or total exclusion of all others (such as free trade and reduction of tax rates).

The Inspectorate had submitted to the authority of a new set of political masters for whom the maintenance of political coalitions and patronage networks often collided with the objective need for efficiency and high performance. Therefore, the Inspectorate's continued existence within the National Government was heavily tied to its ability to maintain its *status quo* as a still well-buffered, well-insulated, fairly autonomous bureaucratic organization. The medium-term goals and approaches of Guomindang political leadership were divided and inconsistent: even those most sympathetic to and admiring of the Salt Inspectorate's efficiency, high performance, and civil service were split between the desire to 'use it (mandating continued *de facto* autonomy) and control it'.[28]

Fortunately for the Inspectorate, it performed services necessary enough to the Nationalist state that the key figures in the immediate political environment of the Ministry of Finance (first Song Ziwen, and then Kong Xiangxi) were inclined to leave it more or less alone as long as the tax receipts kept coming in increasing amounts: when attacked, it could always appeal to its concrete performance in raising tax revenue. More subtly, it played on its success in having established a working, depersonalized, highly efficient civil service—an ideal to which many of the political and administrative elites elsewhere in the National Government were attuned.[29] Internal policy papers and policy reports on personnel administration and organizational effectiveness within the Ministry of Finance were full of admiration for the Inspectorate's ability to institute a ' "scientific" rational administration . . . based on actual experience' that could effectively control corruption, set defined procedures for promotion and demotion, grant security of tenure, and in general 'rigorously implement its regulations'.[30] The Nationalists not only immediately needed the support and funds of an efficient tax-collecting organization; they also contained a number of groups that, in whole or part, looked to the successes of the Inspectorate as a positive model of scientific, rational administration.

Performance and civil service ideals, while extremely important, were not the sole objectives to which Nationalist politicians and administrators aspired. Control and standardization, closely linked with national pride, were also themes that none, not even those in the results-oriented Ministry of Finance, could totally ignore. As a subordinate entity within the Ministry of Finance, the Inspectorate was subject to the Ministry's push towards centralization and amalgamation of various lower-level tax organizations in the mid-1930s. Along with a host of other reorganizations in the Ministry of Finance, the Salt Inspectorate and the Yanwu Shu were formally amalgamated into a new organization known as the Directorate-General of Salt (Yanwu Zongju) in 1936, with a new 'administrative' department (the Yanzheng Si) placed above it for purposes of control and supervision.[31]

In fact, despite the name change, Inspectorate continued as before with only minor adjustments. The Yanwu Shu had long since been absorbed, the 'Directorate-General of Salt' maintained the independent recruitment and personnel system of the old Inspectorate, and appeared to carry on with its daily administration in much the same manner. The leadership of the Inspectorate-cum-Directorate-General of Salt was, for a brief period of time, clearly worried about the intentions and potential controlling power of the new Yanzheng Si, but any obvious 'interference' and change of direction from above by the latter was successfully contained until the early 1940s. For at least the few years after its establishment as a control and supervisory department, the Yanzheng Si served as a relaying station between the Directorate-General of Salt and the rest of the Ministry of Finance. It confined itself to issuing statements of intent regarding salt affairs that the old Inspectorate had consistently pursued for years, such as the establishment of uniform tax rates, the building of storage depots, the suppression of smuggling, and the abolishment of the remaining merchant privileges in preparation for free trade.[32] Although the Ministry of Finance changed the name of the organization and established a new layer of formal control, its only substantive shift in internal management was to attempt to downgrade the status of the Inspectorate's foreign chief inspectors *vis à vis* that of the Chinese chief inspectors.[33]

However, from outside the Ministry of Finance, the inevitable politics and discussions surrounding the reorganization of the Salt Inspectorate and the promulgation of a new Organic Law provided a number of other groups in the government with the platform they needed for launching attacks on the organization. In March 1936, the Legislative Yuan debates surrounding the new Organic Law for the Directorate-General of Salt were fierce, with opinion evenly divided between those who resented the high salaries and influence of foreigners within the Salt Administration and wanted to do away with such forthwith, and those who felt that the foreign component had been a feature of an exceptionally successful organization for quite some time, and that there was no reason why something that wasn't broken should be fixed. Eventually, a version of the Organic Law in which the Salt

Inspectorate's separate civil service system was permitted was ratified by the Legislative Yuan with a vote of 33–31.[34] In mid-1936, the Control Yuan wrote a scathing report in which it recommended that (1) the higher salary scales be reduced and brought into line with the rest of the National governments civil service, and (2) the foreign officers be weeded out.[35] Shortly thereafter, the Ministry of Personnel launched a campaign to do away with the Directorate-General of Salt's independent civil service system in the name of standardization, regularization, and control. Even though the Ministry of Personnel never recognized the existence of this independent civil service and examination system, the Directorate-General successfully resisted the pressure to switch to the standard government classification scheme.[36]

On balance, the defensive strategies of bureaucratization and insulation that were the core of the Inspectorate's pre- Guomindang-era existence continued to preserve it in the more politicized environment of the Nanjing Decade. New political leaders did subject the Inspectorate to a good deal of stress and pressure, but they also allowed the organization the space and opportunity to expand through its takeover of the Yanwu Shu and incorporation of Salt Police in the early 1930s. The government's desire for greater control and nationalist pride determined a somewhat reduced level of influence for the foreigners within the Salt Inspectorate that accelerated by the mid-1930s. But by and large, the organization was able to play on the same types of sensibilities within the Ministry of Finance that it had with its own staff in establishing such a well-institutionalized organization. It adroitly focused on its successes as a function of its ability to implement what aspiring institution-building Chinese elites had by now sought for a generation: to set up a strong, bureaucratic, depoliticized organization based on civil service examination, objective performance, and a career open to talent and hard work. The Inspectorate also provided the government with its most consistent source of funds throughout the Nanjing Decade.[37]

Incipient tendencies to attack, politicize, or take over the Salt Inspectorate were consistent sub-themes from other quarters of the government in the years leading up to the Sino-Japanese War. But formal name changes and reorganizations were cosmetic, and the organization's bureaucratic depersonalization, paired with its continued achievement of important, objective results, enabled it to turn back virtually all of these challenges. In the year that the Inspectorate was reorganized as the Directorate-General, it brought in a net 155,668,100Y to the central government Treasury, an increase of 20,000,000Y over the previous year, and by far its highest yield.[38] With some lapses and strains, informal power sharing between 'pure' administration and political masters appeared to work at least moderately well until the advent of the Sino-Japanese War.

INVASION, MONOPOLY, AND DECLINE, 1937–1945

On the eve of the Japanese invasion in mid-1937, the National Government was on an infinitely more stable course than it had been during most of the previous ten years of its existence, and there was reason for guarded optimism in government circles. Although Manchuria had been lost in 1932, the rest of the country was fairly calm. The 'Bandit Encirclement' campaigns had been successful in driving the Communists out of their base areas in Jiangxi, the large province of Sichuan had just accepted Nationalist administrators in 1936, the examination system was beginning to work a bit better, military expenditures, although still high, took up proportionally less of the still unbalanced budget, and government plans for administrative centralization and amalgamation were beginning to move out of the stage of drafting and discussion and into the realm of implementation—at least in the central government ministries.

The full-scale Japanese invasion into the heartland of China in mid-1937 put an abrupt end to most of these incremental gains in state-building. The government was forced to retreat far into the interior, to areas in which it had previously exercised only minimal control, becoming progressively divorced from its traditional power and resource base in the Yangzi valley delta.[39] Although it took several years in the wartime capital of Chongqing for full-scale demoralization, inflation, and immobilization to set in, the trauma of relocation and the emergencies of wartime generated a range of pressures that the Nationalist regime found increasingly difficult to manage.

The Directorate-General of Salt was far from immune to the general trauma engendered by the war, and, as state organizations went, it was fairly hard hit. Literally up to the point where the Japanese physically took over, the Directorate-General remained a model of high morale and efficiency. As described in the previous chapter, in the important Lianghuai Salt District, due north of Shanghai and Nanjing and therefore particularly exposed to Japanese attack, the staff remained at the salt works, endured bombing raids, worked by candlelight at night, and refused to evacuate until the order came to do so.[40]

If most field staff remained committed, those at the highest levels of the central organization bitterly split. For the first time, a difference of opinion and strategy between the Ministry of Finance and the Foreign Chief Inspector openly emerged. Oliver Lockhart, the Foreign Chief Inspector, believed that he could best serve the interests of the organization by remaining in occupied Shanghai and trying to work out some sort of arrangement with the Japanese, while Kong Xiangxi (H. H. Kung), the Minister of Finance, insisted equally adamantly that the organization retreat and regroup in the interior, after destroying everything in districts likely to fall to the Japanese.[41] At least some of the foreign inspectors disagreed with Lockhart, and remained at their posts in as-yet unoccupied areas or moved to set up new offices inland at enormous personal cost. With the open split and Lockhart's refusal to retreat with the Nationalists, the prestige of foreigners in the organization suffered a severe blow. Before the war, all official documents had to be co-signed by the relevant Chinese District Director and the Foreign District Director, but during the war a practice evolved whereby foreign district directors would be given only a synopsis for review. By the early 1940s, those foreign district directors who remained could at best 'offer opinions' (ti yijian) on a particular course of action: they no longer had the authority to institute or block policy.[42]

Ultimately far more detrimental to the organization than the decline of its foreign staff were the wartime conditions which made it impossible for the organization to continue to pursue its strategies of bureaucratic insulation and objective goal implementation. First, the war caused the loss of one of the critical means by which the Inspectorate had previously insulated itself. The most important revenue-generating salt districts were along the coast or in northern Jiangsu, and these were among the first areas to fall to the Japanese. This loss of revenue, combined with the ruin of the country's transportation system, the relocation of salt offices in the interior, and the general tone and tenor of executive wartime emergency measures, rendered the organization powerless to maintain its insulation consistently.

The years between 1937 and 1945 were critical for the survival of the Nationalist regime, and strained its state organizations to the utmost. In salt administration, the Japanese advance was responsible for the loss of revenue-generating districts and sharp decreases in much needed income to the state. The war interrupted transport and communications between salt-producing and salt-consuming areas of unoccupied China, and, beginning around 1940, successive waves of inflation began to sap morale and lead to widespread speculation and profiteering in commodities in society at large. Like other state organizations, the Directorate-General of Salt was forced to expand tremendously to deal with these contingencies: it quadrupled in size from around 6,000 staff in 1937 to perhaps 20,000–30,000 over the course of the war.[43] This expansion was due in part to the need to relocate and set up scores of new salt offices in parts of the interior in which the National Government's presence had previously been minimal to non-existent, and in part due to the government's shift away from the earlier principle of 'taxation at the yard and free trade thereafter' in favour of monopoly control of salt—with the Directorate-General of Salt taking charge of production, transport, and taxation of salt in the early 1940s.

Such a dramatic expansion would have been difficult for the organization to manage effectively even under relatively stable conditions, and during the Sino-Japanese War conditions were very far from stable. The war led the Guomindang not only to increase the size of its state apparatus, but also to attempt to extend the role and scope of state organizations vastly to establish control and order. Ever fearful of losing control over society, the Guomindang ordered a tremendous expansion of civilian state organizations, thereby causing an organizational paradox. Although rapid expansion was intended to re-establish central control and order, as state organizations grew exponentially and moved to undertake new tasks, they often became weaker and less responsive to the centre as they were flooded by insufficiently trained, uncommitted, undersalaried, or very young and inexperienced personnel.

In late 1941 and early 1942, a series of 'Extraordinary Government' regulations provided for the government monopoly and takeover of many daily commodities—sugar, salt, tobacco, matches, and tea—in order to 'stabilize prices, succour the people, improve quality, return the interests of the merchants to the people, and raise revenue'.[44] If the state had been truly able to implement this sort of official control over collection and transport, a real institution-building breakthrough would have been achieved. But, despite the great expansion in the number and size of salt administration organizations and the attempt of the state to effect total control of key commodities through the establishment of state monopolies, such a breakthrough was not imminent. Under the regulations and form of monopoly control, the salt bureaucracy was as physically incapable as it ever had been to actually control all aspects of salt production, distribution, marketing, and taxation. This, in turn, led to a sort of sub-infeudation reminiscent of the *modus vivendi* in late imperial China. The state proclaimed monocratic authority over the whole of salt administration, and then sub-contracted to exactly those groups it attempted to control, as it 'entrust[ed] merchants with the right to transport salt, the authority over which belonged solely to the government'.[45] Despite its formal claim of monopoly power, The Salt Administration was unable to either establish total control over production at the salt works or to directly manage distribution.

Although the Salt Administration began to bring in tax revenue in impressive amounts by raising tax rates and intensifing production at the salt wells it did control in Sichuan in the last few years of the Sino-Japanese War. (Table 4.3), the attempt to establish government monopolies by asserting broad official control in areas in which its real power was weak was an institution-building strategy that did not work for the Guomindang in wartime any better than it had previously, and was widely perceived to be a failure. Especially as it coincided temporally with an infinitely more difficult external environment in terms of rapid inflation and hyper-expansion, the politically inspired move towards official monopoly and control also had the net effect of signalling the end of the Salt Administration's long history of bureaucratic insulation and 'objectively oriented' effectiveness.

**Table 4.3.** Salt Taxes Collected During the Sino-Japanese War, July 1937–December 1945 (million yuan)

| | 1937–8 | 1938 (Jul.–Dec.) | 1939 | 1940 | 1941 | 1942 | 1943 | 1944 | 1945 |
|---|---|---|---|---|---|---|---|---|---|
| Salt | 141 | 47 | 61 | 80 | 296 | — | — | — | 2,800 |
| Salt surtax | — | — | — | — | — | — | 1,202 | 13,439 | 48,925 |
| Salt monopoly | — | — | — | — | — | 1,180 | 1,823 | 1,089 | 1,781 |
| TOTAL | 141 | 47 | 61 | 80 | 296 | 1,180 | 3,025 | 14,528 | 53,506 |
| Other taxes | 309 | 165 | 422 | 186 | 370 | 2,983 | 12,290 | 19,877 | 48,738 |
| TOTAL TAX COLLECTED | 450 | 212 | 483 | 266 | 666 | 4,163 | 15,315 | 34,405 | 102,244 |
| Salt revenue as % of total revenue | 31.3 | 22.2 | 12.6 | 30.1 | 44.4 | 28.3 | 19.8 | 42.2 | 52.3 |

*Source:* Arthur Young, *China's Wartime Finance and Inflation, 1937–45* (Cambridge, Mass.: Harvard University Press, 1965), 332.

The mid-war years were a period in which *ad hoc* 'Extraordinary Government' regulations proliferated in every conceivable sphere of government action, and the Directorate-General of Salt could not avoid the general trend towards increased politicization, 'interference' from outside the organization, and new layers of reporting, accountability, and control to either the Supreme National Defense Committee (Guofang Zuigao Weiyuanhui), or the newly established Ministry of Audit (Shenji Bu), which was established in order to bring the principles of scientific management and accountability to the Executive Yuan ministries, including the higher levels of the Ministry of Finance itself.

In order to provide some guidelines to the forced expansion of the organization, a series of 'temporary' regulations regarding recruitment and appointments were passed to attract highly qualified technical personnel to the Directorate-General of Salt to run its new, official monopolies. The separate personnel classification and pay scales were retained, but generous provisions for high-level transfers into the organization were made. Temporary regulations stipulated that the previously coveted, nearly impossible to obtain, 'A' rank was now to be made readily available to an individual with seven years of experience and a degree in finance, economics, or commerce; the 'B' rank to be granted to those who had a mere three years of experience in a finance or taxation organization, while those at the bottom levels of the organization still had to take the regular open examination, as before.[46]

In legitimating such a two-tiered system of appointments, the new priorities of wartime struck at the heart of the Directorate-General's stability and presumed fairness. No longer were seniority and the socialization attained through long years of in-house service exclusively rewarded. During the war, external managers uncommitted to the organization's norms and values were given high position, thus disrupting continuity. Within the organization, the exigencies of the moment often forced the personnel offices to grant large promotions and skips in grades to those needed to immediately fill specific positions. In contrast to the years before the war, when 99 per cent of staff came into the organization via the 'regular' examination system and slowly advanced through the ranks, nearly 50 per cent of staff who came into the organization during and after the war were 'irregulars', who had either transferred in or skyrocketed their way through rapid promotions.[47]

In addition to seriously weakening the organization's capacity for insulation by forcing a change in its internal recruitment and socialization, the power sharing that had previously tacitly recognized the Inspectorate's substantial autonomy shifted towards strict control and accountability. At the micro level, staff constantly had to wire to higher levels for approval to take any action.[48] More systemically, by around 1942 the political supervisory department (the Yanzheng Si) began to cause the Directorate-General so much grief over proper authority, jurisdiction, and standard setting that the Directorate was moved to protest to the Minister of Finance.[49] The Directorate-General of Salt's Division of Personnel also convened a work group to monitor 'progress' on examinations, education, training, and evaluations.[50] The endless reports detailing the Salt Administration's adherence to planning and efficiency targets for the Ministry of Audit took up an enormous amount of time and resources as well. At about the same time, the Ministry of Audit acquired the right of audit and final approval over at least the internal promotion exams for lower-level personnel.

Politicization and 'interference' from the outside were in the wind in other ways too, with the expansion of the *xunlian* (training) movement, which explicitly promoted the principles of 'partification and militarization' (*danghua junshihua*) as the means to build a strong nation.[51] In 1941 the Directorate-General of Salt, fearful of being amalgamated into the wider Ministry of Finance's 'All Country Finance Personnel Training Institute', which claimed authority over all personnel, however remotely linked to the Ministry of Finance, petitioned to be allowed to conduct its own *xunlian* course geared to the 'special characteristics and problems associated with setting up the salt monopoly system'.[52] Permission was eventually granted, and the Directorate-General of Salt ran *xunlian* sessions for basic-level personnel at special training centres in Guiyang, Nanxiong, and Pingliang and for advanced personnel at Wutongqiao, just outside of Chongqing, in 1941 and 1942.[53] For those who were not chosen or could not attend the special training centre courses, regional salt offices also ran their own, briefer, versions of *xunlian*.

As it submitted to the general mood of the times in setting up its own *xunlian* courses, the Directorate-General of Salt still seemed to have enough fight left to take defensive steps to limit the scope of politicization and militarization. If 'military training' was a compulsory component of the *xunlian* courses, in most places it seemed to consist of morning physical exercises; the course curriculum downplayed the partification and leader worship that was so prominent a part of the *xunlian* programme at the Central Training Institute, concentrating instead on the functional (*yewu*) aspects of salt administration, and replacing 'small group discussions' on political indoctrination with sessions to discuss the practical problems of administering the salt monopoly.[54]

Although the Ministry of Audit gained the formal right to review the Directorate-General of Salt's examination regime, in practice it seems to have not interfered too much with the organization's continued technical and practical orientation. Even during the latter years of the Sino-Japanese war, virtually all of the examination questions asked by the Directorate-General of Salt on its entry-level examinations were confined to factual material involving the knowledge and application of wartime regulations on salt to specific hypothetical situations. Questions typically asked for particulars on auditing procedures, how employee insurance should be administered, and what accounting methods had been developed for entering the profits from merchant transport of salt. The sole question that could be construed as 'ideological' checked for commitment to the organization's new policy of official control of salt production, transport, and retailing: 'What are the reasons for the suppression of merchant transport in favour of official transport?'[55]

Despite external interference, an outside environment characterized by increasing politicization and militarization, and internal debilitation as its stabilization-oriented norms of slow promotion from within were eaten away by hyperexpansion and transfer in, the Directorate-General was still able defensively to maintain factually oriented, bureaucratic methods of examination and evaluation for at least its lower-level personnel, and to deflect the most severe aspects of militarization and politicization by running its own *xunlian* courses. When seriously stressed by the turbulence and general levels of politicization engendered by the war, the Directorate-General of Salt did not completely or suddenly crumble. Through its handling of the Ministry of Audit over the promotion exams, and in the type of training courses it ran, the organization demonstrated its continued commitment to depoliticized, 'objective' administration whenever there was enough space or discretion for it to do so. Even during a time when it was compromised by the decay of its strategies of insulation, it tried to contain the worst of the damage to its core values while avoiding direct confrontation with its political superiors.

Such defensive actions were but a pale reflection of the organization's morale and effectiveness in the pre-war period. Both directly and indirectly, the Sino-Japanese War destroyed the base upon which the organization had previously grounded its legitimacy and on which it was able to flourish. With the loss of so many of the salt-producing territories in the east, the organization lost a critical component of its justification for continued substantial autonomy—that it produced the goods, and that its distinctive civil service organization and separate ethos of bureaucratic technocracy were indispensible components of its success, components that should best be left untouched by political leaders if they wished to see continued and uninterrupted revenue flows.

Indirectly, but ultimately more importantly, the war created the sorts of conditions under which the Directorate-General of Salt's immediate political superiors shifted their priorities towards vigorous recentralization and the re-establishment of control over every aspect of administrative and political existence. This, more than anything, upset the equilibrium of power sharing between the administrative organization and the state. As the state moved to establish stronger controls over the administrative organization on the basis of its formal authority of position, there was little that the Directorate-General of Salt, as a loyal, depoliticized entity, could do.

The ethos of 'pure administration' upheld by the Salt Administration encompassed two sets of norms that were reconcilable in stable times. First, the administrative machine was to be efficient, effective, and depersonalized, enabling it to be a tool that could serve anyone. But second, it was also expected to be loyal and responsive to the policy preferences and goals of current political leaders. As long as political leaders did not feel compelled to interfere in internal operations, the organization could continue with its key strategies of bureaucratic insulation and objective goal implementation, producing results that more or less satisfied all important parties. However, the bureaucratic, depersonalized norms that had buffered and secured the survival and growth of the organization for so long in one sort of environment were, in the end, insufficient to withstand the shocks of wartime that focused the concerted attention of political leaders on the organization. For the Salt Inspectorate-cum-Directorate-General of Salt, the administrative norms of loyalty and responsiveness ultimately developed during the Nanjing Decade prevailed over the norms of bureaucratization and rule orientation that had been at the core of organizational insulation and identity from the 1910s on. Informal power sharing and a division of labour between politics and administration had, with some bumps and starts, proved to be effective until the advent of the Sino-Japanese War, but it could continue to be so only at the pleasure of its political masters. When circumstances forced a change in the perceptions of the political leadership (as was the case during the Sino-Japanese War), there was little that 'administration' could do besides submit, even though submission meant the ruin of a carefully constructed organizational culture based on the norms of fairness, impersonalism, and objective performance.

Once the insulation of the Salt Administration had broken down, organizational de-institutionalization proceeded apace. After the war, there was an increase in lateral transfer into the organization, and a series of non-emergency policies were as geared to external bureaucratic control as the special wartime monopolies had been. The Directorate-General of Salt got directly involved in 'bureaucratic capitalism', when the organization went in and actually acquired 51 per cent stock and management options in the largest salt-producing companies, thus completely conflating state administration and private profit.[56] Such activities would have been complete anathema to the free trade orientation of Dane and the Inspectorate of earlier years, and well illustrated the degree to which the earlier ethos of the organization had declined.

CONCLUSION

The strategies of insulation, bureaucratic depersonalization, and objective goal implementation that had been so critical to the Salt Inspectorate's early success provided the organization with an adequate base to withstand a number of very serious challenges during the 1920s and 1930s. In styling itself as a depoliticized, purely 'administrative' organization that performed at consistently high levels, the Salt Inspectorate was usually able to work out arrangements with those that threatened its existence. The Inspectorate was willing literally to 'buy' its continued *de facto* autonomy over staff and operations by providing both the warlords and the Nationalist state with a level of resources that few other organizations could match.

Once it was formally absorbed by the Nationalist Ministry of Finance in 1928, the Salt Inspectorate entered a nine-year period of informal power sharing with the Nationalist government. During this period, the Salt Inspectorate accepted the formal authority of new political masters, and in turn was permitted to retain most of its organizational autonomy and absorb the other salt tax organizations. Although not without stresses and strains, informal power sharing worked to the advantage of both parties: the government received increasingly high amounts of salt tax revenue, while the Inspectorate quietly expanded in scope and influence under the new regime. Although a number of groups in the various parts of the National Government intermittently attempted to establish more stringent control over the Salt Inspectorate, the latter maintained its *de facto* autonomy more or less intact until the Sino-Japanese War.

Wartime conditions decisively destroyed the conditions that led to successful power sharing during the early to mid-1930s. The loss of the most important salt works and an open split between the Minister of Finance and the Foreign Chief Inspector seriously eroded the organization's political capital, while the tremendous expansion of the organization ruined its autonomous civil service system.

Although the signals were mixed, during the 1930s it seemed that the interests of both politics and administration could be pursued without overwhelming contradictions as long as political 'power' was willing to listen to technically based 'truth'. The Sino-Japanese War definitively reversed this sort of power sharing by tilting the political leadership towards an assertion of strong control. When it no longer had the space to play on the many ambivalences within the political establishment, the Salt Administration bowed to politics, thus assuring its own decline.

The dual desire monocratically to assert control over administration *and* garner high levels of efficiency and effectiveness from administration were to some degree in tension throughout the Nanjing Decade and beyond. With its highly visible foreign district inspectors and its ties to the group banks, the Salt Inspectorate undeniably provoked many in the Nationalist government to advocate the reassertion of strong central control. But for many others, the Salt Inspectorate served as a model of a strong, effective state organization. The Ministry of Finance lacked the heavy foreign advisor presence that made the Salt Inspectorate so anomalous, but it did possess a similar set of organizational goals and technologies. How the Ministry of Finance adopted parts of the Salt Inspectorate 'model' as it attempted to consolidate, institutionalize, and balance different commitments during the 1930s is explored in the next chapter.

# 5

## The Ministry of Finance and its Range of Institution-Building Strategies

INTRODUCTION

The Salt Inspectorate became a well institutionalized, efficient organization by rigorously insulating its staff, establishing bureaucratic rules for organizational action, providing strong incentives for performance, and allowing senior field officers substantial degrees of professional discretion. In this way, it effectively socialized its staff into identifying their immediate interests with the goals and norms of the entire organization, and prevented the takeover of the organization by particularistic, ascriptive groups. By the late 1920s, the Salt Inspectorate was an especially visible organization for two reasons: first, it had been established in the fairly recent past; and second, it carried out critical tax-collecting functions that were one of the mainstays of the Beiyang government. As such, the Salt Inspectorate attracted much attention from reformers who wished to imitate it, from bureaucrats who wished to control it, and from nationalists who wished to abolish it.

Although the Salt Inspectorate's key institution-building strategies of insulation and goal implementation were in theory widely replicable, the *specific* conditions that enabled the nascent organization to pursue these strategies so vigorously at the very outset were the product of a particular set of circumstances that would not be repeated after the 1910s.[1] In 1914, the Salt Inspectorate's virtual independence from the rest of the Chinese government—its formally separate civil service and system of joint Chinese and foreign authority—was precedented by similar arrangements in the Customs Administration and the postal service. By the mid-1920s, sharply rising mass urban nationalism rendered the Salt Inspectorate increasingly anachronistic and anomalous, widely perceived as a vestige of the humiliations of China's immediate semi-colonial past. With the images of imperial overlordship that the foreign inspectors evoked for many Chinese, even the Chinese reformers who did admire the Inspectorate's efficiency could hardly propose to create new state organizations with an analogous foreign presence.

The Inspectorate's experiences with institution building were non-replicable in another respect as well. Unlike the Inspectorate, most state organizations in early twentieth-century China were not suddenly and artificially imposed from the outside. The vast majority were the products of domestic politics, coalitions, and perceived needs, and most indigenous state organizations in the Republican period could muster neither the initially high degrees of autonomy nor the strong organizational boundaries so characteristic of the Inspectorate during its early years. Since most state organizations could not rely on a heavy foreign presence to set initial agendas, maintain insulation, and enforce results-oriented 'disciplines',[2] their institution-building strategies were of necessity often quite different from those of the Inspectorate.

In order to compare the highly successful Salt Inspectorate with more typical state organizations in Republican China, this chapter will look at the case of the Ministry of Finance. Aside from the military, the Ministry of Finance was responsible for perhaps the most critical set of issues for the Guomindang's attempts to reintegrate the state. In few policy arenas was the state's immediate need to break out of the institution-building dilemma more pressing. Without an efficient, effective, non-corrupt Ministry of Finance, able systematically to extract large amounts of revenue through both taxes and loan flotation, the Guomindang could not pay for the armies necessary physically to unify the state, with catastrophic effects for the state-building effort. In the short term, lack of adequate revenue made for a government that was only precariously viable. Over the medium to long term, the Ministry of Finance portfolio consisted of activities—from currency reorganization to budgeting to equitable tax reform—that were critical building blocks for China's fiscal base, economic stabilization, and future development.

Because of the critical role it played in both short-and medium-term state building in the Republican period, the Ministry of Finance stands as an important case of institution building in its own right. In addition to its intrinsic importance in its own time, the experiences of the Ministry of Finance suggest much about institution-building strategies, and how they relate to a wider process of state building. In terms of goals, technologies, and knowledge bases, the Ministry of Finance and the Salt Inspectorate were strikingly similar. But the Ministry of Finance lacked the foreign administrators and the initial detachment from the Chinese government that made the Salt Inspectorate so atypical; indeed, the Ministry of Finance was one of the cornerstones of the Chinese government itself.

The case of the Ministry of Finance thus provides a useful check and counterpoint to those of the Salt Inspectorate. The following pages will demonstrate how, in contrast to the Inspectorate's rigorous separateness, the institution-building strategies employed by the Republican Ministry of Finance can best be seen as a faithful reflection of the complex and variable range of options exercised by twentieth-century Chinese state-building strategies in general.

THE BEIYANG MINISTRY OF FINANCE, 1912–1927:
ALL DRESSED UP AND NOWHERE TO GO

The 'New Government' *xinzheng* reforms of the late Qing dynasty first proposed, albeit in embryonic form, a number of the key goals to which the Republic's Ministry of Finance aspired. In 1906 and 1907, the Hu Bu (Board of Revenue), with its semi-specialized sub-bureaus and diffused authority, was reorganized into a modernized Ministry of Finance (Zhi Bu), complete with specialized divisions (such as the land tax and currency divisions) and clear lines of responsibility and authority. Alarmed by the increased influence of the provincial and local officials over revenue, the Zhi Bu instituted reforms to bring all financial matters throughout the empire under its control, take over the management of all foreign loans, require full accounts and reports from the provincial governors,[3] and establish a national budget to balance income and expenditures.[4]

Many of these initial centralizing proposals were part of a general financial reform package that was largely dependent on the successful reorganization of the provincial governments. In 1909–10, the Zhi Bu established branch offices in most of the provinces to prevent collaboration between the provincial governors and finance commissioners, and to promote the central reforms. But, as in so many areas, these *xinzheng* efforts came too late, and it was left to the succeeding Yuan Shikai and Beiyang governments to pursue this initial attempt to establish fiscal control.

The Ministry of Finance during the Yuan Shikai period (1912–16) exhibited a strong degree of continuity with that of the late empire. The general intent of the early Republican Caizheng Bu to demarcate its own subdivisions clearly on the basis of functional specialization and to establish strong control over national finance made it the direct descendant of the late Qing Zhi Bu as well as the institutional precursor of the Nationalist Ministry of Finance.[5]

Even before the country dissolved into the anarchy and warlordism of the 1917–27 period, Republican efforts to centralize real administrative control were hampered by systemic conditions and by practices legitimated during the previous century of imperial rule. Since the Chinese state had long tole-rated high degrees of local administrative and fiscal diversity, it was customary and quite usual for even centrally appointed provincial governors to retain much, if not most, of the tax collected for use at the provincial level. The administrative reach of the central state remained extremely limited, the 'modernized' military forces were divided between regions and remained susceptible to further fracture along political and personal lines, and even the most vigorously pro-central government provincial appointee ignored the sensibilities of the local power elites at his own peril.

The conditions for effective centralization were no more favourable during the years of the early Republic than they had been under the late empire. Imperialist pressure was incessant, provincial governors remained powerful, and elites from the provincial level down were hungry for revenue to fund both projects and military expenditure. Increased demand for revenue combined with continued administrative weakness led to the proliferation of assorted surtaxes on both land (*tankuan*) and commerce (*juanshui*), exacerbating both tax farming and local-level 'protective brokerage'.[6] In both the tax farming and protective brokerage scenarios, the 'arbitrariness' of taxation certainly rose, as did (probably) the real rates of taxation, but not in any way that accrued to the centre, as provincial elites, tax farmers, and local protectors were all loathe to give up any significant portion of new revenues being generated.[7]

Given these constraints, the Yuan Shikai government opted for a two-pronged strategy of getting its own house in order through Weberian-style rationalization of the central government finance organization, while projecting central government administrative power into the provinces. Although the full development of the ideology to legitimate this sort of action did not come until ten years later, with Sun Yat-sen's *Fundamentals of National Reconstruction*, the core reasoning behind increased centralization was already well established by 1913–14 and would remain basically unchanged for the remainder of the Republican period. Yuan Shikai selectively drew from both the traditions of imperial statecraft and the latest in Western administrative theory. The way out of China's pressing problems '[was] in reviving the official discipline of government ordinance and in building the prestige of the nation'. For further justification, Yuan turned to Frank Goodnow, an American political scientist and founding father of the American Political Science Association, to draft a constitution favouring a strong executive and to support 'scientifically' the re-establishment of autocracy.[8]

In terms of administrative rationalization and centralization, the early Republican Ministry of Finance extended the trends set in motion with the late Qing reorganization of the Zhi Bu. It replaced a number of Zhi Bu divisions with new departments (*si*) and sections (*ke*), and laboriously drafted documents stipulating the jurisdictions and duties of each. The numbers of junior and senior staff allotted to each division and section were strictly limited. All were responsible to the Minister, who, in turn, was responsible to the President of the Republic.[9]

The relatively small size of the Ministry of Finance rendered it a surprisingly 'flat' organization, with the high-status 'recommended' and 'selected' appointments accounting for around 22 per cent of the total staff.[10] The records do not indicate how appointments to the Ministry of Finance were made in the early 1910s, and the actual quality of personnel was probably quite uneven. But, for at least the upper 22 per cent the finance bureaucrats tended to have had fairly strong, if somewhat mixed, backgrounds in finance or administration under the old regime. All were highly educated by the standards of the time, and they appear to have acquired whatever education they could when the usefulness of the old civil service degrees began to come into question. Of a group of 50 section chiefs and senior assistants, over half (28) had received some sort of traditional civil service degree, and it is likely that nearly all had a classical education. Some of these bureaucrats undoubtedly bought their degrees, since 16 of the 28 had achieved only the type of 'student' or 'probationary' (*fusheng* and *bosheng*) degrees that were often bought and sold in the late empire. But over one-fifth of the total sample (10 of 50) had passed the difficult provincial *juren* examination, and one was even a metropolitan scholar.[11]

This high-status sub-group also systematically widened the scope of their educational credentials. Forty per cent (20 of 50) had studied abroad, the vast majority of these (15 of 20) in Japan. Of the Japan-educated bureaucrats, most (10 of 15) concentrated on government, economics, and law, and the remainder took courses in business and commerce. Another five received degrees from one of the recently established provincial advanced schools of law and government (*fazheng xuetang*). This group of bureaucrats, therefore, had a greater proportion who had studied 'modern' subjects at home or abroad (32 of 50) than it had individuals with classical degrees (28 of 50). The two types of education were not mutually exclusive: 11 of 50 had studied enough modern and classical Chinese subjects to have some sort of degree or credential in both.

In addition to their educations, the middle to upper bureaucrats in the early Republic's Ministry of Finance tended to have a good deal of practical administrative experience. Most had positions either in the Zhi Bu (17 of 50) or in provincial bureaus that specialized in finance or taxation (12 of 50), while an another 7 were former district or prefectural magistrates who undoubtedly would have spent a good deal of their energy on the nuts and bolts of local taxation; 4 individuals also had experience working in the reorganized 'modern' late Qing central government ministries—the Postal Service, Communications, and Agriculture/Commerce/Labour.

The finance bureaucrats that staffed the middle to upper ranks of the early Republican Ministry of Finance were neither traditional Confucian literati generalists nor narrowly specialized technocrats. In their education (and, one surmises, in their outlook as well), they were a transitional generation of elites that had achieved respectable official positions at very young ages: in 1914 the median age for a section chief or senior assistant was 34.[12] Grounded in the Confucian classics, they were 'traditional' enough to have invested heavily in the cult of scholarship and examinations. But as a group they were also practical enough to be aware of the great changes underway, and flexible enough to seek out new sorts of education and training to prepare themselves to deal with an uncertain future. Virtually all held positions in either the central or local government under the Qing, and most probably had some practical grasp of the types of intractable finance problems that China faced.

With the exception of one lone individual with a military background, no one in this group of fifty stands out as obviously ill-suited for a position in central government finance. While one cannot state as much definitively, the written record does not suggest a prevalence of politicization, cliques, or nepotism: relatively few members hailed from the same villages, worked in the same obscure regional tax offices, or went to the same schools.[13] What is instead striking is the diversity within a general pattern of individuals who broadened their educational range and acquired a good deal of practical administrative experience.

Although the curricula vitae indicate that these bureaucrats had fairly strong backgrounds in financial administration, the centralization-oriented President's Office (Da Zongtong) obviously felt that there was great room for improvement. In conjunction with its draft plan for a nationwide civil service examination system, the Yuan Shikai government established a finance studies institute in the Ministry 'to cultivate applied talent in tax collection'. In this internal training unit, a small support staff and twelve instructors ran a year-long training course in the basics of financial administration for promising newcomers who had just passed the upper civil service exam, and for applicants with more than three years' experience in the central government offices. The training programme was designed to educate the staff in the general principles of finance and the specifics of China's new finance regulations and centralizing plans; subjects included general courses in economics, finance, and statistics, as well as more specialized topics such as the implementation of finance regulations, the procedures of customs tax collection, and the principles of the reorganized tobacco and wine tax. In the meantime, probationary periods of one and two years prior to actual appointment became the norm for newly recruited career bureaucrats.[14]

Despite the worsening political and military situation, practical training continued to be promoted in the Ministry of Finance for a number of years after Yuan Shikai's death. Technocratically oriented students returned from abroad were much sought after, and the national examination system set up by Yuan Shikai supplied the Ministry with its first crop of 'regular path' recruits in 1916. In subsequent years, the number of those selected by the civil service exam system increased to levels not matched by the Nationalists until the late 1930s.[15]

Extreme politicization and factionalism does not appear to have been common in the Ministry of Finance until the early 1920s, when increasingly large numbers of staff began to be replaced by people from outside the Ministry. By 1927, as the Beiyang government was nearing collapse, whole departments of councillors and advisors were being removed from office, and the remaining staff members were subjected to an 'official' reappointment.[16] Even in the midst of tremendous external pressure and anarchy, however, the ideals of internal centralization and control, technical competence, civil service examination, and in-house practical training remained important. As late as 1925, the Ministry's general affairs department attempted to single out those without an examination credential for special evaluation and assessment.[17]

The central government elites of the early Republic developed a consistent set of state- and institution-building strategies that continued to inform the later Nationalist period of the 1930s and 1940s: the centralization and rationalization of state structures as the way to build a strong and powerful country, the development of a technocratic elite of state bureaucrats to carry out the centralization drive, and the use of civil service examination and/or advanced degrees (preferably from abroad) as the appropriate means for selecting and rewarding technocratic talent.

The first part of the two-pronged institution-building strategy did produce some positive results. At the level of the central ministry, the Beiyang governments managed to attract 'men of talent', to train them when it perceived serious gaps in knowledge, and to institute mechanisms to recruit civil service examinees. However, the second part of the two-pronged strategy failed miserably. The Beiyang government's efforts were apparent only in areas in which it could exercise real control—within the central government bodies themselves. In theory, the Ministry of Finance in Beijing held authority over all aspects of national finance: in practice, its influence did not extend much farther than the city walls of the capital.

The Yuan Shikai government attempted to extend central government control into the provinces by establishing provincial finance bureaus (*caizheng ting*) and new, specialized bodies accountable to the centre in order to directly administer new national taxes on tobacco and alcohol. The central government's regulations stipulated heavy central control: finance bureau chiefs in the provinces were to report directly to the central Ministry of Finance, and to forward all taxes collected to the National Treasury. In fact, nothing of the sort happened. With the growth of provincial and local militarism after 1916, all taxes not collected by the independent extra-governmental bodies, such as the Customs Administration and the Salt Inspectorate, were retained locally.[18]

Lacking the means to enforce compliance in the rest of the country, the Beiyang Ministry of Finance could not even begin to implement most of its plans for centralization and standardization. Aside from the surpluses from the customs and salt administrations, it had but one option for raising funds: contracting loans from Western banks. From the mid-1920s on, even salt and customs surpluses were regularly retained locally by regional militarists, and foreign loans, readily available in the earlier Beiyang period, were also drying up: 'By the last years of the Peking regime, the Central Government became a virtual mendicant.'[19] Without a modicum of political and military unity in the rest of the country, the Ministry had little scope for implementing its strategies and ideas.[20] After Yuan Shikai's aborted efforts, the central government Ministry of Finance in the early Republican period remained a head without a body: full of intentions and ideas for financial reform, with increasingly less in the way of means to carry them out. The first real steps towards implementation would have to wait until the late 1920s, when the Nationalists secured real territory and established some degree of real control. When they finally did so, the Nanjing government would to a remarkable degree carry on in the trajectory first laid down in the late *xinzheng* and Yuan Shikai periods.

## FINANCE DURING THE NANJING DECADE, 1927–1937

During the Nanjing Decade, the process of building an effective state finance bureaucracy was shaped by two critical factors: the current political and military situation, which set the rough parameters for administrative action, and the continued adoption of late imperial and early Republican methods for working within that environment. Both factors led the Ministry of Finance to adopt institution-building strategies that echoed the state-building efforts of the Guomindang regime.

As described in Chapter 1, the Chiang Kai-shek-dominated Guomindang came to power through an initial revolutionary upsurge and string of military victories, followed by a fairly rapid suppression of the Left. The National Government established its base of operations in the rich Jiangnan delta under conditions of bloodshed, factional infighting and a nearly continual state of emergency. In 1927, given the existence of a rival Guomindang regime in Wuhan, leftist ferment, and the continued presence of undefeated and independent militarists in the north, the Nanjing government's claims were, at best, rather murky; the regime moved quickly to proclaim itself as the sole legitimate government and to institute at least minimal tokens of its authority over the country at large.

The context in which the Nationalist Ministry of Finance was established and the immediate needs it served were quite different from those of the early Salt Inspectorate. The early Nationalist Ministry of Finance was an organization that existed solely to extract revenue for the military machine upon which the regime's survival depended: first in Guangzhou, and then in Nanjing. Under these conditions, immediate institution of Salt Inspectorate-style bureaucratization and rule orientation was unfeasible. Despite the mountains of procedural regulations drafted, the working reality of public finance in its early years revolved around one priority: to supply the central government with enough revenue to consolidate its military and political control.

In the mid- to late 1920s, short-term effectiveness (measured by the real amount of income coming in through whatever means to fund the military) was far more important than efficiency (receipts correlated with administrative costs), or any generalized conception of fairness (the tax burden being apportioned to those who could best afford to pay). Efficiency was not necessarily inconsistent with effectiveness: the two sometimes went hand in hand. Song Ziwen's (T.V. Soong's) reputation as a 'financial wizard' and later standing in the government as Minister of Finance was established on the basis of the clear success and effectiveness of his financial strategies in the Guangzhou Revolutionary Government between 1924 and 1926.[21] During this period gross receipts into the Guomindang treasury multiplied nearly tenfold, from 7,986,000Y in 1924 to 880,200,000Y in 1925. Although some of this increase was, as claimed, due to efficiency gains in the reorganization of tax administration for Shatian income (660,000Y), the alcohol and tobacco tax administration (2,440,000Y), and the system of direct military levies (15,050,000Y), a good deal of the sharp jump in revenue between 1924 and 1925 was due to Song's persuasiveness in floating public bonds (24,283,000Y), as well as simple imposition of new taxes and 'numerous old levies and miscellaneous taxes that were retained, increased, and collected more vigorously than in the past...which weighed most heavily on those who could least afford to pay them'.[22]

With limited means at its disposal in an extremely precarious environment, the Nationalist Ministry of Finance initially turned to whatever sources of revenue were easily accessible. Once the Northern Expedition reached the Yangzi Valley, the efforts of the Ministry of Finance were concentrated on the city of Shanghai and surrounding environs as it levied a whole range of new business taxes and applied both carrot and stick to extract large loans from the Shanghai industrial elites.[23]

Given the degree of uncertainty engendered by internecine squabbling, revolution, and civil war, and the regime's initial fragility, the Ministry of Finance could not immediately recreate the Salt Inspectorate's organizational system: rigorous exclusion and insulation of staff were patent impossibilities at this early stage. The Ministry of Finance needed loyal and competent personnel immediately for its central organization in Nanjing, and at local levels the need for staff with these qualities was even more acute. Faced with such severe shortages, the Ministry of Finance greatly expanded the core finance organization that had been created under the Guomindang Canton Revolutionary Government (1924–6) by formally incorporating pre-existing financial organizations, particularly those with proven track records in tax assessment and collection, as well as absorbing large numbers of individuals who had worked for either the Beiyang Ministry of Finance or local financial administrations.

The circumstances that affected the Ministry's initial creation in 1927–8 continued to influence its processes of institutionalization throughout the 1930s. Although in theory very powerful, in practice the Ministry of Finance was less a monolithic entity than it was a patchwork of different sub-organizations that often had little to do with each other. Although all subsidiary wings of the Ministry of Finance were responsible to and coordinated by the Secretariat of the Ministry, some were more tightly controlled than others. Most of the tax collecting administrations (including the Customs Administration, the Salt Inspectorate, and Consolidated Tax/ Tax Affairs) were formally classified as *shu*, and retained substantial autonomy over their operations, personnel, and local branch offices; General Affairs, Land Tax, Government Bonds, Currency, Treasury, Accounting, and Statistics formed the 'regular' ministry divisions (*si*). While *si* and *shu* were of roughly equivalent status, the former were more directly managed by the Ministry Secretariat than were the latter. The Ministry also organized a number of committees entrusted with establishing tax regulations, accounting, instituting currency reform, and reorganizing local taxes, and took over the Mint and the Beijing Printing Office.[24]

Although the unstable military and political situation in China during the late 1920s produced an environment in which *ad hoc* administration and a wild scramble for revenue were immediately pressing necessities, the Nationalist Ministry of Finance under Song Ziwen (1928–33) and then Kong Xiangxi (1933–44) sought to institute a complete programme for financial reform that went far beyond the daily struggle to keep the government afloat. Like the erstwhile Beiyang Ministry of Finance, the Nationalist Ministry of Finance attempted to centralize and increase its control and diversify its sources of income. In centralizing and extending direct control, it emulated whenever possible the sorts of mechanisms and strategies that seemed to underlie the Salt Inspectorate and Customs Administration's efficiency and effectiveness.

Like the Salt Inspectorate, the Ministry of Finance's priorities were to establish nationwide control over financial administration, to render taxation more efficient through a process of rationalization, and over the long run to promote commerce and fairness by spreading the tax burden more equitably. However, the policy domain of the Ministry of Finance was more wide-ranging than that of the Salt Inspectorate; its functions more diffuse, and, unlike the Inspectorate, which claimed Weberian bureaucratic rationality and efficiency in the hope that when it spoke 'truth to power' powerful political figures would 'listen', the Ministry of Finance was itself an important and intrinsic part of the National Government and as such had some inherent voice in the policy-making process. From a very early date, the Nationalist Ministry of Finance sought to abolish the *lijin* transit tax and all 'irregular' surcharges (*tankuan*), to establish uniform rates for such standing levies as the taxes on imported goods, land tax, and salt, and to diversify its revenue sources.

These goals remained remarkably constant throughout the Nanjing years. During the First National Finance Conference of 1928, Song Ziwen, then minister of finance, announced the Ministry's intention to institute a host of new taxes on consumption, income, inheritance, and commerce, and to carry out currency and banking reform. At this time Song also pointedly referred to the necessity of containing military expenditure to promote investment in national reconstruction. In 1933 friction with Chiang Kaishek over continued deficit spending and Song's increasingly virulent anti-Japanese stance led to Song's resignation as Minister of Finance, whence he was succeeded by Kong Xiangxi (H. H. K'ung). In 1934, the year of the Second National Finance Conference, Kong added the establishment of a national budget and the liquidation of the national debt to the Ministry's list of key objectives, but otherwise changed little, reasserting the importance of establishing control, establishing uniform tax rates, and doing away with all surtaxes.[25]

Despite their differences in personal style, education, and standing within the Guomindang political establishment, Song Ziwen and Kong Xiangxi provided the Ministry of Finance with fairly consistent leadership for nearly twenty years. If Song Ziwen was a sophisticated international financier, much admired by the Westerners with whom he came into contact, he also made a habit of getting Chiang Kai-shek's back up with frequent public breaking of ranks over continued deficit spending, high military expenditure that crowded out economic reconstruction, and the issue of how to deal with Japan. Although Kong Xiangxi retained more links to the provincial Shanxi banking circles from which he came and presented an easy-going and even 'scattered brained' exterior, he was probably the more adept politician in the political environment of Nanjing: much more of an insider, never causing Chiang Kai-shek loss of face through public disagreement, accepting a very substantial degree of deficit spending to finance the Fifth Encirclement Campaign against the Communists without so much as a public murmur, and not objecting nearly as vociferously as had Song to the continued priority accorded to the military.[26]

Whatever their differences regarding the tactics of financial policy in the wider external political and social environment of the Nanjing Decade, as the heads of the organization, Song Ziwen and Kong Xiangxi provided an unusually stable set of goals and priorities for the internal institution-building strategies of the far-flung subsidiaries of the Nationalist Ministry of Finance. Both carried on, more or less unquestioningly, with an orientation and set of goals first articulated in the *xinzheng* period: internal rationalization, differentiation, technical competence and training as the means to bring about both efficiency and effectiveness in building a modern central state and projecting that state's authority far into the hinterland.

Progress in achieving these multiple goals of central projection, rationalization, and efficiency was uneven. The environment in which the Nationalist Ministry of Finance operated placed it in a position somewhere between that of the Beiyang Ministry of Finance and the Salt Inspectorate. Because the Nationalists had established fairly good control over three of the richer provinces in China at the beginning of the Nanjing Decade in 1927–8, its Ministry of Finance was more than a rationalized and differentiated head without a body: it actually had a financial base to manage and secure territory in which to operate. On the other hand, in the late 1920s and early 1930s, Nationalist control over much of the rest of the country to which it claimed authority was nominal or non-existent, the domain of national finance was broad in range, and the Ministry could not implement the high levels of procedural bureaucratization and insulation of staff that made the Salt Inspectorate such a conspicuously successful example of prefectural tax administration.

### THE MINISTRY OF FINANCE: AGENT AND REFLECTION OF STATE BUILDING

Throughout the Nationalist period, the Ministry of Finance occupied a curious organizational niche: it was both an active agent in and a reflection of Nationalist state-building strategies. Both in its immediate policy environment and in its own internal structure, the leadership of the Ministry of Finance systematically attempted to implement bureaucratically oriented centralization, control, and standardization. At the macro, systemic, level, the Nationalist bid to reintegrate the state could only proceed in tandem with effective resource extraction; otherwise, the military advance and civilian integration would collapse for lack of resources. The establishment of effective tax organizations responsive and responsible to the central government thus was simultaneously a cause and an indicator of the state's overall success in carrying out centralization and reintegrative state building.

The Ministry of Finance's large size, varied operations, incorporation of previously autonomous units such as the Customs Administration and the Salt Inspectorate, and extraordinarily broad claims in terms of policy domain required flexibility in terms of internal institution building. The institution-building actions employed by the Ministry of Finance very closely replicated the options inherent in what Thomas Callaghy calls a 'cover-over' strategy of state building: a set of techniques used by aspiring conservative centralizers in historical situations as far removed from each other as Louis XIV in seventeenth-century France to Chiang Kai-shek's National Government in 1930s China to Mobutu Sese Seko's Zaire in the 1970s and 1980s. First, it made a formal, exclusive claim of monocratic authority given formal substance by centrally promulgated administrative laws and regulations, which were backed up by normative appeals. Then, wherever it had the capacity to do so, it sought to make good that claim by establishing centrally controlled and accountable organizations to project its authority outward, either through the creation of new prefectural sub-organizations or through the takeover of old ones. If its influence was insufficient to effect the immediate takeover of previously existing organizations or the establishment of vigorous new centrally accountable sub-organizations, it opted for a set of actions that attempted to render previously competitive and autonomous organizations irrelevant through a process of co-option, absorbtion, and emasculation.[27] Finally, in the least promising scenario of all, when the Ministry's actual capacity was in no way sufficient to begin to realize its claims, it invariably made a general statement declaring its formal authority while in practice looking the other way.

As was the case for the Yuan Shikai government, Nationalist justification for this reliance on centralization came from two quite different sources: the late imperial Chinese political system, and contemporary Western administrative theory. Although their end goals and philosophical values were startlingly different, Confucian bureaucratic elites and Western practitioners of scientific management both habitually reified monocratic authority and hierarchy as intrinsic goods. A commitment to hierarchy and centralization, like the belief in an open civil service examination system as the proper way to recruit government bureaucrats, was one of the few arenas in which the very latest in the 'advanced' West could be correlated with aspects of late imperial Chinese institutions without much cognitive dissonance. The idea of only one source of political and administrative authority had a long pedigree in imperial China, and it fell to the Republican state to attempt to make a concrete reality of the ideal through Western-inspired techniques to generate efficiency and squeeze effectiveness out of the system. Western concepts of 'science' and 'objectivity' tended to be conflated with and enlisted in the service of state centralization and control.[28]

The policy domain that the Ministry of Finance attempted to control was nothing short of staggering. To it fell all responsibility for taxation, bond issuance, loan amortization, currency reform, and budgeting. Each of these areas of finance was characterized by great local diversity, layers upon layers of decades-old *ad hoc* arrangements, and extremely limited central government penetration—all of which contributed to a seeming intractable resistance to rationalization and standardization. The many loans contracted by the Qing and the Beiyang governments meant great indebtedness, and merely keeping up with interest payments was highly problematic. There was no national currency and only a rudimentary national banking system, local and provincial taxation was almost impossibly arcane and complex, and entrenched interests everywhere benefited in some way from the status quo.

Even without continual pressure to produce large surpluses for military ventures, overcoming any of these inherited structural constraints through processes of standardization, centralization, and control was far from straightforward or easy. To the Ministry of Finance's credit, clear results were obtained in two areas by the mid-1930s. In 1935, the Ministry established a national currency (*fabi*) that was stable and popular enough to survive as the preferred tender even in Japanese-occupied areas during the first few years of the war. Progress was made in retiring some of the foreign debt.[29] And second, over the course of the Nanjing Decade the Ministry of Finance succeeded in diversifying sources of government income while more intensively collecting from established sources (see Table 5.1). It was in the arena of tax reform that the Ministry of Finance both diversified and intensified its operations, and it was through tax reform that the Ministry of Finance's institution-building strategies most clearly demonstrated the full range of their potential as well as their limitations.

Issues of taxation were very closely related to the central government's ability to exercise control over society. In the late 1920s and 1930s, the Ministry of Finance had to work within the old paradoxical strictures of needing to extract the revenue necessary to develop an effective state apparatus while remaining hampered by a limited projective capacity. Aside from the Yuan Shikai administration's first, largely ineffective, steps to unify the wine and tobacco tax administration, indigenously administered taxation during the early Republic was highly localized and heterogeneous. Because no nationwide cadastral surveys had been undertaken since the seventeenth century, evasion of the land tax was common.[30] The regionally based Self-Strengthening Movement of the late nineteenth century had sparked *ad hoc* institution of *lijin*, a series of local and provincial taxes on the transport of goods, and had further legitimated the addition of sundry surtaxes on the land tax (*tankuan*) for specific local and regional projects.

**Table 5.1.** National Government Receipts, Fiscal Years 1929–1937[a] (million yuan)

| | 1929 | % | 1930 | % | 1931 | % | 1932 | % | 1933 | % | 1934 | % | 1935 | % | 1936 | % | 1937 | % |
|---|---|---|---|---|---|---|---|---|---|---|---|---|---|---|---|---|---|---|
| Tax | 246 | 56.4 | 451 | 77.1 | 531 | 68.3 | 616 | 80.6 | 582 | 79.8 | 660 | 73.3 | 649 | 62.9 | 622 | 53.2 | 769 | 61.5 |
| Borrowing (domestic bonds, bank loans, overdrafts, and cotton-wheat loan of 1933 | 89 | 20.4 | 101 | 17.3 | 217 | 27.9 | 130 | 17.0 | 112 | 15.4 | 179 | 20.0 | 225 | 21.9 | 276 | 23.7 | 336 | 26.8 |
| Other non-tax revenue (government property, enterprise, and administrative receipts) | 101 | 23.2 | 33 | 5.6 | 30 | 3.8 | 18 | 2.4 | 35 | 4.8 | 32 | 3.6 | 98 | 9.5 | 180 | 15.4 | 101 | 8.1 |
| Cash balance from previous year | | | | | | | | | | | 28 | 3.1 | 59 | 5.7 | 90 | 7.7 | 45 | 3.6 |
| TOTAL | 436 | 100.0 | 585 | 100.0 | 778 | 100.0 | 764 | 100.0 | 726 | 100.0 | 897 | 100.0 | 1029 | 100.0 | 1166 | 99.9 | 1251 | 100.0 |

[a] Fiscal year = 1 July–30 June.
*Source:* Adapted from Arthur Young, *China's Nation Building Experiment, 1927–37,* (Stanford, Calif.: Hoover Institution Press, 1971), 433–5.

Debates continue to rage about the real burden of taxation in the Republican period, and there is good reason to believe that the overall tax burden in Republican China was fairly light and not, at a systemic level, particularly inhibiting to agriculture and commerce.[31] But in at least some times and places, *ad hoc* taxation—generated either by warlords who needed to raise money, by unregulated local elites and tax farmers, or indeed even by the Nationalist government itself—placed unpredictable and onerous burdens on taxpayers.[32] Whatever the economic reality of taxation in the 1920s and 1930s, the growing *political* consensus among Westerners in China, domestic centralizing elites, and critics of the regime alike was that real rates of taxation were highly unfair and uneven, that unrestrained locally collected *lijin* inhibited domestic trade, that the existence of so many *ad hoc* surtaxes dampened productivity, and that the continued existence of independent or semi-independent militarists exacerbated an already bad situation. For example, in the port of Xiamen, in 1924 the local warlord, Cang Zhibing, was reported to have imposed over '70 surtaxes that covered almost anything that could be taxed'. Over five separate surtaxes were levied on pork, three on prostitutes, three on opium, and there were assorted other surtaxes on everything from narcissus bulbs to chicken and duck eggs, flour, trade, paper, firecrackers, tobacco and haircuts.[33]

At least for some locations, the coming to power of the Nanjing Government made little difference in this state of affairs, and indeed in the short run may have made it worse. To cite the case of Fujian again, in August 1929 Samuel Sokobin, then American consul, reported that there were at that time over 150 different taxes being levied in Fujian and that 'it was difficult to conceive of a system of taxation which falls more heavily on the people, the common people . . . [as] pork is the staple meat eaten . . . in one district a total of five taxes are levied on slaughter houses and pigs. In other words, the scrap of pork that a Chinese eats has been taxed five times, and, if the shop tax is added, six times.' With respect to agriculture, 'we have a land tax, a crop tax, a land and grain surtax and a 10% surtax in four out of ten districts, [but] . . . an extra surtax for the compilation of the district annals'. General perceptions were that the taxes were 'generally several times higher than they were four or five years ago', and that there was 'serious opposition on the part of a large body of discontented young men, led chiefly by those associated with education who . . . are unable to obtain their pay regularly, and realize that they are being frozen out by the same type of rapacious military official or higher civil authority . . .'[34]

Even in a 'worst case' scenario such as Fujian in 1929, it ought to be noted that tax rates were highly uneven: if four districts out of ten were singled out as having five taxes and surtaxes on agriculture, the other six were in all likelihood subjected to a much less onerous taxation regime. But by the late 1920s and early 1930s, in state-making circles the ideals of standardization, centralization, and unification were so strong that these principles were axiomatically taken to be positive goods in themselves. Whether the peasants and local commerce empirically did suffer from levels of taxation so high that they disrupted national development and economic growth (and the evidence is such that, at least in some times and some places in the Republican period, they probably did) was quite beside the point for Nationalist state- and institution-building elites. The mere continued existence of such vast differences in local taxation regimes, 'irregularity', and widely varying tax rates carried a resonance far beyond the putative economic havoc it wreaked on commerce and the peasantry. It was a concrete reminder of central government weakness as well as a block on the realization of the centralizing project, and as such was highly obnoxious to the centralizing National Government, as it had been to the Yuan Shikai and Beiyang governments before it.

It is little wonder that, after the obligations of keeping the government in business for another day had been met, the Ministry of Finance was obsessed with its desire to unify and rationalize taxation, to increase efficiency, in order to establish fair and equalized rates, and to clearly demarcate central government finance from local and provincial tax collection—themes that figured prominently in virtually every speech and official publication from the Ministry of Finance over the entire period 1927–49.[35]

Given its limited ability to unify, standardize, and establish immediate control over taxation, the Ministry adopted a multi-tiered approach. It quickly took over what it could, slowly reorganized and amalgamated along centralized lines when its capacity was somewhat weaker, and announced its authority and looked the other way in areas where it had little real influence.

THE EASY PICKINGS: THE TAKEOVER OF CUSTOMS AND SALT

Desiring both to impose its control and immediately to produce large amounts of revenue, the Ministry of Finance focused its attention on the Customs Administration and the Salt Inspectorate very soon after the establishment of the Nanjing Government. Two factors made these organizations attractive initial targets. First, they had structures that had already demonstrated their efficiency and effectiveness in tax collection, and they had cash-rich, intact (or easily restorable) organizations that could generate substantial funds at very little extra cost or investment on the part of the National Government. Throughout the Beiyang years, it was the receipts from these hybrid, largely independent, civil service bureaucracies that kept the northern government afloat, and in 1927–8, despite the disruptions caused by the Northern Expedition's military campaigns, they were still producing far more revenue than any other tax organizations operating in China. Although their relative percentages of overall revenue declined between 1927 and 1937, Customs and Salt remained the first and second 'pillars' of Nationalist finance until the outbreak of the Sino-Japanese War, between them accounting for between two-thirds and four-fifths of the central government's tax receipts in every year of the Nanjing Decade (Table 5.2).[36]

Second, as organizations closely associated with foreigners and foreign influence, neither Customs nor Salt had any natural domestic allies or constituencies, and were therefore vulnerable. When the Customs Administration and the Salt Inspectorate were both formally taken over and placed under the authority of the Ministry of Finance in 1927–8, there was virtually no resistance aside from the initially loud squawks of protest in the foreign language press in Shanghai. The British, who were at this point still the predominant Western power in China, quietly recognized the prudence of giving way to Chinese nationalism, and instructed its nationals Maze and Hussey-Freke, who in 1927–8 were the respective foreign heads of the Customs Administration and the Salt Inspectorate, to do the best that they could under circumstances of takeover by the Nationalists.

As described with regard to the Salt Inspectorate in Chapter 4, the 1930s were characterized by informal power sharing between these two previously independent tax agencies and the Ministry of Finance. In return for a good measure of continued autonomy over personnel and operations, the Customs and Salt Administrations accepted the formal authority of the Ministry of Finance and followed Ministry of Finance directives, which in turn followed the political exigencies of the day: to raise the tax rates, and to turn the efficiency of its organizations to the task of providing the central government with more money. The increases in customs and salt duties served both the government's immediate financial needs and its nationalist pride in reasserting authority over taxation. Nationalists everywhere felt the tariff levels on imported goods into China to be particularly galling, as the unequal treaties of the previous century had fixed import duties at an extraordinarily low maximum rate of 3.8 per cent, giving foreign manufacturers a tremendous competitive advantage, not to mention flagrantly violating China's sovereignty and national pride. Once the Customs Administration was placed under the Ministry of Finance in 1928, tariffs on imported goods increased from 3.8 to 8.5 per cent. In 1931, the Ministry of Finance moved to more fully 'recover tariff autonomy' by proposing a new, elaborate system of tariff classifications, and by 1933 the average rate on imported goods had risen to 25.4 per cent.[37]

A subtle, but no less important, change was the gradual decline in the influence of foreign staff within these two semi-autonomous organizations.

**Table 5.2.** National Government Tax Receipts, Fiscal Years 1929–1937[a] (million yuan)

| | 1929 | % | 1930 | % | 1931 | % | 1932 | % | 1933 | % | 1934 | % | 1935 | % | 1936 | % | 1937 | % |
|---|---|---|---|---|---|---|---|---|---|---|---|---|---|---|---|---|---|---|
| Customs | 179 | 72.8 | 276 | 61.2 | 313 | 59.0 | 370 | 60.1 | 326 | 56.0 | 352 | 53.3 | 353 | 54.4 | 272 | 43.7 | 379 | 49.3 |
| Salt | 30 | 12.2 | 122 | 27.0 | 150 | 28.2 | 144 | 23.4 | 158 | 27.1 | 177 | 26.8 | 167 | 25.7 | 184 | 29.6 | 197 | 25.6 |
| Consolidated Tax | 30 | 12.2 | 41 | 9.1 | 53 | 10.0 | 89 | 14.4 | 80 | 13.8 | 106 | 16.1 | 105 | 16.2 | 135 | 21.7 | 158 | 20.5 |
| Tobacco/wine | 4 | 1.6 | 7 | 1.6 | 9 | 1.7 | 8 | 1.3 | 10 | 1.7 | 13 | 2.0 | 11 | 1.7 | 15 | 2.4 | 15 | 2.0 |
| Stamps | 3 | 1.2 | 5 | 1.1 | 6 | 1.1 | 5 | 0.8 | 5 | 0.9 | 8 | 1.2 | 7 | 1.1 | 10 | 1.6 | 9 | 1.2 |
| Income tax | | | | | | | | | | | | | | | | | 7 | 0.9 |
| Mining | | | | | | | | | | | 2 | 0.3 | 4 | 0.6 | 4 | 0.6 | 4 | 0.5 |
| Bank notes | | | | | | | | | 3 | 0.5 | 2 | 0.3 | 2 | 0.3 | 2 | 0.3 | | |
| TOTAL | 246 | 100.0 | 451 | 100.0 | 531 | 100.0 | 616 | 100.0 | 582 | 100.0 | 660 | 100.0 | 649 | 100.0 | 622 | 99.9 | 769 | 100.0 |

[a] Fiscal year = 1 July–30 June.

*Source:* adapted from Arthur Young, *China's Nation Building Experiment, 1927–37,* (Stanford, Calif.: Hoover Institution Press, 1971), 433–4.

Even though the separate civil service systems in Customs and Salt Administrations remained more or less intact until the Sino-Japanese War, the Guomindang abolished the Customs civil service exam for foreigners in 1928, and announced a policy of replacing retiring foreign staff with Chinese nationals. By 1930 the number of foreign nationals in the Maritime Customs Administration fell to 995 from a pre-1928 figure of 1,321, while the numbers of Chinese correspondingly increased. The slow attrition of foreigners was particularly evident at the central tax division (*shuiwu si*) of the Customs Administration, where the Chinese staff increased from none in 1925 to over a third by 1937.[38]

Since the Salt Inspectorate was a much smaller and younger organization than the Customs Administration, with only some thirty-odd foreigners, the relative decline of foreign influence is much less easy to document. Their numbers did not begin to drop seriously until the Sino-Japanese War. Nevertheless, as was seen in Chapter 4, during the 1930s at least two of the foreign district inspectors within the Inspectorate, Croome and Pearson, were sensitive enough to the presumed efforts on the part of the Ministry of Finance to diminish their independent authority to write lengthy memos decrying the decline of foreign influence, the loss of the Inspectorate's civil service traditions, and their own poor career prospects in the organization. It is also probable that one of the key goals of the 1936 reorganization of the Salt Inspectorate into the Directorate-General of Salt was the reduction of foreign influence, as indeed shortly thereafter the practice of requiring co-signatures by both Chinese and foreign chief district inspectors on orders was quietly phased out, with the foreign district inspectors eventually relegated to advisory status.

The takeover of the Customs Administration and the Salt Inspectorate were the first, easiest, and by any measure the most productive (in terms of yield) of the Ministry of Finance's institution-building strategies. Many Guomindang and other patriotic elites felt uneasy about the continued existence of high-ranking foreigners in these organizations, and the Ministry of Personnel lobbied vigorously, albeit unsuccessfully, to force the Customs Administration and Salt Inspectorate into the 'regular' Chinese civil service *jian jian wei* system of classification. While the influence of specific foreigners in these organizations waned during the 1930s, once formally subordinate to the Ministry of Finance, the Customs Administration and Salt Inspectorate none the less were allowed to preserve most of the civil service autonomy and efficiency-oriented organizational culture that were widely considered to be the crucial factors in their effective and efficient performance in the first place. Under the rubric of formal submission and acceptance of Ministry of Finance directives, this sort of informal power sharing worked to the advantage of both parties. The Ministry of Finance inherited two centralized, highly effective, depoliticized organizations that reliably produced the bulk of the government's tax revenue at virtually no extra cost to the Ministry of Finance, while the Customs Administration and the Salt Inspectorate were allowed to continue to exist and, in their own ways, to flourish under the Nanjing Government. The Customs Administration and the Salt Inspectorate provide an example of the Ministry's first strategy of institutionalization: outright takeover.

### GRADUAL CENTRALIZATION AND AMALGAMATION: INDIRECT TAXATION IN CONSOLIDATED TAX

The Consolidated Tax Administration, which in 1932 became the largest and most important sub-organization under the Ministry of Finance's new Internal Revenue Administration, provided the government with its third largest source of tax revenue after Customs and Salt during the Nanjing Decade. As the most important exclusively Chinese tax administration sub-organization under the Ministry of Finance, the Consolidated Tax Administration illustrates the conditions under which the Ministry of Finance's internally generated institution-building strategies were most successful.

Like the salt gabelle and customs duties, the consolidated tax was an indirect tax on consumption. And like the early Salt Inspectorate, the Consolidated Tax Administration's main thrust was to centralize control and replace highly complicated, overlapping taxes and multiple *lijin* levies with a single consolidated commodity tax that was based on the principle of 'one item, one tax' (*yiwu yishui*), with one set of standard, nationwide flat rates that was assessed at the site of production. After the one-off standard-ized assessment, there were to be 'no barriers to free flow [of goods], resulting in increased receipts... and convenience for merchants and the people'.[39] The consolidated tax was designed to be a national tax to replace the discredited *lijin*, which was increasingly perceived by centralizers to have the doubly negative effects of inhibiting commerce and being beyond the effective purview of the central government. The consolidated tax was to be 'governed by regulations' rather than determined by local power arrangements—a force of standardization in instituting national, uniform tax rates for the same items. In this way, the reorganized consolidated tax would 'increase income, stabilize finance and strengthen control'—a trium-virate of goals dear to the heart of aspiring centralizers in the Nanjing Decade.[40]

During the late 1920s and early 1930s, the Ministry of Finance's Con-solidated Tax Administration pursued a strategy of institution building that in microcosm replicated 'cover-over' state building. In first sought to realize its claims to central authority by claiming exclusive tax collecting authority for the commodities deemed within the jurisdiction of the Consolidated

Tax Administration. Then, where it was able to do so (in the Jiangnan area where the National Government had credible control), it established tax collecting prefectural organizations directly responsible to and managed from the centre. After establishing a core set of sub-offices, the Consolidated Tax Administration then slowly radiated outward to incorporate new geographical areas, amalgamate the numerous pre-existing local tax administrations handling these items, and steadily increase the number of taxable commodities under its control, thus bypassing those pre-existing local tax organizations that it could not incorporate.

Centrality for the Consolidated Tax Administration was realized geographically through its core organizations in the Jiangnan, organizationally through its prefectural administration, and in terms of domain through its early coalescence around the rolled tobacco tax. In 1928–9 the Ministry of Finance began by setting up some eleven bureaus to collect the rolled tobacco tax in areas under firm Nationalist control, primarily in Jiangsu, Zhejiang, and Anhui. From this organizational and geographical core, the Consolidated Tax Administration expanded outward in both domain (the list of commodities claimed to be within its jurisdiction) and space (outward from Shanghai). In 1931 the list of items subject to collection by the Consolidated Tax Administration expanded to include cotton yarn, matches, cement, flour, and flue-cured tobacco, in order to 'replace' locally levied *lijin* transit taxes with one administered by the central government.

At the same time, the Ministry of Finance established a new Internal Revenue Administration (Shuiwu Shu) of formally equal status with the Customs and Salt Administrations. The Consolidated Tax Administration provided the core of Internal Revenue's activities, but in addition the Internal Revenue Administration formally took over the provincially administered wine and tobacco tax bureaus while 'reorganizing' the stamp tax as a central tax 'entrusted' to the post office for collection. In 1933 the mining products tax was added to the Internal Revenue Administration, and in 1935 the alcohol tax was remanded to the consolidated tax system. In late 1936, the Consolidated Tax Administration was drawing up regulations for a new tax on aerated waters, and in early 1937 it took over a special provincially levied tax on firecracker materials in Guangdong.[41]

By 1934 the Internal Revenue Administration, sometimes through establishing new prefectural branches of the consolidated tax system and sometimes through the formal incorporation of pre-existing provincial and local alcohol and tobacco tax offices, had at least established a presence in most regions of China aside from the province of Sichuan, border regions in the north-west and far south-west and the three north-eastern provinces of Manchuria, which by the mid-1930s were totally lost to the Nanjing government. The country was divided into five geographical areas (Jiangsu/ Zhejiang/Anhui, Hunan/Hubei/Jiangxi, Shandong/Henan, Guangdong/

Guangxi/Fujian, and Hebei/Shanxi/Chahar/Suiyuan), each with its own regional managing office, plus a separate office in Shanghai. Each of these regional offices, in turn, managed and audited a sub-complex of district collectorates and local branches. By 1936 a few provincial auditing and collection offices had been established even in the far outlying regions of Sichuan and Gansu, where the Nationalists had historically weak to non-existent control.[42] In the same year, the Internal Revenue Administration began to amalgamate local collectorates on the basis of geographical location rather than the particular commodity handled in an effort to further centralize control, strengthen the consolidated tax system, and increase administrative efficiency.[43]

The Consolidated Tax Administration substantially increased its contributions to the total receipts of the Ministry of Finance in both absolute and relative terms throughout the Nanjing Decade, in part by expanding into new territories, in part by adding more taxes to its collectorates, and in part through intensification and improved efficiency of the offices that already existed. Despite this quite impressive expansion outward in geographical space and organizational scope, the Consolidated Tax Administration remained solidly grounded in its original organizational core. If the Consolidated Tax Administration rose from modest beginnings in the late 1920s to become the 'third pillar' of Nationalist finance by the mid-1930s, then the rolled tobacco tax remained the foundation of the pillar. Diversification and expansion meant that the consolidated tax system would not remain totally dependent either on its original domain in the rolled tobacco tax or on its original geographical core in the Jiangnan. Within the Consolidated Tax Administration, the proportion of revenue provided by the rolled tobacco tax declined from roughly 85 per cent in fiscal 1928–9 (21,140,807Y of 23,196,125Y) to slightly under two-thirds by fiscal 1933–4 (63,750,863Y of 100,160,431Y) (see Table 5.3).[44] While the government publicly lamented that the consolidated tax 'was excessively concentrated in the cities of Shanghai, Wuhan, Tianjin, and Qingdao', its own published reports suggest at least modest geographical diversification out of the Nationalist 'traditional' base in the Jiangnan.[45] Although the city of Shanghai continued to provide the bulk of the receipts for the commodities subject to the consolidated tax throughout the Nanjing Decade, it is worth noting that in 1928–9 the National Government had no tax offices whatsoever in the Shandong/Henan area, but by 1933–4 the Consolidated Tax Administration offices in the Shandong/Henan region provided more revenue than those in the Jiangsu/Zhejiang/Anhui district for rolled tobacco (949,919Y v. 241,142Y), for flour (825,337Y v. 543,350Y), and for cotton yarn (3,487,562Y v. 2,291,216Y). (see Table 5.4).[46] The trajectory of the consolidated tax during the Nanjing Decade illustrated by the figures in Tables 5.3 and 5.4 is clear:

**Table 5.3.**  Consolidated Tax, Fiscal Years 1928–1935[a] (yuan)

| | 1928 | 1929 | 1930 | 1931 | 1932 | 1933 | 1934 | 1935 |
|---|---|---|---|---|---|---|---|---|
| Rolled tobacco | 21,140,804 | 41,110,995 | 47,845,918 | 50,018,279 | 57,435,023 | 63,750,863 | n/a | 76,893,819 |
| Cotton yarn | | | 6,396,771 | 5,656,933 | 17,294,262 | 18,675,028 | n/a | 20,048,491 |
| Flour | | 4,264,917 | 5,107,275 | 5,837,310 | 6,238,153 | 5,467,846 | n/a | 4,678,613 |
| Matches | | | | | 4,887,000 | 6,560,451 | n/a | 9,267,157 |
| Cement | | | | 1,735,292 | 1,368,759 | 2,504,552 | n/a | 2,645,378 |
| Flue-cured tobacco | | | 1,129,368 | 1,584,601 | 2,683,848 | 3,201,691 | n/a | 3,931,107 |
| TOTAL | 21,140,804 | 45,375,962 | 60,479,332 | 64,832,415 | 89,907,045 | 100,160,431 | n/a | 117,464,565 |

[a] Fiscal year = 1 July–30 June.

*Source: Caizheng Nianjian* (The Finance Yearbook) (Nanjing: Caizheng Bu, 1935); *Chinese Yearbook 1937*, ed. Kwei Chungshu (Shanghai and Chungking: Commercial Press, 1937).

**Table 5.4.** Consolidated Tax Receipts, 1933–1934, by Region and Type (yuan)

| | Rolled tobacco | Flour | Cotton yarn | Matches | Cement | Flue-cured tobacco |
|---|---|---|---|---|---|---|
| Internal revenue (Shanghai) | 61,507,606 | 3,181,306 | 9,518,293 | 1,762,105 | 995,757 | 0 |
| Jiangsu–Zhejiang–Anhui | 241,142 | 543,450 | 2,291,216 | 938,401 | 184 | 436,481 |
| Hunan–Hubei–Jiangxi | 6691 | 236,726 | 1,336,483 | 165,432 | 217,052 | 32 |
| Shandong–Henan | 949,919 | 825,337 | 3,487,562 | 2,416,789 | 58,347 | 2,765,178 |
| Hebei–Shanxi–Chahar–Suiyuan | 1,042,185 | 680,110 | 2,017,030 | 1,275,661 | 1,197,940 | 0 |
| Fuzhou branch | n/a | 9,917 | 24,444 | 2063 | 35,272 | 0 |
| TOTAL | 63,750,863 | 5,467,846 | 18,675,028 | 6,560,451 | 2,504,552 | 3,201,691 |

*Source: Caizheng Nianjian* (The Finance Yearbook) (Nanjing: Caizheng Bu, 1935), 951, 960, 972, 982, 988, 995.

increased revenue extraction, continued reliance on both Shanghai and the rolled tobacco tax, and some amount of geographical and product diversification.

Throughout the 1930s, centralizers in the Consolidated Tax Administration both deliberately and unconsciously referred to models of taxation and administration developed in the Salt Inspectorate and Customs Administrations. In addition to the rationalizing principles of centralization and standardization, the 'one item, one tax' slogan sounded very much like the Salt Inspectorate's policy of 'taxation at the yard and free trade thereafter'. Organizationally, the Consolidated Tax made every effort possible to replicate Salt Inspectorate and Customs Administrations' mode of prefectural organization, in which the central office established the rules and guidelines, set the uniform tax rates, and recruited, dispatched, and frequently rotated the personnel to staff the regional field offices. Although it is unclear that the Consolidated Tax Administration was ever successful in so doing, it was a matter of public record that Song Ziwen and other technocrats were much taken with the 'objectivity' and 'results' of the civil service model exemplified by Customs and Salt, and wished to extend the separate civil service systems characteristic of the Customs and Salt Administrations to Consolidated Tax so as to reap the presumed benefits of civil service efficiency and effectiveness.[47] And finally, in 1933 the Internal Revenue Administration set up a special training institute (Yangchengsuo) in Shanghai which was explicitly modelled on the 'Customs College' feeder school into the Customs Administration.[48]

At least in Consolidated Tax, the Ministry of Finance came close to replicating some of the key features of the Inspectorate model—centralization, standardization, bureaucratization, and at least the stated goal of an analogous civil service system—and it did so without a heavy staffing component of foreigners. For the Consolidated Tax Administration, the processes by which it achieved these goals through absorption, amalgamation, centralization, and expansion and diversification was infinitely slower and less dramatic than it had been for the Inspectorate.

But if the methods for pursuing institution building were more incremental, more opportunistic, and broadly parallel to the Nationalists' state-building strategies at large, the eventual similarities in terms of 'success' are quite striking. Both the Salt Inspectorate and the Consolidated Tax Administration built impressively efficient and reliable tax organizations, and as such became organizations that the government was hard put to do without. By the end of the 1927–37 period, the percentage of national revenue derived from consolidated tax had doubled, from 8.8 to 17.5 per cent.[49]

The Consolidated Tax system, like the Salt Inspectorate and the Customs Administration, restricted its domain to a finite, if constantly expanding, list of commodities that were for the most part easy to audit and control. Mines, spinning mills, concrete and match factories were difficult to hide. Most of the factories that could be taxed were concentrated in and around Shanghai, where the government had good direct control and a large number of officials in residence. In the provinces, their numbers were small enough that it was within the plausible means of the centrally appointed, regionally based tax inspectors physically to go out to the factories and assess the tax at the site of production. Other commodities had much more diffuse production and distribution, and were correspondingly difficult to control and audit.[50] Native wine, native tobacco, and the stamp tax all remained problematic for these reasons. The stamp tax was farmed out to be administered through the postal system. Although formally taken into the Internal Revenue Administration and earmarked as national taxes, the central administration of neither the native wine nor the native tobacco taxes was ever quite strong enough to come under the strict implementation guidelines for the consolidated tax.

Although relatively 'efficient' in terms of collection and 'effective' for the needs elsewhere in the government for more revenue, the Consolidated Tax Administration's efficiency was disproportionately trained on those sectors where there was a credible match between its organizational scale and the product it claimed to assess for the central government. For example, during the 1930s there were huge, and evidently increasing, disparities between the rates of real taxation on machine-rolled cigarettes and locally hand-rolled cigarettes, with the former taxed at 80Y per case and the latter at 10Y per case. In 1935 British American Tobacco (BAT) filed a series of complaints about the mushrooming expansion of the hand-rolled tobacco industry in Shandong, Henan, and Anhui and the discriminatory taxation regime, stating that, under these conditions:

As a matter of fact, such [hand-rolled] cigarettes seldom pay any tax at all... it is thus impossible for even the cheapest factory goods to compete with the handrolled product... [as] taxation of the legitimate trade is very high. Consolidated tax rates have been increased five times in seven years. The margin between the cheapest grade of factory goods and hand made goods is now so wide that smuggling and tax evasion have become organized and profitable enterprises.[51]

Kong Xiangxi responded to this set of complaints with a mixture of moral justification (that poor people trying to scratch out a living by hand-rolling cigarettes should not be interfered with), necessity ('the tax on hand-rolled cigarettes has proved ineffective in practice'), conciliation (a timetable to phase out hand-rolled cigarettes, register all cigarette machinery, and strengthen the anti-smuggling division of the Internal Revenue Administration), and a final sharp jab at continued foreign imperialism ('perhaps your Excellency's good offices might be exercised with a view to facilitating the negotiations now suspected between the Internal Revenue Administration and the Settlement Authorities' [with respect to unregulated sale of cigarette paper and leaves in the International Settlement]).[52]

Effective implementation of the centralizing, state-building approach to tax administration was constrained by two factors: the consistent projective power of the organization, and the scale of the domain in which it claimed authority. In the case of the Consolidated Tax Administration, the size of the corps of bureaucrats that could be salaried and administered from the technocratic central government organization and the size of the markets for easily nettable and visible commodities could be brought into rough equilibrium. Like the Salt Inspectorate, the Consolidated Tax Administration was 'fortunate': it operated in a domain in which it could demonstrably extend its control through the establishment of new branch offices and the takeover of pre-existing ones, could increase its effectiveness measured in net receipts, and could raise its efficiency through a lowering of administrative costs, thus buying itself prestige and indispensibility.

The conditions that made the Consolidated Tax Administration's institution-building strategies successful were not generalizable to other areas of tax, nor did they necessarily make for a taxation regime that could claim to be fair. Those items that could be efficiently and effectively taxed by the central government were not those that would spread the tax burden most reasonably or equitably: they were those products that were easy for the Consolidated Tax Administration to identify and control. The National Government drew its lifeblood disproportionately from the relatively small 'modernized' sector that produced goods that were concentrated in points of manufacture or distribution. The Consolidated Tax Administration's strategy of slow expansion, centralization, co-optation, amalgamation, and bureaucratic orientation certainly met with increased efficiency and effectiveness during the 1930s, but the generalizability of its effectiveness was constrained by the nature of the commodities, and the relatively restricted domain in which it dealt.

## DIRECT TAX AND LAND TAX: LATE STARTS AND UNFRIENDLY NEIGHBOURHOODS

Reformers and financial experts inside and outside of the Ministry of Finance certainly recognized the gravity of China's tax administration problems. They were aware that the tax burden fell on too few, that the consolidated taxes fell disproportionately on the small modernized sector, that in the countryside the continued existence of miscellaneous surtaxes on the basic land tax squeezed peasants, and that, although formally abolished, local and provincial *lijin* transit taxes by other names still inhibited internal commerce. These concerns, along with indictments of runaway military expenditures, worries about continued deficits, and the lack of budgetary restraint, figured prominently in every financial report released, finance conference held, and official finance document produced between 1928 and 1937. The central Ministry's limited reach, the average Chinese taxpayer's continued aversion to direct taxation, entrenched interests everywhere, and the technical difficulties inherent in setting up effective administrative organizations for which no precedent existed had the net effect of derailing many of the Ministry of Finance's schemes for complete centralization and rationalization of nationwide tax administration.

One of the most ambitious steps taken by the Ministry of Finance in promoting the goal of rational, direct, and 'fair' taxation came in 1936, when, after several years of preparatory work early in the 1930s, the Direct Tax Administration was inaugurated with a good deal of fanfare. Even though the outbreak of the Sino-Japanese War prevented it from realizing its goals, the Direct Tax Administration stood as the institutional embodiment of what fiscal technocrats aspired to at the height of the National Government's power in the mid-1930s; and for this reason the principles that undergirded the creation of the Direct Tax Administration merit serious attention.

The Direct Tax Administration built on the complex of organizational strategies long since worked through in the Customs, Salt, and Consolidated Tax Administrations and applied these principles to a significantly broader set of goals in extending Republican era national taxation much further and deeper into society than had ever been attempted even by the relatively efficient and effective indirect commodity tax administrations. In terms of organizational design, the Direct Tax Administration replicated the organizational principles of Customs, Salt, and Consolidated Tax, and publicly claimed that its models were taken from 'the example of England, [as well as from] customs, salt and the postal system—which all have similar offices'.[53]

The Direct Tax Administration was established as a *shu*, a formally semi-autonomous organization within the Ministry of Finance with a prefectural administration. Middle to upper-level personnel at the district and branch offices were appointed from the central personnel offices and expected to be rotated fairly often. Office heads had no power of direct appointment; at most they could 'recommend' individuals to be appointed by the central administration.[54] The technocratic ethos of Direct Tax also had much in common with its sister *shu* in the Ministry of Finance: it was obsessed with administrative efficiency, objectivity, rationalization, and centralization, and to this familiar list of positively animating administrative values it added the new one of 'fairness'.

From its very inception, the Direct Tax Administration quite deliberately adopted a set of institution-building strategies that fostered insulation, efficiency, and expertise. Prior to the outbreak of the Sino-Japanese War, the Direct Tax Administration attempted, with at least some initial success, to implement fairly rigorous strategies of insulation by exclusively recruiting a young, college-educated cadre who came into the organization strictly via an open civil service examination held by the Examination Yuan. Kong Xiangxi envisioned the Direct Tax Administration as a working model of youthful, centralizing vigour. In contrast to the Consolidated Tax Administration, which built upon and incorporated old tax units, the Direct Tax Administration was in principle to be 'a new tax run by new people' (yong xinren ban xinshui), or, in a still pithier catch phrase, a 'new tax, new personnel, new spirit' (xinshui xinren xin jingshen).[55]

Pre-entry socialization was then boosted by a rigorous two- to three-month xunlian training course which incorporated military training each day with classroom and practical exercises in such topics as Ministry of Finance regulations, accounting, statistics, theory of finance, and the regulation and implementation of the new direct tax.[56] A total of 158 individuals went through the three direct tax training sessions that were held between September 1936 and the outbreak of the Sino-Japanese War less than a year later, and this cadre continued to provide the 'backbone generation' of much of the Direct Tax Administration well into the war.[57] Even otherwise highly critical observers of Guomindang tax administration rather grudgingly admitted that the pre-war Direct Tax Administration's kaoxun (examination and training) policies 'produced a relatively good atmosphere', as the personnel selected were highly educated college graduates, 'with clean hands'.[58]

Unlike the relatively limited and sharply delineated spheres of the fixed-rate commodity taxes administered by Customs, Salt, and Consolidated Tax, the Direct Tax Administration claimed a very broad mandate. It sought to do no less than ultimately to equalize the tax burden by realizing Sun Yat-sen's ideal of 'taking the tax directly to the people'.[59] The direct tax was in consequence extremely far-ranging, and included projected taxes on income, windfall profits, savings, interest, property, and inheritance. The Direct Tax Administration emphasized in equal measure that direct taxation was a feature of advanced and developed countries that China would do well to emulate; that a direct graduated income tax was inherently fairer than the current tax system (as those who had more income would pay more); and that direct taxation, once instituted, would across the board be lighter, more rational (in comparison with the commodity taxes that fell disproportionately on a few sectors), and more stable as a source of income for the government.[60]

However far apart theory and practice might have been in reality, the dominant trend of Chinese statecraft and tax policy for hundreds of years had idealized a laissez-faire system that enshrined the principle of 'light corvée and minimal taxes' (qingyao bolian), and the Direct Tax Administration's raison d'être flew in the face of this long-held norm.[61] The normative, administrative, and technical difficulties in instituting such a far-reaching set of taxes that in intent were designed to fall on an extremely broad cross-section of the urban population (including those on salaries, those who earned any interest on bank accounts, those with property or anything to inherit, and all businesses) were staggering. Ministry of Finance technocrats and foreign advisers, including those associated with the prestigious Kemmerer Commission, were sensitive to the structural difficulties likely to obstruct the institution of the direct taxes. The problems most often cited included the undeveloped state of China's businesses, the population's customary practice of hiding assets from the government, the potential exodus of capital should interest be taxed, the difficulties in determining 'equitable taxation' or even coming up with a standard for income in a large country with so many regional variations, and the small size of the Direct Tax Administration relative to the policy area over which it claimed control, which it turn would leave the administration no alternative but to rely on self-assessment with, as one official noted drily, 'all of its accompanying defects'.[62]

Despite the cautionary objections, Kong Xiangxi wished to see the principle of equitable taxation given organizational form, and the Direct Tax Administration was inaugurated in 1936, with its first group of trainees beginning in their new offices in November. In the short period of operation between then and the outbreak of the Sino-Japanese War, the Direct Tax Administration started small and 'at home'. In the last quarter of fiscal 1936–7, direct tax intake was very modest at roughly 6,500,000Y. Of this, the vast majority of the direct tax came from, in effect, one branch of the central government paying another. Taxes taken out of the monthly salaries of civil servants on the government payroll accounted for 1,832,341Y, or over one-quarter of the total. Tax taken out by the central and branch offices of the government-controlled central bank, Bank of China, and Bank of Communications accounted for over half of the direct tax, with interest on government bonds accounting for 2,481,063Y, and interest on shares, deposits, and private loans making for another 747,469Y. Direct tax on combined official–merchant enterprises accounted for another 1,180,703Y. The total tax collected on the income of private businesses and professionals was paltry, at 245,690Y.[63] Another, less complete, survey of direct tax collected between October 1936 and March 1937 shows a heavy bias towards Shanghai, with roughly three-quarters of the total remitted through the Shanghai office (see Tables 5.5 and 5.6).[64]

Out in the provincial offices, where there was less concentration of easily detected capital in banks, the administrative tasks at hand were 'troublesome'.[65] Assessing income tax proved to be an administrative nightmare, as there was neither central reporting of income nor standardized forms, and every organization and private business tended to keep its books differently.

**Table 5.5.** Income Tax Collections, October
1936–March 1937 (yuan)

| Office | Collections |
| --- | --- |
| Income Tax Office (Nanjing) | 693,970 |
| Shanghai | 2,957,697 |
| Jiangsu | 123,710 |
| Zhejiang | 18,527 |
| Hubei | 30,182 |
| Sichuan-Xinjiang | 90,723 |
| Guangdong | 14,500 |
| Shandong | 27,636 |
| Henan | 14,053 |
| Other | 36,272 |
| TOTAL | 4,007,270 |

*Source*: Y. Dung, 'Public Finance and Taxation', in *The Chinese Yearbook 1937*, ed. Kwei Chungshu (Shanghai and Chungking: Commercial Press), 448.

**Table 5.6.** Income Tax, 1936–1937

| Source | Amount (yuan) |
| --- | --- |
| Temporary profit-making enterprises | 1,180,703 |
| Civil servant salaries | 1,832,341 |
| Professional salaries | 4,445 |
| Other salaries | 235,479 |
| Interest on government bonds | 2,481,063 |
| Interest on corporate bonds | 11,897 |
| Dividends on stocks | 13,829 |
| Interest on bank deposits | 721,723 |
| Corporate profit tax | 5,766 |
| TOTAL | 6,487,246 |

*Source*: Caizheng Bu, *Banian lai zhi zhijieshui*, p. 7.

Direct Tax regional and branch offices, not surprisingly, concentrated their attention on registering businesses rather than individuals, but staff who went out to register local businesses immediately ran into problems. Local businesses, either through inertia or intent, kept their ledgers in assorted 'old styles' of bookkeeping, and the tax personnel, for all their high-prestige college educations and technocratic training in standard procedures, were unable to fathom these local and variable ledgers. Thus, personnel in the field had little choice but to 'believe what the other was saying, had no real way to discover irregularities . . . and [ultimately] were forced to fall back on estimating income ... opening the door to business fraud', which in turn seriously compromised the whole point of the 'fair' direct income tax.[66]

Whether the Direct Tax Administration could have, with more time, moved out of being so heavily dependent on interest income reported through the banking system, and genuinely could have effected an administrative breakthrough that could 'bring the tax to the people', is unclear: it had only some eight or nine months of operation before the outbreak of the Sino-Japanese War threw the National Government, and with it Nationalist finance and taxation, into chaos. But the intent behind the Direct Tax Administration it was clear: both consciously and unconsciously, it relied on the models of Customs, Salt, and Consolidated Tax to establish a prefectural, well insulated, rationalized organization staffed by well educated and highly motivated personnel that would reach far, deep, and equitably into society.

Although the Direct Tax Administration was beset with problems of reasonably matching its size and the wide scale of its domain, the land tax offered a still more serious set of challenges for Nationalist tax policy during the Nanjing Decade. Because the assessment and collection of the land tax continued as a highly localized affair not subject to any general standards or systematization, the effect of central government decisions regarding fiscal administration remained minimal for the peasantry, who comprised over 80 per cent of China's population. Reorganization and rationalization of the land tax was an item that centralizers everywhere recognized as a positive good, but the administrative obstacles in the way were formidable. The structural impediments to reorganization of the land tax were three: lack of accurate cadastral surveys, the opposition of entrenched interests in both local government and among local elites, and weak central capacity for enforcing the rationalization and reorganization to which it aspired.

Since the most recent national cadastral surveys had last been conducted in the late sixteenth century, well before the destruction and dislocations of the Taiping Rebellion, title deeds had been lost, and reclaimed waste land often went unregistered. The rich and influential in many cases managed to keep their holdings off the books and avoid the land tax altogether, and local administrators kept themselves going by levying *ad hoc* surtaxes on the basic land tax that, typically, the poorer and weaker were least able to avoid. Complete and accurate cadastral surveys were the prerequisite for seriously addressing the inequities and abuses in the administration of the land tax, but neither the central nor local governments had the vast amounts of personnel and liquid resources to carry out such a lengthy, expensive, and undoubtedly divisive project.[67]

The National Government lacked the resources and the projective power to effect any sort of direct reform or rationalization in China's countryside from above: the domain was too diffused, and the central personnel needed were far too many. Perhaps in tacit recognition of the limitations of what it could change, the Ministry of Finance 'delegated' the administration of the land tax to the provincial and county governments as 'local taxes' beyond the legitimate purview of the central government until well into the war, when inflation and the need to feed the army prompted the Guomindang to instruct the government to begin to collect grain tax in kind. While probably unavoidable, given the circumstances of the 1930s, this sort of 'power sharing' between the central Ministry of Finance and local governments produced the opposite effect of the Ministry of Finance's power sharing arrangements with Customs and the Salt Inspectorate. For the land tax, co-optation and formal incorporation of other groups did not strengthen the central Ministry of Finance. As surtaxes such as the ones cited for Fujian continued to grow, and local exactions remained largely unchecked by the Nanjing government, the uneasy co-optive strategy of power sharing with local notables in the countryside spelled the continued detachment of the central government from the millions of peasants over whom it theoretically governed.

## PERSONNEL AND INSTITUTION-BUILDING

The Nationalist Ministry of Finance's personnel policies in the 1930s were varied, and reflected its overall strategies of institutionalization. The Ministry of Finance attempted to promote technical expertise, efficiency, and responsiveness to higher authority, but the Ministry was so large that it operated as a confederation of semi-autononomous units and departments, each with its own policy jurisdiction, personnel office, informal recruitment networks, and *de facto* power over internal promotions. Technically, the Minister of Finance (in the period under consideration, either Song Ziwen or Kong Xiangxi) had to approve promotions and appointments above the level of section member, but in practice approval was seldom withheld.[68] Most sub-units of the Ministry of Finance were not able at the outset to generate the rigid insulation and highly bureaucratic civil service system that characterized the Salt Inspectorate and Customs Administration: aside from the Direct Tax Administration, civil service examinations seldom provided the primary means of entry into the Ministry of Finance. Further, the Ministry as a whole was less bureaucratized and stable with respect to personnel than were the Salt Inspectorate and the Customs Administration: only roughly one-half of the coveted 'recommended' (*jianren*) positions were awarded to those who were promoted from lower-level positions within the Ministry.[69]

Despite this initial lack of an institutionalized civil service and strong institutional boundaries, the Ministry of Finance continued to develop the trends underway in central government finance since the Yuan Shikai period, which pushed the Ministry to approximate at least some of the outcomes generated by the highly bureaucratic and institutionalized Salt and Customs Administrations. In drawing the bulk of its recruits from certain kinds of functionally oriented backgrounds in finance, economics, and practical administration, most working units sought to infuse their personnel with the values of centralization, efficiency, and high performance. Since the Ministry of Finance was widely recognized to be one of two most prestigious state organizations that rewarded talent (along with the Ministry of Foreign Affairs),[70] it did not lack a steady stream of highly qualified and well motivated recruits. In the words of one former division chief, 'it usually wasn't too much of a problem to train staff: most already had some sort of background in finance'.[71]

Even in the first years of the Nationalist regime, the Ministry of Finance's different units tended to select individuals who had very similar sorts of backgrounds as their predecessors in the Beiyang Ministry of Finance, and there was at least a general perception that a significant minority in the Ministry of Finance, particularly at upper levels, had come directly from the Beiyang Ministry of Finance.[72] Surviving records bear out this perception. Of a group of sixty-one Ministry of Finance section members recruited between 1928 and 1932, well over half, or thirty-three, had previous experience in either local finance or a consolidated tax branch office, and an additional seven had come directly from the Beiyang Ministry of Finance. Their lack of overt politicization is quite striking: even during these first years of the Nationalist regime, when the pressure to provide official positions for those who had 'served the revolution' was undoubtedly great, the Ministry of Finance seems to have avoided granting sinecures to clearly unqualified Party members or military figures. Of sixty-one individuals, only five indicated any sort of Party affiliation. The patterns of the small number of recommended and selected appointments from this sample were slightly different. Of the eleven individuals with 'recommended' (*jianren*) appointments, four had been involved with the Guomindang Revolutionary Government in Guangzhou, and all had experience working in finance, either in the Guangzhou Revolutionary Government or in local financial administrative organizations. These four higher-ranking 'selected' appointees (*jianren*) had closer ties to the Guomindang, with all four having served in the early days of the Guangzhou Government. But even they uniformly had a fair amount of practical experience in either prefectural branch offices or local financial administration.[73]

The Ministry of Finance also ignored the Examination Yuan rather less than most. The Examination Yuan began to supply the Ministry with noticeable numbers of new appointees in the mid- to late 1930s, and from 1936 on, with the creation of the Direct Tax Administration, the Ministry of Finance found it positively beneficial to utilize the 'examination route' as the preferred method of recruitment when it had a large number of openings. For the years between 1931 and 1941, only 209 candidates passed the upper civil service exam with a concentration in finance, and undoubtedly not all of the 209 took up appointments in the Ministry.[74]

But once the dust settled after the retreat to Chongqing during the war years, the Ministry of Finance carried on in the trajectory established with the creation of the Direct Tax Administration in 1936 by periodically requesting the Examination Yuan to hold 'special examinations' (*tezhong kaoshi*) at both the upper and basic levels for finance personnel to meet its increased staffing needs. Indeed, in the twelve months between the autumn of 1938 and the autumn of 1939, the Ministry of Finance had the Examination Yuan hold no less than three special finance personnel examinations, which qualified 413 individuals (181 at the upper and 232 at the basic level).[75] Put slightly differently, in just the first year of the wartime Nationalist administration in Chongqing, the Examination Yuan qualified nearly twice as many individuals at the specific request of the Ministry of Finance than it did via the 'general' upper and regular civil service examinations throughout the entire ten years between 1931 and 1941. This trend continued throughout the war years, with at least one, and often two or three, special finance examinations held in every year between 1939 and 1945.

Although the special exams (*tekao*) for finance personnel increased in importance during the Sino-Japanese War, the 'regular' examination route was never the primary path of recruitment into the Ministry during the Nanjing Decade. As was the case throughout the National Government organizations, the vast majority of individuals in the Ministry of Finance got their initial appointments through personal connections and private recommendation, and the informants who guessed that only about two or three per hundred came in through formal examination of any kind during the 1930s was probably quite accurate.[76]

The impressionistic evidence, however, suggests that, once one was in the door of the Ministry of Finance, personal connections counted for less. When compared with other state organizations during the same time period, the Ministry of Finance stands out as *not* particularly factionalized: there was little of the high turnover, personalism, and politicking that existed in other units.[77] When asked, some informants admitted that 'yes, there were informal groups, but one would be hard pressed to identify exactly who belonged with which group', or that 'within the Ministry, of course, some people got along better than others, but one couldn't really call that "factionalism": the really big divisions were outside the Ministry, not within the organization itself.'[78] With their technical and 'results' orientations, the members of the Ministry of Finance were perhaps unusually resistant to Party indoctrination. All interviewees who had worked in the Ministry of Finance insisted that Party membership was completely irrelevant to one's career, that 'one shouldn't project the importance of "the Party" back into the Guomindang period'; and one informant even suggested that by the early 1940s Party prestige had sunk so low that people tried to hide their Party membership from others in the Ministry.[79]

If Party indoctrination and overt factionalism were almost absent from the Ministry of Finance's working units, informal groups and personal relations with others in the Ministry continued to be very important. Unlike the Salt Inspectorate, where promotions were made almost exclusively on depersonalized criteria such as one's seniority in the organization, in most of the Finance units, promotions were made on a combination of personal connections and ability, which was defined as practical technical competence.[80] Although one couldn't do one's work well without being able to get along with one's immediate superior, it was generally agreed that, in the ultimate weightings of 'getting along' and 'ability', personal connections tended to be less important than performance and ability; for, 'if a promotion were made primarily on the basis of private connections, people would talk'.[81] Even without a strictly bureaucratic civil service system, superiors in the Ministry of Finance had every structural incentive to promote subordinates primarily on the basis of ability: section chiefs (kezhang) handled or delegated most of the Ministry's actual business, but the division chief (sizhang) was held responsible for failure.[82]

This, in combination with the relatively quantifiable nature of the Ministry of Finance's operations, led the Ministry of Finance to implement other schemes promoted by the Examination Yuan and the Ministry of Personnel. In 1934 the Ministry of Finance established its own temporary regulations for the evaluation of finance personnel, which were clearly based on the models then being touted by the Ministry of Personnel, and began to institute triennial reviews for senior staff and annual evaluations for regular staff.

Left to its own devices, the Ministry of Finance relied on a combination of its own determination of objective 'performance' and the categories suggested by the Ministry of Personnel, which were then linked to salary increases and promotions for in-house staff. The primary criterion on which office chiefs were evaluated was whether they met their obligations in terms of tax forwarded to superior offices: section chiefs, section members, and assistants were evaluated on the standard Ministry of Personnel format of 'work [gongzuo], behaviour [caoxing], and knowledge [xueshi]'.[83] Nor were the more technocratic aspects of entry level 'training' (xunlian) ignored: the Customs Administration had long had its own pre-entry training curriculum, and different sub-units of the Ministry of Finance, including the Consolidated Tax and the Direct Tax Administrations, both sought to emulate this model through their respective institutes in Shanghai and special training classes in Nanjing.

Even though the Ministry of Finance as a whole lacked the institutionally strong boundaries to set up an insulated, highly bureaucratized civil service in 1927–8, the functional requirements of the jobs that needed to be done, in combination with the technical and measurable nature of the work, slowly pushed the working units of the Ministry in the same direction as the Salt Inspectorate and Customs Administration—to systematically reward the competent, the hardworking, and the efficient.

### THE COLLAPSE OF STATE BUILDING: THE COLLAPSE OF FINANCE, 1938–1945

In a complicated tangle of cause and effect, both the National Government's efforts at state building and the Ministry of Finance's attempts at institution building were brought to the point of near collapse by the pressure of the Sino-Japanese War. The war knocked the heart out of the Ministry of Finance's institution-building strategies in two ways. First, with the Nationalists' military retreat to the interior provinces in late 1937, the government lost its tax base in the rich coastal areas of eastern China. The indirect taxes that the government so disproportionately relied on for its income in the Customs, Salt, and Consolidated Tax Administrations were hard hit by the Japanese advance and had slowed to a trickle by 1940. Virtually all the Customs collectorates were lost outright, as were the primary salt-producing areas in north Jiangsu and around Tianjin. Even the Consolidated Tax Administration lost 'upwards of 90 per cent of its revenue as most factories were concentrated in Shanghai, Wuhan, Qingdao, and Tianjin'.[84]

The shift in the government's fiscal fortunes in terms of taxable resources bases can be seen in Table 5.7. In 1936–7, total government revenue stood at roughly 125.1 million Y, of which the Customs (379 million Y), Salt (197 million Y), and Consolidated Tax Administrations (158 million Y) accounted for well over half (769 million Y). The Internal Revenue Administration's tobacco and wine tax, stamp tax, and mining tax added another 28 million Y and the new income tax a modest 7 million, while internal borrowing provided roughly one-fifth of the government's income (223 million Y), bank loans and overdrafts slightly over one-tenth (113 million Y), and 'miscellaneous' another 68 million Y. The contrast with the situation several years later, in 1940, when inflation was poised to take off, is clear. Total revenue, not adjusted for inflation, stood at 5,425 million Y; Customs revenues dropped precipitously by 85 per cent from 346 million Y in 1939 to 38 million Y in 1940; Salt brought in roughly 80 million Y (or less than half of its 1936–7 receipts); and Consolidated Taxes dropped to less than a third of what it had been bringing in in 1936–7 at 46 million Y. Meanwhile,

**Table 5.7.** National Government Income, 1936–1937 and 1940 (million yuan)

|  | 1936–7 | 1940 |
|---|---|---|
| Customs | 379 | 38 |
| Salt | 197 | 80 |
| Consolidated tax/manufacturing | 159 | 46 |
| Tobacco/wine | 15 | 24 |
| Stamps | 9 | 7 |
| Income tax | 7 | 44 |
| Mining | 4 | 2 |
| Domestic bonds/notes | 223 | 8 |
| Bank loans | 113 | 3,834 |
| Govt property and enterprises | 16 | 29 |
| Govt administrative receipts | 8 | |
| Profit on govt enterprises | 9 | |
| Penalties, fees, estate tax | | 9 |
| Public business and privilege taxes | | 4 |
| Contributions | | 33 |
| Revenue from previous years | 45 | 991 |
| Miscellaneous | 68 | 253 |
| TOTAL | 1,251 | 5,425 |

*Source*: after Arthur Young, *China's Wartime Finance and Inflation, 1937–45* (Cambridge, Mass.: Harvard University Press, 1965), 331–2, tables 39–40.

the assorted direct taxes, including income tax, excess profits and stamp taxes, increased to account for 76 million Y, while 'miscellaneous taxes' accounted for 253 Y million. By 1940 borrowing had increased in both absolute and relative terms to 3,824 million Y, or roughly two-thirds of the government's total revenue, while the annual budgetary deficit jumped from zero in 1936–7 to 3,963 million Y.[85]

Once ensconced in Chongqing, the National Government attempted to meet its wartime financial obligations through a mixture of deficit financing and augmenting its taxation presence in the hinterland of unoccupied China. The latter strategy was carried out by prefectural tax organizations like the Direct Tax, the Consolidated Tax and the Salt Administrations, although direct taxes grew in importance as the receipts from indirect taxes declined in the early years of the war. As the financial position of the government deteriorated and unchecked inflation took off in the early 1940s, the state established a vast tax organization that began to collect the grain tax as a central tax in kind in 1941, to supply the army with its basic food needs and to supplement the wages of civil servants which had been badly eroded by inflation.

Lastly, the government instituted a stop-gap and short-lived attempt to bring inflation under control by establishing government monopolies on the key commodities of sugar, salt, matches, and tobacco in 1942. Rather surprisingly, and certainly contrary to the perceptions both of the time and later, at least some of the tax units established or expanded during the Sino-Japanese War did a fair job in terms of strict 'effectiveness' (i.e. increasing the absolute amount of revenue remitted to the central government budget), especially considering the relative inexperience of the Guomindang in the interior and the National Government's shallow roots in the hinterland of Sichuan.

Far from 'not being able to do much of anything'[86] during the Sino-Japanese War, the Direct Tax Administration posted a tenfold increase in receipts between 1936–7 and 1940 (from 7 million Y in 1936–7 to 76 million Y in 1940), and a further ninefold increase to 6,478 million Y in 1944. Similarly, the Salt Administration revenues, after precipitously declining to a low of 61 million Y in 1939, began to recover at least somewhat as salt wells in the Zigong, Leshan, and Wutongqiao areas of Sichuan were more intensively tapped, with a substantial jump in receipts in 1941 to 296 million Y, and from there to increased extraction in terms of so-called salt surtaxes (from 1,202 million Y in 1943 to 13,439 million Y in 1944), so that the Salt Administration finished out the war more or less as it had begun: as one of the chief pillars of tax administration. However 'inefficient', bloated, and prone to waste and mismanagement the administration of the land tax in kind may have been from 1941 on, most observers agreed that it was certainly 'effective' in so far as it spared the government even higher levels of wartime inflation than otherwise would have been the case, while guaranteeing the armed forces a steady supply of food rations.[87]

Although the indirect commodity taxes of customs and consolidated tax declined sharply in both absolute and real terms during the early years of the Sino-Japanese War, in other arenas the raw tax receipts to the central government rose across the board, often quite substantially, throughout the war years. The Ministry of Finance was to some degree successful in intensifying pre-existing tax sources (salt and direct tax) while implementing some new ones (land tax in kind and wartime consumption tax). What ultimately drove the policies that led to fiscal and organizational de- institutionalization of the war years were factors over which the tax organizations of the Ministry of Finance had little control, rather than failure in the relatively restricted areas over which they could conceivably hope to exert control.

The combination of unrestrained spending on the military and on economic construction projects were decisions that were made outside the Ministry of Finance, and set in train a repetitive cycle of high rates of borrowing, sales of gold reserves, the printing of unbacked money, and the beginnings of hyperinflation. When inflation began to rocket out of control around 1940, this put increasing stress on the Ministry of Finance: even though its tax organizations collected more in absolute numbers, the rapid depreciation meant that the taxes that were collected were worth increasingly less in real terms and had to be converted to an *ad valorem* rather than flat rate tax, which multiplied the administrative difficulties. Worse, the external policy environment meant that tax receipts, no matter how 'effectively' brought in by the Ministry of Finance's assorted tax collectorates, could not meet the needs of the wartime government spending. The government increasingly resorted to inflationary deficit financing, and total tax revenue could bring in only enough to cover roughly 6 per cent of the government's expenditure over the course of the Sino-Japanese War (see Tables 5.8 and 5.9).[88]

For example, the Direct Tax Administration posted steady and impressive gains in the amounts of tax extracted throughout the Sino-Japanese War, as more direct taxes such as the business and inheritance taxes were added, more branch offices opened, and older direct taxes such as the income tax were collected more intensively. Despite the fact that the direct tax was always intended to be a percentage-based tax rather than a flat tax, between 1938 and 1945 the direct tax receipts still increased above the rate of inflation in only one year (1942): in all the other years of the Sino-Japanese War, the direct tax barely kept pace with inflation or even lagged behind it—suggesting that, for all the time and effort invested into deepening and strengthening the direct tax, the Direct Tax Administration only just matched the inflationary external environment, despite the rapid growth of the Direct Tax Administration from 158 individuals in mid-1937 to 'around 3,000' by 1945.[89] In other words, although the Direct Tax Administration cannot be accused of 'having done nothing' during the Sino-Japanese War—merely keeping up with the pace of inflation probably required heroic measures—what it did not manage was to keep ahead of the rapidly changing environment of wartime finance to build incrementally on its previous gains.

If pre-existing tax organizations such as the Direct Tax Administration barely kept up with inflation throughout the Sino-Japanese War, the Ministry of Finance's forays into more direct control of taxation and the economy via the establishment of government monopolies for assorted crucial commodities were still more problematic. Once inflation began to get out of hand in the early 1940s, the government, from a position of administrative weakness, decided to try to institute government monopolies for the production, taxation, and distribution of salt, sugar, tobacco, and matches in 1942 in order to both stabilize prices and increase tax revenues coming in to the government. Unfortunately, according to this set of criteria, the public monopolies failed at the outset. Except for sugar, the government never was able completely to take over production, never

**Table 5.8.** Direct Tax Receipts by Source, 1938–1945 (million yuan)

| | 1938 | 1939 | 1940 | 1941 | 1942 | 1943 | 1944 | 1945 |
|---|---|---|---|---|---|---|---|---|
| Income | 8 | 27 | 44 | 80 | 197 | 751 | 1,145 | 2,009 |
| Inheritance | | | | | 1 | 15 | 49 | 111 |
| Excess profit | | | 25 | 70 | 291 | 884 | 1,189 | 1,833 |
| Business | | | | | 610 | 1,785 | 3,032 | 7,318 |
| Stamp | 3 | 5 | 7 | 16 | 26 | 355 | 1,063 | 3,140 |
| TOTAL | 11 | 32 | 76 | 166 | 1,125 | 3,790 | 6,478 | 14,411 |

*Source:* Arthur Young, *China's Wartime Finance and Inflation, 1937–45* (Cambridge, Mass.: Harvard University Press, 1965), 332, table 40.

**Table 5.9.**   Price Index for Free China, 1938–1945

|      | Price index (June 1937 = 100) | % change from previous year |
|------|-------------------------------|-----------------------------|
| 1938 | 131                           | 31                          |
| 1939 | 220                           | 68                          |
| 1940 | 513                           | 133                         |
| 1941 | 1,296                         | 153                         |
| 1942 | 3,900                         | 201                         |
| 1943 | 12,541                        | 222                         |
| 1944 | 43,197                        | 244                         |
| 1945 | 163,160                       | 278                         |

*Source*: Chang Kia-ngau, *The Inflationary Spiral*, (New York and London: MIT Press and John Wiley, 1958), 371, Table A-2. Chang's data is based upon data compiled by the Directorate-General of Budgets, Accounts, and Statistics, published in the *China Statistical Abstract* (1948).

succeeded in setting retail prices to keep them stable, and thus was unable to increase its real take without passing on higher real prices to already disgruntled consumers.[90]

The government's need for more revenue, and more 'effectiveness' (the increase in absolute revenue collected almost irrespective of the administrative costs), pushed the Ministry of Finance's tax organizations to expand dramatically in size and numbers of personnel. Accurate numbers for the size of the entire Ministry of Finance in either the pre- or post-1937 period are difficult to come by. But the Direct Tax Administration grew by a factor of roughly twenty, from 157 to 3,000; the Salt Administration, despite losing much of its pre-war core, expanded at least threefold; and 1941 saw the establishment of an exceptionally personnel-intensive land tax administration starting from scratch, with over 6,900 collecting sub-offices established by the end of 1941 and with new personnel running into the tens of thousands.[91] The indirect evidence also points to an organization under enormous pressure from external demands, chaotic internal expansion, and inflation that hit those with fixed incomes (such as civil servants) particularly hard. Young and Chang both cite the high administrative costs of the wartime land tax administration, the difficulties of running things with so many young, inexperienced personnel, and the ravaging of salaries by the inflation of the 1940s.[92] Informants suggested an enormous turnaround in the recruitment and promotion practices of the pre- and post-1937 Nationalist government. Before the war, talented individuals were fighting to get *in*to prestige organizations like the Ministry of Finance; by the early 1940s, the Ministry of Finance was sending talent scouts out to the universities that had relocated in the interior to recruit students with any sort of background in finance or economics, whether they had graduated or not, because '[Finance] tasks were becoming more complicated by the day... and the need for personnel greater by the day' (*yewu rifan xuren riduo*).[93]

While the quality of entry-level personnel declined and the numbers concurrently swelled, efforts were made both within outside the Ministry to augment 'training' (*xunlian*) and bring about greater administrative capacity. During the Sino-Japanese War, Ministry-of-Finance-determined 'training', which in the pre-1937 period had concentrated almost exclusively on the functional/technical aspects of training, became increasingly conflated with another, highly politicized and militarized, vision of 'training' which had coalesced in the central party and military during the 1930s. The former version of 'training' was carried out by the ministries themselves, and assumed Weberian technocracy to be both the means and the end of state and institution building: the latter was an extra-ministerial movement with the explicit goal of 'militarization and partification' (*junshihua danghua*) of the entire state and body politic.[94]

In order to carry out the latter programme of militarization and politicization, a Central Training Corps (Zhongyang Xunliantuan) was established in Chongqing in 1939. The Central Training Corps's programme lasted for four weeks, and consisted of morning military drill, followed by lectures that explicated the pronouncements of Chiang Kai-shek and the wisdom of current government policy; late afternoons and evenings were spent on endless diary writing, group discussion, and self-criticism sessions. The first few sessions of the Central Training Corps were attended mostly by military men and high-level Party officials, but they soon expanded to encompass middle- to high-level civil servants, particularly those in the Ministry of Finance, who were assigned *en bloc* to participate in at least the 8th, 12th and 17th Central Training Corps's sessions, held in April 1940, March 1941, and October 1941.[95] Concurrently, the Ministry of Finance's own in-house training programmes began to take on the form, and to some extent the substance, of the Central Training Corps 'model' of training, by incorporating hefty doses of military drill as well as some degree of Party indoctrination to cultivate (*peiyang*) correct throughts.[96]

There is evidence that the technocrats in the Ministry of Finance attempted to resist partification quietly by adopting the surface rhetoric of Central Training Corps programme while in practice continuing to steer the curriculum of the lectures and small group discussions of the *xunlian* sessions towards functional technocracy.[97] But, whatever their quiet rearguard actions, the external environment during wartime was such that technocrats in the Ministry of Finance were unable openly to combat the movement in the direction of politicization and partificiation. *Xunlian* as partification and militarization made eminent sense as an institution-building strategy under resource-short wartime conditions: *xunlian* attempted 'heroically' to mobilize commitments from below while maintaining control from above by appealing to norms and values over incremental, slow, expensive technocratic training. Unfortunately for the Guomindang, inclusivist partification and militarization worked no better than piecemeal functional training as a strategy to generate institutional capacity in a state organization that had lost boundary maintenance and with it most of its quality control.

CONCLUSION

This chapter has illustrated how, in contrast to the Salt Inspectorate, the Ministry of Finance adopted a multi-tiered strategy of institution building that was directly analogous to the concurrent process of state building pursued by the National Government as a whole. The process was often unclear and messy, but during the 1930s the Ministry of Finance began to realize a number of the centralizing goals to which the earlier Beiyang Ministry of Finance had aspired without success.

On the positive side, the Ministry's success in implementing and extending the consolidated tax suggested that, within manageable domains, Inspectorate-style success could be approximated without either a foreign adviser presence or initially very rigid boundaries: that 'cover-over' strategies of centralization, co-optation, amalgamation, and efficiency orientation could be effective if the domain in question were limited enough for the organization to exert direct control over the external environment and some modicum of quality control within the organization. However, the Ministry's institution-building strategies produced but disappointing results in diffused domains where central control was difficult to establish, such as the land tax and direct tax during the 1930s.

The financial and institutional collapse engendered by the Sino-Japanese War illustrates the main shortcomings of top-down and technocratic strategies of institution building: centralization can be sustained only as long as resource bases are reliable, and viable technocracy is viable only in so far as quality control can be maintained and the political leadership in the external environment is willing to listen. Like the National Government of which it was a part, the Ministry of Finance needed a solid core from which to build and expand. When it lost the eastern provinces where it had established a fairly effective and rationalized tax administration by the mid-1930s, it also lost the a good part of the means by which it could continue to pursue its strategies of centralization, standardization, and expansion. Like the Beiyang Ministry of Finance, the Nationalist Ministry of Finance found that the best, most rationally 'scientific' programme could only be built on a reliable resource base with non-interventionist leadership. The

Nationalist Ministry of Finance certainly achieved more during the 1930s than had any previous central financial administration in 20th century China, but it was not enough to survive the loss of its resource core and the hyper-expansion of its internal organization during the Sino-Japanese War.

# 6

## The Ministry of Foreign Affairs:
## Institution-Building in a Generalist Organization

### INTRODUCTION

The Salt Inspectorate and the Ministry of Finance offer very clear examples of strategies for success in institution building. Each maintained a fairly high degree of insulation, which buffered the organization as it promoted professionalization and bureaucratization within. Depoliticization and insulation, however, did not occur either easily or automatically: the degree of real autonomy enjoyed depended on the organization's ability to 'deliver the goods' and effectively to carry out services necessary to the state. The Salt Inspectorate and Ministry of Finance's consistently high levels of performance were, in turn, favoured by two factors. First, both occupied themselves primarily with organizational tasks and technologies that were highly specific and divisible, with agreed upon measures of success. Second, each organization tended to focus on a fairly manageable domain, one in which the resources available to the organization were sufficient to effect noticeable results. When the tasks at hand far outstripped organizational capacity (such as the Ministry of Finance's attempts to institute a progressive income tax), even an otherwise successful organization such as the Ministry of Finance suffered from embarrassing failure.

The evidence from these two cases suggests strongly that in turbulent or hostile environments it is technically based organizations that have the best chance of becoming well institutionalized. The results they achieve are clear and unambiguous; the means by which they attain their goals are specific and divisible. The finite, results-oriented criteria of organizational success is doubly important. It enables the organization to depoliticize itself internally and ward off external, personally motivated incursions. But many, if not most, state organizations in Republican China (and in other developing countries) do not possess a technical orientation with a high degree of specificity. Are these more generalist organizations, dealing with education, culture, and social welfare, then automatically destined to remain poorly institutionalized, highly politicized, and generally ineffective?

In so far as the data allow, the present chapter attempts to explore this question by focusing on a non-technical organization in Nationalist China, the Ministry of Foreign Affairs. This ministry offers an example of a seeming paradox: a fairly well institutionalized, high-prestige organization with an explicitly generalist ethic. In order to contrast the Ministry of Foreign

Affairs with other non-technically based organizations, much more fragmentary findings on the Ministry of the Interior are presented briefly.

## THE MINISTRY OF FOREIGN AFFAIRS: MULTIPLE AGENDAS IN SERVICE OF A WEAK STATE

As a case study of institution building and state building, the Ministry of Foreign Affairs presents a mass of seeming contradictions. Throughout the Republican period, the Ministry of Foreign Affairs served a state that, in the international context in which it operated, can only be described as weak; yet it remained a high-status organization, attracting the best educated young men in all of China and garnering the admiration of the international diplomatic community. In the 1920s, when the minimal attributes of a central state scarcely existed, the Beiyang Ministry of Foreign Affairs functioned surprisingly well, even managing to make incremental progress towards the revocation of some of the unequal treaties and, despite problems with implementation, to wrest from the Great Powers a general statement of principle to phase out the unequal treaties concluded at the Washington Conference in 1921–2. In the 1930s, an era in which the Guomindang and National Government placed great stress on training technocrats and engineers and on fostering 'practical administration', the Ministry of Foreign Affairs remained an unreconstructed bastion of generalist elitism. In the 1940s, when the technocrats in the Ministry of Finance were moving to dissociate themselves from the increasingly discredited Guomindang, Foreign Affairs quietly made Party membership one of the things 'expected' of career officers.

Throughout these decades, the Ministry of Foreign Affairs carried on in an environment that can only be described as highly volatile while retaining its prestige, and consistently eliciting the loyalty and staying power of some of the best educated, most sophisticated, and most urbane men in China. The Ministry of Foreign Affairs combined elements that in other organizations were fundamentally incompatible. It was characterized by a generalist orientation, by goals that were often non-specific and non-divisible, by at best mixed control over its policy domain, and by eventual *de facto* acceptance of the norm of the Party membership. Yet it maintained its high status well into the troubled 1940s.

In addition to being domestically weak and having only partial control over the vast territory of China, Republican-era Chinese governments were dealt an exceptionally poor hand in terms of the international environment in which they operated: lingering Western imperialism was combined with a Japanese expansionism determined to maintain recently won imperialist privileges and exceptionally hostile to rising Chinese nationalism. As the organization that represented China to foreign governments and was entrusted with the day-to-day management of establishing China's credibility as a full member in the club of sovereign states, the Ministry of Foreign Affairs was critically important to the still weak Chinese state.

Although the Ministry of Foreign Affairs, like the Ministry of Finance, carried out functions vital to the state, there were substantial differences between the two. The Ministry of Finance was certainly 'responsive' to outside demands by political leaders (chiefly to raise more taxes), but important political and military leaders outside the Ministry of Finance rarely concerned themselves with the details of how the Ministry of Finance's assorted tax administrations came up with the revenue. The Ministry of Foreign Affairs served as an executor of foreign policy, as did the Ministry of Finance for tax collection. But the generalist nature of foreign policy meant that, when top politicians were moved to involve themselves in foreign policy, large chunks of basic policy setting (particularly policy having to do with China's alignments and 'tilt' towards foreign powers), and often a lot of the details as well, were ceded to top political officials and palace favourites with limited diplomatic experience. Chiang Kai-shek in particular frequently stepped in to reset the broad train of foreign policy (e.g. the appeasement of Japan in the mid-1930s); Chiang's sending of Song Ziwen as a personal emissary in 1933 to the United States to negotiate the Cotton and Wheat Loan, and Madame Chiang's trip to the United States to galvanize support for China's war effort in 1942–3 were also legendary. Unlike the Ministry of Finance and other 'technical' state organizations, the Ministry of Foreign Affairs operated in a domain that was inherently more 'political'. Ends and means were infinitely less clear-cut, and the inherently high visibility of diplomatic initiatives was more likely to attract the attention of political leaders.

Despite the frequent changes in alignment and 'tilt' initiated at the top and a rather unstable leadership during the turbulent 1930s, the Ministry of Foreign Affairs, like the Ministry of Finance and the Salt Inspectorate, was characterized by possession of a set of exceptionally consistent organizational goals from the 1920s to the 1940s: fully reclaiming all aspects of a fully sovereign state by doing away with unequal treaties, concessions, and extraterritoriality, securing international recognition of China's borders, and managing threats to China's security (chiefly Japanese expansionism) through a combination of bilateral relationships and broad appeals to the international community. Unlike technically based organizations such as the Ministry of Finance, whose tasks inherently lent themselves to measurement and specific breakdown, the Ministry of Foreign Affairs pursued a broad set of activities that ranged from the totally bureaucratic (e.g. issuing passports and dealing with consular affairs) to those that were not completely bureaucratized but were amenable to precedent and step-by-step breakdown (e.g. as treaty rewriting, negotiations for retaking foreign concessions, and the painstaking legalese of border delineation), to the highly general (e.g. representing China's interests abroad, containing Japan, making China an intelligible member of the international community, and reacting to assorted foreign relations crises as they occurred). But the agendas were broadly consistent, as were strategies and styles of implementation and the personnel who did the implementing over an exceptionally long period of time.

As part of a larger government that most Western scholarship has hitherto not treated overly generously, the Ministry of Foreign Affairs is often described as perhaps having had good intentions and relatively qualified personel, making some incremental progress in negotiating the conclusions of some of the unequal treaties, but ultimately, like the government of which it was a part, weak, ineffective, and unable to meet the challenges that it faced, at most scoring diplomatic successes only when other powers such as Britain and the United States were in an already conciliatory mood. In short, the argument goes, over the long term, weakness led to more weakness and overall ineffectiveness.[1]

On the contrary, when one considers China's position of military and political weakness throughout the Republican period, the enormity of the tasks at hand and the limited means for dealing with them—revision of unequal treaties, border delineation, managing alignments, representing China abroad as a fully sovereign and sympathetic member in the family of nations, and containing Japan—the Ministry of Foreign Affairs performed astonishingly well in all of these areas except the last. Indeed, if the Nationalist Ministry of Foreign Affairs was unable to contain Japanese expansionism, this could hardly be perceived to be a particularly unique failing, as neither the near unanimous censure of the League of Nations, increasing American hostility, the Nationalist military, nor ultimately the Japanese domestic political system itself was able to curb Japanese expansionist militarism. When one turns to these other activities, even a cursory review suggests that, far from being an ineffective and weak organization, the Ministry of Foreign Affairs was exceptionally adept at manoeuvring and using whatever means it had at its disposal to negotiate favourable bilateral arrangements, to present China in a favourable light abroad, and, if not to contain Japan, then at least to diplomatically and morally isolate Japan, through both bilateral ties and the multilateral forum of the League of Nations.

The tools employed by the diplomats in the Ministry of Foreign Affairs were those of a non-status-quo power attempting to make itself intelligible and sympathetic to an inherently conservative and status quo international system: knowledge of the 'rules of the game', particularly international law and the use of precedent; participation in the big international conferences of the period and in the League of Nations; moral suasion by presenting Chinese nationalism and full sovereignty as just and understandable in a greater evolutionary order; and playing very adeptly on the ambivalent sensibilities of those who represented the status quo through reassurances about their 'interests' (e.g. property rights and bringing the Chinese legal system up to a standard that foreigners need not fear) while appealing to both 'objective' standards of fairness and the power of domestic Chinese nationalism. An obviously aggressive and increasingly militarized neighbour such as Japan, one that at best had only minimal commitment to the rules of the emerging international order, could of course be resistant to even the most artful diplomacy when confronted with a change in a status quo perceived as unfavourable. Diplomacy as opposed to force of arms presumes that there is some possible range in the issues under discussion that both sides can manage to agree on, and the way Japan increasingly defined national interest in the 1920s and 1930s put it on a collision course with Chinese nationalism and self-determination. If one leaves aside the management of a bellicose Japan, the fallout from the bold but diplomatically disastrous adventure in 1929 involving a raid on the Soviet consulate in Harbin, and a brief takeover of the Russian-controlled Chinese Eastern Railway, the Ministry of Foreign Affairs more than held its own in the international community throughout the better part of the Republican period, in service to the Chinese state, astonishingly so in light of the state's domestic and international weakness.

## GOALS AND STRATEGIES OF DIPLOMATIC IMPLEMENTATION

Whatever the shifts in alignment and 'tilt' over the period between the 1920s and the late 1940s, the professional diplomats in the Ministry of Foreign Affairs held to a strikingly consistent set of agendas and sub-goals throughout the Republican period, and consistently resorted to some mix of three basic strategies of diplomacy: (1) taking advantage of the 'wave' of Chinese nationalism and anti-imperial sentiment, and representing Chinese nationalism and full sovereignty as the natural, necessary, and just outcome in the greater evolutionary scheme of national development; (2) the tools of international law and precedence; and (3) a quite astonishing persistence in actual negotiations.

Since the post-imperial Chinese state was not fully sovereign even within its own putative borders, and was saddled with the provisions of unequal treaties, the first, and most consistently pursued, goal of all Republican-era ministries of foreign affairs was fully to recover the rights of a sovereign state: ending unequal treaties and renegotiating on the basis of equality, abolishing foreign concessions and bringing these areas under Chinese government control, and phasing out extraterritorial privileges whereby foreigners in China were not subject to Chinese law—a state of affairs exceptionally far from reality at the beginning of the Republican period. Negotiating the recovery of Chinese sovereignty depended on the above mentioned mix of strategies: taking advantage of historical opportunities, appealing to international forums, and day-to-day dogged patience in negotiating through the conventions of international law to exploit ambiguities either in the text of the original treaty or in more recent international conventions.

As an example of the first strategy, after Germany was defeated in the Great War, the Beiyang Ministry of Foreign Affairs abrogated the standing unequal treaty, negotiated a new one based on equality, and did not permit the Germans to regain either their concessions in Shandong or their extraterritorial privileges. And when the Guomindang was in the process of coming to power on the basis of popular anti-colonial nationalism, it extraordinarily and speedily negotiated the rendition of the British concession in Hankou 'without a shot being fired' in a matter of weeks in the early months of 1927.[2] Once the Nanjing regime had enlisted the services of many of the skilled Beiyang Ministry of Foreign Affairs personnel, the latter were quick to sense the historical opportunities brought forth by what one might call the 'Hankou precedent'. This clearly established a sort of historical momentum towards rights recovery in all spheres in the late 1920s. The National Government unilaterally declared tariff autonomy, and followed through with a series of tariff hikes. The Ministry of Finance's takeover of Maritime Customs and the Salt Inspectorate in 1927–8 proceeded with little more than a flurry of protest in the Western language press. And between 1927 and 1931, a large number of foreign concessions and leased territories, including the British concessions at Hankou, Jiujiang, Jinjiang, and Xiamen, the Belgian concession at Tianjin, and the British-leased territory of Weihaiwei, were all returned to the National Government.

Historical opportunities and momentum were all well and good, but by themselves they did not suffice to turn China into a fully sovereign state and a full player in the emerging international system. As an example of the second strategy of 'bringing China to the international community', Shi Zhaoji (Alfred S. K. Sze), chief Chinese delegate to the Washington Conference in 1921–2, aided by the other members of the Chinese delegation (Wang Chonghui, Gu Weijun [V. K. Wellington Koo], and Yan Huiqing) argued hard, and ultimately persuasively, with 'the great statesmen of the time—Charles Evans Hughes (1862–1948), Aristide Briand (1862–1932), Arthur James Balfour (1848–1930), and Shidehara Kijuro (1872–1951),— for the creation of a new Asian order in which the Powers in concert agreed to a gradualist process of acceptance of Chinese nationalism by the phasing out of foreign concessions, extraterritoriality, and foreign privilege, while providing continual reassurances that stressed China's commitment to international law, its avoidance of unilateral action, and its protection of foreign property.

The Washington System, which was put together with the active participation of Chinese diplomats, was widely perceived to be a diplomatic success at the time. And, although it foundered several years later owing to a combination of France's unwillingness to ratify the treaties and the increasingly militant nationalism and civil war in China itself in the mid-1920s,[3] the principles set forth at the Washington Conference provided the key set of referents to which the Nationalists would return to add legitimacy to its claims for treaty revision and rights recovery once it came to power in 1927–8.

The third strategy, namely a grinding, wearing patience in negotiations, flowed naturally out of some combination of a sense of historical opportunities and the utilization of precedent and international law. Certainly, there was a general lack of political will on the part of the Western powers (particularly Britain and the United States) to fight to maintain continued foreign privilege in the late 1920s and early 1930s; but without the negotiating skills and determination of the Chinese, these changes almost certainly would not have taken place when they did. Chinese diplomats were canny negotiators who were skilled in both legal precedence and interpersonal psychology and were widely recognized by their opposite numbers to be so.

THE RENDITION OF WEIHAIWEI

To some degree, all three of these strategies (i.e. the appeal to historical inevitability, recourse to interpreting international agreements, and patience in long, drawn-out negotiations) were in evidence in the talks surrounding the rendition of the British possession of Weihaiwei, on the Shandong coast. Weihaiwei was a small leased territory, whose primary use for the British was as a summer retreat for the British navy and expatriates. It was unimportant enough, both strategically and in terms of resident foreigners, to be slated for rendition from the days of the Washington Conference, at which Lord Balfour had publicly declared that Weihaiwei would be returned to China 'under suitable conditions'. The conditions agreed to between Lord Balfour and Shi Zhaoji in Washington included continued British access to the port of Weihaiwei and use of naval facilities, and adequate representation of foreign interests in municipal matters.

On the basis of the Balfour Declaration at Washington, an entire agreement for the rendition of Weihaiwei was concluded between Britain and the Beiyang Ministry of Foreign Affairs and was literally awaiting the signatures for ratification in Beiyang when Feng Yuxiang's coup of November 1924 threw the Beiyang government into turmoil; thereafter, the offer was withdrawn pending what the British considered to be sufficiently stable political conditions.[4] 'Suitable conditions' in terms of political stability were a long time in coming, as Shandong was one of the worst bandit and warlord-ravaged provinces in all of China in the mid- to late 1920s.

The British themselves admitted, although certainly not publicly, that 'they wanted to get Weihaiwei off their hands', but, much as they wished to do so, they were markedly reluctant to turn Weihaiwei over to the murderous, rapacious regime of the Shandong warlord Zhang Zongchang, and they were not sufficiently confident of the Guomindang regime's control over the province of Shandong to agree to the immediate rendition that the 'historical momentum' of 1927–8 might suggest.[5] What 'suitable conditions' for the rendition of Weihaiwei meant (in the original language that promised the eventual rendition of Weihaiwei) was obviously in the eye of the beholder, and there were differences within individual branches of the British government as well as between the British and Chinese governments on this question. Two years later, in 1929, bureaucratic infighting between the Colonial Office, which wanted to postpone the rendition of Weihaiwei until political conditions in the province were far more stable, and the Foreign Office, which worried that, if popular Chinese nationalism began to agitate in favour of immediate rendition, the British would get out of Weihaiwei with their reputations considerably more tarnished than would otherwise be necessary, was still going strong, and the status of Weihaiwei had not been decided.[6]

In late May 1929, Miles Lampson, the British ambassador, was authorized by the Foreign Office to ask Wang Zhengting, Minister of Foreign Affairs, if he (Wang) was prepared to sign the text of the 1924 agreement on the rendition of Weihaiwei, which provided for immediate rendition to the Chinese government but guaranteed mooring rights, British navy access, some sort of representation of foreigners on the municipal committee, and a number of buildings designated for exclusive British naval use. Wang responded that all was well 'except for a few outstanding questions about prior mooring rights and specially reserved buildings'; he then engaged in a 'lengthy fencing bout in the course of which [Lampson] attempted to ascertain the precise nature of the modifications he desired without in any way committing to discussing them while he [Wang Zhengting] endeavored to nail [him] down to agreeing or refusing to enter negotiations'.[7] A month later, in a formal interview attended by three representatives from the Ministry of Foreign Affairs and three representatives from the British Legation, Wang Zhengting dropped the bombshell that, since Chinese Navy was planning to turn Weihaiwei into its chief port, it would be impossible for the Chinese government to allow the British navy use of

Weihaiwei as a summer resort; nor could facilities be loaned to the British navy. Lampson, flabbergasted, responded firmly that these were no minor details, that Wang was, in effect, completely tearing up the draft agreement, and that no further discussions were possible until Lampson had received instructions from his government.[8]

In terms of strategy, first by being vague and then by citing the 'incontrovertible' right of a sovereign state to quarter its fleet where it deemed most appropriate, Wang Zhengting was negotiating from a rare position of strength, and making a play to maximize potential gains and to get Weihaiwei returned to the Chinese government virtually unconditionally. It was a gamble that did not pay off in the short term, as the British refused to negotiate on this basis on grounds of principle. But the downside costs of the gamble not paying off were low and the upside gain was probably perceived to be high. Since there was little to be lost in trying (aside from momentary irritation on the part of the British, who in any case were going to have to return to the negotiating table since they had promised the rendition of Weihaiwei at some point in the future), it was quite probably a rational and astute strategy.

Moreover, Wang Zhengting's failure to get the leased territory back virtually unconditionally does not seem to have irrevocably poisoned future negotiating sessions: apparently without hard feelings on either side, the British and the Chinese negotiators sat down the following year, and 'after several hard negotiating sessions' hammered out a signed agreement that dropped all mention of the Chinese Navy turning Weihaiwei into its primary port, provided that Britain would be granted the free use of the territory's naval facilities for ten years with an option of renewal, and promised that foreign property owners would be given new perpetual leases on their property, with compensation to be owed should the government ever decide to close the port. In return, the British turned over the territory, all the government land and infrastructure (some of which the British government had invested in considerably over the previous thirty years), and all the assets that it managed, effective on 1 October 1930[9]—in short, concluding with more or less the provisions of the 1924 agreement.

The British, for their part, were not entirely convinced of the political stability of Shandong in 1930, when the rendition agreement was signed. But they were relieved to get out of Weihaiwei before popular anti-British sentiment was set in motion over British foot-dragging on the issue of Weihaiwei, and were satisfied to have concluded at least a ten-year guarantee of naval access to the port.

Thus, in the case of the rendition of Weihaiwei (and the eventual rendition of the leased territory was never in question—only the *terms* of the rendition were subject to negotiation), Chinese diplomats did not get everything that they asked for; but they showed themselves willing to take a chance to hurry along what they perceived to be the historical momentum (and British lack of resolve) towards full Chinese sovereignty, they argued the fine points of the original Convention for the Leasehold of Weihaiwei and the gray areas of the Balfour–Shi general statement on Weihaiwei, and they certainly proved themselves to be astute and tenacious negotiators over the course of some three years before the details were finally worked out and officially stamped by all concerned.

## THE MANCHURIAN CRISIS AND DIPLOMACY AT THE LEAGUE OF NATIONS, 1931–1933

With respect to China's most pressing problem, namely managing Japanese aggression, the options were rather more limited, as the Japanese were paranoid about the implications of rising Chinese nationalism for their relatively recently won concessions and privileges, particularly in the Three Eastern Provinces (Manchuria) and in north China, and were much less willing than the West Europeans or Americans to negotiate with even a pretence of formal equality between the two sides. To complicate matters even further, events would prove that the Japanese government did not necessarily speak with one voice even after having negotiated agreements.

Once the Manchurian Crisis broke out in late September 1931, despite the unpopularity of the strategy with Chinese activists and Nationalists, the National Government did the only thing that it really could do, given the superior military power of the Japanese and their marked lack of willingness to negotiate in a manner that could in any way be squared with the domestic requirements of Chinese nationalism. It had Gu Weijun, who fortuitously was sitting as China's chief representative to the League in a recently won rotating seat on the Council of the League, formally appeal to the League of Nations on the Manchurian dispute.

China's appeal to the League was not merely on grounds of 'fairness' and 'justice' (that its territory was being violated with impunity), but instead was based on the strictly legal grounds that the original terms of the Charter of the League of Nations were being violated. The Chinese delegation to the League of Nations could legitimately have raised Article X, which called for the respect of the territorial and existing political independence of all members of the League, or Article XII, which held that any dispute between members of the League likely to lead to rupture should be submitted to the League for arbitration or judicial settlement by the Council. But it submitted its complaint on the basis of Article XI, which called for the 'Council to take immediate steps to prevent the further development of a situation endangering the peace of nations', largely because this was the only article that was likely to get the Council to convene immediately.[10]

Veteran Beiyang diplomat Yan Huiqing (W. W. Yen), who along with Gu Weijun and Shi Zhaoji served as the chief Chinese delegates to the League of Nations throughout the Manchurian Crisis, argued that:

naturally, it is for the League itself in the first instance to construe and apply its own fundamental law... [that] the line of least resistance, which has been followed thus far in this as other matters, has been closed by the march of events. Nothing short of a courageous and firm stand now seems possible if the Covenant [of the League of Nations] is to command respect... any ultimate adjustment of Sino-Japanese relations with a view to permanent peace must not only safeguard all rights of third parties, but also be in strict accord with the principles laid down in the Covenant, the Pact of Paris and the Nine-Power Treaty... the League must either reject the Japanese contention [that a disclaimer of permanent territorial ambitions divests one of all aggressive import] or write its Covenant down to a pious declaration that aggression depends on the self-asserted state of mind of the aggressor, thus converting the Covenant from a guarantee of peace into an invitation to war.[11]

By arguing an integrationist conception of China's inviolable territory (that Manchuria 'has from time immemorial belonged to the Chinese national domain; historically, ethnically and politically, it is an integral part of China... repeatedly recognized by the international circles in all treaties bearing on the subject'),[12] the Chinese diplomats fought for, and largely received, international recognition of the inviolability of Chinese territory based on the borders existing at the time of the late Qing dynasty—quite apart from the fact that the Three Eastern Provinces had been open to Han Chinese settlers only for the previous generation or so, that Japan had an accretion of special privileges in Manchuria that dated from only slightly after the restrictions on Han migration were lifted, and that the region known as Manchuria had been run virtually as a separate fiefdom for much of the Republican period with nominal central government control, if any. It is no small measure of their success that they managed to get the League of Nations to swing into action by appointing an independent fact-finding body that came to be known as the Lytton Commission to actually go to Manchuria to investigate the dispute. And they astutely pledged their government in advance to abide by the findings and recommendations of the Commission.

Beginning in April 1932, the members of the Lytton Commission spent roughly one month in China, six weeks investigating conditions in 'Manchukuo', another three weeks in Beijing to begin to organize the materials collected, a final ten days in Japan, and the remainder of the summer to write up the findings. The Lytton Report, when it came out, pulled few punches and largely sided with China's version of events. While it recognized Japan's commercial and strategic interests in Manchuria, it also accepted China's claim to Manchuria as part of its territory and was sympathetic to Chinese nationalism and rights recovery. As for the disputed events of the autumn of 1931, it found no evidence of Japanese legitimate self-defence in the either the original outbreak of hostilities or the continuing military campaigns that drove out the Chinese administration; it discovered that there was no popular Chinese support for the new regime, and described the establishment of "Manchukuo" as impossible without the presence of Japanese troops and the activities of Japanese officials.[13]

The Lytton Report ultimately served as the basis for final report of a specially convened Committee of Nineteen, which recommended a set of proposals to settle the Manchurian dispute in February 1933. Against the backdrop of Japanese recognition for the Manchukuo regime and rumours of a Japanese invasion of the province of Rehe, when the vote came to the floor, all members of the League voted to adopt the report, with the exception of the Japanese, who thereupon left the League forever, and the Thais, who abstained.[14]

Despite the *de facto* hiving off of the Three Eastern Provinces, no country other than Japan ever recognized 'Manchukuo' until Germany, in alliance with Japan, did so in 1938. If it was quite beyond them to actually get the League and the major powers to put their strength where their sympathies were, the Chinese diplomats of the Nationalist Ministry of Foreign Affairs had done a brilliant job in mobilizing world opinion and isolating Japan in an international, multilateral forum through a combination of genuinely having most of the 'facts' on their side, and a translation of those facts into a generally accepted international opinion through recourse to the independent fact-finding commission, appeals to previous international conferences that guaranteed the territory of the Three Eastern Provinces to China, and superior diplomatic manoeuvring among the delegates to the League and in most of the world press.

The Chinese delegates to the League of Nations consciously made themselves and their claims for Chinese nationalism both intelligible and sympathetic to the outside world in a way that the Japanese delegation was never able to manage with quite the same alacrity. In the words of Lord Lytton, 'The Chinese are so articulate—they talk beautiful English and French and can express themselves clearly. With the Japanese it was a surgical operation to extract each word...'[15] Clear expression on the part of Chinese diplomats of this generation may not have made the ultimate difference in the League's eventual censure of Japan, but possessing a cadre of confident, prestigious diplomats who moved easily in international society certainly did not hurt China's cause.

## BOUNDARY DELINEATION: THE ACTIVITIES OF THE SINO-BURMESE BOUNDARY COMMISSION, 1935–1937

The Chinese diplomatic mix of righteous nationalism, appeal to international 'neutral' bodies, knowledge of international law and convention, use of precedent, and grinding patience through protracted negotiations were very much in evidence in the sphere of boundary delineation, particularly in the drawn-out activities of the Sino-Burmese Boundary Commission, constituted in 1934 to fix the border formally along large parts of the Yunnan–Burma frontier.

The problems of border delineation between Burma and Yunnan encompassed virtually every imagineable obstacle: rough country that was impassable to surveying parties during the rainy season; incomplete and unclear maps attached to the original demarcations of the border in 1897 which gave rise to legitimately differing interpretations between the British and the Chinese as to where the border ought to be; the British claiming as Burmese territory everything to the west of the so-called 'Scott line', which was surveyed in 1897, and the Chinese claiming everything to the east of the 'Liuzhen line', which was considerably to the west of where the Scott line was thought to run. To complicate matters even further, this remote frontier was one in which even the provincial government of Yunnan (and much less the central government in Nanjing) had but little control over the paramilitary activities of ethnically Chinese irregulars called the 'Yunnan Province Southwest Frontier Protection League', which made frequent raids into territory that, given the ambiguities of the original maps, could be considered part of British Burma.

Finally, at the beginning of the process of border delineation there were in existence several Chinese sources of differing vintage and provenance that proposed wildly different perameters for where the boundary 'ought' to be set, ranging from only slightly to the west of the undemarcated area to so far to the west that this putative border would bring Chinese territory nearly to Mandalay.[16]

With a disputed boundary and the existence of ill-controlled Chinese irregulars in the area, it was in everyone's interest to get the border fixed once and for all, and the Ministry of Foreign Affairs opened communications to the British on this question of border delineation in a conciliatory vein: 'that the question of the demarcation of the Burma–Yunnan border has been shelved for many years, and it is urgently desired that a settlement should be taken in hand', but that '[the people of China] should not deliberately indulge in talk calculated to give rise to excitement and to stir up trouble in the friendly relations between the two countries regardless of reason and commonsense'.[17]

Several weeks later Xu Mo, the Vice-Minister for Foreign Affairs, formally communicated his government's desire to verify and demarcate the Scott line in accordance with the Anglo-Chinese convention and the Sino-Burma Treaty of 1897.[18] It was speedily agreed between the Foreign Office and the Ministry of Foreign Affairs that a joint boundary commission would be established to determine on the ground and to fix on the map the line presented by the 1897 Convention, on the presumption that, once fixed, the line would form the basis for the subsequent negotiation of adjustments to the border. The Ministry of Foreign Affairs requested, and got, League of Nations assistance in finding a neutral chair of the Commission, a Swiss engineer by the name of Colonel Isélin, who had served as the chair of the Iraqi–Syria Frontier Commission in 1933. In addition, each side presented two commissioners: the British sent M. J. Clague of the Indian Civil Sevice, Commissioner of the Federated Shan States, and F. S. Grose of the Burma Frontier Service, while the Ministry of Foreign Affairs sent two advisors to the Ministry of Foreign Affairs' own Treaty Commission, Liang Yugao and Yin Mingde; in addition, each side had an accompanying surveying party, although the Chinese surveying contingent was much larger than was the British.[19]

The Commission set up camp at a remote site near the disputed boundary in a village called Hohsawn in December 1935 to commence work. From all the evidence, Liang and Yin were from the outset tough negotiators who seized on every available ambiguity in the original mapping and surveying to remake the Scott line in a way that was favourable to increasing the territory on the Chinese side of the border. In the 1935–6 season of negotiation, they brought technical issue after technical issue before Isélin to adjudicate: they successfully challenged large chunks of the putative Scott line by arguing, on the basis of current landscape and the original maps, that the Scott party could not possibly have visited some of the areas where it had fixed the border; and through use of legal logic and a tribunal style of questioning they destroyed the credibility of virtually every local witness that the British brought before Isélin to give their claims based on conflicting details in old maps substance. The British, of course, attempted similar tactics with regard to Chinese witnesses and interpretations of old maps.

There was little that was conciliatory or 'soft' about this first season of technical negotiations.[20] Indeed, the British were so disgusted with the degree to which the neutral Commissioner ruled so often in favour of the Chinese arguments that they considered trying to have him replaced between the first season and the second, fretting in July 1936 that 'the Chairman has conceded to the Chinese along the northern part of the undemarcated frontier a vast salient that cuts into the heart of territory administered by Burma in the last two years'.[21] Needless to say, Colonel Isélin was more than acceptable to the Ministry of Foreign Affairs, who ultimately agreed to pick up half of his off-season salary.

Surveying and adjudication commenced again once the rains stopped in January 1937. A second season of work in the first half of 1937 ground along slowly, with a joint report completed in April. Although the finalization of the border setting was disrupted by the outbreak of the Sino-Japanese War in mid-1937, it still took another *four* years of negotiations between the Foreign Office and the Ministry of Foreign Affairs for a final agreement to be worked out, and the one that was eventually agreed upon was largely favourable to China, ceding to it roughly two-thirds of the disputed territory, and allowing Chinese joint participation in any mining concerns the British might establish in an area outside of the boundary dispute but close to China's historic interests in the area.[22] Incrementalism, recourse to international norms, and an ability to grind down the opposition were strategies that lent themselves particularly well to the technicalities of border delineation, and in this sphere the Ministry of Foreign Affairs truly excelled.

As it pursued its multiple agendas of rights recovery, border delineation, managing alliances and the containment of Japan, and continued to represent China and its interests to foreign countries, the Ministry of Foreign Affairs' organizational goals ranged widely in terms of specificity. The stages (and therefore measurable progress) in renegotiating unequal treaties with the Western powers or coming up with protocol parameters for resolving border disputes were both clearly definable and measurable. There were, after all, finite numbers of foreign concessions and leased territories to be retaken, of unequal treaties to be renegotiated, and of border issues to be agreed on. The larger issues of managing Japan were considerably more diffused, and 'success', even if it existed, was often difficult to correlate with diplomatic initiatives. But the Ministry of Foreign Affairs diplomats in the Republican period were exceptionally adept at utilizing international forums and mobilizing world sympathy for China and against Japanese aggression.

The Ministry of Foreign Affairs' control over its domain was thus a peculiar mix. In terms of external orientation in the wider international community, it certainly could not 'control' policy or outcomes, but it did play the game well and influence world opinion. Domestically, too, the picture was mixed: at the very highest levels, diplomatic initiatives were regularly taken out of its hands by the likes of Chiang Kai-shek, Song Ziwen, and Song Meiling, but in many other ways it had a practical monopoly over its domestic domain. The Ministry of Foreign Affairs was truly the only organization capable of adequately representing China in the international diplomatic community, and, if often it did not decide on the broad thrust of policy (particularly with respect to alignments and strategies of managing Japan), it also was spared domestic constituencies battling over its identity, its organizational missions, or the distribution of its benefits. Patriotic students and activitists may have been frustrated by the Ministry of Foreign Affairs' ineffectiveness in changing the geopolitical realities of representing a large but weak country threatened by a powerful and aggressive neighbour with designs on large chunks of its territory; but this sort of frustration did not translate into widespread patronage, and a weakening of the norms and operations of the Ministry of Foreign Affairs from within. For most of the time frame under consideration here, the Ministry of Foreign Affairs, although generalist, was spared much of the politicization, fractiousness and floundering over goals that beset many other state organizations.

## PERSONNEL IN THE MINISTRY OF FOREIGN AFFAIRS: INSULATION WITHOUT TECHNOCRACY

By almost any criteria, the Ministry of Foreign Affairs was one of the best institutionalized state organizations across the entirety of the Republican period. In the transitions from Empire to Republic, and from Beiyang to National Governments, the organization maintained substantial continuity not only of goals, but also of personnel. From the establishment of the Zongli Yamen in 1861 onward, the organizations that executed China's foreign policy were distinctive and organizationally quite separate from the rest of the 'regular' civil bureaucracy. The Zongli Yamen was originally conceived as an *ad hoc* organization for the management of Western affairs, with a variety of spin-offs, including running a foreign language school (the Tongwen Guan), overseeing the Inspectorate-General of Customs, and at least attempting to coordinate policy in a range of internal affairs having in some way to do with foreigners—missionaries in China, telegraph construction, and modern self-strengthening projects. The Zongli Yamen was hampered by the lack of a charter or statuatory basis, however; and, after the political decline or death of its chief patrons, Prince Gong and Wen Xiang after the mid-1870s, it sank rapidly in prestige, caught between 'aggressive foreigners and conservative foreign officials'.[23]

The Boxer Protocol of 1901 forced the replacement of the Zongli Yamen with a newly created 'proper' Bureau of Foreign Affairs (the Waiwu Bu) on the Qing, which remained in place for the last years of the dynasty. Although much research remains to be carried out on the inner workings of the Waiwu Bu, it was certainly an organization more 'rationalized' than the old Zongli Yamen, divested of its involvement in customs and modern communications such as the postal and telegraph systems. And it was in the Waiwu Bu in the *xinzheng* period that a new ethos of foreign affairs, including rights recovery, assertive nationalism, and the combating of British influence in Tibet, began to to crystallize in the activities of the 'Young China' group, exemplified by individuals of treaty port background and Western education such as Tang Shaoyi and Wu Tingfang.[24]

But it was in the immediate post-imperial period that a slightly younger generation of nationalist Chinese diplomats, with a similar set of educational qualifications and values to those of the 'Young China' group, came to the fore. The (mostly) young men who provided the backbone of the early Republic's Ministry of Foreign Affairs were usually of treaty port background, had foreign experience, were skilled in foreign languages, not infrequently had taken advanced degrees abroad in subjects such as international law, and were 'both prepared and equipped to adopt Western diplomatic practices and deal with foreign powers on those grounds'.[25] In their nationalist foreign policy, stressing the revocation of the unequal treaties through diplomatic negotiation on a basis of sovereignty and equality, and in their defensive protection of China's borders, they established the objectives that would remain central to subsequent generations of China's foreign policy establishment until well into the Sino-Japanese War, when the last vestiges of extraterritoriality and the unequal treaties were abolished by the British and Americans to give a boost to Chinese morale.

Although the degree of personnel carry-over between the *xinzheng*-era Waiwu Bu and the early Republican Ministry of Foreign Affairs is uncertain, Wu Tingfang remained active well into the Republican era; several of the individuals who would go on to prominent careers in diplomatic circles in the Republican period were holders of prestigious imperial degrees (Shi Zhaoji was a Hanlin compiler of imperial examinations, as was Yan Huiqing); and a number of others were sufficiently senior to be granted immediately high positions in the Yuan Shikai government's Ministry of Foreign Affairs (Wang Chonghui, Wang Jingqi, Shi Zhaoji, Wu Chaoqu [C. C. Wu], etc.). What is without question is the extraordinary continuity of personnel between the generation of Beiyang diplomats that came of age in the 1910s and early 1920s (Gu Weijun [Wellington Koo], Guo Taiqi [Quo Tai-chi], Qian Tai, Wang Zhengting, Xu Mo) who continued to dominate the Nationalist Ministry of Foreign Affairs throughout the 1930s and well into the 1940s. There was also considerable carry-over of consular staff between the Beiyang and Nationalist periods. Although some of the individuals who rose to prominence in the Nationalist Ministry of Foreign Affairs had early Guomindang credentials or at least sympathies (Li Jinlun, Wu Chaoqu), the vast majority either did not or were relatively late converts to serving the National Government in exceptionally public roles. Since the Guomindang came to power on the basis of popular anti-imperialism as a revolutionary party with strong incentives to provide patronage for its followers, one must ask why it permitted such a large influx of Beiyang bureaucrats into such a key organization.

For the Nationalist as well as for the Beiyang and *xinzheng* governments, the skills these men possessed were desperately needed and in short supply, and the very rarity and importance of their talents for China seems to have had a sort of 'braking' effect on fostering political patronage in favour of retaining proven ability. Even individuals who by virtue of their previous factional alliances were highly suspect to the Nanjing regime, like Gu Weijun, who had been closely associated with the Zhang Zuolin regime in Manchuria, were eventually brought into the National Government Ministry of Foreign Affairs. (Gu was sufficiently mistrusted that he not once, but *twice*, sought refuge in the British leased territory of Weihaiwei during the turbulent 1920s, the second time from political opponents in the Guomindang regime in 1928.[26]) Gu was later instrumental in galvanizing support for China at the League of Nations during the Manchurian Crisis; he also served as the Chinese counsellor to the Lytton Commission, was rotated in a sequence of ambassadorial positions, and was extremely active in mobilizing world public opinion against Japanese aggression again in 1937.[27]

In terms of positional continuity, there was a sharp split in longevity of tenure between those who held ministerial or vice-ministerial positions, and the career diplomats below the rank of vice-minister. Political appointees in the Ministry of Foreign Affairs, particularly ministers but sometimes vice-ministers as well, came and went more or less in tandem with the diplomatic crises they faced: career diplomats, on the other hand, outlasted both particular crises and the regimes they served.

Unlike the Ministry of Finance, which had extraordinarily stable leadership of proven technocrats throughout the Nationalist era, the Ministry of Foreign Affairs portfolio changed hands with some frequency—sometimes to an individual with substantial experience in foreign affairs, but often not. Wang Zhengting (1928–32) and Luo Wen'gan (1932–3) were career diplomats of long standing. But after the humiliating Tanggu Truce of 1933 made large swathes of north China south of the Great Wall a demilitarized zone, inviting further Japanese expansion, Luo Wen'gan resigned, with the Ministry of Foreign Affairs portfolio going by default to Wang Jingwei, who assumed charge of the Ministry of Foreign Affairs while concurrently serving as head of the Executive Yuan for nearly two years (1933–5), but who had no particular prior experience in foreign affairs.

After an assassination attempt on Wang Jingwei in 1935 forced him into semi-retirement, the Ministry of Foreign Affairs went to a political appointee, Zhang Qun, whose background was in military and Guomindang party affairs. During the first years of the Sino-Japanese war, Wang Chonghui and Guo Taiqi, both respected jurists and diplomats, provided some degree of continuity at the top; after 1941, Song Ziwen, who had previously troubleshooted in foreign policy but whose background was largely in finance, shared the Ministry of Foreign Affairs portfolio with Chiang Kaishek. Serving as Minister of Foreign Affairs in the 1930s could also prove hazardous to one's health: nationalist students physically attacked Wang Zhengting in outrage over concessions made in Manchuria in 1931, and Wang Jingwei was seriously injured while in office.

Below the level of minister and vice-minister, however, both the consular and the diplomatic service remained remarkably constant.[28] Indeed, even for the highly prestigious ambassadorial positions in London, Washington, and Paris and appointment to the League of Nations, Shi Zhaoji, Gu Weijun, Guo Taiqi, and sometimes Yan Huiqing were constantly rotated back and forth throughout the 1930s. Continuity of personnel also reinforced continuity of agenda and organizational goals: after a brief policy debate between conservatives and leftists in the Nationalist Party in 1927–8 as to whether China should retain an 'anti-imperialist' foreign policy or adopt a gradualist approach, the gradualists decisively prevailed when Wang Zhengting, a career diplomat of high standing during the 1920s, became head of the Ministry.[29]

The appointment of Wang as Minister of Foreign Affairs, with the moderate, 'negotiating with the Powers' strategy that it suggested, was closely paralleled by the appointment and ascendancy of Song Ziwen in the Ministry of Finance at about the same time. Song, in his sphere, was a nationalist who was at least sympathetic to the models that hybrid organizations such as the Salt Inspectorate offered as means of building organizational strength. Similarly, Wang Zhengting was a nationalist out to recover rights and eradicate imperial vestiges, but he thought that much could be gained from cultivation of the United States and Great Britain in the process.

Because the Ministry of Foreign Affairs, like the Salt Inspectorate, provided critical services that the central state simply could not do without for any length of time, it was allowed to make the transition from the Beiyang to the Nationalist period with its organization largely intact. It was therefore able to resist or deflect the worst excesses of personalism and politicization during the early years of the Nationalist regime, when the pressures to provide patronage for Party loyalists and co-opt opponents were undoubtedly tremendous. Compared with figures on the Ministry of the Interior, the comparatively small number of appointments during the 1930s in the Ministry of Foreign Affairs that stand out as patronage is quite striking. Gu Weijun, Guo Taiqi, Yan Huiqing, and Wu Chaoqu may have had a lock on the most prestigious ambassadorial positions, but no one could suggest that they were not eminently well qualified to serve in these positions.

When one turns to the rank and file of the commissioned officers of the Ministry of Foreign Affairs during the 1930s, similar patterns are evident. In a sample of 55 Ministry of Foreign Affairs bureaucrats who had entered the Ministry before 1938, a clear majority (35 of 55) had begun their careers with first positions in the Ministry of Foreign Affairs, 11 had previous posts in other central or provincial government organizations, 4 had been professors or instructors in universities, 2 had backgrounds in editing or railroad administration, and only 3 had come in with primary careers in the military or in Party organizations.[30]

In contrast, the personnel records from the Ministry of the Interior during the early 1930s illustrate the typical pattern of attempted co-optation and factionalism so bemoaned by commentators on the National Government.[31] For instance, of 40 *jianren* ('recommended' rank) appointments listed during the early 1930s, 10 'secretaries' (*mishu*) from the weakly controlled Manchurian provinces with no background in interior affairs were appointed *en bloc* in 1931; of the 37 (of 40) *jianren* positions for which information was available, only 2 had previously served in the Beiyang Ministry of the Interior, and an additional 4 more had had any sort of experience in interior affairs for provincial or local government organizations.[32]

Although it did not publicly trumpet the distinctive separateness of its personnel system as the source of its success, as did the Salt Inspectorate, the Ministry of Foreign Affairs replicated the former's key institution-building strategy of promoting insulation from the external environment and fostering a regular, stable system of promotions and incentives within. The Ministry's internal personel system was unique, and it reflected both its connection to the Nationalist central government and its existence as a high-prestige organization with a good deal of discretion and autonomy over internal operations and promotions. For those posted to the central Ministry of Foreign Affairs in Nanjing, it used the '*jian, jian, wei*' (selected, recommended and delegated) system that was standard throughout the National Government. But for its consular and diplomatic staff posted abroad, the Ministry of Foreign Affairs utilized a special system of rankings that was unknown in the rest of the National Government, with special salaries, perks, and many grades but few leaps in status.[33]

Although there were some individuals who came into the Ministry of Foreign Affairs with each sitting of the *gaokao* (upper civil service examination), the Ministry of Foreign Affairs did not set itself up around an impersonal system of open civil service exams as the exclusive means of entry to buffer unwonted politicization, as did the Salt Inspectorate. Nevertheless, the Ministry of Foreign Affairs maintained fairly strong organizational boundaries during the 1930s. It did so by keeping control over recruitment, and not relaxing what appear to have been extraordinarily high informal prerequisites for entry, as the 'Lao Beiyang' (Beiyang Old Timer) generation expected the same sort of educational qualifications and facility with foreign languages that they themselves had acquired. The individuals selected even in the 1920s and 1930s more often than not closely replicated the sorts of educational and social background so prevalent in the *xinzheng* generation of 'new' foreign affairs bureaucrats: foreign experience, facility with foreign language, advanced degrees at prestigious universities, education abroad, and often a treaty port background.

The pool from which the Ministry of Foreign Affairs drew its entry-level personnel was the most cosmopolitan and best educated group of young men in all of China. Fifty-five per cent (30 of 55) had studied abroad; of these 30, 13 individuals had Ph.D. degrees from foreign universities, 6 had MA degrees, and the remainder had taken regular degrees. Of those who had not been abroad, the majority (17 of 25) had attended the most prestigious liberal arts universities in China, with only a relatively small number (7 of 25) getting their degrees from less well known, provincial, or technical colleges, and one lone individual having attended a military school. In addition, five in the sample passed the extraordinarily competitive *gaokao*.[34] With the obvious exception of these five, it is likely that virtually all of those working in the Ministry during the 1930s were informally recruited through personal connections. But the circles to which the Ministry of Foreign Affairs was connected were rarified indeed, and it appears that the Ministry could afford to recruit almost exclusively among the educational and social *crème de la crème*.

In addition to replicating itself through the type of individual it recruited, the Ministry of Foreign Affairs fostered internal stability through a quite conservative process of socialization, stressing organizational continuity and cosmopolitan norms. At least until the outbreak of the Sino-Japanese War, the older, more experienced former Beiyang government bureaucrats controlled most of this by keeping a tight rein on in-house socialization. Through an informal process of mentorship, they trained the younger generation in the skills necessary for the functioning diplomat—mastering the correct protocol, processing documents, correcting mistakes, and giving the inexperienced the 'most uninteresting' work until they had proved themselves after some years of service.[35] The structure of the career path also reinforced organizational continuity. Until the early 1940s, most (42 of 55) in the Ministry of Foreign Affairs were on a clearly discernible 'regular' diplomatic career track that alternated roughly three-year tours of duty abroad with service in the central ministry in Nanjing.[36]

Xiong Yingzha, who came into the Ministry of Foreign Affairs in 1928, had a fairly typical career. Xiong was born in 1905, in Huang'an county, Hubei. He took a degree at National Beijing University and did advanced work at the University of California before being appointed to the central Ministry of Foreign Affairs as a section member (*keyuan*) in 1928. After serving in Nanjing for about a year, he was posted to the San Francisco Consulate as an attaché for a four-year term, and then was promoted *in situ* to the rank of vice-consul, remaining in San Francisco until August 1935, with his Ministry of Personnel *jianren* qualification finally being registered in 1933. He spent the following eighteen months back at the Ministry of Foreign Affairs in Nanjing, in December 1936 becoming a 'specialist' (*zhuanyuan*) for the Ministry of Foreign Affairs. In practice, during the first several years of the war this meant a series of irregular liasion positions between the Ministry of Foreign Affairs and various military units, particularly in the Burma–India theatre. In January 1943 he was rotated back to the Ministry of Foreign Affairs in Chongqing, with a promotion to section chief of the second section of the American continental division.[37]

In a series of policies reminiscent of the Salt Inspectorate, the Ministry of Foreign Affairs also fostered organizational stability by restraining rapid advancement up through the ranks of the organization, and making promotion decisions by committee consensus, which enforced strict quotas on the numbers of individuals allowed the *jia* (highest) rating that qualified one for promotion. The ambassador (or chief of each unit) would rank his subordinates in terms of job performance and make promotion recommendations. If he exceeded his quota, the committee would accordingly reduce numbers. Promotions were usually granted only after years of service: it often took between ten and twelve years to advance from third grade to second grade secretary.[38]

Like the Salt Inspectorate, the Ministry of Foreign Affairs designed its personnel policy around an ethic of organizational insulation. The organization's collective stress on seniority, the continued dominance of the Beiyang elites in terms of training and socializing the new generation, the partially separate personnel classification system through the ranks of a distinctive system of personnel ranks, and the painfully slow climb through the ranks for the average career diplomat were strategies that produced the desired effect. The majority of those who came to the Ministry of Foreign Affairs before 1940 did so early in their careers, and tended to stay with the organization until retirement.[39]

### THE MINISTRY OF FOREIGN AFFAIRS: THE ATTEMPT TO CREATE A 'BLUE GENERALIST' IN THE LATE 1930s

Although the Ministry of Foreign Affairs replicated certain elements of the Salt Inspectorate's institution-building success (insulation, high standards, a tight rein on promotions, and fostering long careers with the organization), in other respects it was strikingly different. Unlike the Salt Inspectorate, the criteria for high performance in the Ministry of Foreign Affairs were often not objectively quantifiable; the organization did not rigorously exclude anything that smacked of Party indoctrination, and yet it still managed consistently to maintain its high status. Even during the early to mid-1930s, Party membership among the career diplomats in the Ministry of Foreign Affairs was fairly common. For the 55 (of 98) who entered the Ministry of Foreign Affairs before 1938, by the time they filled out this particular set of forms, 31 were Party members, 1 was a probable Party member, 6 were clearly non-Party members, 10 were probable non-Party members, and 7 were of unknown Party affiliation. The incidence of Party membership increased dramatically with the group entering the

Ministry in the post-1938 period: of 43 individuals, 32 indicated Party membership, 3 more were probable members, only 1 person appeared as a clear non-Party member, and 6 were of unknown status.[40]

This increased importance of Party membership in the Ministry of Foreign Affairs during the late 1930s and early 1940s can be ascribed in part to organizational expansion and wartime needs. The Ministry of Foreign Affairs did not completely escape the de-institutionalization and militarization that occurred throughout the state bureaucracy during the Sino-Japanese War, and weakening norms of insulation and professionalization accounted for roughly a third of the increase in Party membership. The number of individuals whose primary careers had been in Party or military organizations during the 1930s jumped from 2 (of 55) to 12 (of 43) in the early 1940s. The demands of wartime for large numbers of individuals who could at least speak foreign languages pushed the organization to weaken its norms of rigorous insulation and accept unknown (but probably significant) numbers of *daili* (acting temporary) appointees to man consulates in places such as Xinjiang.[41]

Despite the occurrence of some amount of de-institutionalization during the war years, the indirect evidence suggests that the organization moved to contain these trends in two ways. First, regarding people with primary careers in Party organizations, these 12 had surprisingly elite educational backgrounds that matched general Ministry of Foreign Affairs norms: 7 had studied abroad (2 with Ph.D.s, 2 with MAs, and 3 with regular degrees), 3 had degrees from prestigious universities within China, and only 2 had come from provincial colleges or universities. Furthermore, none of these probable patronage appointments was put into the 'regular' career track of tours of duty abroad, and most were accorded *zhuan* (special) appointments at high rates of pay, but probably with few real responsibilities.[42]

Evidence from a number of sources suggests that Party membership in the Ministry of Foreign Affairs during the late 1930s and 1940s had a significance well beyond its correlation with the de-institutionalization engendered by the war. If 12 of the sample of 43 were probable patronage appointments, the remaining 31 were not. The qualifications of the post-1938 group did not differ substantially from those who came in during the pre-1938 years. Aside from the increased incidence of Party membership and Party connections, most of the individuals who began their careers in the Ministry in the post-1938 period had much in common with their predecessors. They were slightly, but not substantially, less well educated than those who had come in before the war. The proportions of those coming from non-elite schools was 6 of 40 compared with 7 of 55 in the pre-1938 group. Thus, despite greater accommodation to Party norms, elitism, cosmopolitanism, and foreign experience still ruled in the recruitment and personnel policies of the wartime Ministry of Foreign Affairs.

Given the difficulties of higher education and travel abroad under wartime conditions, it was surprising that so many could continue to get their degrees from foreign universities during the war: 11 (of 43) received either a Ph.D. or an MA from a foreign university, and an additional 4 had studied abroad without receiving an advanced degree; 12 had received degrees from one of the key universities within China, and 2 had passed the *gaokao*. The subjects of study for these individuals were practically indistinguishable from those of the pre-1938 group: 25 (of 43) took courses in law, government, economics, or international relations, 5 studied foreign languages or business, 2 had degrees in engineering or journalism, and 8 indicated no major concentration.

The Ministry of Foreign Affairs thus had quietly institutionalized the norm of Party membership in the early 1940s. By this time, the informal pressure on young and ambitious new recruits to become members of the Guomindang was probably quite strong, and even experienced diplomats with years of service in the Ministry were not immune to the organization's increasing expectations of Party membership: during the early 1940s, three individuals whose previous careers were completely devoid of Party involvement suddenly joined the Guomindang.[43] It is likely that by the early 1940s Party membership in the Ministry of Foreign Affairs had increased from somewhat over one half during the pre-1938 period (32 of 55, including one probable Party member) to over three quarters during the Sino-Japanese War.[44]

Although these increased percentages of Party membership may have been augmented by the wider *xunlian* movement to reindoctrinate the ranks of the bureaucracy during the war, the ideal of 'partifying' the Ministry of Foreign Affairs, and of fostering a new type of organizational culture that combined the values of Party loyalty, generalism, and cosmopolitanism, had been in existence since at least the mid-1930s. In 1934 the Guomindang established the Zhongyang Zhengzhi Xuexiao (Central Political Institute), which was renamed the Zhongyang Zhengzhi Daxue (Central Political University) in 1939. The school graduated 'study classes' (*xuexi ban*) and had a regular faculty during the mid-1930s. But after the retreat to Chongqing, when *xunlian* courses began to be instituted throughout the civilian bureaucracy, the university expanded tremendously in scope under the strong sponsorship of Chen Guofu, one of the most prominent of the right-wing Party ideologues.[45] Beginning in 1938-9, the Central Political University granted degrees from its regular university, administered six-month pre-appointment training courses for those who had passed the *gaokao*, and had a section dealing with 'local administration' (*dizheng xueyuan*). Within the regular university section, there was also a small department of foreign affairs (*waijiao xi*), which was established to serve as an eventual feeder school into the Ministry of Foreign Affairs.

The department of foreign affairs at the Central Political University was designed to train a 'new' sort of foreign affairs bureaucrat. In contrast to the Chinese Communist Party, which, in the later formulation of the 1950s, wished to promote both 'redness' (correct 'red' values) and 'expertise', the Guomindang tried to create what might be called a 'blue generalist', as blue was the colour associated with the Party, and the curriculum of the department of foreign affairs continued to stress generalist elitism. A degree from the foreign affairs department at the Central Political University did not guarantee entry into the Ministry of Foreign Affairs; but, since the professors in the department were all affiliated with the Ministry and were expected to recommend their better students for available positions, a student's chances of getting into the Ministry of Foreign Affairs were in theory significantly improved by coming from this foreign affairs department.

The structure of the foreign affairs programme illustrated what sort of values the ideal 'Blue Generalist' foreign affairs bureaucrat was to hold. First, he was to identify strongly with both the state and the Nationalist Party. One could not attend the Central Political University's regular university division without joining the Party, and therefore undergoing a hefty component of political study and training. In return, the Central Political University provided a route to upward mobility for the disadvantaged but bright: it offered a fully subsidized education, complete with pocket money, to those who could get in and who agreed to the requirement of Party membership. In contrast, even the Ministry-of-Education-sponsored Zhongyang Daxue (National Central University), which provided the largest percentage of *gaokao* successes during the 1930s, had some tuition requirements, and private prestigious universities (such as Yanjing and Jinling) were out of the financial range of even more students. The free and good education available at the Central Political University made it choice of many, and the competition for a spot in the foreign affairs department was keen, with an acceptance rate of perhaps only one in twenty.

In terms of the substantive knowledge it wished to inculcate, the foreign affairs department at the Central Political University continued to select for the long held Ministry of Foreign Affairs norms of generalism and cosmopolitanism. The curriculum was fairly similar to that of other social science departments: the courses were general, social-science-oriented, and stressed the acquisition of French and English, literature, economics, and law (particularly international law).[46] The foreign affairs department of the Central Political University amalgamated a number of elements dear to the hearts of leading Guomindang figures since well before the Sino-Japanese War. It combined in one package explicit loyalty to the Party, a generalist elitism, and a channel for upward mobility.

Although interviewees unanimously insisted that the links between the Department of Foreign Affairs at the Central Political University and the

Ministry of Foreign Affairs was the important wave of the future for the 1940s, the available sample of those recruited in the period 1938–42 indicates that in the early years of the war the Department of Foreign Affairs was not yet the presence and feeder school that it later became. In addition to two professors who taught at the Central Political University, there were, in the sample of 98 individuals, only 5 who had come into the Ministry of Foreign Affairs from this foreign affairs department; in the early 1940s, National Central University (with 5), and *gaokao* successes (with 6) were at least as well represented in the Ministry.[47] Because those with *gaokao* qualifications had the right to immediate appointment with the prestigious 'recommended' (*jianren*) ranking, while the recruits from the Central Political University came in with a regular 'delegated' appointment, the latter tended to resent the former. The initial tension between these two groups later dissolved when 'one became much like the other' as most entrants joined the Party and grew to uphold the same values.[48]

Even under the multiple stresses of the late 1930s and the 1940s, the Ministry of Foreign Affairs seems to have remained fairly cohesive. Differences of opinion, when they occurred at all, tended to run along the lines that were broadly generational rather than clearly factional. The older generation of Beiyang Ministry of Foreign Affairs diplomats, who were still very much on the scene into the 1940s, tended to be more conservative, and willing to delay the resolution of issues (such as the demarcation of borders with Burma and Tibet for fear of alienating the British), while the younger generation that came in in the 1930s and 1940s were more willing to push much harder for the immediate resolution of outstanding issues regarding China's sovereignty and borders. However, since the older generation maintained seniority, respect, and control over promotions, differences were quelled in favour of their preferences.[49]

From an institutional standpoint, the cooperation between the Guomindang and the Ministry of Foreign Affairs to produce at least a certain type of 'Blue Generalist' was effective. Even in very unsettled times, the organization did not break down: while some de-institutionalization occurred, it was apparently contained before it spread throughout the organization. Even throughout the Sino-Japanese War, when it accepted a significant number of *zhuan* (special) appointees, the organization maintained its boundaries well enough to remain highly prestigious and attractive to the bright and ambitious. When combined with at least fair maintenance of insulation, the Ministry's generalist, elite orientation enabled it to be flexible along other dimensions, such as incorporating Party membership into its gallery of core values—in genuine contrast to the strict bureaucratic rigidity of the Salt Administration.

In terms of its institution-building strategies, the Ministry of Foreign Affairs was a particularly advantaged organization for a number of structural reasons. Like the Salt Inspectorate and the Ministry of Finance, it performed services so crucial to the state that it behove the regime in power to be extremely careful about subjecting it to too much political interference and pressure. Historically, too, Foreign Affairs was 'fortunate': it stood as the preserve of a small number of twentieth-century heirs to a long-lived tradition of literati generalism.[50] As a fairly small, closed group with a homogeneous set of backgrounds and strong in-service socialization mechanisms, no local constituencies, and no external groups battling over its identity or basic goals, it remained largely immune from serious divisions within and attacks from without. Since it began the Nanjing Decade as an already cohesive and prestigious organization, it did not have to 'buy' or 'earn' its legitimacy during the Guomindang years. It merely consolidated what it already had by bending to the new norm of loyalty through Party membership, and by continuing its tradition of insulation through token political means rather than technical ones.

Because the Ministry of Foreign Affairs had a domestic monopoly in some respects, its lack of clear specificity in its more important operations may have worked to its advantage. Once the Chiang Kai-shek regime was in power and the debate over the merits of 'revolutionary' v. 'gradualist' diplomacy subsided in the late 1920s, those outside the organization did not make a habit of scrutinizing the interior workings of the organization very carefully. Since the Ministry had substantial degrees of autonomy, it was probably able to exclude unrealizable goals (such as stopping the Japanese) from the criteria for 'organizational success', focusing instead on medium- and short-term goals where it could hope to achieve visible results (such as revocation of the unequal treaties, border delineation, and mobilizing world support for its positions).[51]

## CONCLUSION

The Ministry of Foreign Affairs' institution-building strategies replicated those of the Salt Inspectorate and Ministry of Finance in some respects, but diverged sharply in others. As was the case in the Salt Inspectorate, institutionalization in the Ministry of Foreign Affairs depended primarily on continued maintenance of organizational boundaries and prestige, buttressed in part by the visible progress made towards concrete goals (treaty revision, rights recovery, conclusion of treaties on the basis of equality and friendship, border setting).

In contrast to the more technically based Salt Inspectorate and Ministry of Finance, Foreign Affairs' elitism and generalist orientation did render it much more susceptible to infiltration by the Guomindang. Senior diplomats from the Beiyang generation may have quietly decided at various points in the 1930s that, given the type of government they were serving and the inherently 'political' nature of decision making in foreign policy, the best organizational defence of insulation was a good offence: and that pre-emptively proving loyalty and commitment by joining the Party early on would have the net effect of buffering the organization from outside inter-ference in its internal operations and norms further down the road. The 'partification' of the Ministry of Foreign Affairs in the late 1930s and early 1940s did not seem to either factionalize or much weaken the organization, although wartime expansion and chaos did, to a limited effect, subject it to a milder version of the sort of de-institutionalization that was so prominent in the Salt Administration during the Sino-Japanese War. Even when it accepted Party loyalty as one of its core values, the Ministry of Foreign Affairs was still able to maintain most of its pre-existing core values of cosmopolitanism, elitism, and generalism through the curriculum of the department of foreign affairs, and to continue to generate a large amount of insulation by recruiting from a highly educated subgroup of the elite over which it maintained a strong continuity of values through in-house social-ization and promotion policies.

Both domestically and internationally, the Ministry of Foreign Affairs had highly uneven control over its policy domain, but it was often able to compensate for weak effectiveness in one area with strong performance in another. If it often had the 'highest' levels of foreign policy making removed from it, it had a virtual domestic monopoly over the execution of foreign policy. However unpopular the National Government was in terms of its weakness in standing up to the Japanese, and however much the chiefs in the Ministry of Foreign Affairs bore the brunt of that dissatisfaction, the Ministry was, and remained, a highly prestigious organization whose right-ful existence and importance were not often seriously questioned by those in positions of power. Internationally, the Ministry often reflected the weakness and lack of choices of the government it represented, but, given this weakness, it did a remarkably good job of making a little go quite far. Domestically, high prestige, combined with the fact that the Ministry of Foreign Affairs performed crucial services to the state, enabled an already buffered and well insulated organization to remain so under the Nationalists.

Although the Japanese onslaught could not but adversely affect morale, the Ministry of Foreign Affairs managed to avoid being held accountable for failing to realize goals in domains in which it had little real control. Although somewhat weakened during the war, the Ministry, paradoxically probably buttressed by its incorporation of Party membership as a strong internal norm, did not collapse because it was unable to stop the Japanese, as the Salt Inspectorate largely did when it lost its key revenue bases early in the war. Through an astute combination of focusing on short- and medium-term goals that were measurable and provable and proving its loyalty up front through Party membership, the Ministry of Foreign Affairs was able to stick to its initial strategy of generating internal prestige by not relaxing its high standards for entry and continuing to reward those who internalized organizational values of generalism, cosmopolitanism, and loyalty to both Party and state.

# 7

# Conclusion

As in other states throughout the less developed world, the Republic of China attempted to carry out a monumental project between 1912 and 1949: to make a vast country strong and powerful even as it was beset by fragmentation from within and imperialist pressure from without. In so doing, it continued to develop policies adopted in the the very last years of the dynasty, when central elites reversed a late imperial conception of proper government as minimalist and harmony oriented, and began to equate the means to national wealth and power with a classic state-building strategy of increased centralization and rationalization of administrative control. Critical to this process was the creation of strong, pro-active supporting administrative structures able to carry out a greatly expanded state agenda in a wide range of policy areas: taxation, security and police, education, commerce.

But China in the early twentieth century was characterized by a dilemma of institution building common to many non-Western countries. Rising nationalism and anti-imperialism may have suddenly demanded new levels of performance from administrative organizations, but the raw materials with which administrative organizations had to work remained essentially unchanged from late imperial times. Central and auditing control was weak, projective power was extremely limited, salaries were inadequate, and numbers of adequately trained personnel were few. The centuries-old tension between the demands of a universalistic bureaucracy and the social norms of responsiveness to 'human feeling' of providing for one's own were stronger than ever. By the turn of the century, all of the conditions for a 'strong society/weak state' dilemma were present: central government weakness, the rise of regional and local power arrangements, and the relative decline of universalist and bureaucratic norms in favour of ascription.[1]

With the overthrow of the Qing in 1912, these trends intensified, as provincial and local elites contested the last remaining shreds of central authority of the Yuan Shikai government and then were able to ignore the writ of a succession of Beiyang governments in the late 1910s and 1920s. Under these structural and social conditions, the prudent individual who managed to acquire an official position simultaneously ensured his own security and made his life more pleasant by not failing to provide for those near and dear. Therefore, all prospective state organizations had to deal with a dilemma reinforced by the state's structural weakness and compounded by social norms of mutual obligation: how was an aspiring strong state organization to go about building a cadre of committed personnel who identified with the organization's goals and programmes?

## SYSTEMIC STRATEGIES OF INSTITUTION-BUILDING: THE EXAMINATION YUAN AND MINISTRY OF PERSONNEL

During the first half of the twentieth century, the re- integrating Republican Chinese state drew syncretically both from its own long imperial past and from the latest in political ideas and experiments from the contemporary West. The ideas laid out in documents on the 'Five Power Constitution', the 'Fundamentals of National Construction', and the 'Three Principles of the People' suggest that in the mid-1920s Sun Yat-sen and the Nationalists favoured both concentration and division of government power, and both elitist control and popular representation.

Once the Nanjing Government was established in 1927, however, the Nationalists quietly ignored the parts of their revolutionary legacy that stressed popular mobilization and bottom-up political organization in favour of a state-building logic that had been consistently favoured by executive elites in China since the first decade of the twentieth century: extension of central power and control, administrative rationalization, and the creation of strong executive institutions. The reality of the Nanjing Decade (1927–37) was one of military crisis and a large amount of discretionary power ceded to *ad hoc* military leaders, supplemented by growing executive control concentrated in the Executive Yuan, where most of the functional state ministries were placed. But the rhetoric of Nationalist doctrine mandated the establishment of a supra-organizational Examination Yuan and Ministry of Personnel to recruit, standardize, manage, and provide quality control for an effective state government. The second chapter of this book investigated the problems associated with the attempt to do so.

The Examination Yuan faithfully reflected the goals to which the Nationalist state aspired, and its unevenness in implementation equally accurately mirrored the weaknesses of the general co-optive state-building strategy adopted by the Nationalists. The Examination Yuan was designed to implement the values of fairness, pride in China's past, scientific administration, and organizational effectiveness in the state bureaucracy at large. Harking back to the best of the imperial system, the Examination Commission was established to hold open civil service examinations to ensure that 'regular' careers in state service would go to the best qualified on a reasonable and fair basis. The Ministry of Personnel's goals were to bring order, coherence, and standardization to the National Government bureaucracy by reviewing the qualifications of civil servants, registering each at a certain commissioned grade and rank, and 'scientifically' to design promotion and evaluation systems to depersonalize administration.

Although these ideals and goals had longstanding legitimacy and positive valence with bureaucratic elites in China, the Examination Yuan was successful in implementing only a fraction of them over the course of the 1930s. The Examination Commission and the Ministry of Personnel began the decade as weak organizations, and, despite limited and incremental gains, both remained weak throughout the 1930s and 1940s. The Examination Yuan had the misfortune of standing for issues of principle and ideal in the National Government without having been accorded the means to enforce compliance: throughout the Nationalist period, it operated without strong political support in a domain already overcrowded with vested interests. By the time the Examination Yuan was formally established, the functional ministries were already filled with personnel on the basis of some combination of cronyism, co-optation, and merit, and the ministries jealously guarded their privileges of appointment and promotion. Although in principle all agreed on the need for standardization and unification of administration, the Ministry of Personnel had a very difficult time getting the executive ministries to submit the credentials and files of their personnel, and could only reject the smallest fraction of those submitted as 'not being up to standard'. Similarly, the Examination Commission held very difficult, highly prestigious civil service examinations regularly every two years, but could not even guarantee the appointment of those whom it so certified, because the power of appointment resided with the ministries.

Mostly ignored by the political heavyweights of the 1930s and 1940s, the Examination Yuan had but two methods by which it could elicit compliance. The usual strategy was through moral suasion: sending memos to the ministries reminding them of the Examination Yuan's formally superior status and preogatives, and suggesting the names of individuals who had, after all, passed the civil service exams. In extreme cases, the Ministry of Personnel would withold approval, and refuse to give personnel in the ministries their formal appointments. Through some combination of moral suasion, playing on the status sensibilities of the bureaucratic elites elsewhere in the state, and demonstrating the practical usefulness of the examination system, the Examination Yuan did make some inroads during the 1930s. Because they wanted the formal credentials that only the Ministry of Personnel could bestow, the other National Government organizations eventually grudgingly submitted to the Ministry of Personnel's review, and some ministries (such as the Ministry of Finance) came to realize the political and practical advantages of working with the Examination Commission to fill its new departments exclusively through the civil service exam.

But on balance, the National Government's attempt to use the Examination Yuan to build broad civil service institutions was ineffective. Although all could agree on the theoretical desirability of open examinations as the exclusive means of entry into the National Government, the implementation of depoliticized, 'scientific' methods for promoting government bureaucrats, and of the unification and standardization of the national civil service, the Examination Yuan was given none of the backing to make these sweeping ideals feasible. The Examination Yuan's position in policy-making space was unenviable: it combined inherently great intrusiveness in the ministries with only minimal means to enforce compliance or punish deviance. Aside from imparting a minimal standardization of rank classification for the National Government as a whole, the functions of the Examination Yuan were primarily symbolic; and symbols, however positively charged, that remained unsupported by organizational power and influence made a very poor base for institution building. For good or ill, in Nationalist China the realities of institution-building efforts were played out primarily in the ministries themselves.

### ORGANIZATIONAL APPROACHES TO INSTITUTION-BUILDING: THE SALT INSPECTORATE, THE MINISTRY OF FINANCE, AND THE MINISTRY OF FOREIGN AFFAIRS

The second part of this work considered institution-building strategies in three of the more successful state organizations in the Republican period: the Sino-Foreign Salt Inspectorate, the Ministry of Finance, and the Ministry of Foreign Affairs. The workings of these three organizations all challenge the conventional reputation of National government organizations as corrupt and ineffective. None of these organizations shows evidence of being rent by factionalism, all consistently managed to attract individuals of high calibre to their service, and each was widely perceived to be successful and/or highly prestigious in its own time. The Salt Inspectorate, the Ministry of Finance, and the Ministry of Foreign Affairs did, of course, have different administrative histories, occupy different niches in policy space, and pursue varying organizational goals and technologies, and each produced a mix of institution-building strategies that was in some ways some ways unique to the specifics faced by the organization.

The Salt Inspectorate, Ministry of Finance, and Ministry of Foreign Affairs were not 'average' state organizations. The efficiency of the Salt Inspectorate and the Ministry of Finance in tax collection, and the effectiveness of the Ministry of Foreign Affairs in making China an intelligible and sympathetic member of the international community, were services that were absolutely crucial to the larger project of state building and state reintegration. The strategies that these three organizations pursued in achieving their goals were far from random. During the Republican period a proactive, dynamic organization had to distinguish itself from the surrounding environment as a discrete unit with goals, values, and plans for concrete action.

The strategies adopted by these three organizations indicate that, in highly turbulent, politicized environments, successful organizational institutionalization was contingent on two closely related conditions: (1) the organization's ability to insulate itself from the hostile external environment, and to build internal cohesiveness of its personnel around bureaucratic, professional, depersonalized norms; and (2) the organization's high performance in pursuit of its goals, thus reinforcing insulation and building internal morale. Positive results in goal achievement, in turn, were closely correlated with two additional variables: the degree to which medium-term organizational goals were specific, divisible, and clearly related to overall organizational mission, and the extent to which the organization could establish control in its policy domain.

The Sino-Foreign Salt Inspectorate, a tax-collecting organization run jointly by international civil servants and Chinese nationals, was, with periodic changes in name, active for nearly the whole of the Republican period. Of the three organizations analysed in this work, it provided the clearest example of each of these components of institution-building success: insulation from the external environment, bureaucratization and professionalization within, high performance in its policy domain, and a set of organizational technologies and tasks amenable to specific division and breakdown.

Against all odds, the first Chief Foreign Inspector of the Salt Inspectorate, Sir Richard Dane, managed to wrest a fair amount of autonomy for the organization at the very outset by taking over direct control of tax receipts before forwarding them to the Western banks and the Chinese government. Once it possessed the means to insulate itself (by adequately salarying its employees), the Salt Inspectorate turned its energies to implement a two-pronged reinforcing strategy of institution building: internally oriented bureaucratization and professionalization of its staff, and externally oriented goal implementation and high performance.

The cornerstone of the Inspectorate's success was its ability to establish a bureaucratic, depersonalized civil service system that was in practice completely separate from the rest of the Chinese government. Everything about the organization's personnel and recruitment policies reinforced the organization's core values of bureaucratization, depersonalization, and 'fairness'. In providing strong organizational boundaries to deflect the ascriptive claims of family and friends, and offering a steady, stable career, the Salt Inspectorate drew its personnel from a large resevoir.

The organization's policy of recruitment exclusively by open civil service exam tapped into a widely held symbol of legitimacy in statecraft. A personnel system that looked very much like a *zhengtu* (regular path of advancement), including generous salaries, special benefits, and regular merit pay rises, attracted many, as did the generally high standards throughout the organization: promotions were few and seniority-based, and malfeasance in office was unhesitatingly punished.

High performance in pursuit of externally oriented organizational goals further reinforced the organization's internal bureaucratization and insulation. Since the Salt Inspectorate efficiently performed a function necessary to the reintegrating but still weak state, it could 'buy' its continued existence and autonomy by turning over its funds both to warlords and to the Nationalists, as the occasion demandeed. The 'specificity' of the Inspectorate's tasks and technologies further aided internal bureaucratization and depersonalization. Rationalization and standardization of procedures in tax collection, construction of roads and blockhouses to contain smuggling, and experiments with new sorts of evaporation were all types of organizational action that were easily visible, measurable, and reducible to concrete steps. Given this set of organizational technologies, it was fairly easy for the Inspectorate to spot either corruption or exceptional effort, and thus to monitor and evaluate performance. In terms of its own organizational performance, the Salt Inspectorate always had a universally acknowledged bottom line by which it could justify itself to outsiders: the total tax receipts collected in any given year.

Last, the Salt Inspectorate operated in a domain in which it could make significant progress in realizing its goals. It had a detailed blueprint of its organizational mission: rationalization, standardization, and establishment of control over the salt tax. The organization consistently implemented this programme as best it could over the course of thirty years. Warlord depredations, the Nationalist takeover, and the intransigence of local salt merchants often called for tactical retreats; but in general, the Inspectorate managed its domain well until the Sino-Japanese War. It took over other salt administration organizations, increased the amounts of tax revenue it extracted, and strengthened central control over salt administration in the name of the Nationalist Ministry of Finance during the 1930s. In all its key features, the Sino-Foreign Salt Inspectorate was a model of institution-building success. It established its autonomy early, insulated itself rigorously, institutionalized its organizational values of depersonalization and goal achievement through its impersonal civil service system, consolidated its autonomy through its efficiency in performing services necessary to the state, and was fortunate in possessing a series of relatively divisible and specific organizational goals and technologies that further reinforced its core strategies of institutionalization.

Although it was a remarkably successful and well institutionalized organization, the Salt Inspectorate was also anomalous: the existence of a dual Chinese and foreign management structure meant that its experiences in institution building were not generalizable. The foreign presence certainly made it much easier for the organization to insulate and bureaucratize itself so thoroughly at a critical early date in its history. But the organization's system of joint responsibility between Chinese and foreign upper staff and its substantial autonomy from the rest of the Chinese state reeked of Western imperialism to many, and was unlikely to be replicated in other Chinese-directed efforts at institution building.

The Nationalist Ministry of Finance, which formally took over the Salt Inspectorate in 1927–8, provided a much more typical case of attempted institution building in the Republican period. In its goals and technologies (to raise efficiency, extend control over taxation, and rationalize administration), the Ministry of Finance was remarkably similar to the Salt Inspectorate. As a much larger organization without a heavy foreign presence, the Ministry initially had significantly weaker boundaries than did the Inspectorate. Although key figures in the Ministry of Finance admired the Salt Inspectorate's successes, and wished to hold it up as a model for the rest of the organization to emulate, the Ministry could not immediately institute an across-the-board civil service system of recruitment exclusively by examination, and had to rely instead on a gradualist institution-building strategy that almost exactly replicated the 'cover-over' state-building strategy of the Nationalist regime at large, including a mix of outright takeover, co-optation, amalgamation of pre-existing tax administrations, and slowly raising standards for performance.

The results of the Ministry of Finance's efforts suggested that an organization's success in institution building is not necessarily dependent on the nearly total autonomy, insulation, and strong foreign presence that characterized the Salt Inspectorate. Even if it lacked the initially strong boundaries of the Inspectorate, the Ministry of Finance's similar orientation towards efficiency and specific, concrete results meant that in practice it selected for personnel who were experienced, competent, and hard working, thus creating a partial insulation around an ethic of functional orientation and expertise. The intense pressure from above to bring increasing amounts of revenue to the central government through efficient tax collection provided a strong incentive for the Ministry of Finance to avoid recruiting those who were either lazy or unqualified to do the job, and, as new departments and sections were created in the Ministry later in the 1930s, it increasingly turned to open civil service examination as the preferred method of recruitment.

The experience of the Ministry of Finance during the 1930s further illustrated the importance of domain in institution building. If the domain was manageable, as in the Consolidated Tax Administration, where the items to be taxed were concentrated in few points of manufacture or distribution, the organization was able to replicate the Salt Inspectorate's successes. But, where domain was diffuse and beyond the capacity of the organization to directly control bureaucratically, as in the attempts to institute a reformed land tax and direct tax, the Ministry of Finance either informally shared power with the groups it was attempting to control, or was unable to get its programme to have the intended reach and effect.

In contrast to both the Salt Inspectorate and the Ministry of Finance, the Ministry of Foreign Affairs offered an instance of a generalist organization. Despite very different organizational goals, technologies, and types of personnel, the Ministry of Foreign Affairs pursued some institution-building strategies that echoed those of the Salt Inspectorate, and, like the Ministry of Finance, it had no anomalous structure of shared management with non-Chinese nationals. In other respects, however, the Ministry of Foreign Affairs diverged sharply from both the Salt Inspectorate and the Ministry of Finance. Like the Salt Inspectorate, Foreign Affairs maintained a very high degree of insulation. Although an open civil service examination offered but one of several means of entry, the Ministry of Foreign Affairs was a prefectural organization that had a semi-separate system of personnel classifications, rewarded seniority, and kept very strict control over recruitment and promotion. The educational qualifications of the personnel in the Ministry of Foreign Affairs were the highest in the state bureaucracy; a clear 'track' for regular diplomatic service was established; the Ministry's chief goals, personnel, and organizational style exhibited extraordinary continuity; and the organization's prestige remained high throughout the entire Republican period.

Like the other two organizations, the Ministry of Foreign Affairs maintained its insulation and status. But otherwise, the Ministry of Foreign Affairs very much went its own way. Although its internal personnel system was substantially bureaucratized and professionalized, bureaucratization and professionalization did not automatically exclude politics and a degree of partification. Unlike the Salt Inspectorate, whose staff throughout the Republican period remained uninvolved in Party affairs, and the Ministry of Finance, in which membership in the Nationalist Party gradually became a social liability to be suppressed over the course of the 1930s, by the late 1930s the diplomats in the Ministry of Foreign Affairs quietly accepted the norm of Party membership.

The Ministry of Foreign Affairs possessed a set of consistent organizational aims, but, unlike the Ministry of Finance and the Salt Inspectorate, only some of the Ministry's goals (such as the efforts to renegotiate unequal treaties) were reducible to concrete, specific steps that could provide a benchmark for organizational success. Control over policy domain was mixed: domestic political leaders were much more inclined to dramatically intervene and reset foreign policy than they were likely to do for tax policy. In terms of its wider policy domain, the Ministry of Foreign Affairs, like the Nationalist state and indeed the international system of states in the 1930s, was unable to stem Japanese aggression. However, once policy had been decided on, the Ministry of Foreign Affairs continued to enjoy high prestige, and was not often seriously doubted by those in power, at least in part because it represented China's interests in the international community well and managed successfully to implement a number of the longstanding goals of Republican foreign policy: revocation of the unequal treaties, successful conclusion of boundary treaties, and garnering world sympathy in the conflict with Japan.

The Ministry of Foreign Affairs' generalist orientation, its incorporation of the norm of Nationalist Party membership, the acknowledged difficulties of successfully controlling its policy domain and continuing to maintain high standards in personnel administration produced a result slightly different from that of the Inspectorate or the Ministry of Finance: an organization that did not have to literally 'buy' its political legitimacy with immediate results in its policy domain. The Ministry's close ties to the political elite may have ultimately been to its advantage. Since the 'partification' of the Ministry of Foreign Affairs probably reassured political leadership without substantially weakening the organization's standards for recruitment and promotion, institution building in Foreign Affairs could be partially divorced from concrete success in external domains over which the Ministry had little control.

There was no one formula for institution-building success in Republican China. The Salt Inspectorate, the Ministry of Finance, and the Ministry of Foreign Affairs operated in their own particular policy domains, and relied on different proportions of insulation, bureaucratization, and goal implementation. Specificity of goals and manageability of domain also varied from organization to organization, and a lack of clear implementation of one element could be compensated for by the strong presence of another. For example, the Ministry of Finance did not originally possess the strong boundaries and insulation that were typical of the Salt Inspectorate and the Ministry of Foreign Affairs; but the inherent specificity and divisibility of its organizational action helped to reinforce an ethic of performance orientation and depersonalization which built *de facto* organizational insulation over a period of time. In contrast, the Ministry of Foreign Affairs' organizational goals only partially lent themselves to specificity and divisibility; but its high prestige, elitism, strong organizational boundaries, and willingness to make itself politically intelligible to the Guomindang leadership carried it through very trying times.

Although the proportions of insulation, bureaucratization, and success in goal implementation did vary, all three factors were critical to the institution-building strategies of these successful organizations. The Salt Inspectorate's and Ministry of Finance's loss of organizational cohesiveness and effectiveness during the Sino-Japanese War well illustrate their importance. For both, the war caused the loss of the organizations' financial bases, prompted a tremendous expansion of the organizations' size, and focused the attention of political leaders on micro-managing them. Together, these shocks breached both internal insulation and the ability to achieve externally oriented goals. With insulation perforated, the ranks swelled with insufficiently trained young personnel, and increasingly unreasonable demands heaped on by political superiors, rapid de-institutionalization and demoralization set in.

Even the Ministry of Foreign Affairs was compelled to compromise some of its policies of insulation by providing for upper-level 'special' (*zhuan*) appointments during the Sino-Japanese War. Paradoxically, Foreign Affairs avoided far worse de-institutionalization because of its close ties to the ruling elite and its generalist, only partially specifically oriented, goals. Since it had readily incorporated the norm of loyalty to the Nationalist Party, leading political elites felt the Ministry of Foreign Affairs to be politically reliable and in any case indispensible, and they turned their attention to establishing firm top-down control elsewhere in the bureaucracy. When combined with the organization's partially non-specific goals, this relatively *laissez-faire* attitude allowed the Ministry the space to continue to determine its own criteria for organizational success.

The experience of these organizations in Republican China illustrates a common principle. In order to differentiate itself from the environment and have the room to socialize its members into organizational goals, values, and culture, an organization must develop some form of effective insulation. An organization that is felt to be irreplaceable by the state is much more likely to be allowed the space it needs to insulate itself and institutionalize. But organizational insulation, even for organizations at the core of state-building activities, is usually not given free of charge: the organization has to 'buy' and then reinforce its insulation by 'objectively' providing services that the state cannot do without or by otherwise convincing political elites that it is doing an effective job in providing services that the state cannot do without. Organizational effectiveness, in turn, is closely related to additional factors—degrees of bureaucratization, specificity of goals, and manageability of domain.

The Ministries of Finance and Foreign Affairs and the Salt Inspectorate were all 'fortunate' organizations during the Nanjing Decade. All pursued goals that were not only substantially agreed to both inside and outside the organization, but were broadly consistent across a variety of regimes, from the late imperial *xinzheng* era through the period of Nationalist rule. Each of these organizations provided core services, without which the Republican state could not carry out its centralizing and state-building project. Each pursued strategies of institution building that were intelligible to the political leadership: the Ministry of Finance and the Salt Inspectorate in particular implemented programmes of centralization, standardization, rationalization, and amalgamation and undercutting of rival organizations that almost perfectly replicated the logic and strategies of the wider state-building project.

Provision of core services without which the Nationalist state could not pursue its state-building project enabled these organizations to deflect politicization and patronage from the outside. If political leaders were not always willing to 'listen' when the bureaucrats from these organizations 'spoke truth', then they were for the most part amenable to according the organizations large amounts of autonomy over internal operations and refrain from using them as sites for patronage. And, until the shock of the Sino-Japanese War, each used its relative good fortune in insulation to bureaucratize, depersonalize, and professionalize within while pursuing its goals without. Each of these organizations was widely perceived by contemporaries to be, on the whole, successful, which was reflected in the ability of the Salt Inspectorate, the Ministry of Finance, and the Ministry of Foreign Affairs to recruit and train a steady stream of well qualified and committed young men over a period of years.

If the weaknesses of the Examination Yuan in the Republican period illustrate in microcosm the problems inherent to a co-optive strategy of state building, the experiences of the Salt Inspectorate, the Ministry of Finance, and the Ministry of Foreign Affairs suggest ways in which the same co-optive state-building strategy can be successfully pursued by well insulated and goal-oriented supporting state organizations. Far from being the 'yamenized' den of corruption, patronage, and endless paper-pushing described by Lloyd Eastman,[2] the National Government was, at least in the critical sectors of tax and foreign affairs, capable of building strong and pro-active institutions under exceptionally difficult circumstances.

The degree to which the institution-building efforts of these particular state organizations is generalizable to other contexts is a question that awaits further research. Even for Republican China, we know little of the workings of other central state organizations, and still less of state organizations at the provincial and local levels. Until we know a great deal more about different sectors and different levels of Republican government, we will not know whether these institution-building methods were confined to a few core sectors, or were widely pursued throughout state organizations in Republican China. Since states throughout the developing world are subject to many of the same environmental constraints as were the the state- and institution-building elites of Republican China, it would be very useful to compare the institution-building strategies of these core organizations in

Nationalist China with similar organizations in Atatürk's Turkey, Pahlavei Iran, contemporary Africa, or the Commonwealth of Independent States of the former Soviet Union to assess the range and variation of institution-building strategies in different political and temporal contexts. The applicability of the experiences of these organizations in Nationalist China to other times and places can at present be raised only as a possibility, but the prospects for drawing Republican China into a wider comparative framework are promising.

# APPENDIX A
## A Note on Sources

Since very little secondary literature on the Nationalist state bureaucracy exists in any language, constructing the case studies for this study of institution building and state building required a good deal of historical research using primary sources. I was fortunate to be able to spend nearly two academic years in Nanjing, which I used as a base from which to gather most of the data used in recreating the administrative histories and institution-building strategies of the Examination Yuan, the Sino-Foreign Salt Inspectorate (later the Directorate-General of Salt), the Ministry of Finance, and the Ministry of Foreign Affairs.

Between late 1987 and mid-1989, I was able to work in the collection of the No. 2 Republican Archives in Nanjing. Much to my surprise, the No. 2 Archives' materials on the Examination Yuan consisted primarily of drafts of laws and regulations, with only occasionally useful nuggets of information in either correspondence or lists of individuals who passed either the upper-level or regular-level examinations. The most useful, and most unique, materials from the No. 2 Archives provided sets of curricula vitae for bureaucrats from different bureaucratic organizations and different time periods in Republican China. Although the forms were non-standardized, and the information given varied from set to set, curricula vitae typically included the individual's name, native place, schooling, qualifications for his present position, current ranking, previous positions with the government, and occasionally Party or non-Party affiliation. The No. 2 Archives provided extremely useful runs of curricula vitae for Salt Inspectorate in the late 1930s (with a representative cross-sample of 185 Salt Inspectorate bureaucrats) and the Ministry of the Interior in the early 1930s (with a set of 272). Curricula vitae from the Ministry of Finance were incomplete, but were intermittently available over a long time span, with materials from the early 1910s (with a complete set of 234), the early 1930s (with 61), and the early 1940s (with 20 at the 'recommended' *jianren* rank).

After hand-copying these hundreds of curricula vitae, content analysis provided a wealth of information as to the composition of a given organization at a given point in time (what sort of pre-entry training most of its members had, whether the Ministry was obviously invaded with personal networks, whether the organization attracted individuals with experience in its functional areas). For materials on the Ministry of Finance or the Sino-Foreign Salt Inspectorate, where a set of curricula vitae had been preserved late in the 1930s or two sets of curricula vitae had been preserved at different times, it was possible to chart certain aspects of the organization's evolution (i.e. did the organization become more or less politicized over time? Did its proportion of Party members go up or down? Did the organization provide more or less stable careers over time? Did most individuals with moderately high positions come up through the organization, or did they transfer in at high levels?).

In addition to the No. 2 Republican Archives in Nanjing, I was able to spend several weeks at the Guoshiguan Republican Archives in Taipei, which yielded a similar set of 98 curricula vitae for officials from the Ministry of Foreign Affairs in early 1941. The Guoshiguan also held supplementary materials on the Examination

Yuan, which charted the profiles of the examination takers and examination successes throughout the 1930s, and contained some interesting correspondence between the Examination Yuan and the individuals it credentialled in the early 1930s.

Since most archival materials tended to be either excessively broad (e.g. drafts of regulations and administrative laws), or bits of minutiae without a wider context, I turned to a variety of written and oral sources to fill out the medium-range details of organizational function and administrative history. A large number of different written materials were available in libraries or through personal contacts in China, Taiwan, and the United States. Periodicals from the period such as *Dongfang Zazhi* (The Eastern Miscellany) and *Xingzheng Xiaolü* (Administrative Efficiency) offered article-length descriptions of the major problems with different governmental policy areas in tax, salt administration, examination, and personnel systems for the contemporary educated public. Quasi-primary sources such as publically available policy papers, pamphlets put together by ministerial divisions of general affairs, and government-sponsored yearbooks from the 1930s and 1940s offered good reviews of the government organization's goals, self-diagnosis of its problems, and programmes for achieving its goals. Contemporary US Department of State and British Foreign Office analyses provided critical views of China from the outside, and both British and American archives yielded exceptionally long documents from the mid- to late 1930s written by disgruntled foreign district inspectors who, as a byproduct of their complaints, usefully reviewed the entire organizational history of the Salt Inspectorate. Contemporary scholarship from China in the 1930s and 1949s in article and book form contributed critical voices on the government's deep problems in tax and finance, and written memoirs (*wenshi ziliao*) added particular depth to the case studies.

To balance the one-sided nature of the archival and secondary written sources, I was able to interview twenty individuals who had worked for the National Government and/or taken its upper-level civil service examinations in the 1930s and early 1940s. I found retired bureaucrats from the period in both the People's Republic and Taiwan, and interviewed in Nanjing, Shanghai, Suzhou, Beijing, Taipei, and Tainan. At the time of the interviews, the youngest of my interviewees was in his early seventies, the majority were in their eighties, and several were on the far side of ninety. During the interviews, I took notes, and then transcribed as much as possible from memory afterward. Note-taking did not seem to inhibit the flow of recollections: I found almost all of my informants to be remarkably forthcoming and willing to tell their stories and to offer their opinions without guard or pretence, and in several cases they spontaneously added rough diagrams or organizational charts to my notes.

My usual format was first to ask the individual about his own background, family, and schooling, then to ask how he got his job in the government, and what he did there. Once we were talking about the organization for which he had worked, I asked general questions about recruitment and socialization: how others in the organization got their jobs, on what basis people were promoted, whether there was overt factionalism in the ministry (and if so how the factional lines were drawn), and whether organizational life really reflected the personnel policies and programmes I had seen described in the written record. Beyond my standard set of questions, individuals offered quite different information. For example, those who had worked for the Ministry of Personnel waxed eloquent about the personnel system in general, but offered relatively little insight as to the day-to-day inner-organizational dynamics of the Ministry of Personnel, while those who worked in the Ministry of Finance talked a great deal about daily life in the organization, but made only general comments about the systemic problems of tax and finance in the 1930s and 1940s. Although people's memories certainly are selective about events that occurred fifty or sixty years previously, there was little in my informants' stories that was obviously suspect: not only did their information correlate with the written materials, but the data and reminiscences from informants interviewed in the People's Republic did not differ substantially from those of informants who had migrated to Taiwan. Interviews with retired bureaucrats proved to be an invaluable source, which enabled much more effective utilization of the archival data, and provided a great deal of life and texture to the development of the case studies.

# APPENDIX B*
## Biographical List of Interviewees

CHEN GUISHENG. Born in 1919 in Shanxi, but grew up largely in Guangdong and Guangxi, where his father was most often posted as an official with the Sino-Foreign Salt Inspectorate. The younger Chen took the entry-level salt inspectorate examination in 1939, beginning his career in the Salt Inspectorate at the very bottom, as a lowest-level clerk. For several years thereafter he advanced several grades by examination, and then settled into a long career with the Salt Inspectorate, following it through several reorganizations and name changes in the years between 1939 and the 1980s. Chen worked primarily in the personnel division, where he ended his career as a division chief (*sizhang*).

Interviewed on 16 January 1989, Taipei.

CHEN HANZHANG. Born in 1910 in Anhui, but moved to Nanjing at the age of 5 for his father's medical practice. Chen did a degree in humanities at Jinling University, and through the university he got an introduction for his first job in the Division of Archival Reorganization in 1929. On this basis he also entered the Guomindang as a 'special recruit' (*teshu rudang*). Most of his pre-1949 career was spent in a variety of positions in archival and library work: in local, provincial, and national level government units in Sichuan and Jiangsu.

Interviewed on 1 April 1988, Nanjing.

DAI LIYAN. Born in 1901 in a small town in Zhejiang. Graduated from Wusong College with a degree in business, and joined the Nanjing Government Ministry of Finance in 1928, first spending a year in the tax division. When the currency division was formed in 1929, Dai was invited to join it. He remained in the currency division of the Ministry of Finance for twenty years, starting off as a section member (*keyuan*), and eventually rising to the level of division chief (*sizhang*).

Interviewed on 28 November 1988, Shanghai.

DAI YUANCHEN. Born in 1926 in Huzhou, Zhejiang. Because of the war, at the age of 12 he moved to the interior of Fujian, where he attended the Jiangsu Xueyuan and concentrated on politics and economics. He moved to Nanjing in 1946, and through family connections to Dai Jitao, the head of the Examination Yuan, quickly got an appointment as a section member (*keyuan*) in the Ministry of Personnel. But after only one year, Dai passed a Ministry of Finance 'special exam' (*tekao*), and transferred into the Ministry of Finance, where he remained until 1949.

Interviewed on 28 June 1988, Beijing.

* Although every effort was made to ask a standard set of biographical questions of all interviewees, some informants were reluctant to reveal certain details (such as their exact ages, native places, or father's occupations). The information in this biographical list is as complete as politeness at the time of interviewing allowed.

DING WEICI. Born in 1915 in Guiding Xian, Guizhou. Ding went to middle school in Guiyang, but was also taught the classics at home by his grandfather, who had got a *juren* degree under the imperial examination system. Ding's parents both died when he was in his early teens, and after supporting himself through middle school he worked as a reporter and editor in Guiyang between 1936 and 1938. In 1938 he moved to Chongqing, where he enrolled in the Central Political University, studying general social science and Russian between 1938 and 1940. Although he never got a degree, his Russian skills were in great demand: he was asked to be a Russian translator for a military affairs committee in Yining. Then, when the Ministry of Foreign Affairs set up an office in Urumqi geared towards Russian affairs, he was given a temporary (*daili*) appointment as assistant to the representative, where he stayed for three years. It was not until 1944, when he got back to Chongqing, that he was given a formal appointment with the Ministry of Foreign Affairs, and his credentials were not formalized until 1946. Between 1946 and 1949, Ding had a series of entry-level appointments in Nanjing and Moscow. After the retreat to Taiwan, his career in the Ministry of Foreign Affairs stabilized, and he developed new expertise on the Middle East, finishing out his career before retirement at the level of councillor (*canshi*).

Interviewed on 16 January 1989, Taipei.

LI SHUPING. Born in 1902 in Shanghai. Attended a Catholic school, and graduated in 1928 with a degree in politics and economics. Through connections of his in-laws, Li got an appointment as a section member in the Ministry of Agriculture and Mines immediately after graduation. He did not remain there for long; within a few months he was introduced to Song Ziwen, and shortly thereafter was appointed to the Central Party Committee, to work in the Secretariat. Li later had positions in a number of different government and Party organizations as a high-level 'secretary' (*jianren mishu*), but functionally he served as a high-level runner and informer for Song Ziwen. During the war, Li remained in Shanghai with the Central Bank of China.

Interviewed on 28 November 1988, Shanghai.

LI TIEZHENG. Born in 1905 in Nanxian, Hunan. In 1928 Li was accorded an LL.B. degree from National Central University in Nanjing, and the same year he passed the Hunan provincial civil service exam. Li took the first sitting of the upper civil service exam (*gaodeng kaoshi*) in 1931, concentrating on foreign affairs, for which he placed first. After his appointment to the Nationalist Ministry of Foreign Affairs in 1932, he moved up the ranks to reach the rank of first ambassador by 1942. Li resigned in mid-1949, and pursued Ph.D.s in political science and international relations at Columbia University in New York and the University of London. In 1953, when the war in Indochina was widening, Li returned to China and continued to pursue a career in foreign affairs in the People's Republic.

Interviewed on 30 June 1988, Beijing.

LI XUELI. Born in 1910 in Changshu, Jiangsu. Li graduated from Fudan University with a degree in psychology in 1936. Through personal connections, he got an appointment with the Ministry of Foreign Affairs in 1939, but it was an appointment in name only: he never left Shanghai, and never worked for the Ministry of Foreign Affairs. After the war, again through connections, he got an appointment with the newly established Ministry of Agriculture and Forestry, which he considered to be a hollow organization (*kongjia de zuzhi*) that existed to fill patronage positions.

Interviewed 28 November 1988, Shanghai.

LIN JIYONG. Born in 1920 in Fuzhou. Lin attended the Fuzhou Middle School, graduating in 1937. After middle school, he was accepted by several colleges, but was unable to go. When he saw a public announcement for the Salt Inspectorate examinations in late 1939, he took the entry-level examination, embarking on a career in salt administration that would last for over forty-five years, working primarily in transportation and general affairs. Lin retired in the mid-1980s, and at the date of interview was still active in writing about the Salt Inspectorate.

Interviewed 24 January 1989, Tainan.

LIU ZONGHAN. Born in Shuangshan, Liaoning. Liu attended Yanjing University, graduating in 1938, and from there he attended the Central Political University (Zhengzhi Daxue), from which he moved into the Ministry of Foreign Affairs in 1941. In the Ministry of Foreign Affairs he had a succession of posts, including ambassadorial and quasi-ambassadorial positions. At the time of the interview, he had spent nearly fifty years in continuous service in the Nationalist Ministry of Foreign Affairs.

Interviewed on 30 January 1989, Taipei.

LUO WANLEI. Born in 1905 in Xining Xian, Hunan. Luo attended a normal school (*shifan xuexiao*), and continued as the school's principal from 1932 to 1936. In 1936 he took the fourth sitting of the national upper civil service examination (*gaokao*), as he wanted to move out of education and out of Hunan. He passed and was assigned to the Ministry of Personnel as a section member, then returned to Hunan, where he took the local county chief examinations and served as a county chief between 1936 and 1939. When he participated in a party training course (*xunlian ban*) in Chong-qing in 1939, he ran into an old friend, who invited him to come back to the Ministry of Personnel with a position as section chief (*kezhang*) in the salary review section. In 1944, on the recommendation of his boss, he was promoted to division chief (*sizhang*) of the registration department. At the time of the Nationalist Government's removal to Taiwan in 1949, Luo had risen to vice-ministerial rank in the Ministry of Personnel, where he continued to work through the 1950s and 1960s.

Interviewed on 5 January 1989, Taipei.

SONG TONGFU. Born in 1919 in Weihai, Shandong. Song began his studies in Beida's Law and Economics Department, and moved with the school to Chang-sha and Yunnan during the war. After graduating in 1939, he got a position as a researcher/analyst with the Central Bank of China, and then took the special examination for finance in 1940; from there he moved into a series of research/analyst jobs with the Ministry of Finance, remaining there until 1949.

Interviewed 18 November 1988, Shanghai.

SUN JINGGONG. Born in 1908 in a small village in the countryside. Sun attended the Beijing Communications College, but did not finish his programme. Instead, he went to Guangzhou to work for the revolution, where he engaged in political work and education. During the Northern Expedition, he ended up associated with the Wuhan Government, and after the collapse of the latter he went to Moscow for revolutionary training between 1928 and 1931. He returned to China in 1931, taught economics at the college level, and engaged in leftist activities. During the war he retreated to Chengdu, where he taught economics at Chaoyang University. In 1941 he was invited to join the Ministry of Finance as a councillor/adviser to make recommendations on economic policy, and later became a chief secretary (*mishuzhang*). He remained with the Ministry of Finance through the war years.

Interviewed on 29 November 1988, Shanghai.

WU CHENGMING. Born in 1917 in Hebei. Wu took a first degree in economics from Qinghua University, and from there went to Columbia University in New York, where he got an advanced degree in economics. From Columbia he was recruited directly into the newly formed Executive Yuan Economic Advisory Committee in 1940 as a section member (*keyuan*). In 1942 he was promoted to section chief (*kezhang*). After the war he moved into academe, and wrote extensively on economic questions and national finance from the late 1940s to the 1980s.

Interviewed on 21 May 1988, Beijing.

XU GONGXIANG. Born in 1918, Xu spent two years at an upper normal school in Shanghai, and spent the last two years of college in Hong Kong. He got his first position in the Military Affairs Committee (Junshi Weiyuanhui) through private connections in 1940, spent the early war years in Guilin, and then moved to Chongqing in 1943. After the war he got his next position, as a secretary (*mishu*) for the Northeast Army, also through personal connections.

Interviewed on 13 April 1989, Nanjing.

YAN ZEKUI. Born in 1918 to a Hakka family, Yan grew up largely in Hangzhou, and attended the Hangzhou Christian College and Fudan University, from which he graduated with a degree in economics in 1936. Fortunately, at just this time the Ministry of Finance established a new division to handle income tax, and Yan immediately went to work for this division.

Interviewed on 26 May 1988, Beijing.

YIN LUGUANG. Born in 1912 in Shandong, Yin moved early to Henan, Xuzhou, and then Nanjing. He entered the Central Political School (Zhengzhi Xuexiao) in 1932, graduated from the department of foreign affairs in 1936, and then went to the London School of Economics, where he got an MA in 1939. At the end of 1939 he returned to China, and taught at a small college in Shaanxi. He started his civil service career only in 1942, when a friend recommended him into the Ministry of Foreign Affairs with a first position as section chief (*kezhang*) in the Overseas Chinese division. He was then posted to Burma and the Secretariat of the Ministry of Foreign Affairs. By the late 1940s he had become increasingly disillusioned by the government, and elected to remain in China after 1949.

Interviewed on March 11 1989, Nanjing.

ZHONG LIANGZHE. Born in Yongan Xian, Fuzhou, Fujian. Zhong's father died while he was still young, and he began but was unable to complete a degree at Fujian University. In 1941 he took the entry exam for the Salt Inspectorate in Fujian, and was given a position. He started out doing personnel work, but then moved into salt production and transportation. Zhong regularly advanced in the organization, reached the highest grade it offered, and retired in 1984.

Interviewed on 20 January 1989, Taipei.

ZHOU BI. Born in 1911, in the countryside of Tongcheng County, Anhui. Zhou attended Wuhan University, graduating in 1936 with a degree in economics. In 1936 he took a special upper-level examination (*gaodeng kaoshi*) for the Ministry of Finance, which was then setting up a brand new department for the direct tax administration. Zhou was assigned first as an 'upper-level tax staff member' (*gaoji shuiwuyuan*), and was then promoted to section chief (*kezhang*) in the direct tax administration division in 1939. In 1942 he moved from central government tax administration to a series of high-level provincial positions in taxation, and in 1950 he was invited to Beijing to serve in the Ministry of Finance of the People's Republic.

Interviewed on 30 November 1988, Shanghai.

ZHOU WEILIANG. Born in 1911. Zhou's father received a classical education and passed both the *juren* and *jinshi* imperial degrees, but in the 1920s was invited to work for the Salt Inspectorate, where he was involved with salt transport and production. The elder Zhou had a series of appointments with the Inspectorate in Weihaiwei and in the Lianghuai District Office. The younger Zhou graduated from Beiping University in 1932 and followed in his father's footsteps by taking the Inspectorate examination in 1933 and taking up his first Inspectorate post shortly thereafter. Zhou Weiliang spent virtually his entire life with the Salt Administration, first as a child of the service, then as an active member, and finally in retirement, when he continued to engage in research and write essays on the organizational structure and development of the Salt Administration.

Interviewed on 23 January 1989, Tainan.

ZHOU WEIXUN. Zhou grew up in Beijing, but when the war broke out went on his own initiative to Kunming when he was still in his last year of high school. Once in Kunming, he enrolled in the Government Department at Yunnan Daxue, and graduated in 1943. After graduation, he edited a magazine for a while before going to Chongqing, and then to Nanjing after the war was over. After being out of work for months, he finally got a job with the Ministry of Personnel as a section member (*keyuan*) through personal connections, starting work in January 1946. He remained with the Ministry of Personnel as a section member for the remainder of the civil war, and chose to stay in Nanjing after 1949.

Interviewed on 25 March 1989, Nanjing.

ZHU LEIZHANG. Born in 1905 in Kunshan Xian, Jiangsu, Zhu was educated and grew up in Hangzhou, where he attended the Hangzhou School of Law and Government (Hangzhou Fazheng Xuexiao). He then went to Shanghai, where he took a joint degree in electrical engineering and literature at Jiaotong Daxue in three years, graduating in 1931. In 1931 he took the first upper-level civil service exam, with general administration as his sub-field, and he passed with the highest overall score. After the exam, he was first assigned to the Ministry of Communications, where he worked in the division of construction and engineering; then in the mid-1930s he transferred to the Control Yuan, where he served as an auditor until late 1948. After 1949 he remained in China, but was never given a work assignment by the new regime, and lived in abject poverty from the 1950s to the 1980s, sweeping the streets and doing odd jobs to stay alive.

Interviewed on 28 April 1989, Suzhou.

ZHU YUAN. Born in 1914 in Jiangshan Xian, Zhejiang, Zhu was raised in Hangzhou from the age of 5 or 6. He attended Qinghua University, and graduated with a degree in economics in 1936. After graduation, he immediately took the special sitting of the upper-level examination for finance, and went to work for the new direct tax department. Zhu was chosen to participate in a two-year training course within the Ministry of Finance, but by the time the course was seriously underway the war had begun. Zhu moved from Nanjing to Changsha, to Chongqing, to Kunming. In 1943 he was sent by the Ministry of Finance to Washington to do a short course in tax management, and from Washington he went to Harvard University, where he studied for three years and got an MA in Economics. Zhu returned to the Ministry of Finance in China in early 1946, and was posted by the Ministry to be the provincial director of direct tax in Fujian. In 1947 he was transferred to the Currency Division, and in early 1949 he retreated to Shanghai. Once in Shanghai, he began to teach at the Finance Institute, where he has been a professor ever since.

Interviewed on 1 April 1989, Shanghai.

ZHU ZISHUAI. Born in 1897 in Jiangshan County, Zhejiang. Zhu attended primary and middle school locally, and completed a degree at the Zhejiang Upper Normal School in education. Zhu joined the Guomindang in 1924 in Hangzhou, and became associated with the 'Left' Guomindang. After being introduced into the Central Party Organization in 1928, Zhu settled in for a long period with the Guomindang Propaganda Bureau (Xuanchuan Bu), with an eventual position of section chief (*kezhang*). In 1940 Zhu was transferred to the Executive Yuan to troubleshoot for the National Government Library with a newly created position of *zhuren mishu* (managing secretary). Zhu continued library and archival work after 1949 in Nanjing.

Interviewed on 2 April 1988, Nanjing.

# APPENDIX C
## Chinese Terms and Names Used in Text

| | |
|---|---|
| Beiyang | 北洋 |
| bosheng | 撥生 |
| Caizheng Bu | 財政部 |
| caizheng ting | 財政廳 |
| canshi | 參事 |
| caoxing | 操行 |
| Chen Guofu | 陳果夫 |
| Chen Lifu | 陳立夫 |
| chufen | 處分 |
| chushi/zaishi | 初試再試 |
| cizhi | 辭職 |
| Dai Jitao | 戴季陶 |
| daili | 代理 |
| Da Zongtong | 大總統 |
| danghua | 黨化 |
| dangyi | 黨義 |
| daji | 大記 |

| | |
|---|---|
| Da Tong | 大統 |
| deng | 等 |
| Dianshi Weiyuanhui | 典試委員會 |
| dizheng xueyuan | 地政學院 |
| fabi | 法幣 |
| fazheng xuetang | 法政學堂 |
| Feng Yuxiang | 馮玉祥 |
| fusheng | 附生 |
| Gan Naiguang | 甘乃光 |
| gaokao | 高考 |
| gongzuo | 工作 |
| Gu Weijun (V.K. Wellington Koo) | 顧維鈞 |
| Gu Yingfen | 古應芬 |
| guan | 官 |
| Guo Taiqi (Quo Tai-chi) | 郭泰祺 |
| Guofang Zuigao Weiyuanhui | 國防最高委員會 |
| guofu | 國父 |
| Guomindang | 國民黨 |
| houbu | 候補 |

| | |
|---|---|
| Hu Bu | 户部 |
| ji | 級 |
| jia | 甲 |
| jian, jian, wei | 蔣介石 |
| Jiang Jieshi (Chiang Kai-shek) | 簡荐委 |
| jianren ('selected appointment') | 簡任 |
| jianren ('recommended appointment') | 荐任 |
| jiaoguan | 教官 |
| jingshen | 精神 |
| jinshi | 進士 |
| jiuchang zhengshui | 就場征税 |
| ju | 局 |
| juanshui | 捐税 |
| junshihua | 君子 |
| junzi | 軍事化 |
| juren | 舉人 |
| kaoji | 考績 |
| kaoxun | 考訓 |
| ke | 科 |

| kexuehua | 科學化 |
| Keyuan | 科員 |
| kezhang | 科長 |
| Kong Xiangxi (H.H. Kung) | 孔祥熙 |
| lijin | 釐金 |
| Li Jinlun | 李錦綸 |
| ling | 令 |
| lougui | 陋規 |
| luan | 亂 |
| Luo Wen'gan | 羅文幹 |
| Miao Qiujie | 繆秋杰 |
| mishu | 秘書 |
| muyou | 幕友 |
| nei/wai | 內／外 |
| peiyang | 培養 |
| pukao | 普考 |
| Qian Tai | 錢泰 |
| qianshi | 簽士 |
| qingyao bolian | 輕徭薄斂 |

Quanxu Bu            銓敘部

quefa qiantu jingshen  缺乏前途精神

renqing              仁情

renyong kaoshi       任用考試

sanmin zhuyi         三民主義

shen                 審

shengdeng kaoshi     升等考試

shengyuan            生員

Shenji Bu            審計部

Shi Zhaoji (Alfred S.K. Sze)  施肇基

shu                  署

Shuiwu Shu           稅務署

shuiwu si            稅務司

si                   司

sizhang              司長

Song Meiling         宋美齡

Song Ziwen (T.V. Soong)  宋子文

Sun Ke (Sun Fo)      孫科

Sun Zhongshan (Sun Yatsen)  孫中山

| | |
|---|---|
| suo | 所 |
| Tai Ping | 太平 |
| Tang Shaoyi | 唐紹儀 |
| tankuan | 攤款 |
| tekao | 特考 |
| teren | 特任 |
| tezhong kaoshi | 特種考試 |
| ti yijian | 提意見 |
| Tongwenguan | 同文館 |
| Waijiao Bu | 外交部 |
| waijiao xi | 外交 |
| Waiwu Bu | 外務部 |
| Wang Chonghui | 王寵惠 |
| Wang Jingwei | 汪精衛 |
| Wang Zhengting | 王正廷 |
| weiren | 委任 |
| weiyuan | 委員 |
| Wu Chaoqu (C.C. Wu) | 伍朝樞 |
| Wu Tingfang | 伍廷芳 |

Xianzhi caiju fazhan    限制才具發展

Xiangshi Weiyuanhui    襄試委員會

xiao ('owling')        鴞

xiao (filial piety)     孝

*Xingzheng Xiaolü*     行政效率

*Xingzheng Yanjiu Yuekan*    行政研究月刊

xinshui xinren xin jingshen    新稅新人新精神

xinzheng             新政

Xianzheng Bianchaguan    憲政編查館

Xiong Yingzha         熊應祚

xu                   虛

Xu Mo               徐謨

xueshi              學識

xuexiban            學習班

xunlian             訓練

xunlianban          訓練班

xunling             訓令

yamen               衙門

Yan Huiqing (W.W. Yen)    顏惠慶

| | |
|---|---|
| Yangchengsuo | 養成所 |
| yangwu | 洋務 |
| Yanwu Jihe Zongsuo | 鹽務稽核總所 |
| Yanwu Shu | 鹽務署 |
| Yanwu Zongju | 鹽務總局 |
| Yanzheng Si | 鹽政司 |
| yewu | 業務 |
| yewu rifan xuren riduo | 業務日煩須人日多 |
| yi an | 詒安 |
| yin'an | 引岸 |
| yiwu yishui | 一物一税 |
| yong xinren ban xinshui | 用新人辦新税 |
| Yuan | 院 |
| Yuan Shikai | 袁世凱 |
| Zhang Qun | 張羣 |
| Zhang Zuolin | 張作霖 |
| Zheng Hongnian | 鄭洪年 |
| zhengtu | 正途 |
| zhengzhi xuexi | 政治學習 |

zhi an            治安

Zhi Bu            支部

Zhongyang Xunliantuan    中央訓練團

Zhongyang Zhengzhi Daxue ('Zhengda')  中央政治大學

Zhongyang Zhengzhi Xuexiao    中央政治學校

Zhongyang Zhixing Weiyuanhui  中央執行委員會

Zhu Tingqi        朱庭祺

zhuan             專

zhuanyuan         專員

zige kaoshi       資格考試

Zongli Yamen      總理衙門

zu                組

# NOTES

## Introduction

1. Max Weber, *Economy and Society*, i, ii, ed. Guenther Roth and Claus Wittich (Berkeley and Los Angeles: University of California Press, 1978): 54, 56, 902.
2. In addition to Weber, see Michael Mann, 'The Autonomous Power of the State', in John A. Hall (ed.), *States in History*, (Cambridge: Basil Blackwell, 1986): 112; Charles Tilly, 'Reflections on the History of European State-Making', in Charles Tilly (ed.), *The Formation of National States in Western Europe*, (Princeton: Princeton University Press, 1975): 34 and 70; Theda Skocpol, 'Bringing the State Back In: Strategies of Analysis in Current Research', in Peter B. Evans, Dietrich Rueschemeyer, and Theda Skocpol (eds.), *Bringing the State Back In* (Cambridge: Cambridge University Press, 1985): 28; John A. Hall and G. John Ikenberry, *The State* (Minneapolis: University of Minnesota Press, 1989): 1–2.
3. Tilly, *Formation of National States*, 47.
4. The last quarter of the 20th c. has, of course, witnessed a significant retreat of state involvement in states as different as Western states, formerly Leninist states, and states in the developing world. In such key areas as direct economic activity, redistribution of wealth, and the provision of social insurance, an earlier consensus that social public goods and economic development could best be ensured by the state has evaporated; appropriate degrees of state involvement *v.* private initiative are now hotly contested. But even today's 'retreating' states are immeasurably stronger, closer to society, and involved in a wide variety of tasks and service provision when compared to states some several hundred years ago.
5. The phrase is Tilly's, and he suggests that the means of coercion is primarily military, police, and taxation-oriented. For a rational choice rather than an institutional analysis of the same phenomenon, see Margaret Levi, *Of Rule and Revenue* (Berkeley and Los Angeles: University of California Press, 1988). But for many non-Western, pre-modern states, the organized means of internal coercion may have its origins in religion and the sacred; see Patricia Crone, 'The Tribe and the State', in John A. Hall (ed.), *States in History* (Oxford: Blackwell, 1986).
6. The literature on organization theory and behaviour is vast. For an excellent review of most of the main approaches, see W. Richard Scott, *Organizations: Rational, Natural and Open Systems* (Englewood Cliffs, NJ: Prentice-Hall, 1981).
7. Philip Selznick, *Leadership and Administration* (Berkeley and Los Angeles: University of California Press, 1957/1984): 17. Selznick sees this critical institutionalization/infusion with value to be in opposition to the organization's more functional and technical aspects. I see no such dichotomy: in contexts in which functional and technical proficiency is in short supply, technically oriented 'results' and effectiveness may become exactly those values that are institutionalized in new organizations.
8. These key concepts of organizational technology, domain, and task environment come from James D. Thompson, *Organizations in Action* (Pittsburgh, PA

University of Pittsburgh Press, 1967). While these concepts are developed throughout Thompson's work, see pp. 26–7 for succinct definitions of domain and task environment.

9. For example, given the context of 18th and 19th-c. England, a state with notoriously weak central administrative structures *vis-à-vis* the dominant groups in society, Marx's oft quoted comment that the state is but 'the executive committee of the ruling class' makes a good deal of sense. See Karl Marx and Friedrich Engels, 'The Manifesto of the Communist Party', cited in Robert C. Tucker (ed.), *The Marx–Engels Reader* (New York: Norton Press, 1972). In my own view, while degrees of autonomy vary, I see 'the State' and its subsidiary administrative organizations as Janus-faced: simultaneously of society and yet carrying out policies that often reflect broader, autonomous interests of centralization and economic development.

10. See Theda Skocpol, *States and Social Revolution* (Cambridge: Cambridge University Press, 1979), ch. 2; Hall and Ikenberry, *The State*, ch. 1.

11. These states were not, however, necessarily fragile when compared with their contemporary competitors, and still less were they fragile when they chose to train the full power of their coercive capacities on either particular individuals or groups they sought to bring to heel at a given point in time.

12. This discussion of the dynamics of state building in early modern Europe is drawn largely from Tilly, *Formation of National States*, 38–46, 73–6, and in Charles Tilly, *Coercion, Capital and European States, AD 990–1992* (Cambridge and Oxford: Blackwell, 1990 and 1992), ch. 3, 67–95.

13. See Charles Tilly, *Big Structures, Large Processes, Huge Comparisons* (New York: Russell Sage, 1984), ch. 3. Although in this context Tilly applies 'implosion' to the transformation of production during the 19th-c. Industrial Revolution, it seems to me to be applicable to the state-building efforts beginning three to four centuries previously.

14. The conventional historiography on the Nationalist era chronologically demarcates the period into the Nanjing Decade (1927–37), the Sino-Japanese War (1937–45), and the Civil War (1945–9). While this periodization makes a great deal of sense, given the great historical and military conflicts of the Republican period, it makes somewhat less sense for the study of institution building: the processes underway during the 1930s did not come to a sudden halt in July of 1937. Informants repeatedly stressed that, even after the traumatic defeats in the early Sino-Japanese War and the relocation of the government to the interior of China in 1938, 'things only began to get bad' for the National Government around 1940, when inflation began to spin out of control and morale in the wartime capital began to drop: interviews with Zhu Zishuai (2 April 1988, Nanjing), Chen Hanzhang (1 April 1988, Nanjing), Yan Zekui (26 May 1988, Shanghai), and Zhu Leizhang, 28 April 1989, Suzhou).

15. See Ch'ien Tuan-sheng, *The Government and Politics of China* (Cambridge, Mass.: Harvard University Press, 1950); Lloyd Eastman, *The Abortive Revolution: China Under Nationalist Rule, 1927–37* (Cambridge, Mass.: Harvard University Press, 1974), and Tien Hung-mao, *Government and Politics in Kuomintang China, 1927–37* (Stanford: Stanford University Press, 1972).

16. For sympathetic treatments of the Nationalist experiment, see Arthur Young, *China's Nation Building Effort: The Financial and Economic Record, 1927–37* (Stanford: Hoover Institution Press, 1971); Arthur Young, *China and the Helping Hand* (Cambridge, Mass.: Harvard University Press, 1963), and Maria Hsia Chang, ' "Fascism" and Modern China', *China Quarterly*, No. 79 (September 1979).

17. I had access to both major collections of archival documents on the Republican period. In Nanjing, in the People's Republic of China, I worked in the No. 2 (Republican) Historical Archives, where I found a wealth of material on the Ministry of Finance and the Salt Inspectorate from 1913 through the 1940s. In Taiwan, at the Guoshiguan Archives, there were good supplementary materials on the Examination Yuan, and a substantial collection of materials on the Ministry of Foreign Affairs. Secondary sources varied: in both the People's Republic and Taiwan, I found periodicals from the 1930s and the 1940 and concurrent historical scholarship both to be very useful. In addition, while in China and Taiwan I was fortunate enough to be able to interview a number of former bureaucrats from the Nationalist Ministries of Personnel, Finance, Foreign Affairs, the Salt Inspectorate, and a number of other state organizations. For a fuller description of sources and the process of reconstructing these administrative histories, see Appendices A ('A Note on Sources') and B ('List of Interviewees').

## Chapter 1

1. A fairly consistent agenda of maintaining cosmic harmony and order did not, of course, mean that nothing changed during the five and a half centuries between the establishment of the Ming dynasty and the late Qing 'New Government' (*xinzheng*) reforms. Both Ming and Qing emperors were capable of institutional innovation. The Ming presided over the monetization of the economy, while the early Qing rulers, as an alien aspiring dynasty, were particularly sensitive to the need to preserve their cultural distinctiveness while garnering the allegiance of a broad cross-section of Han Chinese elites. The early Qing emperors were adept at modifying certain Ming institutions (e.g. providing for dual board presidencies to ease ethnic tensions), creating hybrid organizations (the Banners), expanding informal organizations and practices to fulfil policy needs (the Grand Council), and establishing a granary system to guard against the downside risk of famine. But institutional innovation occurred to promote results that were fundamentally conservative and maintenance oriented: even the most vigorous of the 18th-c. emperors innovated in a context of re-establishing social and political order.

2. On the establishment and maintenance of the granary system, see Pierre-Etienne Will, R. Bin Wong, and James Lee, *Nourish the People: The State Granary System in China, 1650–1850* (Ann Arbor: University of Michigan Press, 1991).

3. Quoted in Silas Wu, *Kangxi and his Heir Apparent, 1661–1722* (Cambridge, Mass.: Harvard University Press, 1971), 27. In addition to the immediately practical vision of *zhi an*, a more utopian strand of Confucian political theory stressed the desirability of achieving *Tai Ping* ('Great Peace') through *Da Tong*

('Great Harmony'). The 'Great Peace' was an ideal state characterized by tranquility, equality, and lack of differentiation between social classes. However, even those who clearly practised *zhi an* often used the vocabulary and imagery of 'Grand Harmony'.

4. Cited in C. K. Yang, 'Some Characteristics of Chinese Bureaucratic Behavior', in David S. Nivison and Arthur Wright (eds.), *Confucianism in Action* (Stanford: Stanford University Press, 1959), 141.

5. For example, within the Board of Revenue, each of 14 supervisory departments simultaneously was responsible for the tax receipts of a particular province and its own particular Empire-wide functional jurisdiction. The Shaanxi department handled tea administration, the Zhejiang department prepared the annual population census, the Sichuan department wrote the annual report of the Empire's harvest, and so on. These examples are all taken from E-Tu Zen Sun, 'The Board of Revenue in Nineteenth Century China', *Harvard Journal of Asian Studies*, 24 (1962–3), table on 182–3.

6. Esther Morrisson, 'The Modernization of the Confucian Bureaucracy', unpublished Ph.D. dissertation, Radcliffe College (1959), 275. Although clearly not the most efficient way to organize a bureaucracy, these features of redundancy and overlap did perhaps make for a more *effective* organization. By having several different sources of information readily available to high-level decision-makers, distortion was probably reduced.

7. See Thomas Metzger, *The Internal Organization of the Ch'ing Bureaucracy: Legal, Normative and Communications Aspects* (Cambridge, Mass.: Harvard University Press, 1973) on the *chufen* (administrative punishment) laws, and Marianne Bastid, 'The Structure of the Financial Institutions of the State in the Late Qing', in Stuart Schram (ed.), *The Scope of State Power in China* (New York: St Martin's Press, 1985).

8. In fact, the classification system of examinations, types of degree, and ways in which one could eventually obtain office were quite complex. As described below, the 'regular' way of obtaining a degree was through the open civil service exam, held at the prefectural, provincial, and state levels. But alternative degrees to confer imperial favour had always existed, and the state periodically resorted to some selling of offices, especially in times of dynastic weakness. During the Taiping Rebellion, when the state desperately needed to shore up its support with local elites, it greatly expanded its sale of offices. The sale of offices accelerated during the last half of the 19th c.: population pressure greatly increased the competition for regular degrees, but the state did not raise the quotas for each degree. Even so, until the abolition of the imperial examinations in 1905, anyone with aspirations to high status studied hard and began early.

9. These figures are cited in Benjamin Elman, 'Education, Society and Civil Service Examinations in Late Imperial China', unpublished paper, conference on Education and Society in Late Imperial China, June 1989.

10. This calculation, as well as the phrase 'Examination Hell', comes from Ichisada Miyazaki, *China's Examination Hell: The Civil Service Examinations of Imperial China*, trans. Conrad Schirokauer, (New York and Tokyo: Weatherhill, 1976), 16.

11. Cited in Elman, 'Education', and John Watt, *The District Magistrate in Late Imperial China* (New York: Columbia University Press, 1972), 36.

12. See Elman, 'Education'. Elman also notes that wealthy families and lineages would often spread their risk by investing in the education of collateral relatives. Boys bright enough to pass such rigorous examinations were difficult to come by, even in advantaged families.

13. Ibid. 33.

14. The phrase is Max Weber's: Reinhard Bendix, *From Max Weber: An Intellectual Portrait* (London: University Paperbacks, 1959), 112.

15. Baogong is still popular enough as a folk figure that collections of Baogong stories and fables continue to be published in China. See *Baogong Xiqu Gushiji* (A Collection of Stories from Yuan Drama) (Shanghai: Shanghai Wehhua Chubanshe, 1986); and *Baogong Zhuan* (Baogong Stories) (Heilongjiang Jiaoyu Chubanshe, 1986).

16. This discussion is based on T'ung-tsu Chu, *Local Government in China Under the Ch'ing* (Stanford: Stanford University Press, 1962), and Watt, *District Magistrate*.

17. Although such clerks and runners were usually natives of the locality in which they worked, this was not always the case. The wealthy county of Shaoxing managed to produce and perpetuate an impressive network of sub-officials throughout the empire; see James Cole, *Shaosing: Competition and Cooperation in Nineteenth Century China* (Tucson: University of Arizona Press, 1986).

18. See Yang, 'Characteristics', 157–9; and Cole, *Shaosing*, 2–3.

19. Cited in Étienne Balazs, *Political Theory and Administrative Reality in Traditional China* (London: School of Oriental and African Studies, 1965), 59.

20. For the details of the triennial *daji* evaluation, see Huang Liu-hung, *A Complete Book Concerning Happiness and Benevolence: A Manual for Local Magistrates in Seventeenth Century China*, Djang Chu, ed. and trans. (Tucson: University of Arizona Press, 1984), pp. 509–10, and Yang, 'characteristics', 160. On the system of gift giving, see Madeline Zelin, *The Magistrate's Tael: Rationalizing Fiscal Reform in Eighteenth Century Ch'ing China* (Berkeley and Los Angeles: University of California Press, 1984), 55, and Raymond Chu and William Saywell, *Career Patterns in the Ch'ing Dynasty* (Ann Arbor: Center for Chinese Studies, University of Michigan Press, 1984), 14.

21. Certainly, imperial officials themselves complained long and loud about how their careers had been held back by petty jealousies and unsympathetic superiors (Yang, 'characteristics', and Balazs, *Political Theory*). Sycophancy and jealousies were hardly unique to the Confucian bureaucracy. All asymmetrical power relationships have a strong tendency to reward those in lower positions for conforming to the preferences of their superiors. A serious problem arises only when 'yes men' are so exclusively rewarded that alternate or unpopular views are not taken into consideration. Although much work on the imperial bureaucracy remains to be done, it appears that the effectiveness of administrative performance in late imperial China had much to do with the administrative style of the Emperor and the tasks he chose to pursue. Conscientious and vigorous emperors, such as Kangxi and Yongzheng, selected men of proven practical ability, kept open alternate lines of communication, and chose to

pursue only those policies they felt they had the means to implement. Later Qing emperors had to deal with increasingly difficult objective problems, and tended to get trapped by their own rhetoric. See Jonathan Spence, *Ts'ao Yin and the K'ang-hsi Emperor: Bondservant and Master* (New Haven: Yale University Press, 1974); Silas Wu, *Communication and Imperial Control in China: Evolution of the Palace Memorial System, 1693–1735* (Cambridge, Mass.: Harvard University Press, 1971); Zelin, *Magistrate's Tael*; Harold Kahn, *Monarchy in the Emperor's Eyes: Image and Reality in the Ch'ien-lung Reign* (Cambridge, Mass.: Harvard University Press, 1971).

22. The Sino-Japanese War of 1894–5, in which a fast, well equipped Japanese fleet dramatically defeated China, further called the self-strengthening programmes into question.

23. See Knight Biggerstaff, *The Earliest Modern Government Schools in China* (Ithaca, NY: Cornell University Press, 1961), 71–84; and John L. Rawlinson, *China's Struggle for Naval Development, 1839–1895* (Cambridge, Mass.: Harvard University Press, 1967), 61, 104–8.

24. By the 1880s, *houbu* vastly outnumbered officials with regular appointments: Y. S. Leung, 'The Peculiar Institution: Expectant Officials in Late 19th Century China', paper presented at the AAS Pacific Coast Conference, June 1978.

25. The *xinzheng* period remains critically understudied. For more extended treatment of the *xinzheng* reforms, see Esther Morrisson, *The Modernization of the Confucian Bureaucracy*, unpublished Ph.D. dissertation, Radcliffe College, 1959; Mary C. Wright, *China in Revolution: The First Phase*, (New Haven and London: Yale University Press, 1968), 1–63; Ernest Young, *The Presidency of Yuan Shih-k'ai* (Ann Arbor: University of Michigan Press, 1977), ch. 1 and 2; and Paul Hickey, 'Fee Taking, Salary Reform and the Structure of State Power in late Qing China, 1909–11', *Modern China*, 17: 3 (1991), 389–417.

26. See Mary B. Rankin, *Elite Activism and Political Transformation in China: Zhejiang Province, 1865–1911* (Stanford: Stanford University Press, 1986); and Joseph Esherick and Mary B. Rankin (eds.), *Chinese Local Elites and Patterns of Dominance* (Berkeley and Los Angeles: University of California Press, 1990).

27. For a telling exposition of the clashes between these two orientations, see K. C. Liew, *Struggle for Democracy: Sung Chiaojen and the 1911 Chinese Revolution* (Berkeley and Los Angeles: University of California Press, 1971).

28. See Edward McCord, *Power of the Gun: The Emergence of Modern Chinese Warlordism* (Berkeley and Los Angeles: University of California Press, 1993), 10, 310–11.

29. Lloyd Eastman, 'Nationalist China During the Nanking Decade, 1927–1937', in *The Cambridge History of Republican China*, 13: 2 (New York: Cambridge University Press, 1986), 119–24.

30. Analysis of Sun's thought, and of what mixture of top-down 'political tutelage' *v.* bottom-up 'self government' he truly favoured, is a subject worthy of a complete study on its own; see his *Fundamentals of National Reconstruction* (Taipei: China Cultural Service, 1953), and *San Min Chu Yi* (The Three Principles of the People) (Chungking: Ministry of Information of the Republic of China, 1943).

## Chapter 2

1. An earlier abbreviated version of this chapter was first published under the title 'Civil Service as Symbol and Reflection of State Building: The Examination Yuan in the 1930s' in *Modern China*, 20(2), April 1994. The permission of Sage Publications to include this material is gratefully acknowledged.

2. See Lloyd Eastman, 'Nationalist China during the Nanking Decade 1927–1937', in *The Cambridge History of Republican China*, 13:2 (New York: Cambridge University Press, 1986).

3. This translation of the Organic Law is in *The China Yearbook, 1931* (Shanghai: Kelly and Walsh), 577.

4. See Wolfgang Franke, *The Reform and Abolition of the Traditional Chinese Examination System* (Cambridge, Mass.: Harvard Monographs, 1960), on the ultimately ineffective elite attempt to integrate the curricula of thee modern schools with a reformed version of the civil service examinations in the late Qing.

5. The following details on the central government civil service under Yuan Shikai and the Beiyang governments are drawn from *Beiyang Zhengfu Shiqide Zhengzhi Zhidu* (The Political System of the Beiyang Government Period), ed. Qian Shipu, (Beijing: Zhonghua Shuju, 1984), 344–59.

6. Ibid. 346.

7. Except for scattered and impressionistic comments of foreign diplomats, journalists, and participants, there is very little in print on the central government civil service and personnel in the early Republic. For some of these, see Ernest Young, *The Presidency of Yuan Shih-k'ai* (Ann Arbor: University of Michigan Press, 1977), 162–3. To date, no surveys have been done on the composition and previous background on the central government bureaucrats in this period. My own findings on a small group of bureaucrats in the Ministry of Finance in the Yuan Shikai period are presented in Ch. 5.

8. Franke, *Reform and Abolition*, 55–69.

9. Towards what would turn out to be the end of his life in 1915, Yuan launched an unsuccessful bid to install himself as emperor. At this, republicans and the northern military men who had been his erstwhile protegés joined to force him from power. With Yuan gone, there was no longer any central figure powerful enough to command the allegiance of the provincial generals, and China devolved into regionalism and warlordism. On Yuan's fall from power, see Young, Presidency, ch. 8. For the onset of warlordism, see Ch'i Hsi-sheng, *Warlord Politics in China, 1916–28*, (Stanford: Stanford University Press, 1976).

10. *Beiyang Zhengfu Shiqide Zhengzhi Zhidu*, 350, 355–6.

11. Organic Law of the Republic of China, reproduced in English in *The China Yearbook, 1931*.

12. Accurate numbers on the actual size of the Examination Yuan have been hard to find in print, but all those I interviewed suggested that it was a small, relatively low-key operation. Luo Wanlei, who joined the Ministry of Personnel in 1936 and eventually went on to become vice-minister, suggested 'around 400' as a likely number for the 1930s. Dai Yuanchen, who was with the Ministry of Examinations briefly in the late 1940s, thought that the pre-war Examination Yuan had 'about 200' employees. Since most organizations had a

roughly equal number of career officials and support staff, it is probable that
Luo was including support staff in his estimate while Dai was not. The Exam-
ination Yuan, like other state organizations, expanded enormously during the
Sino-Japanese War, probably by a factor of three or four. But compared with
even medium-sized ministries under the Executive Yuan, the Examination
Yuan remained small in both absolute and relative terms.

13. In both the formal and informal descriptions of the Examination Yuan, and
even in the handbooks published by the Ministry of Personnel, the Commission
on Examinations was always listed first, thereby indicating its greater prestige.

14. This listing is drawn from the Organic Law in *The China Yearbook, 1931.*

15. In the ministries that this work considers in detail (Salt Administration,
Finance, and Foreign Affairs), very high levels of factionalism and politicization
seem to have been much less than was the norm in many of the other government ministries (e.g. the Ministry of Interior); see Chs. 3–6.

16. There are no direct statistics on the relative percentages of those brought in
from the 'Old Beiyang' service, and certainly, the numbers varied enormously
from ministry to ministry. See Eastman, 'Nationalist China', and Hung Mao
Tien, *Government and Politics in KMT China, 1927–37* (Stanford: Stanford
University Press, 1972). However, the indirect evidence suggests that, at least
for some ministries, the percentages of 'Old Beiyang' bureaucrats were very
high. To cite one conspicuous example, there was almost total carryover with
the diplomats in the Beiyang Ministry of Foreign Affairs, who were simply
brought down *en masse* to serve Nanjing. This principle of retention also was
in operation for at least some of the lesser known Beiyang offices: in January
1929, the Executive Yuan ordered formal appointments for some 80 individuals
in the previous service of the Beiping (Beijing) Archival Office (Beiping
Dang'an Baoguanchu): GSG Zong 01.2/32.

17. Dier Lishi Dang'an'guan (the No. 2 Historical Archives of China, Nanjing,
People's Republic of China, hereafter abbreviated as DELSDAG) 2/1/276
(Regulations on Civil Service Appointments), file entitled 'Gongwuyuan
Renyong Tiaolie', joint petition signed by some 28 individuals who had passed
the examinations held by the Beiyang governments, prepared for the Secretariat
of the Executive Yuan, dated Apr. 1928.

18. Interviewees and published sources all agree that, until the first wave of
inflation in the early 1940s, official salaries were more than adequate: inter-
views with Zhu Zishuai and Chen Hanzhang; Wang Zhenguo, 'Guomindang
Shiqide Wenguan Zhidu yu Wenguan Kaoshi' (The Civil Service System and
Civil Service Examinations in the Nationalist Period), in *Guomindangde
Wenguan Zhidu yu Wenguan Kaoshi*, Jiangsu Wenguan Ziliao Di 24 Zhuan,
Dec. 1988.

19. Chen Tai-chi (Chen Daqi), 'Examination Yuan', in *The Chinese Yearbook,
1935–36*, ed., Kwei Chungshu (Shanghai: Commercial Press), 268–9; and
'Gongwuyuan Renyongfa' in *Quanxu Bu Niaojian* (Ministry of Personnel Yearbook), 1932, 1–3.

20. DELSDAG 2/1/277, in file entitled 'Gongwuyuan Renyong Tiaolie', an order
(*xunling*) from the Executive Yuan circulated to all Executive Yuan ministries,
dated 6 Nov. 1930.

21. DELSDAG, 2/1/279, file 'Gongwuyuan Renyongfa' (Law on Civil Service Appointments), general order (*ling*) circulated from Ministry of Personnel, dated 12 Mar. 1933.
22. Chen Tai-chi, 'Examination Yuan', 268–9.
23. Interview with Chen Hanzhang. Evidently, until around 1940, Party organizations successfully ignored the calls of the Ministry of Personnel to submit their personnel documents for review.
24. Several interviewees from different organizations had words to this effect in interviews: Luo Wanlei, Zhou Bi, and Li Xueli.
25. These details from interview with Luo Wanlei.
26. Ibid.
27. DELSDAG 92/1/318, 'Gongwuyuan Kaojifa', (The Law on Civil Servant Annual Evaluations), dated 16, Jul. 1935, and 'Xiuzheng Gongwuyuan Kaojifa Shixing Xilie' (Detailed Regulations for Implementing the Revised Law on Civil Servant Annual Evaluations), dated December 1936.
28. Luo Wanlei stated that, 'despite the annual evaluations, real promotions came about as a result of a combination of how well one did one's work and how well one got along with one's boss'. Zhu Leizhang, on the other hand, suggested that, at least until the early 1940s, when the civil service expanded dramatically, the annual evaluation system worked quite well (interview with Zhu Leizhang).
29. DELSDAG 92/1/318, 'Xiuzheng Gongwuyuan Kaojifa Shixing Xilie'.
30. Interviewees repeatedly stressed that the examinations were *qualification* exams (*zige kaoshi*) and not *appointment* exams (*renyong kaoshi*): Dai Yuanchen, Wu Chengming, and Zhu Zishuai.
31. For a much more extensive consideration of the Administrative Efficiency school, see Julia C. Strauss, 'The Cult of Administrative Efficiency: Myth and Statecraft in the Chinese Republic, 1912–37', unpublished paper delivered at the Annual Meeting for the Association for Asian Studies, 25–8 Mar. 1993, Los Angeles.
32. A specially convened Committee on Administrative Efficiency was attached to the Executive Yuan in the mid-1930s and published two periodicals on public administration. *Xingzheng Xiaolü* (Administrative Efficiency), was published on a semi-monthly basis from July 1934 to mid-1936. *The Chinese Administrator* was an English-language version of selected articles from *Xingzheng Xiaolü*, and was published quarterly in 1935 and early 1936. In mid-1936, both the sponsoring committee of the Executive Yuan and the periodical itself changed names. The Committee on Administrative Efficiency became the Research Committee on Administrative Efficiency, and *Xingzheng Xiaolü* became *Xingzheng Yanjiu Yuekan* (Administrative Studies Monthly). *Xingzheng Yanjiu Yuekan* came out as a monthly from July 1936 to July 1937, when publication was suspended by the outbreak of the Sino-Japanese War.
33. Zhao Yuanchong, 'Zemmayang Tigao Zhengzhi Xiaolü' ('How Can Government Efficiency be Raised?'), *Xingzheng Xiaolü* (hereafter cited as *XZXL*), 1:8 (1934).
34. Lei Xiaoling, 'Guanyu Kezhangde Taolun' (A Discussion on Section Chiefs), *XZXL* 1:5–6 (1934).

35. Shen Jianshi, 'Wuquan Xianfaxia Quanxu Zhiduzhi Yanjiu ji Jinhou Yingqu' (Research and Proposals for the Future on the Personnel System under the Five Power Constitution), *XZXL* 3:5 (1936).
36. Gan Naiguang, 'On Administrative Efficiency', *The Chinese Administrator*, 1:1 (1935), 24.
37. Chen Tsun, 'Chiefs of Section in a Ministry', *The Chinese Administrator*, 1:1 (1935). In the same issue of this periodical, Gan Naiguang states that less than 1% of the civil servants had passed the upper civil service exam by 1935.
38. Interview with Luo Wanlei.
39. See Gan Naiguang, 'Administrative Efficiency', and Chen Tsun, 'Chiefs'. Dai Yuanchen thought that, for the entire 20-yr period of Nationalist rule, there weren't more than 2,000 who passed the upper civil service exams: perhaps slightly more passed the advanced special exams. The numbers and percentages of examinees in the ministries varied greatly from period to period and from ministry to ministry. A comprehensive statistical survey of the composition of the entire upper civil service in the 1930s and 1940s is beyond the scope of this study, but in subsequent chapters attention will be devoted to the role of civil service examinations and civil servants for the Salt Inspectorate (Chs. 3 and 4), and the Ministry of Finance (Ch. 5).
40. Starting in the 1920s and continuing for the remainder of the Republican period to the 1940s and beyond, both Guomindang and non-Guomindang individuals and sub-groups created a virtual cottage industry and discourse on public personnel administration and the role of open civil service examinations in the construction of the government bureaucracy. For the most part, period-icals and articles dominated the discourse in the late 1920s and 1930s, with the periodicals *Xingzheng Xiaolü*, *Xingzheng Yanjiu Yuekan*, and occasional articles from *Dongfang Zazhi* (The Eastern Miscellaney) on civil service and examina-tion systems dominating the field: see Zhang Rui, 'Zhongguo Kaoshiyuan yu Meiguo Lianbang Lizhiyuan' (China's Examination Yuan and the United States' Civil Service Commission), *Dongfang Zazhi*, 26:1 (10 Jan. 1929), 25–34. Books on the subject proliferated during the 1940s; for a partial biblio-graphy, see Dai Daoliu, *Kaoxuan Quanxu Jiaoyu Lianxi Fang'an* (A Draft Programme for Connecting Examination, Selection and Education) (Shanghai: Zhonghua Shuju, 1946); Xia Banghou, *Renshi Guanli zhi Lilun yu Shiji* (Theory and Practice in Personnel Administration) (Shanghai: Guoxun Shuju, 1943); Huang Jingbo, *Zhongguo Renshi Wenti Xinlun* (New Discussions on China's Personnel Problems (Chongqing: Shangwu, 1945), which has a lengthy discus-sion of examination systems; and Song Teli (ed.), *Zhidu yu Rencai* (Systems and Talent) (Chongqing: Beidou Shudian, 1944), which goes through the dynasties to ascertain different approaches to the question of administrative talent.
41. The Communists and the quasi-fascist Blue Shirts were exceptions to this otherwise quite general rule.
42. Historical descriptions of the wonders of the examination system through the ages in China began to be published in the 1930s and 1940s, and are still readily available on Taiwan today. More subtle, but no less important, is the tone that pervades much of the official documents of the period, and the way in which interviewees reminisced about the examination system (and its failures) in the

1930s and 1940s. Absolutely everyone agreed that open examination as the route to public office was the way that things 'should have' been done.

43. Several sources stressed the psychological importance of 'examinations as the regular/proper path to official status': interview with Li Tiezheng; Jin Shaoxian, 'Dai Jitao yu Nanjing Guomin Zhengfude Gaodeng Wenguan Kaoshi' (Dai Jitao and the Nanjing National Government Upper Civil Service Exam), in *Guomindangde Wenguan Zhidu yu Wenguan Kaoshi*, Dec. 1988.

44. Shen Jianshi, 'Wuquan Xianfaxia'.

45. Jin Shaoxian, 'Dai Jitao', and Wang Zhenguo, 'Guomindang'.

46. Details from Luo Wanlei and Dai Yuanchen. The regulations governing the administration of the exams can be found in the *Quanxubu Nianjian* (Ministry of Personnel Yearbook), 1932, 50.

47. I could find neither archival sources nor published memoirs which detailed the specifics of examination-taking and examination questions under the Beiyang governments. This analysis is based on the regulations published by the Yuan Shikai government and the much richer documentary evidence from the 1930s and 1940s.

48. Zhu Leizhang, who passed the 1931 upper civil service examination with the highest general score and the highest score for general administration, recalled nearly 60 yrs afterward that the examination had been 'very, very difficult': interview.

49. A complete set of statistics on those who passed the first upper civil service exam is available as a set of appendices in GSG, Guominzhengfu Dangan, 02.7/ fu 101, 'Di'yi jie Gaodeng Kaoshi Zong Baogaoshu ji Tongjibiao' (A complete report and statistical tables on the first upper civil service examination). Another, less comprehensive, set of tables, which spans a wider time frame from the examination of 1931 to the examination of 1940, is reproduced in Chen Bainian, *Kaoxuan Zhidu Dayao* (General Outline on Examination and Selection Systems) (Zhongyang Zhengzhi Xuexiao Renshi Xingzheng Renyuan Xunlianban Jiangyi, 1940). The pass rate of 8.61 is taken from the table 'Lijie Gaokao deng Kaoshi Yingkao yu Jige Renyuan Yingkao Zige Tongjibiao', which is appended to Chen Bainian, as above.

50. These examples are all drawn from Jiang Maicai, 'Wo ying diyijie gaodeng kaoshide huiyi' (My recollections of the First Upper Civil Service Exam); in *Zhongguo Kaozheng Xuehui 50 Zhou Nianjinian Zhuangan* (Taipei: Kaoshiyuan, 1985). See also Jin Shaoxian, 'Dai Jitao', and Wang Zhenguo, 'Guomindang'.

51. Wang Zhenguo, 'Guomindang'.

52. These questions and the officially deemed 'correct answers' can be found in a most interesting volume by Li Feipeng, who passed the second *gaokao* and went on to a long career in the Examination Yuan. In this volume, Li compiled *all* of the questions of the Party Principles section from 1931 to 1953, and supplied a condensed version of the 'correct answer' to each: Li Feipeng, *Lijie Gaodeng, Putong, Xianding Kaoshi Shiti Xiangjie* (Taipei: publisher unknown, 1954).

53. Jiang Maicai, 'Wo ying'.

54. This list of the sub-areas on the examination syllabus is given in a set of reports and tables in GSG 02.7/ fu 101, 'Di'yi Gaodeng Kaoshi Zong Baogaoshu ji

Tongjibiao' (A general report and statistical tables on the first upper civil service examination). The particulars on the examination of 1933 are in Jiang, 'Wo Ying'.

55. This vivid description is drawn from Wang Zhenguo, 'Guomindang', in his detailed recounting of his experience taking the 4th civil service exam of 1936.

56. Zhu Leizhang, 'Wo kaoqu le dishoujie gaodeng kaoshi' (I passed the first upper civil service examination), *Minguo Chunqiu*, 1 (1987).

57. Wang Zhenguo, 'Guomindang'.

58. Li Feipeng, 'Zhongguo Kaozheng Xuehuizhi Tezhi yu Wushi Zhounianzhi Huigu' (The Special Characteristics of China's Examination Institute and Fifty Years of Recollections), in *Zhongguo Kaozheng Xuehui Wushi Zhounian Jinian Zhuankan* (Taipei: Kaoshiyuan, 1985), 6.

59. Interviews with Li Tiezheng and Zhu Leizhang. On the 1931 exam, Zhu passed with the highest score overall, and Li passed with the highest score on the Foreign Affairs section.

60. These generalizations are drawn from statistics and charts in GSG 02.7, fu 101, 'Di'yi Gaodeng Kaoshi Zongbaogaoshu ji Tongjibiao'. Returned students from abroad were a highly visible presence in the middle to upper levels of the civil service in Republican China, and their foreign degrees and presumed expertise made them much in demand. One way or another, they had either the connections or the qualifications to be consistently well represented in the civil service without having to resort to taking the examinations: those who took the exams in the early years almost by definition had not studied abroad. The median age of the successful examination candidate in 1931 was 29. While these young men had taken their degrees at a number of different universities and colleges, the National Central University in Nanjing was particularly strongly represented, with just slightly under a fifth of the successes.

61. GSG. 02.7/1

62. Shortly thereafter, in 1934, the Ministry of Interior began its own police training and examination system with the establishment of the Central Police Academy.

63. These details are all taken from Gu Shouzhi, *Gongzhi Zhi Chugao, Wenzhi Zhidu Kaoxuan* (Recruitment and Selection of Civil Public Functionaries: A Draft), unpublished manuscript (n.d., Taipei).

64. Interviews with Zhou Bi and Zhu Yuan. The case of personnel and examinations for the Ministry of Finance will be dealt with in much greater detail in Ch. 5. In fact, Zhou and Zhu insisted that the examination they took in 1936 was a *tekao*. Fifty years after the fact, the confusion was understandable; 1936 was the last year before Special Examinations for Finance were offered nearly every year as a matter of course.

65. Interview with Song Tongfu. Evidently, the government quickly recognized the loophole potential of the upper civil service exam. Regulations were passed that allowed a new *weiren* appointed official to take an upper civil service examination only after having been on the job for a year, and officials were limited to one attempt per three years on the exams.

66. See Julia C. Strauss, 'Wartime Stress and Guomindang Response: *Xunlian* as a Means to Statebuilding 1938–45', paper given at the 48th Annual Meeting of

the Association for Asian Studies, 11–14 Apr. 1995, Honolulu, for the ways in which different organizations implemented the *xunlian*.

67. The Party Principles section of both the preliminary and secondary exams of 1939 included questions on the differences between the 'correct' Principle of People's Livelihood and 'falseness' of communism (questions found in Li Feipeng, *Lijie Gaodeng*); details on the content of *xunlian* from interview with Wu Chengming.

68. The indirect evidence suggests that the *dangyi* segment, while required, was not deemed to be particularly important in the overall weighting of questions until after the outbreak of the Sino-Japanese War (see Wang Zhenguo, 'Guomindang'). Li Feipeng's study guide to the examinations with its sample questions and answers offers roughly three times the number of questions in the Chinese section as it does in the Party Principles section (Li Feipeng *Lijie Gaodeng*).

69. Interviews with Zhu Leizhang and Luo Wanlei.

70. Gu Shouzhi, 'Gongzhizhi Chugao: Wenzhi Zhidu Kaoxuan' (The Civil Service Selection System: A First Draft), unpublished manuscript (no date, 1980s, Taipei), 42. Interviewees Dai Yuanchen and Song Tongfu also described the 'new' *chushi-zaishi* system in these terms. See also lists of examinations and re-examinations, detailed in DSH 325/2/1 *Kaoshiyuan Gongzuo Baogaoshu* (Examination Yuan Work Report) (September 1939, 3–6), and DSH 325/2/2 *Kaoshiyuan Gongzuo Baogaoshu* (Examination Yuan Work Report) (November 1939, 4–8). The first of the *chushi-zaishi* examinations was a fairly minor *tekao* held in July 1938 for special investigators attached to a new commission for construction in western Sichuan: it preliminarily qualified only six individuals, of whom a mere four made it through the re-examination process. But by November 1938 the first *chushi* were being held on a large scale with a *tekao* for special finance personnel. Henceforth, all 'regular' upper civil service examinations, special civil service examinations, and legal administration examinations followed the *chushi-zaishi*.

71. DELSDAG, 123 (4)/2422, pamphlet entitled *Zhongguo Guomindang Zhongyang Zhengzhi Daxuexiao Gongwuyuan Xunlian Gaodengke Diyiqi Tongxuelu* (Student Record of the First Training Session for Upper Civil Servants at National Central Political University); Chiang Kai-shek, opening speech, p. 3 of pamphlet.

72. See Strauss, 'Wartime Stress'. I discuss the Examination Yuan's own efforts to run special *xunlian* courses for personnel administrators in conjunction with Central Political University on pp. 40–8, and detail the Ministry of Finance's efforts to retain control over its own in-house *xunlian* on pp. 54–75. Despite the enormous variability of *xunlian* sessions, they all subscribed to the same principles of military drill, and all incorporated 'some' amount of partification. The training courses run at the Central Political University as part of the *chushi-zaishi* procedure also varied. Training sessions for groups that passed the 'regular' *gaokao* lasted for six months, training sessions for those who passed the finance *tekao* lasted for three to four months. Each *ban*, or training group, had part of each day devoted to functional training (*yewu xunlian*) in addition to military drill and party indoctrination; but the indirect evidence suggests that those who came in with *tekaos* had proportionally less time spent on partifica-

tion while those coming in through the 'generalist' *gaokao* had more of their programme devoted to such topics as 'spiritual instruction' (*jingshen xunhua*), party principles, and study of current government directives. Certainly all *xunlian* courses shared a 'hard core' of a standardized programme in which the same high-level figures in the Party and Government gave set lectures in areas of their special expertise. Curriculum details for those who passed the *gaokao* of 1939 and 1940 and took the training course are cited in DELSDAG, 123 (4)/2422, *Zhongguo Guomindang Zhongyang Zhengzhi Daxuexiao Gongwuyuan Xunlian Gaodengke Diyiqi Tongxuelu*.

73. There is a vast literature on this topic, mostly with respect to political indoctrination in the People's Republic. Even in the People's Republic, scholarly consensus suggests that political indoctrination from the top down via campaigns and controlled small group meetings tended to lose its effectiveness and take on a routinized quality after a relatively short period of time: see Michel Oksenberg, 'The Institutionalization of the Chinese Communist Revolution: The Ladder of Success on the Eve of the Cultural Revolution', *China Quarterly*, No. 36 (1968), and James R. Townsend, *Political Participation in Communist China*, rev. edn (Berkeley and Los Angeles: University of California Press, 1969), 192–209.

74. These numbers are derived from Gu Shouzhi, 'Gongzhizhi Chugao', and Zhang Ruiying, 'Dai Jitao yu Woguo Kaoquan Zhidu Zhi Yan-jiu' (Research on Dai Jitao and China's Civil Service Selection System), unpublished dissertation, China Cultural Institute, (Taipei, 1978); see pp. 144, and 96–97 for a detailed listing.

75. Interviews with Song Tongfu and Sun Jinggong.

76. See Ch. 3–4 (Salt Administration) and 5 (Finance) for further details on lateral entry and irregular appointments.

77. Details of this sort were spontaneously offered given by Li Tiezheng, Zhu Leizhang, Zhu Yuan, and Luo Wanlei in interviews.

## Chapter 3

1. See Madeline Zelin, *The Magistrate's Tael: Rationalizing Fiscal Reform in Eighteenth Century Ch'ing China* (Berkeley and Los Angeles: University of California Press, 1984). The accumulated informal fees reached between two and three times the regular tax even in the 18th c. which was a era of relative dynastic strength: during periods of dynastic weakness, the prevalence of local fee-taking at onerous levels was undoubtedly much greater. Prasenjit Duara suggests that by the 20th c. a proliferating set of local bureaucratic organizations at the ward level led to the local imposition of *tankuan*, or 'irregular levies', which led to greater real tax burdens without higher-level supervision and control: Prasenjit Duara, *Culture, Power and the State: Rural North China, 1900–1942* (Stanford: Stanford University Press, 1988), 63.

2. Ibid.

3. The image of China as a 'loose sheet of sand' was one that Sun Yat-sen used repeatedly. In *San Min Chu Yi: The Three Principles of the People* (Taipei: China Publishing Company, n.d.) Sun uses the same metaphor on pp. 2, 5, 31, 67, and 75.

4. The organization established in 1913 was called the Sino-Foreign Salt Inspectorate (Yanwu Jihe Zongsuo) and was originally encharged only with the collection and forwarding of the salt tax. Another salt tax organization which handled 'administrative' functions, called the Salt Office (Yanwu Shu), existed alongside the Inspectorate until the early 1930s, when it was slowly absorbed by the Inspectorate. In 1936 the Yanwu Shu and the Inspectorate were formally amalgamated into the Directorate-General of Salt (Yanwu Zongju). Given these successive name changes, I use the names 'the Sino-Foreign Salt Inspectorate', 'the Inspectorate', and 'the Salt Administration' more or less interchangeably, for the period before 1936, and 'the Directorate-General of Salt' and 'the Salt Administration' for the period after 1936. Although in the Republican period the Yanwu Shu was often rendered in English as 'the Salt Administration', I either use the original Chinese or translate it as the 'Salt Office' to avoid confusion.

5. See S. A. M. Adshead, *The Modernization of the Salt Administration, 1900–1920* (Cambridge, Mass.: Harvard University Press, 1970), 21, and Zelin, *The Magistrate's Tael*, chs. 1 and 2, on the pressures and problems that beset the taxation system in late imperial China.

6. Adshead, *Modernization*, 21. The following description of the imperial salt gabelle is drawn from Adshead, ch. 1.

7. Ibid. 25, table 3.

8. Ibid. 52–6.

9. *Yanwu Jisi Ducha Renyuan Yingyou zhi Renshi* (What Anti-Salt Smuggling and Inspection Personnel Ought to Know) (Nanjing: Shoudu Guomin Yinwu Ju, 1935), 5.

10. Adshead, *Modernization*, 82.

11. Adshead also points out that, from the point of view of the Western powers, the *raison d'être* of the loan was as much political as it was financial. The loan was extended 'to enable Yuan to establish a strong central government, one which would maintain the unity of China, and obviate the necessity for extensive foreign intervention'. Therefore, even though the actual negotiations and terms of the loan were conducted by a consortium of international banks, Western governments were also closely involved in an advisory capacity. Ibid. 83.

12. The following details are drawn from Adshead, *Modernization*, ch. 3; Zeng Yingfeng, *Zhongguo Yanwu Zhengshi* (The History of Chinese Salt Administration) (Shanghai: Shangwu Yinshuguan, 1937; reprinted by Shanghai Shudian, 1984), 125–39; Liu Foding, 'Qingmo Lieqiang Geguo Qinfan Woguo Yanzheng Zhuquande Huodong' (The Invasive Activities of all Countries in China's Autonomy over Salt Administration at the End of the Qing), in *Yanye Yanjiu* (Studies in Salt Industry History), 1: 1 (1988); Ernest Young, *The Presidency of Yuan Shih-K'ai* (Ann Arbor: University of Michigan Press, 1977), 123–9; Zhu Dejun, 'Yanwu Jihesuo de Lishi Jianshu' (A Short Description of the History of the Salt Inspectorate), *Tianjin Wenshi Ziliao*, No. 26 (Tianjin: Tianjin Renmin Chubanshe, 1984), 105–7; and Ding Changqing (ed.), *Minguo Yanwu Shigao* (An Outline History of Republican Salt Affairs) (Beijing: Renmin Chubanshe, 1990), 53–8.

13. For one view of the costs and benefits inherent to this form of European domination in Asia, see Adshead, *Modernization*, 212–18.

14. These figures are taken from P. T. Chen, 'Public Finance', in *The Chinese Year Book, 1935–36*, ed. Kwei Chungshu (Shanghai: Commercial Press Limited, 1935), 1298. The total for 1913 of 11,471,000Y was consistent with normal annual collections under the dynasty.

15. Adshead, *Modernization*, 94.

16. Ibid. ch. 4. Although on the surface Dane and the Inspectorate may have seemed like the creatures of the imperialist group banks, the reality was more subtle. Certainly neither Dane nor the Inspectorate ever would have been in China without pressure from the group banks to guarantee their loan, but Dane and the Inspectorate served their own core values of efficiency, neutrality, and technically oriented high performance rather than the immediate interests of the group banks, and on more than one occasion sided with the Chinese government in disputes about the payment of the loan. Subsequent generations of Chinese nationalist scholarship, understandably focus on the Inspectorate's pedigree as an 'imperialist' organization of foreign domination and continued privilege for foreigners; see Liu Foding 'Qingmo', and Ding Changqing, *Minguo Yanwu Shigao*, for this standard, nationalist view.

17. The importance of Dane to the institutionalization of the Salt Inspectorate and the continued existence of foreign advisors at high levels in the organizations throughout the 1930s raises a number of interesting issues. To what extent was the Inspectorate's success and longevity dependent on the foreign presence? Could the Inspectorate have successfully pursued strategies of bureaucratization and insulation with an all-Chinese staff? Dane's role in rigorously establishing a set of impersonal, performance-oriented norms and maintaining insulation was critical for the subsequent evolution of the organization: without Dane's initial vision and practical administrative ability, it is doubtful that the organization would ever have been particularly impressive either in tax collection or as a model for emulation. The later role of other foreigners within the organization is much more difficult to assess. During the Sino-Japanese War, the decline of the Inspectorate and a serious decline in the influence of its foreign staff occurred nearly simultaneously. Although some of the evidence from the 1930s suggests that the role of foreigners in the organization was significantly less than many of the foreign staff liked to presume, it is impossible to state definitively the degree to which the Inspectorate's success was tied to its heavy foreign advisor component.

18. DS 893.51/150; hereafter, this item will be cited as the 'Croome Report'. This long document was written in mid-1936 by one of the Salt Inspectorate's foreign inspectors, J. D. Croome. Croome reviewed at length the history and achievements of the Salt Inspectorate from its beginning in 1913–14 to 1936 in order to protest what he perceived as the recent 'turning away' from the original principles and goals of the organization, which included diminishing career prospects for the foreign staff within the Salt Inspectorate in the mid-1930s. The Croome Report ran to over 100 pages with various paginations and was ultimately forwarded to the US Consul and State Department offices, which Croome hoped would exert some informal pressure on the Nationalist Ministry of Finance. The State Department did no such thing, and the Croome Report appears to have been filed and forgotten. Although clearly biased in favour of

continued foreign dominance in an era when the foreign component of the Inspectorate was beginning to weaken, the Croome Report remains an excellent source for background on the Salt Inspectorate. Another, similarly long and significantly more bilious, report was sent in to the British Foreign Office several months earlier in 1936 by C. G. G. Pearson, the ranking Inspectorate district inspector of British nationality. This item will henceforth be cited as the 'Pearson Report', and can be found in FO 371/2074.

19. *Yanwu Renshi Guize* (Regulations on Salt Administration Personnel), unpublished booklet (Caizheng Bu, date unknown, *c.* 1950), 19–21.

20. *Yanwu Renshi Guize*, 5–8; *Yanwu Renshi Zhidu* (Salt Personnel System) (Chongqing: Caizheng Bu Caiwu Renyuan Xunliansuo, Yanwu Renyuan Xunlianban, 1942), 13–16; *Caizheng Nianjian* (Finance Yearbook) (Nanjing: Caizheng Bu, 1935), 108; interview with Lin Jiyong.

21. These figures, and statistics that will be subsequently referred to in the text, are drawn from Dier Lishi Dang'an'guan (The No. 2 Historical Archives), Nanjing, People's Republic of China, file No. 156/1582. This file, completed around 1936–7, details the entire career histories of some 185 individuals in the Salt Inspectorate until the mid-1930s. Although the file does not contain material on everyone in the Salt Inspectorate, it seems to offer a fairly representative example of the composition of the organization. The base figure of the number of individuals in the sample who entered the organization before 1927 is 104.

22. e.g. only 5% of the total organization was given the highest, 'A', rank.

23. *Yanwu Renshi Zhidu*, 30.

24. Interview with Zhong Liangzhe.

25. Interview with Lin Jiyong.

26. Interview with Lin Jiyong; *Yanwu Renshi Guize*, 26–8.

27. DELSDAG 156/1584. I define these 'high-level administrators' as those who reached either of the top two 'A' or 'B' grades in the Inspectorate's classification system, with a salary of more than 350 Y per month, and I include in this group those who did almost as well but got stuck at the highest step of the 'C' grade, with a salary of 350 Y a month.

28. DELSDAG 156/1584.

29. Clerical and support staff and 'high fliers' did of course have significantly different career patterns. But while one expects the people at the top in a prefectural organization to move a lot, in many prefectural systems, the clerical staff are not rotated, and can prove to be quite obstructionist. The degree to which the Inspectorate seemed to avoid this problem by rotating even its low-level staff is surprising.

30. DELSDAG 266/1584. The fact that the records show some 7% of this group of 185 Inspectorate employees being caught and censured for corruption does not conclusively demonstrate that there were not others in the Inspectorate who managed to avoid having their corrupt activities formally exposed and censured. The records suggest that the Inspectorate was probably unusually rigorous in its censure and expulsion of corruption for two reasons. First, there was a significant difference in the language used by the Inspectorate and other, 'regular' state organizations in Republican China regarding the issue of self-policing. The

Inspectorate clearly recorded merits, demerits, dismissal, and the reasons for each: the personnel records of the ministries of Finance, Education, and the Interior exhibited no clear and unambiguous statements of dismissal for reasons of corruption or irregularity. These 'regular' ministries wrapped whatever disciplinary actions they may have taken in the euphemism 'left office' (*cizhi*). An individual could 'leave office' for any one of a number of reasons, including dismissal, but a broad cross-section of non-Inspectorate government organizations in Republican China opted for euphemism rather than clarity, suggesting that cases of corruption or irregularity, where they existed, were handled informally and quietly rather than procedurally and openly. Second, this set of forms offered two instances of Inspectorate administrators who, by virtue of their previous meritorious service, high position, and long careers, in all likelihood had a great deal of informal 'appeal to human feelings'. They were dismissed anyway, which suggests an unusually bureaucratic, procedurally oriented organization.

31. Croome Report, III-8 and 9, V-5, V-14, V-28, VI-3 and 4, VII-4 and 5, VIII-22–4; Pearson Report, 27–8. Outsiders to the Inspectorate, including very influential ones such as Song Ziwen, also made a direct connection between the Inspectorate's separate civil service organization and its high efficiency and effectiveness. Song referred to the positive 'results' of the Salt Inspectorate and its civil service in the Minister of Finance's Annual Financial Report of 1931 (reproduced in *China Year Book, 1933* (Shanghai: Kelley and Walsh), 338).

32. DS 893.51/235, F.E.L. Dobbs, Associate District Director, Confidential Memorandum on the Chinese Government Salt Revenue Administration, Dated 15 Jun. 1939, 1.

33. Interview with Lin Jiyong.

34. DELSDAG 156/1582. This figure is based on the sample of 185 forms completed in the mid-1930s. The 15 'high fliers' were those that reached either the 'A' or 'B' grade, and had average tenures of 17.06 years. The 12 'near high fliers' remained in the top rank of the 'C' grade, with a slightly longer average tenure of 17.33 years. Although there was no comparable set of forms from the early 1940s, it is likely that most of these individuals continued their service for the organization well beyond the mid-1930s. Informants reiterated that many, if not most, of those who had begun to work for the Inspectorate in the 1910s and 1920s were still with the organization in the 1940s (interviews with Chen Guisheng and Zhou Weiliang).

35. Interviews with Chen Guisheng and Zhou Weiliang.

36. Interview with Lin Jiyong.

37. Interviews with Chen Guisheng and Zhou Weiliang.

38. DS 893.51/137, Report by Charles Reed, Vice Consul, 15 Sept. 1932.

39. DS 893.5/230, Dobbs and Y. C. Yao, joint memo.

40. This list is set forth in the Croome Report, III-5–10.

41. This definition is taken from Arturo Israel, *Institutional Development* (Baltimore and London: Johns Hopkins University Press, 1987), 48. Israel further proposes that the higher the degree of specificity, the more intense, immediate, identifiable, and focused the effects of a good or poor performance will be.

42. In these ways, the technology and goals of the Salt Inspectorate were favourable to either a 'programmed' type of decision-making or an 'experimental' type of decision- making, because the goals were agreed upon within the organization, and in many cases the technology for achieving those goals was also known. See James D. Thompson and Arthur Tuden's 'Strategies, Structures and Processes of Organizational Decision', in J. D. Thompson *et al.* (eds.), *Comparative Studies in Administration* (Pittsburgh: University of Pittsburgh Press, 1959) for a complete description of the typology.

43. Much ink has been spilled over the proper definition of the term 'professionalism', and a good deal has been written about the degree to which 'professionalism' conflicts with 'bureaucracy'. I follow Wilensky's fairly minimalist definition: 'professionalism' is characterized by 'autonomous expertise and a service ideal' (Harold Wilensky, 'The Professionalization of Everyone?' *American Journal of Sociology*, 70:2 (Sept. 1964). Although they were certainly not doctors, lawyers, or ministers (the classic instances of 'the professions' in the West), by these criteria the Inspectorate's high-level district and assistant district inspectors were fairly professionalized in much the same way as were the forest rangers in the US Forest Service: see Herbert Kaufman, *The Forest Ranger* (Baltimore: Johns Hopkins University Press, 1960, 1967). As prefectural administrators out in the field, both forest rangers and district inspectors had substantial autonomy, frequently exercised their judgement, justifying their decisions on a combination of their technical expertise and the presumed benefits that would accrue to their clients.

44. Croome Report, VII-44 and 45.

45. *Yanwu Jisi Ducha Renyuan Yingyou zhi Renshi* (Important Knowledge for Anti-Salt Smuggling and Inspection Personnel) (Training Group for Anti-Salt Smuggling and Inspection Personnel, 1935) repeats several of these methods of stopping 'salt leakage' (*yanlou*) on pp. 13–14; and *Shinian Lai zhi Yanzheng* (The Past Ten Years of Salt Administration), compiled by the Yanzheng Si (Chongqing: Caizheng Bu, 1943), 3, states explicitly that the experiments in Huaibei with storehouses and depots were 'extended to Hubei, Hunan and Anhui'.

46. The Croome Report describes in some detail the lack of distinguished leadership in the Salt Inspectorate after Dane's departure: pp. VI-7 and 8, VII-15, VII- 24 and 25. The case of the Inspectorate suggests quite strongly that for highly bureaucratized technical organizations charismatic organizational leadership may be unnecessary and perhaps even inappropriate. Erwin Hargrove makes a similar argument for the case of the TVA, suggesting that the organization might have been much better off had it not felt compelled to pursue heroic missions and charismatic leadership and instead opted for conservation-oriented strategies of administration: Erwin Hargrove, *Prisoners of Myth: The Leadership of the Tennessee Valley Authority, 1933–1990* (Princeton: Princeton University Press, 1994), especially 1–15.

47. Croome Report, V-29 and V-9.

48. Interview with Lin Jiyong.

## Chapter 4

1. For the most influential proponents of this image of administration, see Frederick Taylor, *Principles of Scientific Management* (1911); Max Weber, *From Max Weber: Essays in Sociology*, ed. H. H. Gerth and C. Wright Mills (New York: Oxford University Press, 1946, 1958: ch. 8); and especially Woodrow Wilson, 'The Study of Administration', *Political Science Quarterly*, 56:4 (December 1941), in which he formulated a very explicit 'policy/administration' dichotomy. See also Martin Landau, 'On the Use of Metaphor in Political Analysis', in Landau, *Political Theory and Political Science* (Atlantic Highlands, NJ: Humanities Press, 1972, 1979) for the prevalence of mechanistic imagery in this conception of administration.

2. 'Croome Report', VI–4.

3. For the genealogy of what John Fitzgerald calls 'a revolution misconceived', see Fitzgerald, 'The Misconceived Revolution: State and Society in China's Nationalist Revolution, 1923–26', *Journal of Asian Studies*, 49: 2 (May 1990).

4. This discussion of the dynamics of the warlord system is drawn from Hsi-sheng Chi, *Warlord Politics in China* (Stanford: Stanford University Press, 1976); James Sheridan, *Chinese Warlord: The Career of Feng Yu-hsiang* (Stanford: Stanford University Press, 1966); Diana Lary, *Region and Nation: The Kwangsi Clique in Chinese Politics* (Cambridge: Cambridge University Press, 1974); and Arthur Waldron, *From War to Nationalism: China's Turning Point, 1924–25* (New York: Cambridge University Press, 1995).

5. DS 893.51/134, report by Charles Reed, American Consul in Guangzhou, dated 5 Nov. 1932. Although this phrasing comes from an incident of local authority seizure of salt district funds during the Nanjing Decade, both the problem and the methods of dealing with the problem were familiar to senior field staff. During the 1920s, Inspectorate offices in Sichuan, Yunnan, and Jiangsu were inviting, and sometimes frequently visited, targets for warlord depredations.

6. DS 893.6371/41, report by JVA MacMurray, written in July 1927 as the Nanjing government was being consolidated. This report referred back to a set of arrangements made between Jiangsu authorities and Salt Inspectorate offices in 1925, and stipulated explicitly that the 'share' of the salt funds was half to the local authorities and half remaining with the Inspectorate.

7. These figures are drawn from *The Chinese Yearbook, 1935–36*, ed. Kwei Chung-shu (Shanghai: Commercial Press), 1299.

8. These details are from a memo by E. W. Mead, chief English secretary of the Salt Inspectorate, to B. C. Newton, 6 Jan. 1928: FO 371/13201.

9. *Chinese Year Book, 1935–36*, 1308–10; and *Yanwu Nianjian* (Salt Affairs Yearbook) (?Nanjing: Yanwu Shu, 1929).

10. Memo by J. T. Pratt, 18 Jun. 1928, with appended comments by Embassy staff. These comments make it quite clear that the British, while not sanguine about the National government's ability to continue to meet its debts over the long run, understood that nationalism in China was running high, that the Chinese government with good reason found the Reorganization Loan agreement and the existence of a virtually independent foreign chief inspector for the Salt

Inspectorate to be 'specially obnoxious' as a product of an unequal treaty, and that the National Government's 'solemn undertaking to respect its loan obligations must be accepted as sufficient': FO 371/13291. On several other occasions in the late 1920s and 1930s, either banking interests or foreign inspectorate staff would attempt to appeal to either the British or US governments to intervene to safeguard some aspect of the Inspectorate's workings, and in each case the request fell on deaf ears.

11. Hung Mao Tien, *Government and Politics in Kuomintang China, 1927–37* (Stanford: Stanford University Press, 1972). These percentages are drawn from a Tien's charts, p. 83.

12. Zhou Weiliang, personal communication, dated 25 Aug. 1995.

13. P. T. Chen, 'Public Finance', in *Chinese Year Book, 1935–36*, 1313.

14. From Song Ziwen's Annual Financial Report of 1931, cited in the *China Year Book, 1933* (Shanghai: Kelley and Walsh), 338. Referred to also in the *Yanwu Nianjian*, 83. The Croome Report approvingly notes Song's understanding and appreciation of the Inspectorate in the late 1920s and early 1930s: pp. VIII–11 and 12.

15. The Croome Report, VIII–8, details the first erosion of the 'strong civil service traditions of the Inspectorate' beginning in 1929, when Zhu Tingqi appointed Chen Rong, his old teacher, to the relatively high position of associate district inspector. Judging from the complaints of Croome, Pearson, and Dobbs in the mid- to late 1930s while Zhu was still in office, Zhu did very little to prevent the progressive erosion of the status of the foreigners who worked in the Inspectorate. However, during the 1930s, despite the slow decline in the prestige of foreigners in the organization and the precedent of a few non-'regular' appointments (where before the 1930s there had been virtually no irregular appointments), the Inspectorate's *basic* norms remained the same.

16. Croome Report, VIII–15, VIII–22–26, notes the 'erosion' of 'the Inspectorate Spirit', and practically waxes hysterical on the subject of personal appointments, in particular the appointment of Chen Rong in 1928. The Pearson Report drips vitriol on the subject of the decline in influence of foreigners in the organization on virtually every page. But, while the importance of foreigners in the organization certainly began a long decline during the 1930s, the Salt Inspectorate's ethos, operations, and large amounts of *de facto* autonomy with respect to daily operations exhibited a strong continuity with the 1910s and 1920s.

17. Interviews with Chen Guisheng and Lin Jiyong.

18. All informants—Chen, Lin, Zhong, and Zhou—who were themselves recruited in the mid- to late 1930s, agreed on this point.

19. DS 893.51/150. This quote is taken from a précis of the Croome Report, which serves as an introduction to the much longer Report itself: 2 Sep. 1936.

20. Since the duty rates and assorted surtaxes varied substantially from district to district, it is no easy matter to come up with an aggregate rate of salt tax for all of China during this period. Ding Changqing *et al.* cite seven instances of the salt tax being increased by the central government during the Nanjing Decade, in 1929, 1931, 1932 and 1933, 1934, 1935, 1936, and 1937: Ding Changqing *et al, Minguo Yanwu Shigao* (Outline of Salt Affairs in the Republican Period)

(Beijing: Renmin Chubanshe, 1990), 220–41. However, tax rates were highly variable to begin with, and not each increase was directed at the same district. Tellingly, many of these increases were justified in the name of amalgamation, unification, and simplification of the salt tax.

21. This figure is based on the 'Salt Inspectorate Statistical Review of 1934', reproduced in part in the *Chinese Year Book, 1935–36*, 1316.

22. Ibid. 1321.

23. Interviews with Chen Guisheng and Zhou Weiliang.

24. Zhou Weiliang; Zhou Weiliang, 'Yanjing yu Jisi' (Salt Police and Smuggling Control), in *Yanwu Jiyao* (Summary of Salt Affairs) (internal publication, n. d.).

25. DS 893.51/147, report by C. E. Gauss, American Consul General, 7, Apr. 1936; and Croome Report, VIII–25.

26. DELSDAG, 156/1584 and 156/1582. In addition to the group of 185 administrators from the 156/1584 file cited earlier, I added consideration of a list of some 30 post-1927 recruits from file 156/1582. Only 2 of these 30 were of 'high flier or near high flier' status. The incorporation of the Salt Police personnel was most interesting: 7 of the Salt Police officers appointed in 1935–6 entered at the relatively high salary of 160Y, and 4 others started off at even higher grades. The Salt Inspectorate obviously tried to contain and mollify the previously autonomous Salt Police by granting them much higher salary levels and status than was normally the case for new recruits.

27. My informants Zhong Liangzhe, Zhou Weiliang, and Lin Jiyong, who spoke of these features so glowingly some 50 years later, all insisted that the system still worked 'in accordance with regulations, the way it was supposed to' during the 1930s.

28. I am indebted to Liu Foding for this phrasing.

29. The Croome and Pearson Reports cite these themes on virtually every page, but most official publications from the Salt Administration took this up as well. For two examples see *Shinian Lai zhi Yanzheng* (The Past Ten Years of Salt Administration) (Chongqing: Caizheng Bu, 1943), 2–3, and *Yanwu Jisi Ducha Renyuan Yingyou zhi Renshi*, 17–18, 30–1.

30. DELSDAG, 266/2738, 'Yanwu Renshi Guanli Zhidu' (The Administrative System of Salt Personnel) (pamphlet, Ministry of Finance, 1943).

31. DELSDAG, 266/2923, report in the file, 'Yanzheng Si 1936 Niandu Jingguo Gongzuo yu Chengji' (The Work and Results of the Salt Administration Department in 1936); interview with Chen Guisheng.

32. DELSDAG, 266/2923 (as above).

33. Predictably, both Pearson and Croome complained about this long and loud in the reports they submitted. In July 1936, in the wake of the promulgation of a new Organic Law for the Directorate General of Salt, Oliver Lockhart, who was by then foreign Chief Inspector, pressed Kong Xiangxi to commit to the principle of continued joint responsibility between Chinese and foreign officers in the Salt Administration: DS 893.51/158. Kong was suitably bland in his responses, and the trend towards the diminution of joint responsibility continued unchecked.

34. Report on the 52nd Meeting of the Legislative Yuan, 29 Mar. 1936, Guomin News Agency, appended to a file sent to Anthony Eden, Foreign Office, FO 371/

20274. The Legislative Yuan did not, of course, in this period have a great deal of power: at best, it operated as a consultative body. Nevertheless, on this issue at least, for a rubber-stamp legislature it exhibited a great deal of spirit. It ratified the proposed legislation by only a slim margin, and probably well illustrates the ambivalence that educated state elites felt towards the Inspectorate.

35. DS 893.51/154, report from Huang Huiying, with translation of a letter of the Control Yuan's list of recommended action with respect to the Salt Administration, signed by Yu Youren, President of the Control Yuan, 28 Jul. 1936.

36. Interview with Chen Guisheng. Indeed, up to the 1970s in Taiwan, the Ministry of Personnel was still complaining about the continued existence of the Salt Administration's separate rank classifications, to no avail.

37. Customs revenues supplied more funds in total, but customs tax fluctuated a good deal from year to year. Thus, salt was seen to provide the more reliable, predictable tax funds.

38. This figure comes from *The China Year Book, 1937* (Shanghai/Germany: Council of International Affairs), 419.

39. See Lloyd Eastman, 'Nationalist China at War', in *Cambridge History of Republican China*, 13:2 (New York: Cambridge University Press, 1986), ch. 5

40. DS 893.51/232, joint report by F. E. L. Dobbs and Y. C. Yao, Dec. 1937.

41. DS 893.51/180, report on status of the Salt Administration, 21 Feb. 1938.

42. Interview with Lin Jiyong.

43. Reliable figures on the size of the salt administration over the course of the Republican period have been difficult to find. The Croome Report, VI–10, puts the size of the Salt Inspectorate at 5,422 individuals in 1922; the figure of 6,000 in 1937 is mentioned by one of the foreign district inspectors in DS 893.51/230; and Ding *et al*, in *Minguo Yanwu Shigao*, 165, state that in 1931 the Salt Inspectorate consisted of 8,288 individuals, with an additional 26,129 in the Salt Police. It is unclear what is behind the discrepancy in these numbers; perhaps Ding's figures include personnel Yanwu Shu offices, which were then in the process of being absorbed into the Inspectorate. For the Sino-Japanese War there are no reliable aggregate numbers anywhere. Ding *et al*. suggest a 'rough' figure of 'more than 40,000' in 1942 (p. 355). Zhou Weiliang guessed at somewhere between 20,000 and 30,000, or 'a three to four-fold increase'. (interview and personal communication, 25 Aug. 1995). Given the similar ballooning of other organizations during this time, a tripling to quadrupling in size was not unlikely.

44. *Shinian Lai zhi Yanzheng* (The Past 10 Years of Salt Administration), pamphlet compiled by the Yanzheng Si (Nov. Caizheng Bu, 1943), 14–15. See *Kangzhan Shiqu Zhuanmai Shiliao* (Historical Materials on Monopolies during the Sino-Japanese War) (Taipei: Academia Historica, 1992), 297–314, for reproductions of original documents establishing temporary regulations for the wartime salt monopoly.

45. *Shinian Lai zhi Yanzheng*, 12.

46. 'Caizheng Bu Zhuanmai Shiye Renyuan Renshi Guanli Zhanxing Banfa Cao'an' (Ministry of Finance Draft Methods on Temporary Implementation of Monopoly Work and Personnel Management), pamphlet printed by the Ministry of Finance for internal circulation, 1942: DELSDAG, 266/2738.

47. Interview with Lin Jiyong. Zhong Liangzhe also insisted that until the war 99% of staff came in the 'regular' way (interview with Zhong Liangzhe).

48. Lin Jiyong cited the constant radio communication as a real change from before the war (interview with Lin Jiyong).

49. DELSDAG 266 (4)/156, from file 'Yanwu Zongju Renshichu Zhiyuan Renmian Dongtai', 1943–44: Document from Directorate-General of Salt to Minister of Finance (n.d. *c.* 1942), no cover sheet.

50. DELSDAG 266/158, Directorate-General of Salt, Division of Personnel document (November 1943).

51. See Julia C. Strauss, 'Wartime Stress and Guomindang Response: *Xunlian* as a Means to Statebuilding', paper given at the Association of Asian Studies Annual Conference, Honolulu, 11–14 Apr. 1996, MS pp. 17–19, 22–4, 26–32, for the goals of the *xunlian* movement and the 'model' that was set forth by the Central Training Institute (the Zhongyang Xunliantuan) with respect to both values and curriculum. For a particularly concise description of the ethos of the *xunlian* movement as 'partification and militarization', see Wang Dongyuan, *Zenyang Shixing Xunshi* (How to Implement Training) (Chongqing: Zhongyang Xunliantuan, 1940), 8–12.

52. GSG Microfilm No. 307000000D, 0313/7817, 139–40, Request from the Department of Salt (Yanzheng Si) to the Ministry of Finance Department of Personnel, dated 26 Jun. 1941.

53. DELSDAG 266/9721, 1–3, file entitled 'Shenji Bu Yanwu Zongju Shenji Bu Banshichu Juanzong Shiti'; GSG Microfilm 307000000D, 0313/7817, 'Caizheng Bu Yanwu Zongju Choushe Yanwu Renyuan Xunlianban Jihua', 30–1; and interviews with Lin Jiyong and Zhong Liangzhe.

54. Strauss, 'Wartime Stress', 79–81, 84–87; Zhong Liangzhe and Lin Jiyong also remembered the Guiyang *xunlian* session as being academically and practically oriented, stressing economics and the technical aspects of Salt Administration under wartime conditions, rather than the latest Party platform or the speeches of Chiang Kai-shek.

55. The answer was: 'That merchants use transport to get rich, they rig and monopolize the market. Therefore, official transport reduces exploitation, speculation, and stabilizes prices'; DELSDAG 266/9721, 1–3, file 'Shenji Bu Yanwu Zongju Shenji Banshichu Juanzong Shiti' (Assorted Files on Examination Questions from the Ministry of Audit and the Directorate-General of Salt's Auditing Office).

56. Interview with Zhou Weiliang and personal discussion with Liu Foding, Tianjin, 24 June 1988. See also Liu Foding, 'Zhongguo Jindai Liangyan Yunxiao Zhidude Bianhua' (The Changes in the Salt and Grain Transport System in Modern China), *Nankai Jingji Yanjiusuo Jikan* (Nankai Economics Institute Quarterly), 2 (1985).

## Chapter 5

1. As reviewed in Ch. 3, had it not been for the Western banks' concern about the status of their loans to the Chinese government, the Inspectorate never would have come into existence. Without Dane's administrative vision and immediate practical ability, the organization in all likelihood would not have established

initial control over the disbursement of the salt tax from the districts, and without this critical access to funds, the organization might very well have never established its early autonomy from the rest of the Chinese government.

2. See Albert Hirschmann, *Development Projects Observed* (Washington: Brookings Institution, 1967).

3. This was in contrast to the central government's previous practice of simply being content with the proportion of provincial funds 'customarily' remitted to the centre.

4. This list is taken from Esther Morrisson, *The Modernization of the Confucian Bureaucracy*, unpublished Ph.D. thesis, Radcliffe College, 1959, 1041–70.

5. The terms 'Zhi Bu' and 'Caizheng Bu' are both translated as 'Ministry of Finance', and stand in contrast to the term 'Hu Bu' (Board of Revenue), which covered finance, taxation, and household registration in the empire until 1907.

6. On the concept of protective brokerage, see Prasenjit Duara, *Culture, Power and the State: Rural North China, 1900–42* (Stanford: Stanford University Press, 1988), 42 and *passim*.

7. Ernest Young, *The Presidency of Yuan Shih-kai* (Ann Arbor: University of Michigan Press, 1977), 166–7; see also Duara, *Culture, Power*, 66–7.

8. Both of these examples are from Young, *Presidency*. The Yuan Shikai quote is cited on p. 99, and the involvement of Goodnow is discussed in detail on pp. 220–1.

9. This description is a summary of a long document that outlined the organization of the Ministry of Finance, *c.* 1913: DELSDAG 1027(2)/220.

10. DELSDAG 1027/804 (1). These and subsequent figures are based on a file that contains 234 curricula vitae for what appears to be the entire central Ministry of Finance from roughly 1913 to 1915. At least during the tenure of the Yuan Shikai Government, the quotas setting the size of the Ministry seem to have been followed. In 1914–15, the central Ministry of Finance had only 234 registered members, including members of advisory commissions. In contrast to the later Nationalist Ministry of Finance, which had relatively few section chiefs (*kezhang*) over masses of section members (*keyuan*), 55 of the 234 members had relatively high prestige appointments. This ratio of high-status appointees to regular section members is probably due to the strong continuity of finance personnel in the transition from the *xinzheng* to the Yuan Shikai period. Because so many had had official positions under the Qing, it may have been necessary to offer these individuals ranks in the new system that were commensurate with their former status. Most of the 55 fell into the category of *qianshi* (senior assistants), a classification with status only slightly lower than that of section chief. This particular rank was not continued under the Nationalist personnel system.

11. This trend was even more noticeable at higher levels. For the highest ranked division chiefs (*sizhang*) the percentages of Metropolitan graduates increase greatly. Of the 50 section chiefs and senior assistants, only one passed the Metropolitan (*jinshi*) exam, while of the 5 division chiefs, 2 did.

12. DELSDAG 1027/804 (1). Of the group of 50 section chiefs and senior assistants, 9 were born in 1884–9, 25 in 1878–83, 7 in 1872–7, and 7 in 1867–71.

13. The relatively high concentration of individuals who studied at Waseda University in Japan (nearly half of the 15 who studied in Japan, and 7 of the 50 overall) is the only exception to this trend. Otherwise, at no point could I identify more than three individuals who had obvious native place, or old school ties.

14. DELSDAG 1027 (2)/220.

15. DELSDAG 1027/176 (2). This file contains a list of Ministry of Finance appointees who passed the first examination cycle shortly after the death of Yuan Shikai. In 1917, 18 individuals who passed the upper civil service exam, and another 27 with the general civil service credential were assigned to the Ministry for a two-year training period.

16. DELSDAG 1027/179, 1027/181, 1027/188 (1). These files contained lists of those appointed to positions in the Beiyang Ministry of Finance throughout the 1920s. The pattern revealed in these appointment lists is clear. In the late 1910s the Beiyang Ministry of Finance was staffed by a surprisingly stable group of bureaucrats who, by the standards of their time, had substantial claims to expertise in the realm of finance and taxation. But as the 1920s wore on, the Ministry of Finance was under increasing external political and military stress; this was reflected in the wholesale de-institutionalization, replacement of the personnel of whole departments, and the sorry state of the appointment forms themselves, which often were not completely filled in.

17. DELSDAG 1027/183 (1).

18. DELSDAG 1027 (2)/220; also *Shi Nian Lai zhi Caiwu Xingzheng* (The Past Ten Years of Finance Administration) (Chongqing: Caizheng Bu, 1943), 3.

19. Ch'ien Tuan-sheng, *The Government and Politics of China, 1912–49* (Stanford: Stanford University Press, 1950/1970), 212. See also Arthur Waldron, *From War to Nationalism: China's Turning Point, 1924–25* (Cambridge University Press: Cambridge and New York, 1995), 120–4, on the Beiyang government's fiscal difficulties on the eve of the Second Zhili-Fengtian War in 1924–5.

20. Intensification of militarization and the rising expenses of larger-scale internal warfare in the provinces throughout the 1920s blocked revenues customarily remitted to the central government and in addition made even modest central control an increasingly less politely observed fiction. On the growth of military expenditure and intensification of regionally based warfare, see Ch'i Hsi-sheng, *Warlord Politics in China, 1916–28* (Stanford: Stanford University Press, 1976), 135–42, 167–72, and Waldron, *From War to Nationalism*, 55 and passim.

21. Tan Yankai, reported in *Shenbao*, 9 January 1928; cited in Wu Jingping, 'Song Ziwen Lun'gang' (Outline Discussion on Song Ziwen), *Lishi Yanjiu* (Historical Studies), No. 6 (1991), 117.

22. These figures are from *Caizheng Nianjian* (The Finance Yearbook) (Nanjing: Caizheng Bu, 1935), 17, and the quote is from John Fitzgerald, 'Increased Disunity: The Politics and Finance of Guangdong Separatism, 1926–1936', *Modern Asian Studies*, 24:4 (1990), 754. Fitzgerald also suggests that, although there were 'some' efficiency gains in direct military levies, which forced the sale of bonds, increased taxation and taxes levied as much as a year in advance were the primary means by which the Guomindang was able to finance the Northern Expedition.

23. Lloyd Eastman, *The Abortive Revolution* (Cambridge, Mass.: Harvard University Press, 1974), 228–39. For an excellent study of the complex and ambivalent relationship between the Guomindang finance establishment and the Shanghai business elite, see Parks Coble, *The Shanghai Capitalists and the Nationalist Government, 1927–37* (Cambridge, Mass.: Harvard University Press, 1986).

24. This list is based upon an organization chart of the Ministry, found in *Caizheng Nianjian* (The Finance Yearbook) (Nanjing: Caizheng Bu, 1935), 35.

25. The Ministry of Finance's key goals were set forth in the official reports on the First and Second National Finance Conferences of 1928 and 1934. Song Ziwen's Report of 1928 can be found in *The Chinese Yearbook, 1929–30* (Shanghai: Kelley and Walsh), 665–6. Kong Xiangxi's address to the Second National Finance Conference of 1934 is reproduced in *The China Yearbook, 1935–36*, ed. Kwei Chungshu (Shanghai: Commercial Press), 1174–6.

26. On the differences between Song Ziwen and Kong Xiangxi, see Coble, *Shanghai Capitalists*, 161–3, and Tan Guang, 'Wo Suo Zhidao de Kong Xiangxi' (The Kong Xiangxi I Knew), in *Wenshi Ziliao Xuanji*, No. 25, Wenshi Ziliao Yanjiuyuan Huiyi (Beijing: Wenhua Shuju, 1962), 218. Tan further states: 'Although the common view was that Song was brightly intelligent while Kong was mediocre and incompetent, in fact it was not this way. If Kong sometimes played the fool [*zhuang hutu*], it was always to suit a particular situation, and indeed he could be as wily as a thousand-year-old fox.'

27. The highly evocative concept of a 'cover-over strategy' of state building and its application to both early modern Europe and Zaire in the 1970s is elaborated in Thomas Callaghy, *The State–Society Struggle: Zaire in Comparative Perspective* (New York: Columbia University Press, 1984), esp. 96–9. Callaghy himself contrasts the socially conservative 'cover-over' strategy of state building with a more explicitly revolutionary approach that seeks to effect a 'revolutionary breakthrough' in the transformation of state and society. Although Callaghy focuses on a wide-ranging process of state building, the concept of 'cover-over' involving some mix of persuasion, normative appeals, outright coercion, co-option, and emasculation is equally applicable for intermediary levels of institution building, and is particularly accurate to describe the actions of both the Nationalist state and its handmaidens of state building: organizations involved with war making and resource extraction.

28. See Ch. 2 for the genesis of the 'Administrative Efficiency' school.

29. On currency reform, see Arthur Young, *China's Wartime Finance and Inflation, 1937–45* (Cambridge, Mass.: Harvard University Press, 1965), ch. 14. On the retiring of the foreign debt, Hung Mao Tien is more critical: he suggests that, while some debts were retired by the mid-1930s, the Nationalists systematically concentrated on those loans whose default would have adverse international consequences while significantly raising the level of internal debt during the 1930s: Tien Hung Mao, *Government and Politics in KMT China* (Stanford: Stanford University Press, 1972), 77.

30. Although an attempt was made to conduct a national cadastral survey in the mid-17th c. in the reign of the Shunzhi Emperor, it ended in failure when it became clear that local officials either could not or would not report truthfully

on actual land holdings. The last national cadastral survey had been carried out under the Ming in 1578–82, and was seriously outdated by the turn of the 20th c. See Yeh-chien Wang, *Land Taxation in Imperial China, 1750–1911* (Cambridge, Mass.: Harvard University Press, 1973), 20–8.

31. The 'received wisdom' on Republican China has long assumed that the period was characterized by an onerous burden of taxation as well as a weak and ineffective government: R. H. Tawney, *Land and Labor in China* (New York: Octagon Press, 1972) and Arthur Young, *China's Nation Building Effort, 1927–37* (Stanford: Hoover Institution Press, 1971), 69. Studies of individual warlords similarly focus on the inexorable search for more revenue: see Donald Gillin, *Warlord: Yen Hsi-shan in Shansi Province* (Princeton: Princeton University Press, 1966), 138, and James Sheridan, *Chinese Warlord: The Career of Feng Yü-hsiang* (Stanford: Stanford University Press, 1966), 24. For a revisionist view that argues quite the opposite—that, despite weak and ineffective governments during the Republican period, taxes were on the whole low and fell disproportionately on those best able to pay—see Thomas Rawski, *Economic Growth in Prewar China* (Berkeley: University of California Press, 1989), esp. 13–32. Prasenjit Duara offers an analysis that is consistent with both positions: real state income in terms of extraction was rising throughout the first half of the 20th c., but was not rising as fast as revenue extracted by a proliferating set of local entreprenurial brokers, who kept themselves going via almost totally unreported and unauthorized 'provisional taxes' (*baidi tankuan*) that were felt to be onerous: Duara, *Culture, Power*, 78, 84–5.

32. Arthur Waldron applies very much the same argument in his analysis of the political and social consequences of the second Zhili-Fengtian War: see Waldron, *From War to Nationalism*, 120.

33. DS 893.512/232. A similar set of taxes was reported from the American consulate in the city of Qingdao in DS 893.512/1000, and such taxes were probably common elsewhere during this period.

34. DS 893.512/982: Samuel Sokobin, consular report, August 1929.

35. The Ministry of Finance's 'agenda' of tax rationalization and unification was first raised publicly in Song Ziwen's speech to the 5th Plenum of the 5th Plenary Session of the Nationalist Party Central Committee on August 1928 and subsequently figured prominently in virtually all of the Ministry of Finance's official proclamations, reports, and accounts throughout the remainder of the Republican period. For Song's speech, see *The Chinese Year Book, 1935–36*, ed. Kwei Chungshu (Shanghai: Commercial Press), 1177. A partial and incomplete list of the venues where these key concerns of tax standardization and unification were put forth include: *Caizheng Nianjian* (1935), 1, 935; *Shinian Lai zhi Huowushui* (The Past Ten Years of Commodity Tax), ed. Caizheng Bu Shuiwushu (Chongqing: Caizheng Bu, 1943), 3, 5–6, and the First and Second Finance Conferences of 1928 and 1934.

36. The Customs Administration supplied between 36.5% and 58.4% of the central government tax revenue, and Salt generated between 8.8% and 27%. These calculations are from Tien, *Government and Politics*, 78.

37. Ci Hongfei, 'Guanyu Guomindang Zhengfude Guanshui Zhengce' (On the Nationalist Government's Custom's Tax Policy), *Shehui Kexue* (Social Science)

(March 1985), and Xingzheng Yuan Xinwenju (News Office of the Executive Yuan), *Guanzheng* (Customs Policy), free pamplet (1947), 8–9.

38. *Ibid.*

39. *Shinian Lai zhi Huowushui*, 2.

40. Ibid. 2–3; Liu Bing, '1927–33 Nian Nanjing Guomin Zhengfu Banli Tongshui Jiangshu' (The National Government's Administration of Consolidated Tax, 1927–33), *Minguo Dangan*, 3 (1987); *Caizheng Nianjian* (1935), 59; and Y. Dung, 'Public Finance and Taxation', in *The Chinese Yearbook* 1937 (Shanghei: Commercial Press), 424–7.

41. This list of commodities, and the dates they were brought in to the Consolidated Tax/Internal Revenue system, is provided in P. T. Chen, 'Public Finance', *The Chinese Year Book, 1936–37* 639–40); Y. Dung, 'Public Finance and Taxation', *The Chinese Year Book, 1937* (Shanghai: Commercial Press, 1937), 423–27; See also Liu Bing, '1927–33 Nian Nanjing'.

42. *Shinian Lai zhi Caiwu Renshi* (The Past Ten Years of Finance Personnel) (Chongqing: Caizheng Bu, 1943), 12–13; Liu Bing, '1927–33 Nian Nanjing'; *Caizheng Nianjian* (1935), 61–3.

43. Dung, 'Public finance', 427.

44. *Caizheng Nianjian* (1935), data drawn from 949–50, 960, 972, 982–3, 988, and 994.

45. *Shinian Lai zhi Huowushui*, 7.

46. These figures are drawn from *Caizheng Nianjian* (1935), 950–1, 960, and 972. However, the Jiangsu/Zhejiang/Anhui district did not include the consolidated tax receipts from the city of Shanghai. Consolidated taxes from the Shanghai collectorates were remitted directly to the much larger Internal Revenue Administration: *Caizheng Nianjian* (1935), 950.

47. The evidence as to whether the consolidated tax ever did succeed in establishing a totally separate civil service system, complete with higher salary scales and non-convertability back into the 'regular' *jian jian wei* personnel system, is mixed, but the cachet of the civil service 'model' in Nationalist technocratic and financial circles during the 1930s is without question. In his Financial Report of 1933, Song Ziwen spoke glowingly of the high efficiency engendered by the strong civil service systems in both Customs and Salt, and stated that a civil service system had 'mostly' been instituted for the Consolidated Tax Administration: see *The China Year Book*, ed. H. G. W. Woodhouse (Shanghai: Kelley and Walsh, 1935), 483–84. Later 'official' reports in the 1930s were less sanguine on this point: Y. Dung's (Deng Xian) official review of 'Public Finance and Taxation' in the *Chinese Yearbook*, Council of International Affairs (Shanghai: Commercial Press, 1937), suggested that, 'although prominent administrators had long recognized the merits of a civil service system, "for obvious financial reasons" it had proved impossible to extend civil service systems to other [i.e. non-Customs, non-Salt] departments of the government': p. 357.

48. *Caizheng Nianjian* (1935), 72.

49. Tien., *Government and Politics*, 78.

50. This point is made by Ma Yinchu in his critical summary of Nationalist era finance, *Caizhengxue yu Zhongguo Caizheng* (Study of Finance and Chinese Finance) (Shanghai: Shangwu Yinshu, 1948), 332.

51. FO 371/19291: letter from Archibald Rose, British American Tobacco, to Mr Orde, Foreign Office, 4 January 1935.
52. FO 371/19291: official letter with appended report, H. H. K'ung (Kong Xiangxi), Minister of Finance, to Alexander Cadogan, British Minister, 27 May 1935.
53. Gao Bingfang, *Zhongguo Zhijieshui Shishi* (History and Practice of China's Direct Tax) (Chongqing: Zhongguo Zhijieshui Congshu, 1943), 59.
54. Ni Shaojiu, 'Anhui Zhijieshui Shimo' (The Beginning to the End of Direct Tax in Anhui), *Zhongguo Renmin Zhengzhi Xieshang Huiyi Anhui sheng Weiyuanhui Wenshi Ziliao Yanjiu Weiyuanhui* [no number] (Anhui Renmin Chubanshe, 1988), 157.
55. Both of these slogans were often enunciated and obviously stuck in the memories of all those who were associated with the Direct Tax: in interviews with Zhou Bi and Zhu Yuan, both mentioned the 'new tax run by new people' slogan with some enthusiasm as summing up the ethos of the Direct Tax Administration in its early days. Also cited in *Shinian Lai zhi Caizheng Renshi* (The Past Ten Years of Finance Personnel) (Chongqing: Ministry of Finance, 1943), 4, and Gao Bingfang, *Zhongguo Zhijieshui Shishi*, 60. The 'new tax, new personnel, new spirit' (*xinshui xinren xin jingshen*) variant is mentioned in Li Jianji, 'Jiefangqian de Lanzhou Zhijieshui' (Preliberation Direct Tax in Lanzhou), *Gansu Wenshi Ziliao*, No. 14, (Lanzhou: Gansu Renmin Chubanshe, 1983), 99, and in Chen Yugan, 'Fujian de Zhijieshui' (Direct Tax in Fujian), *Fujian Wenshi Ziliao*, No. 13 (Fuzhou: Fujian Sheng Weiyuanhui Wenshi Ziliao Yanjiu Weiyuanhui, 1986), 116.
56. *Caizheng Nianjian* (1943), 52; interviews with Zhu Yuan and Zhou Bi. Both Zhu Yuan and Zhou Bi, who took the 1936 civil service examination and went through the training course, remembered the training as *yewu* (functional) training that 'prepared you for what you needed to know in the division to which you were assigned'.
57. *Caizheng Nianjian* (1943), 52; *Banian Lai zhi Zhijieshui* (The Past Ten Years of Direct Tax) (Chongqing: Caizheng Bu 1943), 20; Chen Yugan, 'Fujian de Zhijie Shui', 121; Li Jianji, 'Jiefangqian', 99.
58. Chen Yugan. 'Fujian de Zhijieshui', 125.
59. Interview with Sun Jinggong.
60. Zhang Zhijie (ed.), *Suodeshui Zhanxing Tiaolie Xiangjie* (A Detailed Introduction to the Temporary Implementation of Income Tax Rules) (Shanghai?: Shangwu, 1941), i, 12–15; and Caizheng Bu Zhijieshui Shu, *Zhijieshui Shuifa Gaiyao* (General Outline of the Tax Laws for Direct Tax) (Nanjing: Caizheng Bu, 1946), 6–8.
61. Ma Yinchu *Caizhengxue*, 255, 227.
62. Dung, 'Public Finance', 440. The Kemmerer Commission also recommended strongly against the introduction of a direct tax as early as 1929, on the grounds that China had neither the skilled administrators nor the accounting procedures to make the tax viable. Arthur Young and Oliver Lockhart, who stayed on to advise the government on fiscal matters after 1929, both considered the direct tax experiment 'premature' in 1936, and recommended against it: see Young, *China's Nation Building Effort*, 67–8.

63. This information is drawn from a table on the different varieties of direct tax collected in fiscal 1936 in *Banian Lai zhi Zhijieshui*, 7. See also Dung, 'Public Finance', 447–8, for a slightly different set of figures.
64. These figures are drawn from Dung, 'Public Finance', 447–8.
65. Interview with Zhu Yuan.
66. Chen Yugan, 'Fujian de Zhijieshui', 119.
67. Young, *China's Nation Building Effort*, 5; Tien Hung Mao, *Government and Politics*, ch. 4; and P. T. Chen, 'Finance', in *The Chinese Yearbook, 1935–36*, 1417.
68. Interview with Song Tongfu.
69. In a group of 14 who achieved recommended (*jianren*) appointment status by 1941, only 6 had been promoted from within the Ministry and 8 had transferred in from the outside with the recommended appointment classification: DELSDAG 27/71 (1 and 2). Informants also stressed the difficulty of promotions from within: interviews with Wu Chengming and Sun Jinggong.
70. Interviews with Sun Jinggong and Zhu Yuan.
71. Interview with Dai Liyan.
72. Interview with Sun Jinggong; Li Jianji, 'Jiefangqian', 99.
73. DELSDAG 27/72. These 61 section members and 11 recommended and selected appointments were all recruited between 1928 and 1932.
74. DELSDAG 37/206. These figures are the Examination Yuan's own statistics of how many it qualified through the upper civil service examination with a concentration in finance in the years between 1931 and 1941.
75. *Caizheng Nianjian* (1943), 39–40.
76. Interviews with Song Tongfu and Li Xueli.
77. See Ch. 6 for comparative data from the Ministry of the Interior.
78. Interviews with Dai Liyan and Zhu Yuan.
79. Interviews with Wu Chengming, Song Tongfu, and Zhu Yuan.
80. Interviewees Zhu Yuan, Zhou Bi, Sun Jinggong, Dai Liyan, and Wu Chengming all agreed on this point.
81. Interview with Dai Liyan.
82. Interview with Zhou Bi.
83. *Shinian Lai zhi Caiwu Renshi*, 14–15, 17.
84. *Shinian Lai zhi Huowushui*, 7.
85. Chang Kia-ngau, *The Inflationary Spiral: The Experience in China, 1939–50* (New York and London: MIT Press and John Wiley, 1958), 124 (for table on government expenditure and revenue, 1936–45).
86. Interview with Zhu Yuan.
87. Wartime finance and inflation have been comprehensively studied and evaluated both by Arthur Young, in *China's Wartime Finance*, and by Chang Kia-ngau in *The Inflationary Spiral*. Both Young, who on the whole was sympathetic to the government's efforts and Chang, who was considerably more critical, wrote from a post-1950 perspective in which all analysts, sympathetic or not, implicitly evaluated the Nationalist regime in light of its failure in 1949. Even the critical Chang points out that, were it not for this highly unpopular land tax in kind, 'expenditure for 1941–42 and 1942–43 would have been greater by about 30 and 80 percent, respectively, and that for 1943–44 and 1944–45

would have been about 80 and 85 percent higher' (p. 142). It is not at all surprising that a brand new tax administration to collect a grain tax in kind, with personnel hastily recruited and given only rudimentary training, should be riven with problems, including inequitable levying, financial irregularities, and administrative waste. It is still less surprising that the land tax in kind was inherently difficult to convert into Chinese yuan equivalents, which enormously complicated government accounting (Young, pp. 25–7; Chang, pp. 142–4). What is surprising is that such a wartime administration functioned at all, and succeeded, albeit for a brief period of time, in bringing central government penetration and agents further and deeper into the countryside of China than had ever before been the case under extremely adverse conditions.

88. Chang, *The Inflationary Spiral*, 150.
89. Chen Yugan, 'Fujian de Zhijieshui', 119.
90. The original orders that created the wartime government monopolies for salt, sugar, tobacco, and matches can be found in Shi-mi Ho, *Kangzhan Shique Zhuanmai Shiliao* (A Documentary Collection on Monopoly during the Sino-Japanese War) (Taibei: Guoshiguan, 1992). Critical assessment of the public monopoly system can be found in Chang, *The Inflationary Spiral*, 135–7 and Ma Yinchu, *Caizhengxue*, 384–8, 397–8.
91. In only its first full year of operation, the land tax administration accounted for 1,075 of the individuals in the Ministry of Finance who attended *xunlian* (training) courses, and certainly not all of those recruited made it into the *xunlian* course: *Shinian Lai zhi Caiwu Renshi*, 9. Those in the new land tax administration who were fortunate enough to receive formal training were only a fraction of staff. By the end of 1941, 1,243 county administrations had set up nearly 7,000 sub-collectorates responsible for administering the land tax in kind: *The China Handbook, 1937–43*, compiled by the Chinese Ministry of Information, (New York: MacMillan, 1943), 201.
92. Chang, *The Inflationary Spiral*, 130–2; Young, *China's Wartime Finance*, 24–5.
93. Interview with Song Tongfu: Gao Bingfang, *Zhongguo Zhijieshui*, 6.
94. Wang Dongyuan, *Zenyang Shixing Xunshi?* (How to Implement Training Instruction), pamphlet (Chongqing: Zhongyang Xunliantuan, 1940), 3. The following discussion is drawn from my unpublished paper, 'Wartime Stress and Guomindang Response: *Xunlian* as a Means to Statebuilding'.
95. There may well have been other, later *dangzheng xunlian* sessions at the Zhongxuntuan that particularly targeted Ministry of Finance personnel, but the documents preserved on this topic dry up from 1942 until 1946, when the Zhongxuntuan ran a *xunlian* course specifically for finance personnel: GSG 0313.16/5050, pp. 346–79, 'Zhongyang Xunliantuan Caiwu Renyuan Xunlian Ban Xunyu Shishi Xize' (Detailed Regulations on Training Implementation for Finance Personnel in the Central Training Corps).
96. The Ministry of Finance ran at least two in-house training organizations during the Sino-Japanese war. The first, which was an *ad hoc* training course for successful new examinees from the special finance civil service examinations of 1938–9, stressed functional (*yewu*) training, but incorporated two hours of daily military drill into its programme. A more formal organization, called the All-Country Training Institute for Finance Personnel (Quanguo Caiwu Renyuan

Xunliansuo), was established by the Ministry of Finance in 1942. This institute blended the ethos of continued Weberian tenets of standardization and technocracy, with the form, if not the substance, of the partification so prevalent in the Central Training Corps: *Caizheng Nianjian* (1943), 46–7.

97. *Caizheng Nianjian* (1943), 47–51: e.g., the Ministry of Finance divided its trainees into groups by functional work area, which strongly suggests a heavy *yewu* technocratic component. And in sending over its personnel to participate in the Central Training Corps *xunlian* sessions, it seems to have quietly lobbied to increase the 'practical' component, even going so far as to have its own senior personnel go over to the Central Training Corps to deliver lectures on the latest in wartime financial policy and run the discussion sessions: DELSAG 3(1)/ 1574. Ministry of Finance, 'Caizheng Bu Yuxunban Caiqu zu Gonguo Taolunhui Jilu' (Ministry of Finance Working Group on the Adoption of Training: Record of Discussion Meeting), dated 16 October 1941.

## Chapter 6

1. For explicit statements of this view, see David Pong, 'The Ministry of Foreign Affairs during the Republican Period 1912–1949', in Zara Steiner (ed.), *The Times Survey of the Foreign Ministries of the World* (London: Times Books, 1982), esp. 146–47; and Edmund S. K. Fung, 'Nationalist Foreign Policy, 1928–37', in David Pong and Edmund Fung, (eds.), *Ideal and Reality: Social and Political Change in Modern China, 1860–1949* (Lanham, Md: University Press of America, 1985), esp. 211–12.
2. William C. Kirby, 'The Internationalization of China: Foreign Relations at Home and Abroad in the Republican Era', *China Quarterly*, forthcoming, p. 11 of typescript.
3. Arthur Waldron, *From War to Nationalism: China's Turning Point, 1924–25* (Cambridge and New York: Cambridge University Press, 1995), 31–2.
4. FO 371/13219: Reginald Johnston, Commissioner of Weihaiwei to L. S. Amery, Colonial Office, memo describing the history of the outstanding (and in 1928 still unratified) agreement, 14 Dec. 1928.
5. FO 371/13219: Miles Lampson to Sir Austen Chamberlain, recommendation dated 19 Nov. 1927. Lampson put his objections in exceptionally strong language: 'His Majesty's Government have bound themselves to hand back the territory and there is of course no going back on that pledge. In existing circumstances, however, to turn over a peaceful, law abiding and prosperous community of nearly 200,000 souls to the appalling misrule of Chang Tsung-chang [sic] would be little less than criminal...' To which the appended minutes of G. Mounsey read: 'I am afraid that Sir Miles Lampson is perfectly right and that much as we should prefer to get this off our hands, we cannot give Weihaiwei back to the worst of the Chinese bandits.'
6. FO 371/13899: Foreign Office to Miles Lampson, 12 Jan. 1929.
7. FO 371/13899: Lampson to Foreign Office, 21 May 1929.
8. FO 371/13899: Minutes of interview between Lampson *et al.* and Wang *et al.*, Ministry of Foreign Affairs, Nanjing, 22 Jun. 1929.

9. Pamela Atwell, *British Mandarins and Chinese Reformers: The British Administration of Weihaiwei and the Territory's Return to Chinese Rule* (Hong Kong: Oxford University Press, 1985), 162; and Appendix B, 'Convention between His Majesty and the President of the National Government of the Republic of China for the Rendition of Weihaiwei and Agreement Regarding Certain Facilities for His Majesty's Navy After Rendition', 18 Apr. 1930, reproduced on pp. 216–24.

10. Ian Nish, *Japan's Struggle with Internationalism: Japan, China, and the League of Nations, 1931–33* (London and New York: Kegan Paul International, 1993), 30; Manley O. Hudson, *The Verdict of the League: China and Japan in Manchuria* (Boston: World Peace Foundation, 1933), 73.

11. *The Sino-Japanese Dispute from September 18, 1931 to February 22, 1932* (statement of the case with all the relevant facts submitted by the Chinese Delegation to the League Council in conformity with Article XV, Paragraph 2, of the Covenant of the League of Nations), Information Bulletin No. 1 [Nanking: Intelligence and Publicity Department, Waichiaopu], 10 Apr. 1933, 2–3, and 5.

12. Ibid. 5.

13. *The Report of the Commission of Enquiry of the League of Nations into the Sino-Japanese Dispute* ('The Lytton Report') (New York: League of Nations, 1932); see esp. pp. 71–2 on Manchuria as coming under the *de jure* authority of the Chinese government, pp. 74–5 on Japan's 'claims to a "special position" in Manchuria, p. 142 on the aggressiveness of Japanese military operations on 18 Sep. 1931, and pp. 197–8 and 219–25 on Manchukuo as a creation of the Japanese army and officials and the overwhelming hostility to the new regime on the part of the majority Chinese.

14. Nish, *Japan's Struggle*, 213.

15. Quoted in ibid. 240.

16. FO 371/18066: Harding, Consul-General at Yunnanfu, to Alexander Cadogan, report, with appended map of frontiers claimed according to Chinese publications of various dates, 3 Jul. 1934.

17. FO 371/18065: Wang Jingwei, Minister of Foreign Affairs, speech at the Weekly Memorial Service, Nanjing, 16 Apr. 1934.

18. FO 371/18065: Xu Mo, Vice-Minister of Foreign Affairs to Alexander Cadogan, memo, 2 May 1934.

19. FO 371/19270: 'Draft Terms of Reference for the Sino-Burma Boundary Commission', 3 Jan. 1935; FO 19273: 'Communication to press' (re: the composition of the Boundary Commission), 11 Jul. 1935.

20. FO 371/20236: confidential report, typescript, dated Camp Hohsawn, 18 Jan. 1936; sent in by J. Clague, Senior Commissioner of the Boundary Commission, including a joint report on the proper demarcation of the Kunlong Circle (a disputed area) by Liang and Yin, and the British counterview by Clague and Grose.

21. FO 371/20238: Harcourt-Smith to Pratt, 8 Jul. 1936.

22. 'Exchanges of Notes on Sino-Burmese Frontier Delimitation', in Shao Yu-lin, 'Foreign Relations', *The Chinese Yearbook*, (1943), 244–50.

23. Immanuel C. Y. Hsü, 'The Development of the Chinese Foreign Office in the Ch'ing Period', in Steiner, *Times Survey*, 128–9.

24. Louis Sigel, 'The Diplomacy of Chinese Nationalism, 1900–11', in Pong and Fung, *Ideal and Reality* 238–41.
25. Sigel, 'Diplomacy', 237. Sigel uses this phrase in the context of the 1900–11 generation of 'Young China' diplomats, but it applies equally for the subsequent generation of young Beiyang bureaucrats.
26. Reginald Johnston, the last British Commissioner of Weihaiwei, could not restrain himself from committing to print exceptionally barbed comments on the subject of Gu's second asylum in Weihaiwei. 'Although Dr. Koo is one of the Chinese statesmen who have advocated the abolition of the "unequal treaties" and foreign concessions, he has on several occasions shown himself very ready to avail himself of the protection which those treaties and concessions afford to Chinese who happen to find themselves in an uncomfortable situation . . . it will be remembered that at the time of the [1924 Feng Yuxiang] *coup d'état* that Dr. Koo held the post of Foreign Minister, and that had it been postponed for a month or two he would have signed on behalf of the Chinese government the Anglo-Chinese Agreement relation to the rendition of Weihaiwei.' Johnston also noted that, as he sought asylum in Weihaiwei for the second time in 1928, Gu showed no evidence of wanting the speedy return of Weihaiwei to the Chinese authorities. FO 371/13219: Reginald Johnston to L. S. Amery, Colonial Office, communication dated 24 Jul. 1928.
27. See Pao-chin Chu, *V. K. Wellington Koo: A Case Study of China's Diplomat and the Diplomacy of Nationalism, 1912–1966* (Hong Kong: Chinese University Press, 1981).
28. Interview with Liu Zonghan.
29. Fung, 'Nationalist Foreign Policy', 188–9, 191.
30. These numbers come from a collection of 98 curricula vitae of Ministry of Foreign Affairs bureaucrats in the early 1940s. Although this particular group of curricula vitae lends itself best to analysis of the organization in the late 1930s and early 1940s, there is still substantial (if incomplete) data on the early to mid-1930s. Over half of the bureaucrats in this sample (55 of 98) had joined the Ministry of Foreign Affairs before 1938, while 43 of 98 entered during the years of the Sino-Japanese War: GSG, files 910.1/2.2 (1–3).
31. Both contemporary writers and later analysts stressed the endemic factionalism and patronage within the bureaucracy: see Lloyd Eastman, *The Abortive Revolution* (Cambridge, Mass.: Harvard University Press, 1974), esp. ch. 1, and articles throughout *The Chinese Administrator* (English version), published in Shanghai in 1935–36, and *Xingzheng Xiaolü* (Administrative Efficiency), Chinese language version, both published 1934–6 by the Executive Yuan Committee on Administrative Efficiency.
32. These figures are based on DELSDAG 12/2/1062–1065. These three files contain what appears to be a complete list of CVs for the personnel in the National Government Ministry of Interior during 1933–4, and covers most of the appointments made in the years 1929–32. While these files do not trace the development of the Ministry of Interior over time, they do offer a fairly good snapshot of the central Ministry at a particular point in the early 1930s.
33. Interview with Liu Zonghan.

34. GSG 910.1/2.2(1–3). I included National Central, Beijing, Jinling, Yanjing, Fudan, Nankai, Lujiang, Zhongshan, Qinghua, and Aurora on the list of 'prestige' universities.
35. Interviews with Liu Zonghan and Li Tiezheng.
36. An additional 8 individuals (in a sample of 98) had otherwise stable careers in the central government's Foreign Affairs office with no foreign postings: GSG 910.1/2.2 (1–3).
37. GSG 910.1/2.2/Vol. 3. Xiong's curriculum vitae was No. 58 from a total of 98.
38. These details on the Ministry of Foreign Affairs' personnel system are from an interview with Liu Zonghan.
39. Ibid.
40. GSG 910.1/2.2 (1–3). Obtaining accurate statistics on membership in the Guomindang from the available curricula vitae involves some amount of guesswork, and therefore probable error. Each ministry had its own CV forms, and even within the same ministry the layout of the forms changed from year to year. Although forms usually had a space to indicate one's Party membership, owing to either carelessness or political considerations individuals often left these spaces blank. In organizations where Party prestige was low, such as the Ministry of Finance, there would be every incentive to conceal one's Party membership on these forms; in fact, those who filled out the personnel forms from the Ministry of Finance seldom indicated Party membership. In organizations such as the Ministry of Foreign Affairs, where Party membership became increasingly important to one's career, the reverse was true: non-Party members had every incentive not to draw attention to their lack of Party membership by leaving that set of spaces blank. To account for the largest number of individuals in the sample, I came up with the categories of 'probable' and 'unlikely' Party membership to supplement the findings on definite Party membership and non-membership, where Party membership was clearly indicated or denied. Those deemed 'probable' Party members were those who indicated no Party membership, but belonged to more than one Party or military organization before joining the Ministry of Foreign Affairs. Those categorized as 'unlikely' Party members were those whose CVs contained no evidence of membership in Party or military organizations at any time, and who had long careers in the Ministry. The group remaining in the 'unknown' category were those people whose CVs gave no strong hints one way or the other of Party membership: typically, they had only one short affiliation with a Party or military organization during the Northern Expedition as a *jiaoguan* (instructor).
41. The numbers of such *daili* appointments can only be guessed at. None were recorded in the GSG files, but they certainly existed. One informant managed to get himself into the Ministry of Foreign Affairs in 1942 simply because he had known some Russian, and was willing to undertake *ad hoc* liaison missions in the border areas of Xinjiang. Nearly 50 years after the fact, he was still obviously loathe to admit that he had come into the organization as an 'irregular' who later obtained a regular appointment: interview with Ding Weici.
42. GSG 910.1/2.2 (1–3). The surprisingly elite background of these 12 suggests that in the early 1940s individuals who combined high educational

qualifications with service in Party organizations were rewarded with a post in the Ministry of Foreign Affairs.
43. Interviews with Yin Luguang, Li Tiezheng, and Liu Zonghan. The three bureaucrats who suddenly joined the Party late in their careers were found in the GSG sample of 98.
44. The data in GSG, 910.1/2.2 (1–3) shows that by the early 1940s 66 individuals (of 98) definitely belonged to the Party, with another 4 probable Party members for a total of 70 of 98. It is likely that these figures err on the side of caution: probably many of the individuals for which there was no information were also Party members.
45. Although the *xunlian* of the late 1930s and early 1940s certainly provided a hospitable wider environment for partification, the trend 'proving' one's loyalty to the state through joining the Guomindang pre-dated wartime *xunlian* by several years in the sphere of foreign affairs. Zhengzhi Daxue was established as a Party school with special links to the Ministry of Foreign Affairs well before the war.
46. This rich detail on the establishment and operations of the foreign affairs department at Zhengzhi Daxue was provided by Yin Luguang and Liu Zonghan, who both attended the school in mid- to late 1930s, in interviews.
47. GSG 910.1/2.2 (1–3). Although the records from the early 1940s do not bear out the memories of my informants (Li Tiezheng and Yin Luguang were interviewed in the People's Republic, Liu Zonghan was interviewed in Taipei) as to the importance of the Department of Foreign Affairs as a feeder programme into the Ministry of Foreign Affairs, the unanimity of the memories suggests that, at some point a bit later in the 1940s, the Department of Foreign Affairs *did* begin to send substantial numbers of new appointees to the Ministry of Foreign Affairs.
48. Interviews with Li Tiezheng, Yin Luguang and Liu Zonghan.
49. Interview with Liu Zonghan. Li Tiezheng also stressed the lack of any overt factionalism.
50. Of course, the content of the generalism was different for Confucian literati elites and Foreign Affairs bureaucrats. The former studied archaic literary texts, while the latter acquired knowledge of foreign languages and international law. But in its strong sense of in-group elitism based on a generalist high culture, Ministry of Foreign Affairs personnel more closely replicated the *modus vivendi* of the old bureaucratic elite than others in state organizations during the Republican era.
51. David Pong and Edmund Fung both stress the ineffectiveness and overall weakness of the Ministry of Foreign Affairs during the Republican period. The Ministry was, after all, unable to resolve (or, perhaps even significantly, to influence) the most pressing diplomatic issue of the time—Japanese aggression and expansionism. While Pong and Fung concede that the organization made 'limited gains' in its gradualist strategy of revising the unequal treaties, they see this issue as a minor accomplishment (Pong and Fung, *Ideal and Reality*). From the perspective of eventual ends and historical outcomes, Pong and Fung are undoubtedly correct: not only the Ministry of Foreign Affairs, but also the Party, Nationalist military organizations, the National government as a

whole, and a host of other international actors such as the League of Nations failed to resolve the issue of Japanese imperialism. From an *institutional* perspective, however, the Ministry of Foreign Affairs' pursuit of other activities (treaty revision, border establishment, opening direct diplomatic relations with other countries), and its unwillingness to stake its entire prestige on an endeavour where its range could hardly be expected to produce the desired results, was institutionally and ultimately politically quite astute.

## Chapter 7

1. See Joel Migdal, *Strong Societies and Weak States* (Princeton: Princeton University Press, 1988).
2. Lloyd Eastman, *The Abortive Revolution: China Under Nationalist Rule, 1927–1937* (Cambridge, Mass.: Harvard University Press, 1974), 9–12, 14–20.

# BIBLIOGRAPHY

## Archival Materials

Dier Lishi Dang'an'guan (the No. 2 Historical Archives), Nanjing, Jiangsu, People's
Republic of China
*Abbreviation*: DELSDAG
Guoshiguan (National Palace) Archives, Taipei, Taiwan, Republic of China
*Abbreviation*: GSG
Guomindang Dangshi Weiyuanhui (Committee on Party History), Taipei, Taiwan,
Republic of China
*Abbreviation*: DSH
Foreign Office Archives, Public Record Office, Kew, London
*Abbreviation*: FO 371
Department of State, Records with Special Reference to the Internal Affairs of
China, 1930–1939 Washington, DC
*Abbreviation*: DS


## Published Works

Adshead, S. A. M., *The Modernization of the Salt Administration, 1900–1920* (Cam-
bridge, Mass.: Harvard University Press, 1970).
Balazs, Étienne, *Political Theory and Administrative Reality in Traditional China*
(London: School of Oriental and African Studies, 1965).
*Banian Lai zhi Zhijieshui* (The Past Ten Years of Direct Tax) (Chongqing: Caizheng
Bu, 1943).
*Baogong Xiqu Gushiji* (A Collection of Baogong Stories from Yuan Drama) (Shang-
hai: Shanghai Wenhua Chubanshe, 1986).
*Baogong Zhuan* (Baogong Stories) (Heilongjiang Jiaoyu Chubanshe, 1986).
Bastid, Marianne, 'The Structure of the Financial Institutions of the State in the
Late Qing', in Stuart Schram (ed.), *The Scope of State Power in China* (New York:
St Martin's Press, 1985).
Bendix, Reinhard, *From Max Weber: An Intellectual Portrait* (London: University
Paperbacks, 1959).
Biggerstaff, Knight, *The Earliest Modern Government Schools in China* (Ithaca, NY:
Cornell University Press, 1961).
*Caizheng Nianjian* (The Finance Yearbook) (Nanjing and Chongqing: Caizheng
Bu, 1935 and 1943).
Callaghy, Thomas, *The State–Society Struggle: Zaire in Comparative Perspective* (New
York: Columbia University Press, 1984).
Chang Kia-ngau, *The Inflationary Spiral: The Experience in China, 1939–50* (New
York and London: MIT Press and John Wiley, 1958).
Chen Bainian, *Kaoxun Zhidu Dayao* (General Outline on the Examination and
Selection System) (Zhongyang Zhengzhi Xuexiao Renshi Xingzheng Renyuan
Xunlianban Jiangyi, n.d., early 1940s).

Chen, P. T., 'Public Finance', in *The China Yearbook, 1935–36*, ed. Kwei Chungshu (Shanghai: Commercial Press).

——*Recent Financial Developments in China, 1934–36* (reprint of essay from *The Chinese Year Book, 1936–37*, No. 2) (Nanjing: The Chinese Year Book Publishing Company, 1937).

Chen Tsun, 'Chiefs of Section in a Ministry', *The Chinese Administrator*, 1: 1 (1935).

Chen Yugan, 'Fujian de Zhijieshui' (Direct Tax in Fujian), *Fujian Wenshi Ziliao*, No. 13 (Fuzhou: Zhongguo Renmin Xieshang Huiyi Fujiansheng Weiyuanhui Wenshi Ziliao Yanjiu Weiyuanhui, 1986).

Ch'i Hsi-sheng, *Warlord Politics in China, 1916–28*, (Stanford: Stanford University Press, 1976).

Ch'ien Tuan-sheng, *The Government and Politics of China, 1912–49* (Stanford: Stanford University Press, 1950/1970).

*The China Handbook, 1937–43*, compiled by the Chinese Ministry of Information (New York: Macmillan, 1943).

*The China Yearbook*, series years 1928–1935, ed. H. G. W. Woodhouse (Shanghai: Kelly and Walsh).

*The China Yearbook, 1937* (Shanghai and Germany: Council of International Affairs).

*The Chinese Administrator* (Shanghai: Executive Yuan, Committee on Administrative Efficiency, 1935–6).

*The Chinese Yearbook*, series years 1935–45, ed. Kwei Chungshu (Shanghai and Chungking: Commercial Press).

Chu Pao-chin, *V. K. Wellington Koo: A Case Study of China's Diplomat and the Diplomacy of Nationalism, 1912–1966* (Hong Kong: Chinese University Press, 1981).

Chu T'ung-tsu, *Local Government in China under the Ch'ing* (Stanford: Stanford University Press 1962).

Ci Hongfei, 'Guanyu Guomindang Zhengfude Guanshui Zhengce' (On the Nationalist Government Customs Tax Policy), *Shehui Kexue* (Social Science) (1985).

Coble, Parks, *The Shanghai Capitalists and the Nationalist Government, 1927–37* (Cambridge, Mass., and London: Council on East Asian Studies, Harvard University Press, 1986).

Cole, James, *Shaohsing: Competition and Cooperation in Nineteenth-Century China* (Tucson: University of Arizona Press, 1986).

Cohen, Paul, *Discovering History in China* (New York: Columbia University Press, 1984).

Crone, Patricia, 'The Tribe and the State', in John A. Hall (ed.), *States in History* (Oxford: Basil Blackwell, 1986).

Dai Daoliu, *Kaoxuan Quanxu Jiaoyu Lianxi Fang'an* (A Draft Programme for Connecting Examination, Selection, and Education) (Shanghai: Zhonghua Shuju, 1946).

Ding Changqing (ed.), Minguo Yanwu Shigao (Outline of Affairs in the Republican Period) (Beijing: Renmin Chubanshe, 1990).

Duara, Prasenjit, *Culture, Power and the State: Rural North China, 1900–42* (Stanford: Stanford University Press, 1988).

Duus, Peter, 'Japan's Informal Empire in China, 1895–1937: An Overview', in Peter Duus, Ramon H. Myers, and Mark R. Peattie, *The Japanese Informal Empire in China, 1895–1937* (Princeton: Princeton University Press, 1989).

Eastman, Lloyd, *The Abortive Revolution* (Cambridge, Mass.: Harvard University Press, 1974).

—— 'Nationalist China during the Nanking Decade 1927–1937', in *The Cambridge History of Republican China*, 13: 2 (New York: Cambridge University Press, 1986).

—— 'Nationalist China at War', in *The Cambridge History*, 13: 2 (New York: Cambridge University Press, 1986).

Elman, Benjamin, 'Education, Society and Civil Service Examinations in Late Imperial China', paper presented at the conference on Education and Society in Late Imperial China, June 1989.

—— 'Delegitimation and Decanonization: The Trap of Civil Examination Reform, 1860–1910' (Diyi jie Guoji Qingdao Xueshu Yanjiu Taolun Wenji) (Taipei: Guoli Zhongshan Daxue Zhongwenxi, 1993).

Esherick, Joseph, and Rankin, Mary B. (eds.), *Chinese Local Elites and Patterns of Dominance* (Berkeley and Los Angeles: University of California Press, 1990).

Fitzgerald, John, 'The Misconceived Revolution: State and Society in China's Nationalist Revolution, 1923–26', *Journal of Asian Studies*, 49:2 (May 1990).

—— 'Increased Disunity: The Politics and Finance of Guangdong Separatism, 1926–1936', *Modern Asian Studies* 24: 4 (1990), 745–75.

Folsom, Kenneth, *Friends, Guests and Colleagues, The Mu-fu System in the Late Ch'ing Period* (Berkeley and Los Angeles: University of California Press, 1968).

Franke, Wolfgang, *The Reform and Abolition of the Traditional Chinese Examination System* (Cambridge, Mass.: Harvard University Press, 1960).

Fung, Edmund S. K., 'Nationalist Foreign Policy, 1928–37', in David Pong and Edmund S. K. Fung (eds.), *Ideal and Reality: Social and Political Change in Modern China, 1860–1949* (Lanham, Md: University Press of America, 1985).

Gao, Bingfang, *Zhongguo Zhijieshui Shishi* (History and Practice of China's Direct Tax) (Chongqing: Zhongguo Zhijieshui Shiwu Congshu, 1943).

Gillin, Donald, *Warlord: Yen Hsi-shan in Shansi Province 1911–1949* (Princeton: Princeton University Press, 1966).

Grieder, Jerome, *Intellectuals and the State in Modern China* (New York: Free Press, 1981).

Gu Shouzhi, 'Gongzhi Zhi Chugao, Wenzhi Zhidu Kaoxuan' (Recruitment and Selection of Civil Public Functionaries:' A Draft), unpublished manuscript (Taipei, date unclear).

Hall, John A., and Ikenberry, G. John, *The State* (Minneapolis: University of Minnesota Press, 1989).

Hargrove, Erwin, *Prisoners of Myth: The Leadership of the Tennessee Valley Authority, 1933–1990* (Princeton: Princeton University Press, 1994).

Hirschmann, Albert O., *Development Projects Observed* (Washington: Brookings Institution, 1967).

Huang Jingbo, *Zhongguo Renshi Wenti Xinlun* (New Discussions on China's Personnel Problems) (Chongqing: Shangwu, 1945).

Huang Liu-hung, *A Complete Book Concerning Happiness and Benevolence: A Manual for Local Magistrates in Seventeenth-Century China*, trans. and ed. Djang Chu (Tucson: University of Arizona Press, 1984).

Israel, Arturo, *Institutional Development* (Baltimore and London: Johns Hopkins University Press, 1987).

Jiang Maicai, 'Wo Ying Diyijie Gaodeng Kaoshide Huiyi' (My Recollections of the First Upper Civil Service Exam), in *Zhongguo Kaozheng Xuehui 50 Zhou Nianjinian Zhuangan* (China's Examination and Government: A 50 year Commemorative Volume) (Taipei: Kaoshiyuan, 1985).

Jin Shaoxin and Zhenguo Wang, 'Dai Jitao yu Nanjing Guomin Zhengfude Gaodeng Wenguan Kaoshi' (Dai Jitao and the Nanjing National Government Upper Civil Service Exam), in *Guomindangde Wenguan Zhidu yu Wenguan Kaoshi, Jiangsusheng Wenshi Ziliao*, No. 24 (December 1988).

Kahn, Harold, *Monarchy in the Emperor's Eyes: Image and Reality in the Ch'ien-lung Reign* (Cambridge, Mass.: Harvard University Press, 1971).

Kaufman, Herbert, *The Forest Ranger* (Baltimore: Johns Hopkins University Press, 1960, 1967).

Kirby, William, 'The Internationalization of China: Foreign Relations at Home and Abroad in the Republican Era', *China Quarterly*, forthcoming.

Landau, Martin, 'On the Use of Metaphor in Political Analysis', in Martin Landau, *Political Theory and Political Science* (Atlantic Highlands, NJ: Humanities Press, 1972/1979).

Lary, Diana, *Region and Nation: The Kwangsi Clique in Chinese Politics* (Cambridge: Cambridge University Press, 1974).

Lei Xiaoling, 'Guanyu Kezhangde Taolun' ('A Discussion on Section Chiefs'), *Xingzheng Xiaolü* (henceforth *XZXL*), 1: 5–6 (1932).

Leung, Y. S., 'The Peculiar Institution: Expectant Officials in Late 19th Century China', paper presented at the AAS Pacific Coast Conference, June 1978.

Levi, Margaret, *Of Rule and Revenue* (Berkeley and Los Angeles: University of California Press, 1988).

Li Feipeng, *Lijie Gaodeng, Putong, Xianding Kaoshi Shiti Xiangjie* (A Detailed Introduction to Examination Questions on the Upper and General Civil Service Examinations) (Taipei: publisher unknown, 1954).

—— 'Zhongguo Kaozheng Xuehuizhi Tezhi yu Wushi Zhounianzhi Huigu' (The Special Characteristics of China's Examination Institute and Fifty Years of Recollections), in *Zhongguo Kaozheng Xuehui Wushi Zhounian Jinian Zhuankan* (Taipei: Kaoshiyuan, 1985).

Li Jianji, 'Jiefangqian de Lanzhou Zhijieshui' (Pre-liberation Direct Tax in Lanzhou), *Gansu Wenshi Ziliao Xuanji*, No. 14 (Lanzhou: Zhongguo Renmin Zhengzhi Xieshang Huiyi Gansu Weiyuanhui Wenshi Ziliao Yanjiu Weiyuan hui, 1983).

Liew, K. C., *Struggle for Democracy: Sung Chiao-jen and the 1911 Chinese Revolution* (Berkeley and Los Angeles: University of California Press, 1971).

Liu Bing, '1927–33 Nian Nanjing Guomin Zhengfu Banli Tongshui Jiangshu' (The National Government's Administration of Consolidated Tax, 1927–1933), *Minguo Dangan*, 3 (1987).

Liu Foding, 'Qingmo Lieqiang Geguo Qinfan Woguo Yanzheng Zhuquande Huodong' (The Invasive Activities of all Countries in China's Autonomy over Salt Administration at the End of the Qing), *Yanye Yanjiu* (Studies in Salt Industry History), 1:1 (1988).

—— 'Zhongguo Jindai Liangyan Yunxiao Zhidude Bianhua' (Changes in the Salt and Grain Transport System in Modern China), *Nankai Jingji Yanjiusuo Jikan*, 2 (1985).

Ma Yinchu, *Caizhengxue yu Zhongguo Caizheng* (Study of Finance and Chinese Finance) (Shanghai: Shangwu Yinshu, 1948).

Mann, Michael, 'The Autonomous Power of the State', in John A. Hall (ed.), *States in History* (Oxford: Basil Blackwell, 1986).

Marx, Karl, and Engels, Friedrich, 'The Manifesto of the Communist Party', in Robert C. Tucker (ed.), *The Marx–Engels Reader* (New York: Norton Press, 1972).

McCord, Edward, *The Power of the Gun: The Emergence of Modern Chinese Warlordism* (Berkeley: University of California Press, 1993).

Metzger, Thomas, *The Internal Organization of the Ch'ing Bureaucracy: Legal, Normative and Communications Aspects* (Cambridge, Mass.: Harvard University Press, 1973).

Migdal, Joel, *Strong Societies and Weak States* (Princeton: Princeton University Press, 1988).

Miyazaki, Ichisada, *China's Examination Hell: The Civil Service Examinations of Imperial China*, trans. Conrad Schirokauer (New York and Tokyo: Weatherhill, 1976).

Morrisson, Esther, 'The Modernization of the Confucian Bureaucracy', unpublished Ph.D. dissertation, Harvard University, 1959.

Ni Shaojiu, 'Anhui Zhijieshui Shimo' (From the Beginning to the End of the Anhui Direct Tax), *Jiang huai Gongshang* (Anhui Wenshi Ziliao) (Anhui Renmin Chubanshe, 1988).

Oksenberg, Michel, 'The Institutionalization of the Chinese Communist Revolution: The Ladder of Success on the Eve of the Cultural Revolution', *China Quarterly*, No. 36 (1968).

Pong, David, 'The Ministry of Foreign Affairs during the Republican Period, 1912 to 1949', in Zara Steiner (ed.), *The Times Survey of the Foreign Ministries of the World* (London: Times Books Limited, 1982).

Porter, Jonathan, *Tseng Kuo-fan's Private Bureaucracy* (Berkeley: Center for Chinese Studies Research Monographs, No. 9, 1972).

Qian Shipu (ed.), *Beiyang Zhengfu Shiqide Zhengzhi Zhidu* (The Political System of the Beiyang Government Period) (Beijing: Zhonghua Shuju, 1984).

*Quanxu Bu Nianjian* (Ministry of Personnel Yearbook), (Nanjing, 1932).

Rankin, Mary B., *Elite Activism and Political Transformation in China: Zhejiang Province, 1865–1911* (Stanford: Stanford University Press, 1986).

Rawlinson, John L., *China's Struggle for Naval Development, 1839–1895* (Cambridge, Mass.: Harvard University Press, 1967).

Scott, W. Richard, *Organizations: Rational, Natural and Open Systems* (Englewood Cliffs, NJ: Prentice-Hall, 1981).

Selznick, Philip, *Leadership and Administration* (Berkeley and Los Angeles: University of California Press, 1957/1984).

Shen Jianshi, 'Wuquan Xianfaxia Quanxu Zhiduzhi Yanjiu ji Jinhou Yingqu' (Research and Proposals for the Future on the Personnel System under the Five Power Constitution), *XZXL*, 3:5. (1936)

Sheridan, James, *Chinese Warlord: The Career of Feng Yu-hsiang*, (Stanford: Stanford University Press, 1966).

*Shinian Lai zhi Caiwu Renshi* (The Past Ten Years of Finance Personnel) (Chongqing: Caizheng Bu, 1943).

*Shinian Lai zhi Caiwu Xingzheng* (The Past Ten Years of Finance Administration) (Chongqing: Caizheng Bu, 1943).

*Shinian Lai zhi Huowushui* (The Past Ten Years of Commodity Taxation) (Chongqing: Caizheng Bu, 1943).

*Shinian Lai zhi Yanzheng* (The Past Ten Years of Salt Administration), compiled by the Yanzheng Si (Chongqing: Caizheng Bu, November 1943).

Sigel, Louis T., 'The Diplomacy of Chinese Nationalism, 1900–1911', in David Pong and Edmund S. K. Fung (eds.), *Ideal and Reality: Social and Political Change in Modern China, 1860–1949* (Lanham, Md: University Press of America, 1985).

Skocpol, Theda, *States and Social Revolution* (Cambridge: Cambridge University Press, 1979).

—— 'Bringing the State Back In: Strategies of Analysis in Current Research', in Peter B. Evans, Dietrich Rueschemeyer, and Theda Skocpol (eds.), *Bringing the State Back In* (Cambridge: Cambridge University Press, 1985).

Song Teli, *Zhidu yu Rencai* (Systems and Talent) (Chongqing: Beidou Shudian, 1944).

Spence, Jonathan, *Ts'ao Yin and the K'ang-hsi Emperor: Bondservant and Master* (New Haven: Yale University Press, 1974).

Strand, David, *Rickshaw Beijing: City People and Politics in the 1920s* (Berkeley and Los Angeles: University of California Press, 1989).

Strauss, Julia C., 'The Cult of Administrative Efficiency: Myth and Statecraft in the Chinese Republic, 1912–37', unpublished paper, presented at the 1993 meeting of the Association for Asian Studies, March 1993.

—— 'Wartime Stress and Guomindang Response: *Xunlian* as a Means to State-building', unpublished paper, presented at the 1996 meeting of the Association for Asian Studies, 11–14 April 1996.

Sun E-Tu Zen, 'The Board of Revenue in Nineteenth Century China', *Harvard Journal of Asian Studies*, 24 (1962–3).

Sun Yat-sen, *Fundamentals of National Reconstruction* (Taipei: China Cultural Service, 1953).

—— *San Min Chu Yi: The Three Principles of the People* (Taipei: China Publishing Company, n.d.).

Thompson, James D., *Organizations in Action* (Pittsburgh: University of Pittsburgh Press, 1967).

—— and Tuden, Arthur, 'Strategies, Structures and Processes of organizational Decision', in J. D. Thompson *et al.* (eds.), *Comparative Studies in Administration* (Pittsburgh: University of Pittsburgh Press, 1959).

Tien Hung Mao, *Government and Politics in KMT China, 1927–37* (Stanford: Stanford University Press, 1972).

Tilly, Charles, 'Reflections on the History of European State- Making', in Charles Tilly (ed.), *The Formation of National States in Western Europe* (Princeton: Princeton University Press, 1975).

—— *Big Structures, Large Processes, Huge Comparisons* (New York: Russell Sage, 1984).

—— *Coercion, Capital and European States AD 990–1992*, (Cambridge and Oxford: Blackwell, 1990 and 1992).

Townsend, James R., *Political Participation in Communist China*, rev. edn (Berkeley and Los Angeles: University of California Press, 1969).

Waldron, Arthur, *From War to Nationalism: China's Turning Point, 1924–25* (Cambridge and New York: Cambridge University Press, 1995).

Wang Yeh-chien, *Land Taxation in Imperial China, 1750–1911* (Cambridge, Mass.: Harvard University Press, 1973).

Wang Zhenguo, 'Guomindang Shiqide Wenguan Zhidu yu Wenguan Kaoshi' (The Civil Service System and Civil Service Examinations in the Nationalist Period), in *Guomindangde Wenguan Zhidu yu Wenguan Kaoshi, Jiangsu Wenshi Ziliao*, No. 24 (December 1988).

Watt, John, *The District Magistrate in Late Imperial China*, (New York: Columbia University Press, 1972).

Weber, Max, *Economy and Society*, i and ii, ed. Guenther Roth and Claus Wittich (Berkeley and Los Angeles: University of California Press, 1978).

——*From Max Weber: Essays in Sociology*, ed. H. H. Gerth and C. Wright Mills, (New York: Oxford University Press, 1946).

Wilensky, Harold, 'The Professionalization of Everyone?' *American Journal of Sociology*, 70:2 (September 1964).

Will, Pierre-Étienne, and Wong, R. Bin, *Nourish the People: The State Civilian Granary System in China, 1650–1850* (Ann Arbor: University of Michigan Press, 1991).

Wilson, Woodrow, 'The Study of Administration', *Political Science Quarterly*, 56:4 (December 1941).

Wou, Odoric, 'The District Magistrate Profession in the Early Republican Period', *Modern Asian Studies*, 8:2 (April 1974).

Wright, Mary C., *China in Revolution: The First Phase*, (New Haven and London: Yale University Press, 1968).

Wu Jingping, 'Song Ziwen Lun'gang' (An Outline Discussion on Song Ziwen), *Lishi Yanjiu*, No. 6. (1991).

Wu, Silas, *Communication and Imperial Control in China: Evolution of the Palace Memorial System, 1693–1735* (Cambridge, Mass.: Harvard University Press, 1971).

——*Kangxi and his Heir Apparent, 1661–1722* (Cambridge, Mass.: Harvard University Press, 1971).

*Xingzheng Xiaolü* (Administrative Efficiency) (Executive Yuan, Committee on Administrator Efficiency, 1934–6).

*Xingzheng Yanjiu Yuekan* (Administrative Study Monthly), (Executive Yuan, Administrative Efficiency Study Group, 1936–7).

Yang, C. K., 'Some Characteristics of Chinese Bureaucratic Behavior', in David S. Nivison and Arthur Wright (eds.), *Confucianism in Action* (Stanford: Stanford University Press, 1959).

*Yanwu Jisi Dicha Renyuan Yingyou zhi Renshi* (Important Knowledge for Anti-Salt Smuggling and Inspection Personnel) (Training Group for Anti-Salt Smuggling and Inspection Personnel, 1935).

*Yanwu Renshi Guize*. (Regulations on Salt Administration Personnel), unpublished booklet, (Caizheng Bu, date unknown, *c.* 1950).

Young, Arthur, *China's Nation Building Effort, 1927–37* (Stanford, Calif.: Hoover Institution Press, 1971).

——*China's Wartime Finance and Inflation, 1937–45* (Cambridge, Mass.: Harvard University Press, 1965).

Young, Ernest, *The Presidency of Yuan Shih-k'ai* (University of Michigan Press: Ann Arbor, 1977).

Zelin, Madeline, *The Magistrate's Tael: Rationalizing Fiscal Reform in Eighteenth Century Ch'ing China* (Berkeley and Los Angeles: University of California Press, 1984).

Zeng Yingfeng, *Zhongguo Yanwu Zhengshi* (The History of Chinese Salt Administration) (Shanghai: Shangwu Yinshuguan, 1937; reprinted by Shanghai Shudian, 1984).

Zhang Ruiying, 'Dai Jitao yu Woguo Kaoquan Zhidu zhi Yanjiu' (Research on Dai Jitao and China's Civil Service Selection System), unpublished dissertation, China China Cultural Institute, Taipei (1978).

Zhao Yuanchong, 'Zenyang Tigao Zhengzhi Xiaolü' (How Can Government Efficiency be Raised?), *Xingzheng Xiaolü* 1:8 (1934).

*Zhijieshui Shuifa Gaiyao* (General Outline of Direct Tax Laws) (Nanjing: Caizheng Bu, Zhijieshui Ju, 1946).

Zhou Weiliang, 'Yanjing yu Jisi' (Salt Police and Smuggling Control), in *Yanwu Jiyao* (Salt Affairs Summary) (internal publication, n. d.).

Zhu Leizhang, 'Wo Kaoqu le Dishoujie Gaodeng Kaoshi' (I Passed the First Upper Civil Service Examination), *Minguo Chunqiu*, 1 (1987).

# INDEX

administration, prefectural 67, 73, 131, 177
administrative appointment 15
  acting (*daili*) 39, 174 n.41
  in Beiyang Ministry of Finance 109–10
  delegated (*weiren*) 30, 41, 46
  in imperial bureaucracy 15
  recommended (*jianren*) 30, 38, 41, 46, 52,
    109, 177
  in Salt Inspectorate 92
  selected (*jianren*) 30, 31, 38, 41, 52, 109
  special (*teren*) 30
'Administrative Efficiency' School 42–4
  and civil service examinations 46
administrative organizations 2–3
  dualism of 3, 7
  relations with political leaders 81, 104
  weakness of in Republican period 155
  *see also* state, institutions
administrators, *see* personnel
authority
  formal, in Examination Yuan 33
  shared in late imperial bureaucracy 14
  state 16
autocracy 109
autonomy
  of Salt Inspectorate 68, 87
  of state 4, 212 n.9
  of Ministry of Foreign Affairs 178

Balfour, Arthur James 157, 158
Baogong 16
Beiyang
  bureaucrats 35
  government 22, 25, 29, 112–13
    carry over into National
      Government 218 n.16
  Ministry of Finance 112
Briand, Aristide 157
bureaucracy
  effectiveness of 214 n.6, 215 n.21
  formal 20
  importance of 28
  innovation in 12, n.1
  late imperial structure of 13–14
  values in 17–19
bureaucratization 8–9
  in Salt Inspectorate 66, 68–70, passim
  *see also* Weberian, institution building

cadastral survey 119, 124 n.30, 138
Cang, Zhibing 121
capacity

in land tax 138
  organizational 5, 10
  organizational in late imperial China
    16–17
  of state in *xinzheng* period 22
  *see also* goal implementation, institution
    building, state, state building
Central Executive Committee (Zhongyang
  Zhixing Weiyuanhui) 26, 54, 84
Central Political School (Zhongyang
  Zhengzhi Xuexiao) 53
Central Political University (Zhongyang
  Zhengzhi Daxue) 53–5, 175–6
Central Training Corps (Zhongyang
  Xunliantuan) 53
  and Ministry of Finance 149–50
centralization 8
  and 'Administrative Efficiency' School 43
  attempted in *xinzheng* period 20–2
  in Consolidated Tax Administration 127
  limits of 108–9
  in Ministry of Finance 117–18
  of state structures in late imperial
    China 11–12, 13, 16
  *see also* Weberian, *xinzheng*
Chang, Kia-ngau 242 n.87
chaos (*luan*) 25
Chen, Guofu 175
Chiang Kai-shek 7, 24, 113, 116, 154, 169
*The Chinese Administrator* 219 n.32, 43
civil service
  in Consolidated Tax Administration 239
    n.47
  linkages to Yuan Shikai and Beiyang
    periods 29, 32
  in National Government 28
  qualifications 37
  ranks and salaries in 35–6
  regularization of 52
  in Salt Inspectorate 67–73
  in Yuan Shikai and Beiyang periods 29,
    32
  *see also* examination system, Examination
    Yuan, Ministry of Personnel, personnel
Clague, M. J. 165
Committee on Administrative Efficiency
  (Xingzheng Xiaolü Weiyuanhui) 42
Committee on Examinations (Dianshi
  Weiyuanhui) 33, 46
concessions
  rendition to National Government 157
  *see also* Weihaiwei, Washington System

Consolidated Tax Administration (Shuiwu
   Shu)
   cover over strategy of institution building
      in 126 passim
   institutionalization in 10
   as 'Third Pillar' of Nationalist
      finance 128–31
   use of Customs and Salt Administration
      'models' 131–2, 239 n.47
   wartime decline of 143
cooptation
   of elites in late imperial China 15
   in National Government 35, 81
   in personnel system 37
corruption 12, 67
cosmic harmony 12
Croome, J.C. 226 n.18, 92
culture
   of Chinese and civil service
      examinations 49–50
   informal bureaucratic 18
   of literati elite in late imperial China
      15–16
Customs Administration 59–60, 64
   takeover by Nationalist Ministry of
      Finance 124–5

Dai, Jitao 45, 49
Dane, Sir Richard 66–7, 75–6, 78
de-institutionalization 189–90
   in Ministry of Finance 143 ff
   in Salt Administration 98, 100, 102–3
differentiation in late imperial
   bureaucracy 14
Direct Tax Administration (Zhijieshui Shu)
   administrative difficulties of 135–6
   domain 137–8
   and examinations 52, 135, 139
   goals 134–5
   replication of customs, salt and
      consolidated tax model 134
   results 136
   in Sino-Japanese War 145, 146–7
Directorate General of Salt (Yanwu
   Zongju)
   decline of foreign influence in 96–7
   establishment of 94–5
   relocation inland 97
   wartime de-institutionalization 100–3,
      143
   wartime expansion 97
   wartime transport and production
      monopoly 97
   see also de-institutionalization,
      Sino-Foreign Salt Inspectorate
discretion
   of local officials in the late Empire 14

of Salt Inspectorate senior
   administrators 77–8
district magistrate 13, 16–17
domain 187–8, 189
   of Consolidated Tax 131–2
   of Ministry of Finance 119
   of Ministry of Foreign Affairs 166–7, 179
   of state 4
   see also task environment

Eastman, Lloyd 191
education
   of Beiyang Ministry of Finance
      personnel 110–11
   Confucian 15, 17
   of diplomats in the Republican
      period 168, 171–2, 175 passim
   of Nationalist Ministry of Finance
      personnel 140
effectiveness
   of Consolidated Tax Administration 132
   government need for during Sino-Japanese
      War 148
   in late imperial bureaucracy 214 n.6, 215
      n.21
   organizational 8, 118, 190
   of Salt Inspectorate 89, 93, 145
efficiency
   of Consolidate Tax Administration 132
   of Salt Inspectorate 65, 89–90, 93
   as a value in the imperial bureaucracy 14
elites
   bureaucratic in the Republican period 22,
      23
   local 17, 73
   Nationalist, dual office holding 26
   in the post-Taiping period 21
   and relations with the late imperial
      state 17
   and the salt tax 63
   split in 1911–12, 22
environment, hostile
   impact on institutionalization 58, 152
   international and impact on state building
      in Republican China 25, 44
   and Salt Inspectorate 68 and passim, 79,
      102
   and state building 3, 8
European states 5–6
   impact of on non-Western world 1–2
   system of 1
evaluation
   of officials in late Empire (daji) 16
   system during the Nanjing Decade
      (kaoji) 40–1
'Examination Hell' 15
examination system